Talking Politics

This book is a philosophical examination of some of the basic concepts of political discourse. It focuses on what is said by politicians, newspapers and people in pubs rather than on the works of political theorists. The theorists are not ignored, but are not given centre stage. This is a work *of*, but not *on* political theory.

There have been other books on political concepts, but the philosophical ones are primarily concerned with what other philosophers have said. The non-philosophical ones, much more often than enough, go in for slick moralism and smart cynicism; appealing to popular prejudice, rather than challenging it. While trying to detect obfuscation, deliberate or unintentional, the author is aware that there can be honest muddles and that what seems to be sheer waffle may be a confused attempt to state the complex.

The author's attitude is critical, but not cynical. He is independent, but not aloof. He does not believe that 'philosophy leaves everything as it is', but does believe that philosophy must be a patient listener.

A. W. Sparkes is very well qualified to write a philosophical analysis of a political subject. He has taught philosophy for some thirty years and has had a lifelong fascination with politics. He has also worked in the library of an Australian state parliament and was a member of the staff of a university politics department. He is now Professor of Philosophy at the University of Newcastle, New South Wales.

This book is essential reading for students of politics and of philosophy. It will also appeal to (and provoke) others with a thoughtful interest in politics.

Also available by the same author from Routledge:

Talking Philosophy
A wordbook
A. W. Sparkes

Talking Politics

A wordbook

A. W. Sparkes

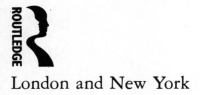

London and New York

First published 1994
by Routledge
11 New Fetter Lane, London EC4P 4EE

Simultaneously published in the USA and Canada
by Routledge
29 West 35th Street, New York, NY 10001

© 1994 A. W. Sparkes

Typeset in Garamond by
EXCEPT*detail* Ltd, Southport
Printed and bound in Great Britain by
T. J. Press (Padstow) Ltd, Padstow, Cornwall

British Library Cataloguing in Publication Data
Sparkes, A. W.
  Talking Politics: A wordbook
  I. Title
  320.01

Library of Congress Cataloging in Publication Data
Sparkes, A. W.
  Talking Politics: A wordbook/A. W. Sparkes.
     p.   cm.
  Includes bibliographical references and index.
  1. Political science—Terminology. I. Title.
JA61.S62 1994 93-38021
320'.014—dc20

ISBN 0-415-10807-1 (hbk)
ISBN 0-415-10808-X (pbk)

To my parents and to Veronika, Connie, Daniel and Mary

Contents

Acknowledgements

I owe much to many people. I thank my colleagues at the University of Newcastle, D. W. Dockrill, C. A. Hooker, J. M. Lee and J. N. Wright. I have learnt much from the writings of Conal Condren, and also from many students, amongst them Rosemary Lovell, Mike Coulson, Harry Hodges, Colin Wilks and Wayne Christensen. I have great debts to two remarkable men, both now, sadly, dead, C. D. Rowley and Stanley Benn. I must mention also three of my early teachers, J. S. Campbell of St Joseph's Christian Brothers' College (Gregory Terrace) and Eric Dowling and Louis Durell of Queensland University. My first school of politics was the Parliamentary Library of Queensland, of which I have many lively memories.

Mrs Dorrit Nesmith typed the manuscript with extraordinary care, patience, efficiency, tact and good sense. I am grateful for the assistance of Richard Stoneman, Victoria Peters and Sarah-Jane Woolley of Routledge; and my hawk-eyed copy editor, Margaret Deith. Three libraries have been very helpful: the State Library of NSW, the Lake Macquarie City Library and, most of all, Newcastle University's Auchmuty Library and its thaumaturgical Inter-Library Services section.

I owe much also to many people whose names I do not know.

I would like to thank the John Fairfax Group Pty Limited and the *Sydney Morning Herald* for permission to use the cover photograph.

A book like this needs many quotations and I acknowledge with gratitude those listed below. All items are fully described in the bibliography and the page references below refer to this book. If I have in any instance left undone those things which I ought to have done, I apologise for it: R. J. Hawke *The Resolution of Conflict* (p. 197) by kind permission of the Australian Broadcasting Corporation; Paul Addison *The Road to 1945* Jonathan Cape (p. 183); Alfred A. Knopf Inc. for Eric Ambler *The Light of Day* (p. 32); A. J. Milne 'Reason, Morality and Politics' from B. Parekh and R. N. Berki *The Morality of Politics* Allen & Unwin (pp. 58, 88); Alternative Publishing Co-operative for blurb to Métin, 1977 (p. 216); Benedict Anderson *Imagined Communities* Verso (p. 135); Aristoleian Society (pp. 14, 281); D. M. Armstrong *'The Nature of Mind' and other Essays*, 1980, University of Queensland Press (p. 223) and 'An Intellectual Autobiography' (p. 192); *The Australian*

Journal of Political Science for J. Pemberton and G. Davis "The Rhetoric of Consensus" (p. 199); extract reproduced from *The Thatcher Phenomenon* by Hugo Young and Anne Sloman with the permission of BBC Enterprises Ltd (p. 78); Tom Barrass (pp. 26, 83); J. C. M. Baynes *Morale: A Study of Men and Courage* Praeger (p. 266); Kellie Bisset (p. 258); Blackwell Publications for P. T. Geach *Reason and Argument* (p. 2), P. H. Partridge "Some Notes on the Concept of Power" (p. 33), John Wisdom *Philosophy and Psycho-Analysis* (p. 6), Ludwig Wittgenstein *Philosophical Investigations* (pp. 2, 8, 9, 97, 289, 290); Blanche Marvin for Nigel Balchin *A Sort of Traitor* (p. 77); Amanda Buckley (p. 83); Angela Burger *Neville Bonner* Macmillan (Australia) (p. 260); Burns & Oates Ltd for Jack Dominian *Authority* (p. 39); Tom Burton (p. 160); Cambridge University Press for Bertrand de Jouvenel *Sovereignty* (p. 58) and *The Pure Theory of Politics* (pp. 135, 199), and for Stuart Hampshire *Public and Private Morality* (p. 221); Cambridge University Press (USA) for Ernest Barker's translation of O. von Gierke *Natural Law and the Theory of Society* (p. 104); the J. L. A. Cary Estate and Andrew Lownie for Joyce Cary *Not Honour More* (pp. 79, 189); Churchill Livingstone Inc. for *International Dictionary of Medicine and Biology* (p. 216); Timothy Cribb (pp. 242–243); David Campbell Publishers for the Everyman Rousseau (p. 266) and Euclid (p. 4); Kenneth Davidson (p.21); Bernd Debusman (p. 87); extract from "Social Sciences" in *Encyclopaedia Britannica* 15th edn (1987) (p. 44); David Evans (p. 159); Raymond Evans (p. 210); Alfred Duggan *Conscience and the King* Faber & Faber (pp. 180, 242); Faber & Faber and Harcourt Brace for T. S. Eliot *The Idea of a Christian Society* (pp. 190–191) and *Collected Poems 1909–1962* (p. 72); Bruce Felknor *Dirty Politics* Greenwood Press (p. 106); Michael Frayn *Constructions* Wildwood House (pp. 266–267); Nicholas Freeling *Lady Macbeth* Penguin (p. 83); J. D. B. Miller *The Nature of Politics* by permission of Gerald Duckworth & Co. Ltd; Alan Gill (p. 26); Greg Hall and Revd Frank Fletcher (p. 26); R. H. S. Crossman *The Charm of Politics* Hamish Hamilton Ltd (p. 30); Harper Education for A. W. McCoy *Drug Traffic* (p. 176); HarperCollins (Australia) for P. B. Westerway "Pressure Groups" in J. Wilkes *Forces in Australian Politics* (p. 108), John Anderson *Studies in Empirical Philosophy* (pp. 121–122, 125), A. J. Baker *Anderson's Social Philosophy* (p. 125) and James McAuley *Collected Poems 1936–1970* (p. 141); HarperCollins Publishers for Kate Millett *Sexual Politics*, Barry Hindess *The Decline of Working Class Politics* (pp. 58–59) and J. A. K. Thomson's translation of Aristotle's *Ethics* (p. 170); Owen Harris for his Latham Memorial Lecture (p. 266); Peter Hartcher (p. 258); *National Reconciliation: The Speeches of Bob Hawke* Fontana/Collins (p.262); the estate of the late S. M. B. Orwell and A. M. Heath & Co. for *The Collected Essays, Journalism and Letters of George Orwell* (pp. 26, 40, 103, 237); Hodder & Stoughton/New English Library for A. Sampson *The Changing Anatomy of Britain* (p. 201); Theodore Saloutos *Poulism: Reaction or Reform?* Holt Rinehart & Winston (p. 158); Philip Wheelwright *The Burning Fountain* Indiana University Press (p. 63); John

Fairfax Group P/L for extracts from *The Sydney Morning Herald* (pp. 138, 160); Andrew Kruger (p. 243); J. T. Lang *The Turbulent Years* Alpha Books (p. 291); Stephen Leeder (p. 26); Leo Cooper for F. M. Richardson *Fighting Spirit* (p. 181); *The Listener* for W. I. Jennings 'How to Transfer Authority' (p. 36); Hutchinson Group for *Eamon de Valera* ©The Earl of Longford and Thomas P. O'Neill (pp. 145, 157, 188); Longman Cheshire for P. J. Boyce *et al. Dictionary of Australian Politics* (pp. 120, 178) and James Walter and Kay Dickie "Johannes Bjelke-Petersen: A Political Profile" in Alan Patience *The Bjelke-Petersen Premiership 1968-1983* (p. 159); Bruce Loudon and M. G. G. Pillai (p. 160); Catherine Lumby (p. 213); Peter Loveday "Representation" (p. 174); McDonald and Janes Publishers Ltd for Constantine Fitzgibbon *The Blitz* (p. 105); McGraw-Hill Book Company for W. V. Quine and J. S. Ullian *The Web of Belief* (p. 266); and *The New Catholic Encyclopedia* (p. 240); Ralph McInerny *The Search Committee* Athenaeum (p. 258); Charles Maclean *Island on the Edge of the World* (p. 212); Frank McManus *The Tumult and the Shouting* Rigby (p. 48); Macmillan Publishers Ltd for L. B. Namier *The Structure of Politics at the Accession of George III* (p. 1), Bernard Crick *Basic Forms of Government* (p. 122) and N. K. Smith *A Commentary of Kant's Critique of Pure Reason* (p. 8); Macmillan and Free Press for extracts from *Encyclopedia of Philosophy* (p. 30) and *International Encyclopedia of the Social Sciences* (p. 129); Manchester University Press for J. D. B. Miller *Politicians* (p. 79); S. L. A. Marshall *Men against Fire* Peter Smith (p. 181); Massachusetts Institute of Technology Press and Harvard University Press for N. Glazer and D. P. Moynihan *Beyond the Melting Pot* (p. 254); Methuen for Michael Oakeshott *Rationalism in Politics* (pp. 64, 71) and G. R. Elton *England Under the Tudors* (p. 233); Glenn Milne (p. 21); Stephen Murray-Smith *Sitting on Penguins* Hutchinson (Australia) (p. 258); *The Newcastle Herald* (pp. 26, 127, 160, 250, 258, 262, 269); News Limited for excerpts from *The Australian* (pp. 21, 87, 160); *The Weekend Australian* (p. 27), *The Daily Telegraph* (p. 180), *The Daily Telegraph Mirror* (pp. 159, 202), *The Sunday Telegraph* (p. 256); H. G. Nicholas *To the Hustings* Cassell (p. 203); Richard Nolan (p. 24); Brad Norington (p. 160); Dr Julius Nyerere, Betty E. Burch and Van Nostrand Inc. for *Dictatorship and Totalitarianism* (pp. 186–187); Oxford University Press for excerpts from J. L. Austin *Philosophical Papers* 1979 (pp. 70, 192); *The Complete Clerihews of Edmund Clerihew Bentley* 1981 (p. 106), Alan Bullock and Maurice Shock *The Liberal Tradition from Fox to Keynes* (1967) (pp. 223–225), H. W. Fowler *Modern English Usage* 2nd edn 1974 (p. 206), R. M. Hare *The Language of Morals* 1963 (p. 124), C. H. Rolph *Further Particulars* 1987 (p. 104), Richard Tuck *Hobbes* 1989 (p. 222), K. C. Wheare *The Constitutional Structure of the Commonwealth* 1960 (p. 253) and for quotations from its indispensable dictionaries (pp. 8, 34, 42–46, 55, 116, 140–144, 173, 199, 208, 212, 240, 244, 255); Pan Books for Roger Scruton *A Dictionary of Political Thought* (pp. 20, 41, 100, 129–130, 213); Alan Pattison (p. 256); Penguin Books Ltd and Curtis Brown Group Ltd for Tom Harrisson *Living Through the Blitz* (pp. 105, 182–184, 193); the *quotation from The Devils* (©David Magarshack 1963) is reproduced by permission of Penguin Books Ltd; excerpts from Evelyn Waugh's *Scoop* (p. 242) and Hilaire Belloc's *Sonnets and Verse* Pimlico, a division of Random Century (p. 209) are reprinted by permission of the Peters Fraser and Dunlop Group Ltd; Princeton University Press for Michael Howard and Peter Paret's translation of Clausewitz *On War* (p. 181); Peter Quiddington (p. 25); Alan Ramsay (p. 256); *The Review of Politics* for 'What Does "Political" Mean?' (p. 6); Senator Grahame Richardson (p. 126); Alek Schulha (p. 242); Jack Simons (pp. 100–101); *The Spectator* (p. 200); Mike Steketee (p. 101); Joanna Strangwayes-Booth *A Cricket in the Thorn Tree* Hutchinson (p. 51); Anne Summers *The Curse of the Lucky Country* National Centre for Australian Studies (p. 265); John Tate (p. 25); Thomas Nelson for A. de Crespigny and A. Wertheimer *Contemporary Political Theory* (p. 32); excerpts on pp. 246–249 copyright Time Australia, 1988; Paola Totaro (p. 245); Hannah F. Pitkin *The Concept of Representation* University of California Press (p. 65); University of Michigan Press for W. H. D. Rouse's translation of Xenophon's *Anabasis* (p. 180); University of Queensland Press for C. A. Hooker "On deep versus shallow theories of pollution" in Robert Elliott and Arran Gare *Environmental Philosophy* 1983 (pp. 9, 10), Kett Kennedy 'William McCormack: forgotten Labor leader' in D. J. Murphy *et al. The Premiers of Queensland* 1990 (p. 78); Anthony Walker (pp. 202–203); Alan Watkins (p. 200); Leicester C. Webb *Politics and Polity* Australian National University (p. 60); Weidenfeld & Nicholson Ltd for Bernard Crick *In Defence of Politics* (p. 149); Arnold Wesker *Words as Definitions of Experience* Writers and Readers Publishing Cooperative (p. 39); Mrs Neil Bedford Whitlock for Randolph Bedford *Naught to Thirty-Three* (pp. 47, 51, 263); Hugo Young and *The Guardian Weekly* (p. 83). Section 11.10 of this book is a revised version of an article which appeared in *Dialectic: Journal of the Newcastle University Philosophy Club* XXII (1984).

Abbreviations

AFR	*The Australian Financial Review*
APD	*The Attorney's Pocket Dictionary*
APF	*Australian Political Facts*
BPF	*British Political Facts*
CBA	Commonwealth Bank of Australia
CDC/DJ	Canada – Department of Communications/Department of Justice
'CdR'	'Cola di Rienzo'
CODCE	*Concise Oxford Dictionary of Current English*
CT	*The Canberra Times*
CW	*The Catholic Worker*
DHI	*Dictionary of the History of Ideas*
DPCP	*The Dictionary of Physiological and Clinical Psychology*
DT	*The Daily Telegraph* (Sydney)
DTM	*The Daily Telegraph Mirror* (Sydney)
EP	*Encyclopedia of Philosophy*
EPsy	*Encyclopedia of Psychology*
ER	*Encyclopedia of Religion*
ERE	*Encyclopedia of Religion and Ethics*
FDMT	*The Fontana Dictionary of Modern Thought*
Fed	*The Federalist or, The New Constitution*
GSE	*Great Soviet Encyclopedia*
IDMB	*International Dictionary of Medicine and Biology*
IESS	*International Encyclopedia of the Social Sciences*
IM	*The Independent Monthly*
LCdR	*The Life of Cola di Rienzo*
LPA	Liberal Party of Australia
MCWS	*Marxism, Communism and Western Society*
NCE	*The New Catholic Encyclopedia*
NEB	*The New Encyclopaedia Britannica*
NH	*The Newcastle Herald* (New South Wales)
NS/S	*New Statesman/Society*
OCCL	*The Oxford Companion to Classical Literature*
OCCM	*The Oxford Companion to the Mind*

ODCC	*The Oxford Dictionary of the Christian Church*
ODQ	*The Oxford Dictionary of Quotations*
OED	*The Oxford English Dictionary*
OxLD	*Oxford Latin Dictionary*
PI	*Philosophical Investigations*
PPW	*Political Parties of the World*
PSCC	*Political Scandals and Causes Célèbres*
QPD	*Queensland Parliamentary Debates (Hansard)*
SMH	*The Sydney Morning Herald*
SOED	*The Shorter Oxford English Dictionary*
SPD	*Serving the People with Dialectics*
ST	*The Sunday Telegraph* (Sydney)
TA	*Time (Australia)*
TDNT	*Theological Dictionary of the New Testament*
TP	*Talking Philosophy*
VPD	*Victoria Parliamentary Debates (Hansard)*
WNWDAL	*Webster's New World Dictionary of the American Language*
WPLD	*Words and Phrases Legally Defined*

Introduction

This book is concerned with certain words which seem basic to political discourse. Though a work of theory, it is not primarily a work *about* theory (conscious or deliberate theory, anyway: see *TP* 5.5D, E). It concerns itself primarily with words as elements in the vocabulary of politicians and activists, commentators and 'the general public'. Most philosophical works on 'key political concepts' have been focused on the writings of philosophers and other theorists. Less technical works tend to be philosophically crude and too thoroughly biased by prejudices about the incurable wickedness of politicians, etc. I try to take 'ordinary' political discourse seriously and to use philosophical techniques to bring out its full flavour, its strengths, its weaknesses. The 'Masters of Political Thought' (Plato, Aristotle, Hobbes, etc.) are not totally ignored. They help to keep our telescope steady and reorient it from time to time, but it will be focused on ordinary political thought. (Our telescope is also a microscope.)

This is a wordbook. Like a dictionary, it lacks a plot. It is not designed to be read through from beginning to end. In other ways, it is unlike a dictionary. The words chosen need to be treated at length, so their number is limited, and treatment at length must be controversial. Hence, the book lacks the dictionary-beseeming virtues of comprehensiveness and impartiality. Another non-dictionarial feature is that articles are arranged not alphabetically but topically. If someone asks 'But why *this* topical arrangement?', my only short and general reply is 'Why not?' There are many cross-references and a copious index to help readers find their way about. Chapter 1, which deals with some methodological and 'foundational' issues, is something like a 'real chapter'; i.e., it approximates to having a beginning, a middle, and an end. Most of the others are really *gatherings*: each is more like a gallery than a painting. There is no need to 'begin at the beginning, and go right on to the end, then stop'. The matters discussed in chapter 1 deserve a place at the beginning of the book. That in no way implies that the reader must read it first. Though the book lacks a plot, it does not lack a unifying thesis, and that is: the incurable contestability and controversiality of the language of politics (1.17). This thesis is stated, argued for, and exemplified throughout. But the book is not one continuous whole. It could not do its own kind of job if it were. It has a beginning, but it has neither a middle nor a finish.

I have selected words which are central to political discourse and have dealt in passing with less central words which are closely related to them. I do not claim to have dealt with every word which is central to political discourse. There are three particularly glaring omissions: 'freedom', 'equality', 'justice'. There is a great need for a study of the role of these words in actual, day-to-day political discourse, but that task could not be accomplished in less than a volume apiece.

I am writing primarily for students, though with hope of also interesting scholars, academics and members of 'the general public'. The book is introductory (or almost so), but I beg all readers to remember that, as Anthony Kenny has said, 'Philosophy has no shallow end.'

1 Hunting the wild concept

I took pains to determine the flight of crook-taloned birds, marking which were of the right by nature, and which of the left, and what were their ways of living, each after his kind, and the enmities and affections that were between them, and how they consorted together.
(Aeschylus, *Prometheus Vinctus*, 488–492. Quoted, Namier, 1957: p. ii)

INTRODUCTORY

1.1 'National unity', 'the people', 'popular opinion', 'general interest', 'democracy': these are familiar, important and troublesome terms. Though they are in no way technical, esoteric or exotic, it is not always easy to understand statements in which they figure. They are loaded with theory and ideology, sometimes with very diverse and conflicting theories and ideologies (*TP* 5.5D, 7.2D). There is sometimes bitter warfare between different ideological tribes, each wishing to make the Sacred Object (i.e., one of these terms) its own exclusive property (i.e., the words are *contestable*: see 5.34 and *TP* 8.10B). Often, the terms are used by people who are not knowingly adherents of any of the warring tribes and each tribe will insist that the use of the term commits the artless user to its side only. Such claims are in urgent need of critical investigation.

1.2 These words are *wild*, in a special sense. Unlike technical terms, they have not been bred in captivity. (Even carefully bred technical terms can escape and become wild. They sometimes mate with words which are thoroughly wild and the progeny can be terrifying.) The words we are interested in are terms of everyday political discourse. They are used in talking *about* politics, but it is important not to misinterpret that 'about'. A doctor uses various terms, technical and non-technical, to talk about a patient's digestive system. Those terms themselves are not part of the patient's digestive system, but the terms we are interested in are themselves part of politics. 'Political power', according to a grossly overrated thinker, 'grows out of the barrel of a gun.' Perhaps, but it also grows out of human mouths and ears. Politics is, amongst other things, an essentially linguistic activity (see Ball *et al.*, 1989: pp. 1–5; see also 2.14H). Words and facts are often contrasted, but, if we are trying to understand politics, words are some of the facts which we have to understand.

We are concerned with political words, with (e.g.) 'representation'. Should we concern ourselves only with 'representation in the political sense'? I think that that would be a mistaken way to begin. For one thing, there may be nothing very 'the' about it; i.e., the political concept of representation may not be unitary (see *TP* 1.14A, 5.30). Another difficulty is that such a way of beginning assumes too easily that the political use(s) of word *W* is/are entirely independent of or detachable from its non-political uses. According to a certain ideal, technical terms should be like that: any connection with non-technical uses is, at most, of historical interest. Non-technical *W* casts no light on technical *W*, and vice versa. There are some technical terms which approach or even attain that ideal. 'Distribution' in logicians' lingo is light years away from the distribution of a leaflet or of wealth. Physicists apply the words 'charm' and 'strange' to particles, but the only connection with non-technical uses of those words is a joke (like the relation between their 'quark' and the same word in *Finnegans Wake*). And there are some political terms like this, e.g. some of the terms of parliamentary and electoral procedure (e.g., 'division'; 'declaration'). There are also jargon-words of political studies: 'polyarchy', 'electoral swing', 'two-party-preferred vote'. These are, at least in intention, precise, unitary, strictly definable, and having only just so much connection with non-technical discourse as the theorists allow. The language of political debate is usually not like this. The words of that language come (in Austin's phrase, 1979(a): p. 201) 'trailing clouds of etymology' and carrying all sorts of associations, acknowledged and unacknowledged, with non-political talk. They should be treated as wild until definitely shown to be non-wild. Their use frequently embodies tacit beggings of relevant questions (*TP* 4.23) and mutually incompatible values and demands.

ABOUT (AND LARGELY AGAINST) DEFINITIONS

> I certainly could not define either 'oak-tree' or 'elephant'; but this does not destroy my right to assert that no oak-tree is an elephant, nor will my readers find this thesis hard to understand or be likely to challenge it.
>
> (Geach, 1976: p. 390)

> When philosophers use a word – 'knowledge', 'being', 'object', 'I', 'proposition', 'name' – and try to grasp the *essence* of the thing, one must always ask oneself: is the word ever actually used in this way in the language-game which is its original home?
>
> (Wittgenstein, *PI* pt I, §116 1958(a): p. 48)

1.3   Am I in search of definitions? The reply 'It depends on what you mean by "definition"' is irresistible and also true (if not very helpful). There can be no doubt that people think that definitions are important. They certainly regard 'But how do you define "X"?' as a legitimate and powerful move in controversy. Geach cites philosophers who refuse to admit that a proper name is a word unless a 'rigorous definition' of 'word' can be produced and others who respond to the argument 'Machines are not alive and therefore cannot think' by demanding a definition of 'alive' (1972: p. 34). And, of course, as Geach also points out (1976: pp. 38–39), it is people in general who go on like this, not just philosophers. What is it that they are demanding when they demand a definition of 'X' (or of X)? It would seem that they want a formula which:

(i)   gives the meaning of the word;
(ii) will cover all and only those things which can be correctly described as Xs or as X things (almost invariably, it is substantives, including verbal nouns, and adjectives which people want defined);
(iii) will not only identify the Xs or the X things, but will also state what it is that makes them Xs or X things.

It seems also to be assumed that, though arriving at such a formula may be a long and difficult task, the formula once arrived at should be both succinct and luminously clear, a portable X-detecting device. I think it makes sense to say that this demand for a definition of 'X' is a demand for a specification of *Xness*: a definition, as popularly conceived, is an essence-stating formula. The motivating thesis for demanding a definition of 'X' is that, unless we can give one, we do not know, or do not *really* know, what we mean by 'X' and are in danger of misidentifying non-Xs as Xs, failing to identify genuine Xs, and misconceiving the whole point of being concerned about Xs. Sometimes an even stranger thesis is also at work: that, unless somehow a speaker can explicate every detail of what he is saying, he cannot be understood by his audience (9.18).

1.4   Most people, I think, have that in mind when they ask for a definition, but it is not the only thing they have in mind. Whatever else it may be, defining is drawing limits, giving something a shape, or indicating what shape it has. That, of course, is part of the history of the word (see Robinson, 1962: p. 55) and it is also part of its present. Shapes as seen in a mist can lack definition: one may not be able to see where they end. To define my rights and duties is to draw a limit to what I may do, to what I must do, to how I must be treated. If the Pope defines a dogma, he gives a limit, a shape to what is to be treated as agreed, thus limiting both the area of freedom and the area of obligation with respect to the topic. The popular belief, as I read it, is that definition (in the sense of an essence-stating formula) is essential to definition (in the sense of delimiting, indicating a shape) of a word, concept, idea, term. That is a view I reject. Definition in the second sense is (or can be) of great importance, but definition in the first sense is not always a necessary means to definition in the second sense. Indeed, it may be a hindrance. Definitions of the kind talked about by Socrates and by numerous logic textbooks[1] flourish in geometry:

1 A POINT is that which has no parts, or which has no magnitude.
2 A line is length without breadth.
3 The extremities of a line are points.
4 A straight line is that which lies evenly between its extreme points.
5 A superficies is that which has only length and breadth.
6 The extremities of a superficies are lines.

(Euclid, 1933: p. 1)

But geometry is an artificial world of ideals. Its relations to the familiar world of experience, though real and significant, are oblique. In geometry, the definitions create the terms or objects. No wonder they fit so well! To define terms or objects of ordinary experience is not to create but to (try to) exhibit what is already there. How should one define the word 'chair'? *Concise Oxford*'s answer seems as good as we are likely to get: 'Separate seat for one, of various forms.' Notice, though, that it provides no answer to the question 'Is it *really* a chair?' when 'it' refers to a fortuitously, but conveniently shaped rock or to a priceless, frail antique on which no one could safely sit. That is not a weakness of *Concise Oxford*'s answer, upsetting as that might be to the very tidy-minded. If it did provide a 'Yes' or 'No' answer to that question, it would misrepresent ordinary usage. If ordinary usage were so precise as to allow such an answer, it would be less adequate to deal with the plurality and polymorphism, the 'etceteraness' of human interests and purposes.

1.5 Not too long ago, I set a first-year essay on *conscience*. I suggested that, as a starting point, an essay-writer might sketch two or three situations in which the words 'conscience' and 'conscientious' are used, and that, after reading some of the things on the reading list, s/he might then ask what these uses of the words committed the speakers to. No one did that, which was rather a pity. 'Conscience' and 'conscientious' are not just some philosopher's technical terms, invented by him and meaning exactly what he wants them to mean, neither more nor less (*à la* Humpty Dumpty: see 2.1), still less are they empty forms waiting to be filled in with whatever anyone chooses. They are part of the moral discourse and moral experience of mankind and can, therefore, be expected to be pretty complicated, not the sort of thing which can be accurately 'defined' in one crisp little sentence. But the students had been advised by earlier teachers, 'Always begin with a definition,' and (by golly!) they did. 'Conscience', I was told more than once, 'may be defined as an interior voice which instructs an individual about the rightness and wrongness of actions.' I suppose it *might* be so defined, but is there any good reason why it *should* be, still less why it *must* be? When one's philosophical investigations have to do with words like these (words, that is, which are very much common property), it is better to talk, not about *defining terms*, but about *analysing concepts*. The concept of X is (*very* roughly speaking)[2] what is done, can be done and might intelligibly be done with the word 'X', with its cognates ('xious', 'xify', 'xification', etc.), and with at least some of its kinwords and contrasters.[3] One analyses a concept by observing, participating in, and reflecting on the appropriate area of human experience and human discourse (i.e., thought and talk). That is hard work, much harder than plucking a definition out of the air or out of an introductory text but it is much more worth doing. Unless one does that kind of conceptual analysis, there is a strong danger that one's theory will simply be at cross-purposes with reality. The definition of (e.g.) 'conscience' may be neat. The arguments may be elegant and even, in their way, sound. And they may have *no relevance at all* to what we do with the word 'conscience' when we are actually dealing with moral perplexities. And what is true of that word is true of the vocabulary of politics.

1.6 An investigation of the concept of X seeks (*inter alia*) to determine criteria for the reasonableness of claims, questions, etc. embodying Xish words. It aims at establishing such lines of demarcation as can be established and counts the establishing of a fuzzy line as just as much a discovery as the establishing of a neat, clear line or of a clearcut distinction (cf. Wittgenstein, *PI* §71, 1958(a): p. 34). Indeed, in such an investigation, neat, clear lines and clearcut distinctions are *prima facie* suspect. When people fuss about definitions, the word in the 'X'-place is almost always an abstract noun whose primary importance is as a label for a problematical *area of discourse*, not as the name of an *elusive essence*, an etherial Beast Glatisant, which is the quarry of our search (cf. White, 1962: pp. 21–24, 150–151). There is not a substance (e.g. Politics, or Democracy or Unity) whose essence is to be captured in a definition of the corresponding noun (cf. Wittgenstein, 1958(b): pp. 1, 7) – or, rather, even if there is, it is not true that all other questions about the area of discourse must wait on that capture. The appropriate image for an investigation like this one is not the hunt for a mysterious beast, but the patient work of an ornithologist trying to understand systematically the behaviour of birds of a very familiar species. And the most striking feature of most concepts is not their unitariness and purity but their complexity. See Pitkin, 1967: pp. 10–11, 255.

1.7 Essence-hunters always focus on abstract substantives (i.e., nouns) and that is a mistake. Abstract nouns are derivative from their non-substantive cognates and their substantive but non-abstract cognates, not the other way round. The habit of treating nouns as more significant than non-nouns has caused far more trouble than enough. 'Solar' is junior to 'sun' (in Latin *sol*), but 'privacy' is junior to some uses of 'private', hence a concentration on the question 'What is this thing called "privacy"?' might well be self-frustrating.

1.8 'My concern', says one philosopher, 'is with concepts not merely with words' (Milne, 1972: p. 48). I think I might say the same (though I would not say it in a form which suggests that one can be concerned with concepts without being concerned with words). Chapter 3 concerns the word 'politics'. If I were concerned *merely* with the word (or with the mere word), the facts that it has eight letters and rhymes with 'tricks' and 'fix' would be matters of some importance to my enterprise, but they are not. I am concerned with the words 'politics' and 'political' as instruments in our attempts to understand and manage the world and ourselves. That is my notion of what it is to be concerned with a concept. Another philosopher objects that 'Defining "political" in terms of the principle of "meaning as use" is likely to lead . . . to a thoroughgoing conventionalism' (E. F. Miller, 1980: p. 57). He expects us, I think, to reel backwards in horror, saying 'No! No! Anything but that!' My reaction is rather different. I simply wonder what he is talking about. If we are trying to understand a concept, we are trying to understand a *social institution*, i.e., a product of convention. Saying that is in no way to denigrate it. I do not know what he means by 'a thoroughgoing conventionalism'. I think I know what *a thoroughgoing conventionalism* in morality would be. It would be the thesis that there can be no moral appeal against a morality established in a society. But the thesis that looking for the meaning of a word should be a matter of watching how the word behaves entails nothing like that. The same writer asks 'Does . . . [the] meaning [of "political"] depend simply on its use, as the followers of Wittgenstein have argued? Do we mislead ourselves when we search for the real meaning of "political" in things to which it might refer?' (ibid.: p. 65). But my notion of investigating the use of a word in no way involves renouncing a consideration of things to which the word might refer. Indeed, it requires just that. The phrase 'real meaning', however, is worrying. It suggests some occult object like a Platonic *eidos* or form, existing apart from the world in which people talk and argue. (See 3.2–3.3.)

1.9   But, with respect to the central words of political talk, the essence-hunters are not entirely misguided. We cannot fob them off by quoting Geach's wisecrack about oak-trees and elephants. For the most part, to ask for a definition of 'oak-tree' or 'elephant' would be a matter of either pure science or pure bloody-mindedness. If someone tells us that his oak-trees are in danger, or that he has a plan to protect the elephant, we do not ask him 'What is an oak-tree?' or 'What is an elephant?' We ask him what the danger is, how bad it is, what or whom he wants to protect the elephant from and how. But the words I want to consider are closely tied up with complex interests and complex conflicts of interests. That makes them worth investigating for their own sakes and also to avoid bamboozlement, including self-bamboozlement, but it would be a mistake to assume that a successful investigation must produce neat little formulas. We need to improve definition, but definition*s* may be no help at all.

A VERY FAMILIAR CLASS OF ANIMALS

> Every philosophical question is a request for a description of a class of
> animals – of a *very* familiar class of animals.
>
> (John Wisdom, 1953: p. 112)

1.10   The opinion that, without a definition of Xness, we are quite ignorant about Xs is one which is often attributed to Socrates. We frequently find him saying such things in Plato's earlier dialogues; e.g., he ends a discussion on friendship by saying:

> Well, Lysis and Menexenus, you young fellows and I have made proper

fools of ourselves today. Anyone listening to us could say that, even though we regard ourselves as friends, we haven't been able to find out what a friend is.

(Lysis 223b)

Such remarks should not be taken literally. They are paradoxical hyperboles meant to spur us on to greater intellectual endeavour. If they are taken literally, they are very discouraging, very destructive, even corrupting: if you don't really know what crookedness is, why go to the bother of opposing what is called crookedness? (Cf. Geach, 1972: pp. 34–35.) But there are logical flaws as well. If Socrates, Lysis and Menexenus can distinguish friends from non-friends, friendly from non-friendly behaviour, etc., then they *do* know what a friend is, even if they cannot say what it is. *Their* question 'What is a friend?' is totally different from a culinary ignoramus's 'What is a roux?', or 'What is snurging?', asked by a puzzled reader of Barbara Pym's diary (1984: pp. 355, 20, 30), that being an undefined word of her own invention.

1.11   The 'define-your-terms-Oh-you-can't-then-you're-ignorant' element of the Socratic heritage seems to be the one which has soaked most deeply into popular western culture, but, in Plato's writings, there is another and counteracting notion of the knowledge being *there*, but implicit and in need of being made explicit. This is summed up in the metaphor of Socrates as an intellectual midwife, bringing ideas to birth out of the mental wombs which enclose them (see Guthrie, 1971; pp. 97–129; Crombie, 1964: pp. 16ff., 37ff.). This led Plato to adopt doctrines of innate ideas and of knowledge acquired in a previous existence. There we need not follow him. I do not want (here, at any rate) to criticise these doctrines on metaphysical grounds (*TP* 7.22A). Rather, I think that, even if true, they miss the point because they see the knowledge concerned as being a set of propositions implicit in (i.e., locked up in) individual minds, rather than implicit in the relations of individuals with one another and with their world, organic and non-organic.

1.12   We are members of a speech community which has, as part of its linguistic and conceptual equipment, such expressions as 'the people', 'general interest', etc. We therefore already have some knowledge of what the words mean – knowledge which is more implicit than explicit (cf. Dreyfus & Magee, 1987; Polanyi, 1958; Grene, 1966), knowledge which is closer to *knowing-how* than to *knowing-that* (cf. *TP* 8.14B; Ryle, 1949: pp. 27–32), but knowledge nonetheless.[4] The methodological pretence that we lack such knowledge may sometimes be useful, but its fruitfulness has been greatly overrated. Sometimes, it is confusing self-deceit. We believe that we have 'made a desert of our consciousness', but have not. A result is that our pre-existing beliefs are free to influence us in a totally uncriticised fashion. A more fruitful beginning is to take stock carefully of our actual situation with respect to the concept under investigation. Usually, the degree of ignorance we have actually attained is quite enough.

1.13   Thus, the appropriate way to investigate concepts like these is an *internal* way. I do not mean *simply* that the investigator should search his own mind (though he should), nor even simply that he should search within the discourses of people using the concepts (though, most emphatically, he should). What I mean primarily is that, when we reflect on such concepts as politics, unity, the people, they are not things externally related to us (as are the concepts of a roux or of snurging), neither are they merely things inside our minds. Rather, we are inside them. They are concepts in use *pervasively* in our speech-community, so we are working from within them (or at least, within something of which they are pervading elements). They are not mysterious little black boxes which we are trying to open. They are part of the air we breathe. 'Knowledge', as Kemp Smith says (1923: p. xxxviii), 'starts neither from sense-data nor from general principles, but from the complex situation in which the human race finds itself at the dawn of consciousness' – or, more likely, at the dawn of the consciousness that we have a problem, i.e., at the many dawns of many consciousnesses. ('If you look at a thing nine hundred and ninety-nine times,' says G. K. Chesterton, 'you are perfectly safe; if you look at it the thousandth time, you are in frightful danger of seeing it for the first time' (1960: pp. 16–17).)

1.14   Hence, John Wisdom's epigram about 'a *very* familiar class of animals' is not a pure metaphor. We need to treat it as a hyperbole, philosophy being more various than it seemed in the 1930s and 1940s to even so generous a metaphilosopher as Wisdom: but its talk of 'a *very* familiar class of animals' is entirely literal. In trying to understand concepts which are deeply rooted in our culture, we are trying to understand ourselves. When we make such an investigation of a key concept in another culture, we are doing anthropology. When the key concept belongs in our own culture, we are making 'that circular journey, from the familiar to the familiar, which is philosophical analysis' (another 'Wisdomism', quoted in Strawson, 1952: p. 259). Our condition, when we are puzzled by such concepts, is described well by Ludwig Wittgenstein:

> We want to *understand* something that is already in plain view. For *this* is what we seem in some sense not to understand.
>
> Augustine says in the *Confessions* ['What is time? If no one asks me, I know, but if I want to explain it to a questioner, I do not know.'] . . . something that we know when we are supposed to give an account of it, is something we need to *remind* ourselves of. (And it is obviously something of which for some reason it is difficult to remind oneself.)
>
> (*PI* pt I §89, 1958(a): p. 42)

As I said, we do not need to pretend more ignorance than we have if we are to become better acquainted with what we (in a very cloudy way) already know.

Taking a fresh and comprehensive look at the familiar can present difficulties, but the difficulties are greater when the thing we are thinking about is part of the structure of our thinking. If objectivity is possible only when what is being studied is clearly 'out there', clearly detached or detachable from ourselves, then objectivity is not possible in the investigation of these concepts. But objectivity is a very slippery notion and the proposition that *that* kind of objectivity is not possible does not imply that *no* kind of objectivity is possible. (The concepts we are investigating are not subjective. Being shared, they are *inter*subjective. I see no point in pursuing the question 'Are they objective?' (see *TP* 8.1B).)

1.15   When artists philosophise about the nature of art, they often confuse the questions 'What is art?' and 'What is the kind of art I practise?' Philosophers philosophising about philosophy are given to making the same mistake, with much less excuse. At one stage, those who went in for the clarification of concepts tended to claim that this was all that philosophy is and that people who seemed to be doing other kinds of philosophy were really either disguised clarifiers or non-philosophers. Another fault which philosophers (less venially) share with everyone else is a tendency to throw babies out with bathwater. Conceptual analysts[6] rightly rejected the notions of philosophy as the master-science and the philosopher as a universal expert, but, in doing so, they sometimes turned their backs on urgent practical problems. A notorious passage in Wittgenstein's *Philosophical Investigations* seemed to proclaim an extreme version of this creed:

> Philosophy may in no way interfere with the actual use of a language; it can in the end only describe it.
> For it cannot give it any foundation either.
> It leaves everything as it is.
>
> (pt I §124, 1958(a): p. 49)

I think that it is this that C. A. Hooker has in mind when he denounces: 'the irresponsible claim that philosophy is only conceptual clarification'. '[T]he suggestions of a non-committal clarificatory role disguise a deep-seated conservatism of intellect as well as of political persuasion' (1983: p. 59). Even if the Wittgensteinian pronouncement is taken entirely literally,[7] this is misguided. He says that *philosophy* leaves everything as it is. Radiology also leaves everything as it is. It merely depicts, clarifies, portrays, and then it collects its fee and lifts not one finger to rectify any unhealthy condition. Does that make radiology unduly conservative? No. It is for other branches of medicine to make the interventions. If the clarificatory role of philosophy is as 'noncommittal' as that of radiology, then the claim that philosophy is only conceptual clarification is not irresponsible or unduly conservative at all. It is as philosophers that we show that the Emperor has no clothes (or – oh, how paradoxically! – that he is quite adequately clothed). It is as something else that we decide what to do about him. Wittgenstein is unduly conservative only if he says, 'Philosophy leaves everything as it is, and it is impossible that philosophical findings should ever affect non-philosophy.' He does not say that; neither does he think it. Where Wittgenstein is wrong is in his suggestion that making changes must be a non-philosophical activity. The elaboration of a plan for change in a conceptual framework or in a morality is itself a philosophical task, which does NOT imply that only or all professional philosophers are good at making such an elaboration.

1.16   Hooker says, 'The philosopher's role is much more than auxiliary analyst, it involves the articulation of a wise way of life and the diagnosis of the deep roots of unwisdom in extant cultures' (ibid.: p. 59). That is something that *some* philosophers can do, and lots of good luck to them, but they will be helped by the clarification of concepts, which is my task in this book. I do not pretend to be noncommittal. I neither plead guilty to nor do I boast of irrelevance to the sweaty controversies of practical politics.

1.17   At the same time, one must not exaggerate the eirenic powers of conceptual clarification. There is a much-quoted anecdote of the American philosopher, William James (1842–1910). Someone dreamt up this example: A squirrel is clinging to a tree trunk. A man stands on the opposite side of the tree. He wants to see the squirrel, so he moves round the tree, but the squirrel moves in the opposite direction and keeps the tree between itself and the man. This dance continues and the man never sees the squirrel. Does the man go round the squirrel or not? James found a group of people furiously divided over that question. He tells us that he 'assuaged the dispute' by pointing to an ambiguity in 'to go round': the man is successively to the east, south, west and north of the squirrel (and so, in one sense, goes round it), but is never behind its back (and so, in another sense, does not go round it). Thus, there was no real disagreement once the language was understood (1975: pp. 27–28). Some regard that as the paradigm example of the relation of 'the philosopher' to 'practical people'. The practical ones are disputing hotly. Along comes the philosopher and shows them that they really do not disagree, and, as a result, they can get on with the job, peacefully and efficiently. But the clarification of concepts sometimes reveals that the differences between the disputants are greater even than they imagine. Philosophers have no business 'saying "Peace, peace" when there is no peace'.

Suggested reading

Austin, 1979(b); Geach, 1976: ch. ix; Pitkin, 1967: pp. 1–12; Skinner, 1989(a); R. Williams, 1983; Wittgenstein, 1958(a): p. 71.

WORDS IN THEIR NATIVE HABITAT: SOME PRACTICAL ADVICE ON STUDYING THEM

1.18   Dictionaries – *some* dictionaries – *can* be very useful in conceptual investigation. All too often, however, dictionaries are used in such a slapdash fashion that they are a snare and a delusion. A writer takes a quick look at a concise (or 'desk') dictionary, writes the sentence, 'According to the dictionary, "democracy" means "government by all the people, direct or representative"', and goes on from there, classifying this or that polity, practice, policy, etc. as democratic or not. Thus is a complicated concept analysed! That just will not do. It is misguided from the very beginning. Using the phrase 'according to the dictionary' is a very bad habit. It suggests that there is just one dictionary, which, really, is not true, and, though many dictionary-makers simply crib from other dictionary-makers, they do not all agree on everything. Say *which* dictionary. Further, 'according to the dictionary' encourages a sort of lexicographical fundamentalism: 'The Dictionary' becomes Holy Writ, to which nothing may be added, from which nothing may be subtracted. Dictionary entries should be read carefully and critically. In conceptual analysis, they are to be used as a guide to the living discourse which they profess to be summarising. The 'original home' of words is not 'The Dictionary' (or even *a* dictionary or dictionaries collectively), any more than the original home of streets is a book like *Gregory's Guide* or the London *A to Z*.

1.19   The fault is often in 'The Dictionary', not just in its use, especially if it is a concise (or 'desk') dictionary. Too often their treatment of words likely to be keywords of controversy is simply inept. The *Concise Oxford* (*CODCE*) on 'democracy' is a masterpiece of unhelpful superficiality. In conceptual investigations, 'desk' dictionaries, if useful at all, are useful primarily as sources of 'kin-words'. A good thesaurus (e.g., *Macquarie* or the Penguin *Roget*) can be much more useful. Sometimes, a 'desk' dictionary can give us a quick overview of a concept – a quick overview which solves no problems, but at least helps us to see what the problems are. *The Oxford English Dictionary* (*OED*), however, is the source of much more, and is indispensable. There are many, many Oxford dictionaries, even many of English, but only one is *The* Oxford Dictionary. In 1989, its second edition was published in twenty black folio volumes. The entries for a quite familiar word might fill several columns. Such entries are to be read carefully *and savoured*, especially the many illustrative quotations. The *OED* is streets ahead of *Webster*, even the genuine *Webster* (the vagaries of American copyright law have allowed a multitude of false pretenders). *Webster* has nothing like the detail of *OED* (though its pictures – *OED* has none – are a great delight). *The Shorter Oxford* (*SOED*) can also be helpful (though shorter than the *OED*, it is much longer than any 'desk dictionary'), but there is nothing like the *OED*.

1.20   When we are investigating a concept and using a dictionary as an aid, we should not look only at the entries for the abstract substantive (i.e., abstract noun), but pay equal attention to the entries for *cognates*; e.g., an investigation of 'representation' should take us also to entries for 'represent', 'representative', etc. Dictionaries do not *end* a conceptual investigation. Used sensibly (alertly, critically, savouringly), they are a way of beginning it well. Even the best dictionaries have their limitations. The most obvious one is that they stand still while the language wanders, meanders, gallops on. Raymond Williams's introduction to *Keywords* is well worth reading, as is *Keywords* itself, though Williams shamelessly exaggerates his own originality and most unjustly denigrates the *OED* (see Burchfield, 1976). While dictionaries and books like *Keywords* are immensely helpful, it is also important to keep one's eyes and ears open, noticing how words work in living discourse. Just about everything you read is a set text, as is what you overhear on the bus or in the coffee-queue. The method recommended by Austin (in 1979(b): pp. 186–187) can be very helpful, but there are other methods, e.g., taking a piece of theory and seeing how it squares with ordinary talk or simply amassing a great number of instances and seeing what order one can establish amongst them. I began this chapter with Namier's quotation from Aeschylus, because the kind of investigation which I recommend has much in common with Namier's approach to history: the collection and systematisation of a vast amount of detail.

2 Humpty Dumpty and various social objects

DECIDING MEANINGS

2.1 Humpty Dumpty and decisionism

'I don't know what you mean by "glory",' Alice said.
Humpty Dumpty smiled contemptuously. 'Of course you don't – till I tell you. I meant "there's a nice knock-down argument for you!"'
'But "glory" doesn't mean "a nice knock-down argument",' Alice objected.
'When *I* use a word,' Humpty Dumpty said in rather a scornful tone, 'it means just what I choose it to mean – neither more nor less.'
'The question is,' said Alice, 'whether you *can* make words mean different things.'
'The question is,' said Humpty Dumpty, 'which is to be master – that's all.'

(*Through the Looking Glass* ch. vi. Carroll, 1974: p. 193)[1]

That is the classical statement of the *decisionist* (or *extreme nominalist*) theory of meaning.[2] There are two scraps of truth which can be disentangled from it. One is that words do not have their meanings 'by nature'. The other is that, in certain circumstances, a very limited decisionism can be useful; e.g., one can say, 'I'm using the word "student" to include undergraduate students and those doing other coursework degrees, but not research students', or 'For the sake of brevity, I'll use the word "artist" to include/exclude writers.' The same sort of thing is found in the 'interpretation' section of an Act of Parliament; e.g., in the Public Assemblies Act [NSW], 1979:

3. In this Act, except in so far as the context or subject-matter otherwise indicates or requires –
'Commissioner' means the Commissioner of Police;
'court' means the Supreme Court of New South Wales or the District Court of New South Wales;
'organiser', in relation to a public assembly in respect of which a notification

has been given to the Commissioner as referred to in section 4 (1), means the person referred to in section 4 (1) (3) (i) by whom the notification is signed;

'public assembly' means an assembly held in a public place and includes a procession so held;

'public place' means public road, public reserve or other place which the public are entitled to use.

The Australian Military Regulations used to, perhaps still, say '"Horse" includes mule.'

In cases like those, the meanings of words are being extended or trimmed for special (and limited) purposes. A user of the language is declaring the meaning that he will give to certain specified words in a specified piece of discourse. That is, of course, perfectly legitimate, but it is legitimate because it is limited and occurs against a background of words used ordinarily, conventionally. What Humpty Dumpty overlooks is that a large part of the point of language is to *make oneself understood,* and, if someone acts on the principle that he can make any word mean whatever he wants it to mean, then, in a very literal sense, *we cannot really trust a word he says.* If everyone were to slap words about in that fashion, then we should have sheer chaos, the Tower of Babel; i.e., a linguistic counterpart of Hobbes's 'state of war' (*Leviathan* ch. xiii, 1991). Even limited decisionism can be hard to maintain. Common usage, driven out with a pitchfork, can return surreptitiously. (Common usage is a 'second nature'![3] See Geach, 1976: pp. 42–43.) In 2.2–2.7, I do a little mild Humpty-Dumptying with the aim of establishing some *instrument-words,* i.e., technical terms, *tools-of-trade* words. From 2.8 on, I am engaged in the non-Humpty-Dumptyan (and even riskier) business of *critical unpacking*.

SOME INSTRUMENT-WORDS

2.2 **Social object** (instrument-word)

A useful technical term introduced by Anthony Quinton:

> a group or institution which contains or involves a number of individual human beings, such as a people, a nation, a class, a community, a society . . .
> (Quinton, 1975: p. 1, see *TP* 1.15B)

2.3 **Collective** (instrument-word)

This word can stir the emotions. For some, it is a Boo-word, evoking all the worst horrors of subsidised medical care and the Pure Food Act. For others, it is a Hooray-word, an ideologically cosy substitute for 'committee' or 'club'. Those are equal and opposite sillinesses which have nothing to do with the use of the word in this book. Here it has a technical sense, thus defined:

Just about everything we can think of or experience can be regarded in two contrasting ways: as a *unit* (one thing of some kind) and as a *collective* (something made up of other things of some kind or kinds).

Some things (e.g., social objects) are more notably collectives than others (e.g., a rock). A human being is more of a unit than a society is.

2.4 Team of action (instrument-word)

Human social collectives vary greatly, not just in scale, but also in kind. One of the basic kinds is the *team of action* (Jouvenel, 1957: ch.iv): a group of people which comes into existence in order to achieve a specific result, e.g., half a dozen people pushing a car with the hope of persuading the engine to work. Polities are, usually, not like that. We know the aims and objects of the people trying to get that car going. We know the aims and objects of the Bantam Breeders Association or the Newcastle University Philosophy Club (both more complicated than those of that gang of car-pushers). But what of *Australia?* What are its aims and objects? The question is crazy. Australia just is not that kind of group. It approximates to a team of action in times of total war: the war needs to be won. That is the overall goal. And, once that is achieved, we can go back to our usual pursuits which do not add us up to a team of action. See also 5.41–5.45.

2.5 Polity (instrument-word)

I shall use this word to refer to such things as Australia, the UK, Iraq, Fiji, Canada, etc.; i.e., I am using it as a substitute for *some* senses of 'nation', of 'country' (7.17–7.18) and of 'state', words which are far too ambiguous and entangled to serve as instruments. Polities have heads of state, flags, central governments, and national anthems. In the twentieth century, they issue postage stamps and are (with rare exceptions) represented at the United Nations. Socrates would say that he doesn't understand this, but that is only because he is in the grip of a false theory (1.11–1.13). He would, however, be right if he said that I had done only half the job of explication. What is needed is a careful unpacking of the concept, aimed at finding the *rationale* (or *logos*) of its application to an agreed set of examples and its non-application to other social objects, such as firms, clubs, cities and the Commonwealth of Nations. But, here and now, I have neither the time nor the space. I do, however, something like that with *state* (2.6).

In modern colloquial English, 'polity' has few (if any) connotations or associations, which is why I prefer it to 'state', 'country' or 'nation', but it is A Word With A Past, and has had many other meanings, taking after its Greek original, *politeia*, which could mean a *system of government*, or a *constitutional system of government* (as distinct from government by means of what Locke called 'extemporary Arbitrary decrees'),[4] or a *system of government, neither purely democratic* (rule by the entire citizenry) *nor purely oligarchic or aristocratic* (rule by a small body), *but combining elements of both systems.*

(See Sinclair, 1951: chs iii, xi; Bury, 1951: ch. xi.) It could also be a near-synonym of *polis* (3.1). The Greek title of Plato's *Republic* is *Politeia*. 'Polity' can also mean *system of government*, as in Richard Hooker's *Of the Laws of Ecclesiastical Polity*. See *OED* 'Polity'.

2.6 State

A troublesome word, not only ambiguous, but trailing clouds of far too many mutually inconsistent and sometimes barely intelligible theories and doctrines. 'State' meaning *unit of a federation* ('state (1)') is no problem, provided that it is not confused with 'state' in the discourse of international relations ('state (2)'). There, it and my technical term 'polity' *refer* to the same thing, but it can *mean* a lot more (or sometimes less), because of those trailing clouds. The most troublesome of all senses is 'state' as in 'the state and the individual', 'state intervention', etc. I shall call this 'state (3)'. This state is the complex of such institutions as legislature, ministry, courts, public (civil) service, police, etc. We may be able to pin it down further, thus:

(i)   Primarily, the state (3) is the system whereby a differentiated, specialist group (or groups) make and enforce norms and decisions binding on the polity as a whole. The *typical* method of acquiring membership of a polity is not deliberate joining, and the claim of the state (3) to direct any member is based, not on his decision to join, but on his presence within the polity.

(ii) Further, a state (3) system is not itself subject to another state (3) system. Any agency outside the polity which issues norms, etc., binding on the polity is, to the extent that it does that, part of the state (3) system.

(iii) *Derivatively*, the state (3) is that differentiated specialist group (or those groups) considered as such.

(iv) The state (3) need not be one united and unanimous collective of people engaged in making the same norms. It may well be a collective of interacting sources of norms and sanctions and there may well be conflict amongst these different sources (see, e.g., Weller & Grattan, 1981).

State, in this sense, is sometimes contrasted with *civil society*, meaning (it would seem) the rest of the polity, especially its 'unofficial' systems of authority and customary regulation, but the line between state and civil society is not always easy to draw. The term 'civil society' has a nice, crisp, technical sound about it, but it is used in such very diverse ways that it is not always very helpful. (See, e.g., Scruton, 1983: p. 66; Benn & Gaus, 1983: index.)

Clause (ii) introduces the notion of *independence*, which admits of degree. It may be quite impossible to say precisely when, as a matter of politico-legal fact (as distinct from formal declaration), the European Community has moved from being an assemblage of treaty-bound states and become one federal state. See also 2.10 (*sovereignty*).

In that last sentence 'state' is used in its international-relations sense which can be given domestic flesh-and-blood thus:

A state (4) is a polity which has a state (3).

That, perhaps, is the sense 'state' has in 'for the protection of the state', 'in the interests of the state', but uses of such phrases should be scrutinised carefully. They have often been used to justify brutality. Apart from that, those in power sometimes have a tendency to confuse themselves with the state. Louis XIV, as an absolute monarch, could get away with saying 'L'état c'est moi' ('The state? That's me'), but less archaic governors sometimes behave that way and should not be permitted to get away with it. (They often get away with more than *le Roi-Soleil* could even have dreamt of.)

What is the relation between state (3) and state (4)? The state (3) as an institution is only one of many sources of regulation and control in *most* states (4). (For totalitarian states, see 2.16B.) It is the one with widest scope, in a way the most powerful, though this may be so only because it treats other institutions within the polity with respect, and, at least apparently and usually, conducts its activities according to commonly accepted moral rules.

A federal polity is a state (2) and (4), i.e., has a state (3), because, though power is divided between the centre and the units of the federation according to law, the powers of each and their limits are clearly defined. In feudalism, however, boundaries, both internal and external, both purely legal and geographico-legal, were too fluid to allow talk of a state (3) or state (4). For *acephalous* societies, see 2.7A below. For *society*, see 2.12A n. 17. (In intent, these remarks on *state* are a piece of critical unpacking, rather than of even mild Humpty Dumptyism, but some readers have disagreed so strongly with this view of it, that I put it here, rather than in the second large part of this chapter.)

Suggested reading

Scruton, 1983: pp. 446–448; Burnheim, 1985: pp. 19–50; Crick, 1973: pp. 38–51; d'Entrèves, 1973; Head, 1984; Krader, 1968; Graubard, 1980; Oakeshott, 1975(b): ch. iii; R. Robinson, 1964: pp. 158–173; Skinner, 1989(b). For *state-worship*, see 11.10C.

2.7 Government, governance (instrument-words)

A Lucy Mair draws a distinction between *having government* and *having a Government*. There are or have been many societies (e.g., Australian Aboriginal societies, and some societies in East Africa and Melanesia) which have lacked not only the state (3), but anything like it. (These are called *acephalous* (i.e., 'headless') societies.) There may perhaps be a chief or elders who are respected and generally followed, but have no power to coerce the disobedient. The members of such a society, however, recognise a distinction between fellow-members and non-members. They also possess rules of behaviour and recognised procedures for the redress of wrongs and the resolution of disputes.

In other words, they lack *a* government, but they do have government. They are far from being either in Hobbes's 'state of war' (*Leviathan* ch. xiii, 1991: p. 89) or in a clash-free, norm-free social nirvana. (For *anarchy*, see 2.9D. See also Pilgrim, 1965.)

It follows that the State or *a* government is not logically necessary for social order. It does *not* follow that every society would remain orderly if it were without a state or *a* Government. Arguing that because the Mbuti Pygmies manage to live in a stateless society we should do so too, is like arguing that because the Nuer, a very dark people in a very hot climate, get along without clothes, the Eskimos and melanoma-prone Westerners should do the same.

There is a more important lesson to be drawn from accounts of acephalous societies. If we turn from them to societies of the kind we are used to, we find that, even there, though the State may be indispensable, it is not the only maintainer of order, and that it would not be able to maintain order if it were not for less formal institutions, some of them remarkably like the informal institutions of an acephalous society. That is one reason for the near-ubiquity of potential 'political relevance' (3.40–3.44).

Suggested reading

Mair, 1962: pp. 7–122; 1965: chs vii–ix; Emmet, 1972; Meggitt, 1966; Parker, 1976; Roberts, 1979; Rowley, 1973; G. C. Lewis, 1898: pp. 18–19.

B   The word 'government' is, of course, ambiguous. The near-archaic 'governance' can be used for the *activity of government* (as distinct from the institution which performs that activity) (Laver 1983) is a lively discussion of what governments are and do and why we need them and when we do not.

CRITICAL UNPACKINGS (see 2.1 above)

2.8 The Ship of State

Our word 'government' comes from the Latin *gubernatio*, which comes from the Greek *kubernetes*, which means 'helmsman'. The metaphor of the Ship of State has been with us for a long time. In a not very systematic search of just three books of quotations, I found thirteen distinct uses of the ship as a political metaphor. There were eleven others which either *might* be political or were so general (about Life and all that) that they could be applied to politics. The metaphor itself can be steered in different directions. Two very influential uses of it are Plato's (criticised by Bambrough) and Oakeshott's (criticised by Crick and by Crossman), and it makes a difference whether the emphasis is on the shiplikeness of the polity or on resemblances between the task of the politician and that of the sailor.[5] Plato's is of the former type (as is Mao's) and Oakeshott's is of the latter.

One serious limitation of the Platonic analogy is this: the various duties of the members of a ship's company are directed towards one end, getting the ship to its destination. There seems no good reason why, in normal circumstances, we should expect every member of a society to be working towards a single end. A ship's company is a *team of action* (2.4), but polities are not. Totalitarianism (2.16B) is the attempt to organise a polity on these lines, and even a free polity moves in that direction under conditions of total war, but it is a bad mistake to use that as a model for the polity under *all* conditions (see 5.41–5.45). But all analogies have their limitations and it would be foolish to suspect every user of this one of being a possible totalitarian.

The all-in-the-same-boat metaphor sees a polity as a perhaps ill-assorted collection of people who need to find a way of living together (5.6 *et seq.*, 10.30) and have a common interest in staying afloat. This view of the polity can be challenged (6.17–6.29). 'Spaceship Earth' is an adaptation of this metaphor which, in addition, stresses the finitude of resources.

Suggested reading

Plato *Republic* 488A–489B (1974: pp. 282–283); Bambrough, 1956; Oakeshott, 1962: p. 127; Crick, 1982: pp. 111–123; Crossman, 1958: p. 135; Herbert, 1948: pp. 181–188, 243–246; Bartlett, 1980: pp. 62, 74, 127, 273, 511, 520, 599; *ODQ*, 1959: pp. 124, 190, 316, 425, 560, 566, 567; Stevenson, n.d.: pp. 52, 431, 824, 1095, 1161, 1774, 2152, 2246.

2.9 Ocracies and ocrats, archies and archs:[6] Forms of government; Imperialism

A   *Kratia* is a Greek word meaning something like 'power', 'government', 'rule'. *Arche* means much the same. By and large, 'xocracy' means *the system of rule by x* and an xocrat is either an advocate of xocracy or one of the xs who rule. By and large, 'xarchy' is (or would be) equivalent to 'xocracy'. *An xarch*, though, is *more likely* to be a *ruling x* than just an *advocate of rule by x*. But verbal habits here are very messy and tidy formulas are likely to be false. An advocate of monarchy (or of a particular monarchy – an important difference, that)[7] is not a *monarch* but a *monarchist*, whereas an *oligarch* can be either one of the ruling few or an advocate of rule by a few. A list of 'archy' and 'ocracy' words can be found in Roget, 1984: §5.2 para. 733 (pp. 326–327). Roget's list is incomplete and does not include 'coprocracy', a word which I have sometimes found very useful. For more on *ruling*, see 4.15.

B   Hobbes argues that by definition there can be only three forms of government:

> For the Representative must needs be One man, or More: and if more, then it is the Assembly of All, or but of a Part. When the Representative is One man, then is the Common-wealth a MONARCHY: when an Assembly of All that will come together, then it is a DEMOCRACY, or Popular Common-

wealth: when an Assembly of a Part onely, then it is called an ARISTOCRACY.
Other kind of Common-wealth there can be none.

(*Leviathan* ch. xix, 1991: p. 129)

Very neat, but it depends on the assumption that the only basis for a
classification of governmental forms is 'How many governors?' There are
other questions that matter: 'How are they recruited?'; 'How do they exercise
their governance (2.7B)?'; 'In what ways (if at all) and to whom are they
accountable?'; 'Is it possible to change governors peacefully?' etc. The *manner*
of Hobbes's argument is very much his own, but there is nothing idiosyncratic
about the mistake on which it is based. Although many of the archy/ocracy
words are indispensable, every one of them embodies in its very shape the
possibility of bad error. These matters are taken up in 8.20–8.27, which deal
with *democracy* and what I call the *kratic error*. (*Bureaucracy* is discussed in
2.13.) Alexander Pope's lines are much quoted:

For forms of government let fools contest.
Whate'er is best administered is best.

(*An Essay on Man* Epistle III ll.
303–304, 1966: p. 267)

They are themselves rather foolish, since they overlook the possibility (and it is
much more than a possibility) that some forms of government are more
conducive to good government than others and some more susceptible to abuse.
C   (i) Bernard Crick (1973) also maintains that there are three basic forms of
government: autocratic, republican, totalitarian. He emphasises 'basic' and says
that many sub-varieties are possible (1973: p. 88). His classification is based on
the question: *In what way does this form of government attempt to solve the
basic problem of the adjustment of order to diversity?* (5.31).

'Republican', in Crick's terminology, has nothing to do with what the head-
of-state is called or even with how s/he got there in the first place. In his
terminology, many (probably most) existing polities called 'republics' are
either autocratic or totalitarian and many (perhaps most) existing monarchies
are republics.[8] Crick loves to shock, but his classification is by no means
perverse and deserves to be taken seriously. He uses 'totalitarian' more or less
as most other people do (see 2.16B). By *autocracy*, he means a form of
government 'which attempts to solve the basic problem . . . by the enforcement of one [only] of the diverse interests' as the goal of government. Other
interests are made subservient to it (1973: p. 53). Standard use of the word is,
however, better represented by Scruton: 'rule by an agent who holds all power
himself, . . .and exercises . . . [it] in an arbitrary manner' (1983: p. 33). When
I speak of 'the autocrat' in 2.16A(ii), I am thinking of a rather pure, undiluted
instantiation (*TP* 1.9A) of that concept. For 'arbitrary', see *TP* 9.5B.
(ii) The word 'republic' is derived from Latin *res publica*, literally 'the public
thing', that which involves all the citizens as distinct from the many *res*

privatae (private things), each of which involves only some of them. (Notice that the *involvement* of all the citizens can be more or less or not at all active. See Barrow, 1949: ch. i; Benn & Gaus, 1983: chs i, xv.) Used that way, the word could apply to any polity, regardless of its form of government, but it can also carry the flavour of *that which exists for the good of all* (6.17–6.29), hence it becomes a word worth capturing, and it has been captured (sometimes by presidents-for-life who are succeeded by their offspring).

'Commonwealth' began as a translation of *res publica* with all its ambiguities and all its hopes and blandishments (hence, Australia's official title, on which see Murray-Smith, 1987: pp. 69–72). Its meaning, however, has been almost totally confounded by (a) its Cromwellian use (i.e., non-monarchy), (b) its application to the loose association of former British colonies, and (c) the American practice of using it as part of the title of its internally self-governing colonies. In 1991, the word was adopted as a name for an association of former units of the USSR. This suggests that use (b) has developed into a generic term for a loose association of polities. A messy development. See also 2.12A, B (*community*).

D *Anarchy* etymologically means *the absence of rule*, and is ambiguous between *the absence of [effective] rules, with consequent disorder and chaos* and the *absence of rulers, especially the state* (2.6). Most people use it in the former sense, to the great annoyance of people who call themselves *anarchists*, and use it in the latter sense. They are also (justifiably) irritated by the belief that an anarchist is a Bearded Man with a Bomb. See Scruton, 1983: pp. 15–16; Labedz & Ryan, 1988; Ryan, 1988(a); R. Williams, 1983: pp. 37–38; Bone, 1991; Docker, 1972; Ehrlich *et al.*, 1979; Guérin, 1970; Tier, 1975.

E Econocrat

> . . . the econocrats are creating a monopoly . . . in order to promote artificial and contrived competition . . .
>
> (K. Davidson, 1991)

> . . . the Government is mounting a concerted attack on Dr Hewson[9] as a dangerous, one-dimensional econocrat, an unfeeling professor of economics driven by computer models rather than feelings for real people.
>
> (G. Milne, 1991: p. 5)

I cannot recall meeting this word in any source earlier than September 1991. It refers disparagingly to *economists*, or, more specifically, to *economic advisers to governments* and *devisers of economic policy*. The adjective 'cold' tends to go with it. Thus, it imputes a preference for figures[10] over human beings, ill-founded arrogance, and undeserved, irresponsible power. It chimes well with the old characterisation of economics as *the dismal science* and with Burke's distaste for 'sophisters, oeconomists, and calculators' (1968: p. 170). It is close to 'ideologue' in one of its nastier senses. See *TP* 7.2D.

F Imperialism

α: Imperialism is actually not dead yet.

β: The nomadic Penans should be settled into modern homes and integrated into society.

Those two assertions were reported in the one newspaper story (*SMH*, 1991(b)). The fact that β was said might seem confirmation of the truth of α, particularly as the report makes clear that the assertor of β means *whether they like it or not*. But both assertions were made by the same person, Dr Mahathir, Prime Minister of Malaysia. The 'imperialism' he objects to is foreign criticism of his government (cf. 8.19 n; see also 7.1–7.21 (*nation*, *nationalism*), 12.44 (*autochthony*)).

> In almost every instance in which the rule of the Queen has been established and the great Pax Brittanica has been enforced, there has come with it greater security to life and property, and a material improvement in the condition of the bulk of the population.
>
> (Joseph Chamberlain, 1897. Quoted, Leigh, 1979: p. 71)

A wild (and disgustingly smug) hyperbole. What would it be if we deleted everything from 'in which' to 'enforced' and substituted 'of decolonisation?' Cf. 7.15.

'Empire' is an interesting word. In Henry VIII's Act of Appeals (1533), 'empire' means *sovereign polity* (2.10), one free from 'the authority of any foreign potentates', but earlier kings had claimed to be emperors in a sense more familiar to us: they claimed to rule more than one kingdom (Elton, 1974: p. 161). Contemporary use tends to stress the dominance of one nation or people (7.1–7.21, 8.1–8.16) over others. Contemporary users, however, are a little selective about what instances of dominance they are prepared to recognise explicitly. Despite obvious Russian dominance, few people ever called the USSR an empire (Reagan did, but without any clear idea of what he meant) and anyone who called Indonesia an empire would upset many people (especially the Australian Department of Foreign Affairs). This is not the sort of habit of usage which constitutes or changes the meaning of a word. Rather, it is an example of careless or dishonest classification. The inconsistency could be cleared up by writing in either of these assumptions: (1) Nothing is an empire unless it calls itself one; (2) Nothing is an empire unless there is a striking difference in skin colour between the parties involved. But that would make the word too silly for words.

Suggested reading

Scruton, 1983: pp. 215–216; Andreski & Bullock, 1988; Ritter, 1986: pp. 223–228; Gefter, 1976; Lichtheim, 1974; Schmidt & Mommsen, 1972; Stretton, 1969; Vasser, 1976.

2.10 Sovereignty

This is a dreadful word. I have a choice amongst three possibilities: (i) Ignore it altogether; (ii) Write a book about it; (iii) Say something brief and hope that it is neither silly nor misleading. Possibility (i) is pusillanimous and the word is too important to be ignored. Possibility (ii) is out, if only because I am writing *this* book. That leaves possibility (iii). There are two principal senses of 'sovereignty':[11] one international, the other intranational. In the 'intra' sense, a collective is a sovereign polity to the extent that its legal system and jurisdiction on that legal system are internal to the collective. An institution within a polity is sovereign to the extent that its decision-making capacity is not subject to that of any other body. Where I say 'to the extent that' in these definitions, some would say 'if and only if'. I am not sure whether sovereignty is a useful notion at all. I am sure that it is more likely to be if it is regarded as a matter of degree rather than an all-or-nothing matter. Some have asserted that, *as a matter of logic*, there must, within each polity, be a body which is absolutely sovereign: 'an uncommanded commander' of all within the polity (John Austin), 'a supreme, irresistible, absolute and uncontrolled authority' (Blackstone). That is clearly false. Try to find such a body within Australia or the United States. In the international sense, sovereignty is *independence*. A polity is sovereign to the extent that its governance (2.7B) and relations with other polities are performed by institutions internal to it. See also 2.6 (*state*).

Sovereignty is a species of *authority*, rather than of *power* (2.14–2.15). An Australian State parliament cannot impose a customs duty on goods imported from another State. That is a limit on its sovereignty, on what it legally can do (cf. 11.13B). If a government reacts to forces beyond its control by taking action which it would prefer not to, that shows a limit on its *power*, not on its sovereignty. Nevertheless, in both international and intranational senses, we can distinguish *nominal* from *factual* sovereignty. A puppet state is nominally sovereign, but in fact has to follow the will and seek the approval of the state that pulls the strings. From 1903 to 1977, the Panama Canal Treaty 'granted' Panama a different kind of merely nominal sovereignty over the Canal Zone. The United States was granted in perpetuity all the rights 'which it would possess *if* it were sovereign of the territory' (quoted, Greene, 1984: p. 14, my italics). Thus nominal legal Panamanian sovereignty was recognised while actual sovereignty (legal authority, not merely power) was given to the United States.

Some have argued that the closer political integration of the member-polities of the European Community would involve no diminution of their sovereignty or that of their legislatures, but rather a *pooling of sovereignty*. But if 'pooling' implies that a central legislature can make laws which legally apply to Xland against the wishes of the Xlandic legislature or that a central court can declare an Xlandic statute null and void, then Xlandic sovereignty has been diminished and talk of 'pooling' as something other than diminution is a sophistical obfuscation.

Suggested reading

Scruton, 1983: pp. 440–442; Hickey, 1971; Benn & Peters, 1959: ch. xii; Lindsay, 1962: ch. ix; Hart, 1961: ch. iv; Graubard, 1980: see index; Hinsley, 1966; G. C. Lewis, 1898: ch. v; *Spectator*, 1990; Brittan, 1990; Stankiewicz, 1969.

2.11 *Gemeinschaft* and *Gesellschaft*

A   These two German words (translatable as 'community' and 'association') were used by Ferdinand Tönnies (1855–1936) to contrast two types of societies. A pure *Gesellschaft* is a set of social relationships based on contractual relations and division of labour between purely self-interested individuals. The *Gesellschaft* is a means of harmonising their interests, so that painful clashes are minimised. The members' 'loyalty' (5.1–5.11) to it is simply a matter of seeing it as a useful instrument. In German commercial law, '*Gesellschaft*' means something like 'public limited company'. Members of one of Tönnies's *Gesellschaften* are, as it were, *shareholders*. *Gemeinschaft*, on the other hand, is a set of relationships based on kinship or affection or simply on a sense of belonging. The members see these relationships not as a means to an end, but rather as themselves an end. (But PLEASE, let's not get starry-eyed. See 10.14–10.15.) *Gesellschaft* is associated with *bureaucracy* (2.13).

B   These concepts are *pure* (or *ideal*) *types*, i.e., their use does not imply the existence of societies which display ONLY *gemeinschaftlich*[12] features or ONLY *gesellschaftlich* features. Rather, the concepts are tools for sorting out the almost limitless complexity of actual societies and social relationships (see Andreski, 1968(a); Ritter, 1986: pp. 201–206).

Suggested reading

Manley, 1968; Raphael, 1976: pp. 32–35; Kamenka, 1982; Tönnies, 1955; Loomis & Beagle, 1957; Chesterton, 1905: ch. xiv. See also 2.12A.

2.12 Community

A   *Services to the community* may earn you a 'gong' in the New Year Honours List. On the other hand, a minor conflict with the law may earn you a sentence of two hundred hours' *community service*. But that is not the full story of the strangeness of this thoroughly ordinary word. In one kind of use, 'community' is virtually synonymous with certain senses of 'the public' or 'the people': 'The persons belonging to a place, or constituting a particular concourse, congregation, company, or class' (*OED*; see also 8.6).

> Budget deficit notwithstanding, we must distribute the load between all sections of the community in a position to carry it.
>
> (Nolan, 1986)

To render industrial processes free from pollution costs money; ultimately this cost is met by the community.

(Tate, 1982)

A *community facility* is one available to people in general. 'The community', in this sense, can be used interchangeably with 'the taxpayer':

Tunnel cost blow-out: taxpayers face $1 bn bill

A secret report into the economics of the Sydney Harbour Tunnel shows that the project is set to generate huge losses – estimated to cost the community in excess of $1 billion.

(Quiddington, 1990)[13]

'Community' can be used also with a qualifying phrase, to pick out classes within that wider community: 'the local community', 'the business community', 'the ethnic community'[14] even 'the criminal community'.[15]

Another use of 'the community' makes it virtually synonymous with 'the public' in another of its senses: the public as *the rest* relative to some smaller group or some institution (cf. 8.8–8.9). 'Out there in the community' is a typical phrase. 'Community policing' means (roughly speaking) the involvement of miscellaneous non-police in police work. When a political candidate declares himself to be 'community-based', he is (I think) declaring that his contacts, experience, opinions are not derived solely from his party (if he has one). He claims 'contact with the grass-roots' (on which, see Sperber & Trittschuh, 1964: p. 179). Cf. *civil society* (2.6).

To apply the word 'community' in one of those senses to a group says nothing about the kind of interrelationships holding amongst its members. We could, without absurdity, apply the word to Colin Turnbull's atomised, unloving, unlovable, emotionally and intellectually desiccated Ik (see Turnbull, 1974). As we speak of *the business community* or *the migrant community* we could also speak of the *utter-isolate community*, i.e., the class of all and only those, within a given polity, who are each utterly isolated. But quite clearly, that is not the sort of community which people go *in quest of*, seek for a *sense of*, lament the *end, collapse* or *eclipse of*, hope for the *rebirth of*, etc. 'Community' in that sense is approximately equivalent to *Gemeinschaft* (2.11), *approximately* since it embraces the notion of *community spirit*, which is often seen as a *gemeinschaftlich* leavening of a *gesellschaftlich* lump.

'Community' is, therefore, a dangerous (though indispensable) word. It can apply to the small, sympathetic, face-to-face group of intimates, or to the entire population of a huge polity. It is, as Kenneth Hudson remarks (1977: pp. 39–40), a 'warm' word, but it is applicable also to social relationships and systems which are not warm and, in some cases, cannot be.[16] In the 1980s, we were told that psychiatric patients (with the exception of those dangerous to themselves or to others) should not be kept in institutions, but should be cared for *in the community*. (See, e.g., Laurance, 1987; Rollin, 1987) 'Institution' is a very cold word indeed, and the message sounded splendid, but, in this case, 'the community' refers to the whole polity minus the psychiatric hospitals, and that is no warm, caring nest.[17] Here we have a euphemism which ranks with those memorably condemned by George Orwell:

> Millions of peasants are robbed of their farms and sent trudging along the roads with no more than they can carry: this is called *transfer of population* or *rectification of frontiers*.
>
> (Orwell, 1970(e): p. 166)

Suggested reading

Orwell, 1970(e); R. Williams, 1983: pp. 75–76; *FDMT*, 1988: pp. 148–149; Banks, 1979; Bonjean, 1971; Gusfield, 1975; König, 1968; Janowitz, 1961; Nisbet, 1976; Plant, 1974; Stein, 1960; Vanier, 1979.

B *'Community' and 'society'*

> A man was vigilant and determined when he followed a panel van used in a robbery . . . until he got its registration number, a judge said yesterday . . . . He commended Mr W for his service to the *community*.
>
> (*NH* 1991(b), my italics)

> Mr H also was given a two-year jail term to express *the community*'s disapproval of his attempt to attack the judge in the court-room during the trial.
>
> (*NH* 1991(a), my italics)

Not so very long ago, those judges would have said 'society' rather than 'community', but 'society' has become a *complaining* word:

> . . . the way society has controlled and manipulated people . . . through sanctions and laws about sex.
>
> (Leeder, 1984)

> . . . a champion of values which modern society has discarded as old hat – temperance, the importance of family life, and reliance on work.
>
> (Gill, 1984)

> The funny little old man became the object of society's taunts.
>
> (Barrass, 1985)

> '. . . the death penalty is a vengeful and dehumanising act, especially when the persons killed are those whose lives society has twisted up literally from birth.'
>
> (Quoted, Hall, 1990)

The Man-from-Mars could be forgiven for thinking that there are two quite distinct entities, Community (which, on the whole, is reasonable and worthy of respect[18] and Society (which is tyrannical, insensitive, stupid: in short, a stinker). But Society is merely Community *misliked* (to borrow a word from Hobbes: *Leviathan* ch. xix, 1991: p. 130). This pejorative use of the word 'society' is not itself new (see, e.g., Hardy's *Tess*, ch. xxiii, 1975: p. 174). What is (at least comparatively) new is its total victory, in popular speech, over non-pejorative uses[19] and the replacement of those by 'community'. A journalist tells us that remnants of the USSR chose to call themselves a commonwealth because 'It is the loosest form of . . .organisation on offer, looser than federation, confederation or community' (Dejevsky, 1992). Any notion looser than 'community' is loose indeed.

2.13 Bureaucracies, etc.

A *Public/civil servants and services*

In Australia, we say 'public servant'. The corresponding term in the UK and US is 'civil servant'. 'Civil' here means *non-military*. (The Man-from-Mars might believe that 'Primus is a public servant' means either 'Primus is at everyone's beck and call' or 'Primus is a public benefactor of great humility', but Mars is far away.) These terms have strict and less strict senses. They also have standard examples. Strictly and legally, public/civil servants are those who are appointed under a piece of legislation governing the public/civil service. This can produce clashes with popular usage. In Queensland, a member of the staff of the State Library is, in law, a public servant. Someone doing similar work at the Parliamentary Library is not, even though he, too, is paid from the State Treasury. This is more than a mere legal quirk,[20] but both would (intelligibly and sensibly) be popularly styled *public servants* (i.e., government employees).

Under most anglophone legal systems, judges,[21] soldiers, teachers in government schools, and policemen are not public servants, and neither are 'ministerial advisers', appointed by and entirely responsible to their ministers. Those who legally have the status of public servant are a heterogeneous bunch: typists, medical officers, permanent heads of department, cleaners, etc. In common usage, the standard examples are *administrative and clerical officers employed by government departments*. That too is a very mixed class.

Suggested reading

Boyce *et al.*, 1980: pp. 216–219; Page & Painter, 1993; Scruton, 1983: pp. 65–66; Aberbach *et al.*, 1981; Crisp, 1972; Hawker, 1981; Niskanen, 1973; Weller, 1989.

B *'Bureaucracy', 'bureaucrat', 'bureaucratic' in popular parlance*

In popular and journalistic parlance, these are invariably terms of reproach, complaint or disrespect. If saying 'you politicians' can be a little risky (4.12), saying 'you bureaucrats' is dynamite. If someone calls himself *a bureaucrat*, he does so in the same spirit as a journalist may say 'we hacks', or as you or I might say 'I *am* a fool.' (We are not grateful if someone says 'How true!') When we do not want to reproach, complain or be disrespectful, we say 'civil/ public service/servant' (government) or 'administration' (more general).

Primarily, the term 'bureaucrat' is applied to *clerical and administrative officials*. The standard and central cases are members of the civil/public service (see A above), though any organisation with a large administrative–clerical wing can be intelligibly said to have its bureaucracy. The word, however, is not always purely descriptive. It often tends to suggest such traits as inefficiency, sloth, 'legalism' (*TP* 8.5A), undue privilege, needless and self-serving complication, pointless prolixity of language, etc. The participle 'bloated' tends to go with it, the proposition that there are too many bureaucrats being frequently treated as an axiom (though no one is happy at being kept waiting when he visits an office).

This use of 'bureaucracy', etc. frequently expresses a fear lest (or a full-grown conviction that) too much of the resources of an organisation are being consumed by its clerico-administrative wing. This is part of a fear that administration may or has become an end in itself or even a society operating primarily for the good of its members (see 9.31–9.44 on *corruption*). Especially in non-State bodies (but also in (e.g.) health services and armies), those doing 'The Real Work' of those bodies[22] rightly resent any suggestion that the clerico-administrative wing is the centre (or heart or brain) of the body. The senior officials of a certain university once proposed to name a new administrative building The University Centre. That did not please those engaged in study and teaching.[23]

These fears are just, though it would be foolish to imagine that they are always realised or that they justify unremitting hostility to all things called '*bureaucracies*'. There are various paradoxes or insoluble surds involved. The larger an organisation becomes, the more bureaucratic (in *some* sense: see A above and C below) it *must* become, and that opens the possibility of bureaucracy (in some nasty sense). It is obviously true that the primary duty of policemen is to police, just as that of philosophers is to philosophise, and that performance of those primary duties can be badly hindered if they have to do much clerico-administrative donkey-work (which they may not be much good at, anyway). But releasing them from such tasks inevitably increases the numbers of full-time clerico-administrative workers (and/or non-workers), thus worsening those fears sketched above and perhaps leading to a situation where those doing The Real Work have lost control over it. Here, as so often elsewhere, a large part of sanity is a continual effort to strike an unstrikable balance (cf. 4.8, 10.31, 11.10E). See D. Emmet, 1966: especially ch. ix; Morris-Jones, 1949.

C 'Bureaucracy' in technical discourse

Sociologists and political theorists endeavour to use 'bureaucracy', etc., descriptively and neutrally. Their starting point is the work of Max Weber (1864–1920) whose notion of bureaucracy included these characteristics: a salaried administrative staff, the members of which have definite areas of jurisdiction, governed by written rules. The offices held by these people are arranged in a definite hierarchical order. They hold their offices by legal appointment, not by birth. Their promotion is governed by seniority or merit. Any authority that these office-holders have is derived from the office held and is not a personal possession. See M. Weber, 1948(a): pp. 196–244.

There are various questions asked about this: How well does it apply to the things actually called *bureaucracies?* Does it adequately distinguish bureaucracies from non-bureaucracies? Is bureaucracy something peculiarly modern (11.5)? Can bureaucracy co-exist with the computer or do they get along together all too well?[24] See especially Brown, 1979. Bureaucracy is associated with *Gesellschaft*, not *Gemeinschaft* (2.11).

Suggested additional reading

Albrow, 1968; 1970; Scruton, 1983: pp. 46–47; D. Bell, 1988(a); Kamenka, 1989; Kamenka & Krygier, 1979; Murray-Smith, 1988: pp. 8–11; B. C. Smith, 1988.

D *Apparatchik*

The governing apparatus of the Communist Party of the Soviet Union was known as *The Apparat*. An *Apparatchik* was, primarily, a member or agent of the Apparat, though the word could also be a euphemism for 'agent of the secret police'. It has also been used for functionaries of other political parties, though never of party-leaders. It is not complimentary. *OED* (2nd edn) has some interesting quotations.

2.14 Power

A *Power* and *authority* are concepts basic to political discourse, and, being basic, they are difficult to talk about. Another difficulty is the extraordinary breadth of the words. At its broadest, any ability, even any potentiality, can be called a *power*. We need to narrow it down. 'The power of a man . . .' says Hobbes, 'is his present means, to obtain some future apparent Good' (*Leviathan* ch. x, 1991: p. 62), but that also is too broad for our purposes. Having the price of a meal is a means to some future apparent good, but not even a small instance of *political* power. Political power is a form of power *over people* (and it is part of Hobbes's story[25] that having power in the sense of *his* definition requires that someone has political power over people, including oneself). Politicians, we are told, Only Want Power. Richard Crossman, a British MP for twenty-nine years, disagrees:

[T]he most cursory examination of the character of politicians is sufficient to contradict this old wives' tale. There are, of course, Members of Parliament whose object is to shape the affairs of men in their own likeness and whose keenest pleasure is the mastering of a crisis. But they are few in number; and . . . they are usually suspected or even disliked by their colleagues. The vast majority of British politicians . . . shudder if ever the moment comes when decision is unavoidable and power must be exercised ruthlessly.

[What an ex-Member misses is] certainly not *personal* power. Treading the lobbies under the cold eyes of the Whips, queueing for skinless sausages in the tea-room at 3 a.m., or failing to catch the Speaker's eye for a whole day – the average Member enjoys less power than a sergeant in the Army or a London bus conductor.

. . . Politicians are ambitious not to *make* important decisions but to *say* important things – and to read them next day in Hansard. . . . The politician has a streak of the actor in him. . . . What he desires is public life – to 'be in' on great events, preferably as a star, but, if not, with a one-line part.

(1958: pp. 3–4)

'. . . to shape the affairs of men in their own likeness . . . the mastering of a crisis . . . to make important decisions . . .': Most politicians, Crossman says, do not desire power and, hence, do not desire these things, but power must have other instances as well, since bus conductors hardly shape the affairs of men in their own likeness, etc., and the words seem not to fit quite comfortably on the activities of an Army sergeant, though he comes closer to it than the conductor does. But the sergeant does, like the Centurion in the Gospels,[26] 'say to this man, Go, and he goeth; and to another, Come, and he cometh; and to [yet another], Do this and he doeth it'. Even the bus conductor, when he says, 'Move down the centre there' or 'The bus is carrying a full load. No more on', can usually expect ready compliance with his orders.[27] Like the centurion, or the sergeant, the bus conductor can get people to move in a manner and a direction which he nominates. And that, Crossman says (by implication), is something which the average MP cannot hope for. (He may have overstated his case, but, even if so, it is a valuable overstatement.)

B   The last few paragraphs are not a definition of political power (or of anything else), but they do suggest some of the things involved in power-talk. Stanley Benn's 'power paradigm' is useful:

X, by his power over Y, successfully achieved an intended result, r; he did so by making Y do b, which Y would not have done but for X's wishing him to do so; moreover, although Y was reluctant, X had a way of overcoming this.

(1967(b): p. 424)

Benn does not present this as a Socratic definition of *power*; i.e., as a set of characteristics which every instance of power must have and no instance of non-power may have. He does, however, present it as a set of characteristics which most[28] instances of power have to some extent, though the absence (or only weak presence) of one or two does not inevitably rule out something as an instance of power. Considerable absence or weakness of several might reasonably lead us to say, 'Not exactly power. "Influence" is a better word.'

Benn's paradigm enables us to single out different aspects of an instance of power; e.g., how did X induce Y to do b? How much was persuasion? How much was coercion? And what kind of persuasion? It is useful also because it draws our attention to cases which do not quite conform to it; e.g.:

Y was not reluctant, but, if it had not been for X's instigation,[29] the possibility of r would not have entered Y's head

OR

Y was not reluctant, but would have been if the proposal had come from anyone but X

OR

So far from being reluctant or unaware, Y ardently desired r, but r would not have come about without X's instigation

OR

Y may not do b (thus frustrating the achievement of r), but, in that case, X can make Y suffer severely.

The last kind of case raises the possibility that what is a striking demonstration of power seen from one angle may, seen from another, be a marked failure. But we need those qualifying phrases about angles. Some theorists have presented analyses of power which imply that to cut someone's head off is not to exercise power over him. And that means that their analysis is badly holed below the waterline.

There are other cases of power which are further away from Benn's paradigm; e.g., 'veto-ing' or 'spoiling': Y cannot hope to initiate anything successfully on his own, but can make things very difficult for X and his projects if X disregards the wishes of Y. Or: Does X's reliance on Y as an underling or an instrument mean that Y has (some) power over X? (Or, perhaps: In what circumstances would such an assertion be more than a play on words?) Consider Mill on the government of Russia:

The Czar himself is powerless against the bureaucratic body; he can send any one of them to Siberia, but he cannot govern without them or against their will.

(*On Liberty* ch. v, 1972: p. 166)

C   Nothing of what I have said is an objection to Benn's paradigm of power. Again, it is not a definition. The fact that it can provoke such questions is a strength, not a weakness. But it needs supplementation lest it, too, suffer that hole-below-the-waterline. I propose the following as a supplement, not as an alternative:

> X has power over Y to the extent that X can significantly (and intentionally) affect Y's interests for good or ill, AND to the extent that Y cannot comparably affect X's interests.

Benn's paradigm stresses the effect on Y's actions (i.e., on Y as *agent*). Mine stresses the effect on Y as enjoyer and sufferer (i.e., on Y as *patient*[30]). In most (?all?) cases, what falls under (*TP* 1.9A (ii)) Benn's paradigm (or thereabouts) will fall under mine also. Some of the cases which fall under mine will not fall under his. But we need both if we are to do justice to human discourse and human experience:

> When one of the old sultans was preparing to receive [foreign ambassadors] . . . he would always keep them waiting a long time, perhaps a whole day. Then, when he thought they had been sufficiently humbled, he would give the order – 'Let the dogs be fed and clothed.' After that, they would be . . . given food and robed in caftans.
>
> (Ambler, 1962: p. 155)

Any analysis of political power which ignores that sort of thing has lost its way badly.

D   The editors of an anthology containing two essays on power say:

> [The writers] agree on several major points. First, both suggest that power must be defined in morally neutral terms, stripped of any moral or emotional connotations. Power has long been considered an 'evil', but this view must be avoided at all costs if the concept is to be useful.
>
> (de Crespigny & Wertheimer, 1971: p. 15)

I myself have not noticed that power has long been considered an evil, with or without inverted commas: dangerous, yes; sometimes corrupting (9.31–9.44), but hardly *an evil*. 'Is water clean or is it not?' would be a silly question. 'Is power an evil or is it not?' is no better. (In both cases, we concern ourselves with specific types or individual instances.) If avoiding such silliness requires a definition 'in morally neutral terms', then so be it. But what exactly is to be 'stripped of any moral or emotional connotations'? The *definiens* or the *definiendum*?[31] If the concept has 'moral or emotional connotations', removing them is not stripping, but amputation, even butchery. To try to explicate political concepts while steadfastly ignoring human hopes, fears and aspirations is to refuse to do the job properly.

E   Why do certain uses of the word 'power' give people a queasy feeling? Why is 'X is fond of power' rarely a compliment? Why does 'Y is in X's power' usually suggest that Y is in an unfortunate position and X in a morally dubious one? Partly, it is because the ordinary user of the word is more aware of the 'patient' aspect than social theorists seem to be, and primarily because these phrases say *only* that Y is subject to X, that X can get Y to do things that X wants him to do or that X can hurt Y. They say nothing about any rules that may limit that subjection, or about any purposes that may legitimate it, or about any contractual or quasi-contractual act of Y's that constituted a voluntary institution of his relationship to X, or about any loyalties or affection between X and Y. The phrases say nothing about the interests of anyone but X.

If X is a teacher and Y is one of his pupils, then X has power over Y in a quite 'Benn-ish' sense (i.e., X can get Y to carry out his instructions, etc.). If X is an examiner or a surgeon and Y is a candidate or patient, then X has power over Y in a different sense (i.e., X can affect Y for Y's weal or woe). In all three cases, Y is subject to X. But if that is, in X's eyes, the most important thing about his relationship to Y, if that is the thing he most *likes* about it, the aspect which *appeals* to him, then X should not be in such a job. It might even be a good idea to lock him up. (See also 2.16A(ii).) At the end of his essay on power, P. H. Partridge says:

> . . . if we happen to be interested in moral issues connected with power and its operation, it is very obvious that such well-worn assertions as Acton's 'power tends to corrupt and absolute power corrupts absolutely' . . . are not in an undissected form either illuminating or interesting.
>
> (1963: p. 125)

Tosh. Acton's remark states one of those truths we know, but often try to forget, so it is both illuminating and interesting. If it were not, there would be no point in reading essays such as that of Partridge. See 9.30 (*Realpolitik*, etc.). For power as *coercion*, see 2.15C.

F 'Being in power' and the perks thereof

The phrase 'in power'[32] usually means 'in office' and a party in office can usually do more of the things it wants to do when it is in office than when it is out. Hence, it is appropriate that a political party should strive for power. Crossman tells us (in effect) that an individual MP has little of the 'Go-and-he-goeth' kind of power, but what he says about the excitement of '"being in" on great events' indicates clearly enough that being in on them as a government MP must have a special charm.

But does the politician seek power as a means or as an end?

The question misconstrues the means/end distinction. Obviously, there is such a distinction. In a Roget's-*Thesaurus* fashion 'means' and 'end' are opposites, mutual contrastives, but their opposition is not like vertebrate/invertebrate (*TP* 10.1B). It is closer to academic-staff/student. To identify something as a vertebrate is to identify it as not an invertebrate and vice versa. On the other hand, someone can be both a member of the academic staff and a student. The means/end distinction is like that. That might sound a bit odd, because we do tend to have the habit of thinking of means and ends as if nothing could be both. An example, however, will show that that is a mistake. A person's job is a means to getting his livelihood. But (if he is lucky) his job may also be one of his ends, something he is interested in for its own sake. In that case, getting his livelihood is also a means to continuing in his job. For the politician, power (in the shape of office and the influence which goes with it) can be both an end and a means. Power is an end because it is something he tries to get. Power is a means because it is something he must have if he is to achieve anything else. Cf. 11.6A.

The politician likes the tangible perks of office.[33] As an American senator said, 'After you have once ridden behind a motorcycle escort, you are never the same again.' Do we say that these are aspects of power or do we say, 'No. They're *consequences* of power'? I do not care, but, if we are trying to get an understanding of political power as an object of desire, competition, contempt or fear, we must take them into account.

G *The powerful and the powerless*

These are contrary, not contradictory opposites (*TP* 10.1B). The words 'great' or 'greatly' occur in all *OED*'s definitions of 'powerful'. For 'powerless', it says 'without power', 'devoid of power or ability', 'helpless'. Hence, it is possible to be neither powerful nor powerless. Somehow, we manage to get along without a single word meaning 'having a moderate amount of power'. It needs to be noticed, however, that *OED*'s definition of 'powerless' states an extreme limit.[34] Most actual usings of 'powerless' are elliptical for 'virtually or significantly powerless', just as 'Tom is penniless' is not proved false if Tom can buy a sandwich. For most societies, 'Society is divided into two classes, those with power and those without' is at best a hyperbole. It will be an illuminating hyperbole about some societies; literally true only rarely. We should make sure that it is one or the other before we assert it, otherwise our political thinking is in danger of degenerating into a jumble of slogans and caricatures.

The Benn analysis, the Hobbes definition, and the formula about capacity to affect for good or ill (see B and C above) can be plausibly represented as alternative senses of the word 'power' (alternatives, though converging in many of the actual occurrences of the word), but 'powerful' and 'powerless' partake of all three simultaneously (a further reason for being cautious about accounts of power which depart from common usage: see D above).

'Primus is powerless' implies that Primus is not *in power*, that he lacks *power over* others, but that is not (or should not be) the main point. The main point is that, to a very significant degree, *he is unable to further and defend his own interests*. If Secundus has that ability, it does not follow that he has power over anyone, but he does have power *with respect* to others. There are limits to *their* power over *him*. That ability (like power in the sense of Hobbes's definition) is an important form of *non*-powerlessness (as it were): a necessary (but not sufficient) condition for being powerful, but a necessary-and-sufficient condition for not being powerless (*TP* 4.16). Is it a form of political power? Yes or no? I do not mind what answer is given to that, so long as it is recognised as a politically important form of power.

H   Is it true that 'Politics is all about power', that 'Power is the central concept of political theory'? I think we should be wary of superlatives, of all-abouts, of nothing-buts, of phrases like 'the central' (*TP* 5.19, 5.30). Certainly, power is a very important concept in politics, but, if we go all superlative about it, we may give ourselves the impression that every political event is the product of someone's decision, which is far from being true (*TP* 5.29). Politics is about power and its limits and how they are to be coped with: 'the art of the possible', yes, but the art of coping with the impossible, too. As for the motives of politicians, they are as mixed and muddled as those of the rest of us. See also 3.12–3.17, 3.27, 4.8, 4.13–4.15, 8.27, 9.25–9.28. For *power-politics*, see 9.30. Not even military power is a matter of brute force and *nothing* else. As Hume remarked:

> The sultan of Egypt or the emperor of Rome might drive his harmless subjects, like brute beasts, against their sentiments and inclinations; but he must, at least, have led his Mamelukes, or praetorian bands, like men, by their opinion.
>
> (1951: p. 148)

See also 10.1–10.5 (*morale; morale and physical factors*).

Suggested reading

Benn, 1967(b); Dahl, 1968, 1970: chs i–iii; Scruton, 1983: pp. 366–367; D. V. J. Bell, 1975; de Crespigny, 1968; Duffy, 1986; Jouvenel, 1952; Kernohan, 1989; R. King, 1986: ch. vi; Lucas, 1967: see index; Lukes, 1977: ch. i; W. J. M. Mackenzie, 1975; Neumann, 1950; P. H. Partridge, 1963; Pasquinelli, 1986; Pfeffer, 1981, 1992; Riker, 1964; Russell, 1928; E. V. Walter, 1964; Wartenberg, 1988.

2.15   Power and authority

A   The first thing to say about these is that they need to be carefully distinguished. The second thing is that, in some contexts, the two words are interchangeable.

B   One distinction is between, on the one hand, what X can do and succeed in getting done (in some way comparable to Benn's paradigm (2.14B–C)) and, on the other, what X is entitled to do or have done in that way. The entitlement may be moral or legal. Charles I, when brought before a court set up by his enemies, refused to plead, saying that the court was illegal and spurious. Bradshaw, its President, said:

> . . . it . . . [is] not for you, nor any other man to dispute the jurisdiction of

the supreme and highest authority in England. . . . [Y]ou are . . . to find you are before a court of justice.

The King replied, 'I see I am before a *power*.' One reporter did not hear the words, but caught the tone and guessed that he had said, 'Pish, Sir! I care not a straw for you' (Wedgwood, 1964: pp. 142–145), and that was a fairly accurate report. The King had said that he was in their power, but their power over him was illegitimate and unworthy of respect; they lacked authority. In this sense, 'power and authority' is synonymous with 'might and right'.

The distinction can work in the other direction as well: X may have a legal or moral entitlement but his rulings and orders may be disregarded. Charles I was perfectly aware that his would not be followed by his captors. That great draftsman of violated and discarded constitutions, Sir Ivor Jennings, wrote:

> . . . nobody can transfer power, except in a purely legal sense. What is transferred is legal authority and legal authority does not necessarily confer power. If you have legal authority to knock a man down, you still have to knock him down; and he may prefer to knock you down. Similarly, if a group of nationalists have legal authority to govern, it does not follow that they have the power or capacity to govern.
>
> (1961: p. 337)

He cites the Congo in 1960 as an example. There have been others, not all of them in Africa.

C There is another quite different distinction drawn between authority and power. To the extent that people do X's bidding because of their respect for him, for his office, or for what he has said, X is exercising authority. To the extent that they do his bidding out of fear of what he can have done to them if they do not, X is exercising power. 'Power' here = 'coercion', which it did not on the previous distinction. Authority as dealt with in this distinction need not be the same as in the previous distinction, since we can recognise that the Pirate King's men obey him not out of fear but out of respect, without committing ourselves to the legitimacy of his rulings and orders. (Authority here is power in a 'Benn-ish' sense (2.14B).) Similarly, an expert or someone regarded as wise may have authority (in the sense that the fact that s/he has made some utterance makes that utterance seem special and worthy to be followed within some community or other), but have no *power of enforcement* whatsoever.

D Jennings speaks of 'power . . . in a purely legal sense'. That is a sense in which 'power' and 'authority' can be used interchangeably. Section 51 of the Australian Constitution begins:

> The Parliament shall . . . have power to make laws for the peace, order, and good government of the Commonwealth with respect to:–

Then follows a list of the topics on which legislation by the Federal Parliament will be valid. For 'power', read 'authority' and no difference is made.[35] See also 11.13B (*ultra vires*).

E   In a rough, wide, general fashion, we can say that X has authority (i) to the extent that his pronouncements are (or (ii) to the extent that he is entitled to have them) accepted and/or followed. (The entitlement referred to is entitlement in terms of some set of rules or values.) To the extent that X has authority of the (i) type, he is a person in *de facto* authority. To the extent that he has authority of the (ii) type, he is a person in *de jure* authority. These Latin phrases mean, respectively, 'as a matter of fact' and 'by right or by law' (the latter ambiguity will trip us up sooner or later, but it need not do so here). An instance of authority may be both *de jure* and *de facto*.

Someone might object that this definition implies that just about everyone has *some* authority. True, but I do not think that matters. Any reasonable definition of intelligence or creativity would imply that just about everyone has *some*, but not that it is informative and non-misleading to apply the predicates '. . . is intelligent' or '. . . is creative' to just about everyone.

When we talk of *de jure* or *de facto* authority, the pronouncements which we have in mind are primarily *prescriptive*: commands, rules, laws, appointments, etc. (*TP* 5.12A). But there is a parallel notion which concerns descriptive or propositional pronouncements. This is *being-an-authority-on* . . . . If X has (or is believed to have) more than usual knowledge of or experience in a special field, then X's pronouncements about that field will be received (or should be received) with more credence than those of someone without that special knowledge or experience. This is the authority of the expert.

F   There are some curious *non*-entailments within authority-talk (i.e., entailments which the Man-from-Mars would mistakenly think were there):

(i)   I ask you the time. You say 'Five past two'. I believe you.
      In that case I accept that it is 2.05 *on your authority*, but it does NOT follow that I have treated you as (or am committed to the proposition that you are) *an authority on time*.

(ii) Primus signs a legal document *giving Secundus authority* to do the following things on Primus's behalf: to sign cheques, convey property, receive debts, sue, etc.[36]
      It does NOT follow that Primus has appointed Secundus to a position of authority. (It would be different if Primus had appointed Secundus to manage his (Primus's) factory.)

Suggested reading

Benn, 1967(a); Davie, 1969; McMorrow, 1967; Peabody, 1968; Scruton, 1983: pp. 32–33; E. D. Watt, 1982; De George, 1976.
   Additional reading: Anscombe, 1981: ch. v; Cameron, 1966; Cassinelli, 1961; Flathman, 1980; Friedrich, 1967: lectures IX, X; Jouvenel, 1957: pt I,

1963: pt IV; Manschreck, 1971; Nisbet, 1973; *Nomos* 1958, 1987; Raz, 1990; Rhodes, 1969; Tuck, 1972.

G   'Defer' meaning 'postpone', etc., and 'defer' meaning 'pay respect', etc. are mere *homonyms* (*TP* 2.6B). The latter (which is always followed by 'to') is the one I am concerned with. The *OED* entries for this and its cognates should be read in full. If Primus pays deference to Secundus, then he treats Secundus with respect, perhaps as his superior, either in general or in some particular matter. If Primus believes that Secundus is an authority (2.15E) on fish, then he may revise his own opinions on fish *in deference* to Secundus. The most common adjectival form is 'deferential', not 'deferent' (I do not know why).

Someone called *the deferential voter*[37] has played a big role in political sociology. People have argued thus: 'In Britain, Labour is the party of the working class. The Conservatives are the party of the middle and upper classes. The working class is more numerous than the middle and upper classes, but the Conservatives often win elections. It follows that a substantial number of working-class people vote Conservative. Why?' This has been called 'the problem of the Tory workingman' ('working-class Tory' would be better). One hypothesis was that the working-class Tory voted *deferentially*, i.e., because s/he believed that ruling should be done by those of higher status. Then, along came the opinion-surveyors who found (it is said) that the number of deferential working-class Britons was, in fact, much too small to account for the working-class Tory vote.

So, new hypotheses were needed. Perhaps they *don't know* they are working-class. Needler (1991: p. 84) says that the Conservatives are the party of other things beside the middle and upper classes. They are, he says, the party of the Anglican Church and also of what he tendentiously calls 'national chauvinism' (5.40), and perhaps one or both of these may outweigh class in the minds of working-class Tories. Some daring thinkers have suggested that working-class Tories may vote Tory for the same reason that Lord Mountbatten[38] voted Labour: they choose their party because they prefer its policies or believe it to be more competent.

'Deference' should not be confused with 'diffidence' (from Latin *diffidens* = 'lacking in confidence or in trust'), nowadays meaning 'lacking in *self*-confidence', though, in the seventeenth century, it was closer to its Latin origin. See Hobbes's *Leviathan* ch. xiii (1991: pp. 87–88).

Suggested reading

Needler, 1991: ch. viii; R. McKenzie & Silver, 1968; D. C. Moore, 1976; Nordlinger, 1967; Parkin, 1967; R. Rose, 1974(b): pp. 527–530; Shils, 1975: pp. 276–303.

2.16   Authoritarian; Totalitarian; *Gleichschaltung*

A   (i) Jack Dominian says:

I . . . believe that authority and law are an inescapable part of human life
. . . [A]t the same time . . . [I believe] that, however necessary both are,
they can never be the principal means through which life is sustained.[39]

(1976: p. 11)

And so say all of us, I suppose. Or almost all of us. Some might reject it, not
precisely because they want to write 'do not' in front of one or other of those
two inscriptions (*TP* 1.7) of 'believe', but because they fear that such a
formulation might be used as the thin end of an objectionable wedge (*TP*
9.5D), authoritarian or libertarian. Apart from such cagey people, just about
everyone could happily sign his name beneath the quotation without telling us
a great deal about himself, but that does not mean that it is an *empty* truism
(*TP* 3.18). For one thing, it can provoke the question 'Right-oh. What *are* the
principal means?' (Dominian's answer is likely to be different from G. E.
Moore's (1903: pp. xxiv–xxvii and ch. vi) and both would differ considerably
from the answer of Gordon Gecko or a life-member of Hell's Angels.)

But there is another thing that makes it interesting: it suggests a rough scale
on which one can place opinions, one's own and those of others. 'Authoritarian' is to *some* extent a dirt-is-matter-in-the-wrong-place word: i.e., it is used
to complain about excessive or inappropriate uses of (or emphasis on)
authority. Or, even when it is not a complaint, it can be used to talk about a use
or emphasis which is unusually strong (cf. 9.22). I do not object to the
existence of armies, but I might say 'An army is an authoritarian environment'
to make the point that there is a greater emphasis on obedience, rank and
conformity in an army than in most other environments.

The rough scale works like this: Primus has a view concerning the
importance of authority and law to the sustaining of life. Someone who gives a
much higher importance to authority and law is a person whom Primus is
committed to regard as an authoritarian. This does *not* make the word wildly
ambiguous, though it can make it indeterminate until you know what his
criteria are. See *TP* 2.3 (*meaning and criteria*).

(ii) As Arnold Wesker says:

. . . evil must be carefully measured and accurately named . . . or we might
find ourselves drawing blood . . . when to spit would be enough.

(1976: p. 8)

'Authoritarian' is not a mere rude noise or posh substitute for 'bullying' or
'arrogant', neither does every instance of bullying or arrogance deserve that
title. Some are too small, many too big. A person who overemphasises law and
authority might also give high value to justice and fairness, and, even, within
his own narrow limits, succeed in being often just and fair. By my criteria,
General De Gaulle, Captain MacWhirr and Sir James Murray[40] were all
authoritarians, and, to some extent, living with or under any of them would
(therefore) have had its tiresome aspects, but anyone who thinks that the

difference between them and Hitler is merely one of degree is linguistically, morally and psychologically tone-deaf.

The autocrat (2.9C) (e.g., the bully, the tyrant (political or domestic)) is addicted to power, not to authority. The authoritarian is legalistic (*TP* 8.5A), but the autocrat is anti-legalistic and arbitrary (*TP* 9.5B). He may disguise himself in the costume of authority (e.g., Mussolini's appropriation and debauchment of ancient Roman symbols, especially the *fasces*), but it is power he loves and the most spectacular use of power is to inflict pain and harm, to destroy people's hopes, or, alternatively, to bestow benefits capriciously. The authoritarian overemphasises law and order, but the autocrat despises law and order.[11] He glories in inconsistency and disorder (so long as it is his own), because that prevents his subjects from making sense of their situation, of 'knowing where they stand'. The autocrat wants even truth to be his creature (*TP* 8.21B). The authoritarian would purge the *kosmos* (*TP* 1.10D) of much of its variety. The autocrat would purge it of order. The autocrat wants to be a 'law unto himself' and an incalculable chaos to everyone else. If Hitler had lived much longer than he did and if he had succeeded in imposing his 'New Order' on Europe, he himself would have had to disrupt it, lest it become intelligible to others. That, after all, is what Stalin did. Such a person 'declares [him]self infallible, and at the same time attacks the very concept of objective truth' (Orwell, 1970(b): p. 163). Rule by De Gaulle, by MacWhirr, by Murray would be a pain in the neck, but it would be light years away from autocracy (2.9C) or totalitarianism (B below). Perhaps we need a new word for those Hitleroids who are avid for power: '*potestarian*' (from Latin *potestas* = 'power').

(iii) For the psychological notion of the *authoritarian personality*, see Schmitt-Mummendey, 1972; Madge, 1962: see index; Rokeach, 1960: see index; Adorno *et al.*, 1964. This work is interesting and important, but badly flawed by a failure to draw the distinctions which I have mentioned above. (See Friedrich, 1958: pp. 32–36.) It has also been put to some odd uses. There are groups in which Adorno *et al.* is treated as a sacred text and all fundamental dissent is 'written off' as a symptom of The Authoritarian Personality (i.e., objections are met not with argument but with 'psychiatric' diagnosis). This has been called the *All-authoritarians-should-be-shot syndrome*. Cf. 11.14A, D. See *TP* 8.10B (self-stultification).

(iv) The contradictory opposite (*TP* 10.1) of 'authoritarian' is simply 'non-authoritarian' and we can use 'anti-authoritarian' for positions in contrary opposition to it. What about its direct, hostile opposite, i.e., the sort of thing we might call 'the opposite extreme'? In A above, I used 'libertarian'. Other possibilities are 'individualist' and 'anarchist' (2.9D), but all three bristle with other meanings, so that professed libertarians, individualists or anarchists might complain of misrepresentation. 'Antinomian', being less idiomatic, might be better, provided that we can say that antinomianism can be a matter of *degree*. (Most dictionaries call it a rejection of *any* element of law.) See D. L. Edwards, 1988; Hill, 1975: see index; *ODCC*, 1974: p. 65; Scruton, 1983: p. 19.

But perhaps thinking that there must be something which can be called 'the opposite extreme' is simply a bad habit which we should have grown out of years ago. (On *extremes*, see 11.12.)

(v) Scruton (1983: p. 32) uses 'authoritarianism' in a different sense:

> The advocacy of government based on an established system of authority, rather than on explicit or tacit consent.

It is *possible* that government of the former kind could be mild and freedom-favouring. It is possible that government of the latter kind could be authoritarian (in the sense I have outlined): 'Our government rests on consent; so you'd better agree with it or else.' Rousseau and Hobbes deployed consent-theory in a very authoritarian way (*Social Contract* bk I, ch. vii, 1973: p. 175; *Leviathan* ch. xviii. 1991: 123–124). On consent, see 10.32.

B Totalitarianism

> . . . for the Fascist, everything is in the State, and nothing human or spiritual exists, much less has value, outside the State. In this sense Fascism is *totalitarian*, and the Fascist State, the synthesis and unity of all values, interprets, develops and gives strength to the whole life of the people.
>
>   (Mussolini,[42] 1932: §7; 1939: p. 166. My italics)

'Totalitarian' was then a brand new word, coined to characterise Mussolini's Fascism. Notice that he accepts the characterisation. A Fascist of our time might not (see 8.13, 8.19). A political system is totalitarian to the extent that it conforms to or aspires to conform to the following specifications:

> There is a single party or movement (5.2, 5.36) with a monopoly on legal political activity. This party is fused with the governing apparatus, and all other permitted organisations are under its control. Divergent conceptions of the general interest or of the good life are not permitted. There is an official line on all significant questions. Art, science and education (and religion, if permitted) are all subject to party-control and are part of its monopoly of the means of communication. A political police, using methods of espionage and terror, is a central part of the system.

It is a matter of fact that no actual political system has succeeded in maintaining that degree of control, but some have come very close to it, far too close for the comfort of many inhabitants. Some theorists have argued that the concept of totalitarianism is of no great use in talking about twentieth-century politics. They are wrong. Worse luck.

Suggested reading

Scruton, 1983: pp. 466–467; Buss, 1964; Burch, 1964; Crick, 1973: ch. xii; Friedrich, 1964; Groth, 1964; Grunberger, 1974; Mosse, 1966; Needler, 1991: pp. 13–23; Orwell, 1954; Spiro, 1968.

C *Gleichschaltung*

This is the German word for *co-ordination*. Sometimes, it can also be translated as 'synchronization', 'unification', 'streamlining'. During the Nazi period, it meant the Nazification of every aspect of life and the violent elimination of all dissent. See Mosse, 1966; Grunberger, 1974.

2.17 Representation

A   'Ambition' is etymologically connected with *walking* and 'candidature' with *wearing a robe the colour of pipe-clayed webbing*. But that is *merely* interesting: informative about election campaign procedures in ancient Rome, but no more than that. In some cases, however, the etymology is both enlightening and bewildering. That of the 'represent' family is certainly the latter and may well be the former as well. *OED*'s first entry for 'represent' is:

> To bring into presence; esp. to present (oneself or another *to* or *before* a person).

Amongst the six examples are

> Representeth your self smartely to this judgement, by ordre, as ye shal be clepyd. (1413)

> She [the soul] . . . leueth her body and her representeth unto hym unto his blessyd pleasure. (1502)

> In the day time they did represent themselves before the Gouernours. (1585)

To represent, in this sense, is *to make present*. There may be some suggestion of a special kind of making present, a connection with authority; i.e., it is not merely that the 'represented' is made or makes himself present, but (?also?) that he is brought or brings himself *into the presence* of a superior or official (cf. the *Presence Chamber* in royal palaces). The stress is on the *presence of* the authority-figure and the special kind of space or place which is his circumambience. He is *present*. The inferior is *there*. Being *in the presence of* (in this sense) is an *asymmetrical* relation (*TP* 10.6). However that may be, it is important to note that *hauling someone into court by the scruff of his neck* is a species of *representing someone* in this sense and *representing oneself* in this sense has no necessary connection with speaking up for oneself, but perhaps that is just round the corner – or round a couple of corners.
B   That is a *spatial* kind of representing. There is also an epistemological/ rhetorical kind ('getting things across', 'bringing them before the mind') (*OED*'s 'represent' 2.a):

> To bring clearly and distinctly before the mind, esp. (to another) by description or (to oneself) by an act of imagination.

Some of the examples are:

> Wherefore, representing your Majesty many times unto my mind . . . I have been . . . possessed with an extreme wonder at those your virtues. (1605. Bacon to James I)

> Of all external things, Which the five watchful Senses represent, She forms Imaginations. (1667. *Paradise Lost* v. 104)

> Why is God said to have a head and hands? To represent Him the better to our capacities. (1708)

> Man may have knowledge which he cannot represent to his formal reason. (1856)

> It remains, therefore, to complete the work by representing the character of the country. (1879)

(See also *OED*'s 'represent' 2.b, 2.c, 3.b.) Other connected uses concern *making manifest, exhibiting, performing or producing a play, acting a role in a play,* etc.

C   Some of these uses shade into others which concern the making of an image of the thing said to be represented:

> 4.b. *spec.* To exhibit by means of painting, sculpture, etc.; to portray, depict, delineate.

>> The Painter meaning to represent the present condition of the young ladie. (Sidney, *Arcadia*, 1586)

>> What is commonly considered the whole art of painting, that is, the art of representing any natural object faithfully. (Ruskin, 1843)

> 4.c. Of pictures, images, etc. To exhibit by artificial resemblance or delineation.

>> There is one over the Gate, representing in bas relief our Saviour's riding into Jerusalem upon the ass. (1687)

>> Two allegorical pictures by . . . Holbein, representing the Triumph of Riches and the Triumph of Poverty respectively. (Pattison, 1861)

(Cf. 'Representation' 2.a–d)

There are three important points to note about these examples:

(i)   in some of the cases, the representer (i.e., that-which-represents) resembles the represented; in some, it does not.

(ii) in all of them, the representer makes present, *as it were*, something which literally and/or physically is not present.

(iii) If X represents Y, then X is *not* identical with Y (cf. example about God in B above and see *OED* on 'representational' and 'representationism'), so that representing is a *very* special way of making something present.

D 'Represent' and 'resemble' become mutually replaceable in the obsolete 7.b, though the element of metaphorically making-present diminishes:

7.b. To present the figure or appearance of, to resemble.

On their outside they [the valves of the veins] represent the knottes that are in the branches of plants. (1615)

Sampling is another kind of making present which involves resemblance:

9.a. To serve as a specimen or example of (a class or kind of things); hence, in *passive*, to be exemplified (*by* something).

A soup in which twenty kinds of vegetables were represented. (1858)

E Symbolisation can be a form (?or several forms?) of making-present-(as it were)-of-that-which-is-not-present, but *OED* has run together several significantly unlike things in its 6.a:

6.a. To symbolize, to serve as a visible or concrete embodiment of (some quality, fact, or other abstract concept).

The Stewart and Thesaurer in his absence, within this Courte, represents unto the estate of an Erle. (1483)

The sueird of conquis . . . Be borne suld highe before the in presence, To represent sic man as thou has beyn. (Dunbar, 1508)

An Appell of Golde, representynge the shape of the rounde worlde. (1560)

No sovereign has ever represented the majesty of a great state with more dignity and grace. (Macaulay, 1849)

The phrase 'some quality, fact, or other abstract concept' is rather too sweeping, but that need not detain us. 6.a overlaps somewhat with 7.a (and also with 4.b and c: see 4.19 above):

7.a. Of things: To stand for or in place of (a person or thing); to be the figure or image of (something).

Peple honoure non thynge in theyme [images] but God, or for God and for seyntes, whiche they represente to us. (1432–1450)

Before him burn seaven Lamps as in a Zodiac representing The Heav'nly fires. (1667. *Paradise Lost* xii 255)

If we represent the Sun by a globe about two feet in diameter . . . (1868)

6.a overlaps also with 8.a (directly, not via 6.a's overlapping of 7.a):

8.a. To take or fill the place of (another) in some respect or for some purpose; to be a substitute in some capacity for (a person or body); to act for (another) by a deputed right.

> Our Generall sent Cap. Jobson, repraesentinge his person with his authorite, as his Leiftenante Generall. (1595)

OED records corresponding cognate uses as follows:

> 7.a. The fact of standing for, or in place of, some other thing or person, esp. with a right or authority to act on their account; substitution of one thing or person for another.

> No Parliament can begin without the Kings Presence, either in Person, or by Representation by Commissioners. (1671)

> 2.a. Standing for, or in place of, another or others, esp. in a prominent or comprehensive manner.

> A king or queen, as representative persons in a nation. (1861)

6.a, 7.a, and 8.a are all representations of the type, making-(as it were)-present-of-the-not-physically-present. Symbolising seems to be a form of representation, but it would seem that not all representation is symbolising. What is the difference? It might be something like this: if α symbolises β, then α, considered in itself, is generically and significantly different from β. The Governor represents the Queen. At certain kinds of military parade, she is represented by the Royal Standard. She is symbolised by the Royal Standard, but not by the Governor. The parade can give the Royal Salute to the Standard, as it could to the Queen if she were physically present. In either case, the salute is equally to the Queen. The Royal Standard, however, cannot go and have lunch afterwards in the officers' mess, neither could it perform the various ceremonial and constitutional duties which the Governor performs as representative of the Queen, and, after the parade, they do not sprinkle the Governor with naphtha flakes, fold him up and put him in a cupboard to await the next big ceremony. It might begin to look as if the difference between symbolic representative and non-symbolic representative is merely that the non-symbol is more versatile, but that is not it. The Governor might, on Anzac Day, be represented at the City Callathumpian Church by Colonel Chinstrap, whose representative function is discharged in full by that attendance. He is, as it were, a Royal Standard in human form for an hour or so, but no one would call him a symbol of the Governor. (He may symbolise various social forces, just as the Queen may, or just as the Queen represents the nation, but whatever the ontological status of social forces and nations, it is not the case that a nation or a social force is an individual human being. Thus, there is still a categorial (*TP* 3.4A) difference between symbol and symbolised.)

F   *OED*'s 'represent' 8.a is clearly relevant to politics, as some of the examples show, but 8.b is wholly within politics, as are corresponding entries for cognates:

'*Representation*' (noun)

8.a. The fact of representing or being represented in a legislative or deliberative assembly . . . the position, principle, or system implied by this.

It would be with great discontent that I should see Mr Thrale decline the representation of the Borough. (1780. Samuel Johnson)

'*Representative*' (adjective)

2.b. *spec*. Holding the place of, and acting for, a larger body of persons (esp. the whole people) in the work of governing or legislating; pertaining to, or based upon, a system by which the people is thus represented.

'*Representative*' (noun)

2.a. One who (or that which) represents a number of persons in some special capacity; *spec*. one who represents a section of the community as member of a legislative body . . . .

That, I suppose, is 'representation in the political sense', the definition with which, according to many, I should have begun, cutting all the cackle about other kinds of representation, but if this is it, if this is what it *really* is, the essence refined and bottled, I must admit to a certain feeling of anticlimax, of disappointment. The reason is not hard to find. *OED* in its defining formulas says nothing of what constitutes someone or something as a politically representative thing, neither does it say much about the function of a representative: *how* he represents, what counts as doing the job, what counts as doing it well or as doing it badly. Some of the quotations are more informative. Obviously, election has something[43] to do with constituting someone or something as a representative. Some of the quotations support that. Burke ('representation' (noun) 8.a) speaks of representation as a necessary condition of legitimate taxation. The representatives' role of 'empowering' (and presumably 'disempowering') governments is also mentioned (important in 'Westminster' systems, but not in all others) ('representative' (noun) 2.a). That is something, but it is not a great deal.

G   That, however, is no complaint against *OED*. To 'define "representation" in the political sense' in such a relatively uninformative way is the best that can be done, granted certain important aspects of the dictionary-maker's task. The dictionary-maker needs to be, so far as he can be, neutral between conflicting doctrines, world-views, programmes, and he is not allowed to let one word or word-family take over the whole book. Political representing is a shifting (perhaps even shifty) concept. That cry of 'No taxation without representation' was of great historical significance and can still stir the blood (not just American blood, either), but few of those who raised it originally were radical democrats. They did not mean 'No one should be taxed unless he has a vote', but 'No one should be taxed unless the territory he resides in elects a representative to the assembly which imposes the tax', which may be (and was) a very different thing indeed. Political notions of representation are very much parasitic on non-political varieties of representation.[44] But precisely *how much* is drawn from *which* non-political uses of 'represent', etc., is a matter of where one stands politically, i.e., of one's political outlook, but often also of what is, at the relevant time, in one's political or personal interests. Here, one Australian politician defends his colleagues by relying heavily on the elements of *resemblance* and *sampling*:

> [T]he mediocre critic demands, in the one breath a Parliament representative of all the people, and a Parliament of all the virtues and intelligences . . . . Parliament represents not only the votes of the public but the public's qualities, their goodness and badness and honesty and fraud, their generosity and meanness. A Parliament composed of geniuses and altruists would emphatically be misrepresentative of the people, who are neither genius nor altruistic. . . . Parliaments as they are, with one or two men above the average intelligence and many men of average intelligence, and more men little better than morons, represent the nation – any nation.
>
> (Bedford, 1976: pp. 180, 242)[45]

Parliament is much *less* representative than Bedford says. The percentage of people of *very* high or *very* low intelligence will be *lower* than in the general population: the very low, for obvious reasons; the very high, for reasons only slightly less obvious: they get involved in other time-consuming pursuits. For similar reasons, mystical contemplatives (rare anywhere) and artists will be underrepresented in Parliament. The shy, the unambitious, the self-doubting: Will there be *any* of them? I think not. Neither will there be any of those who have absolutely no interest in politics and regard all politicians as incompetent and dishonest. It follows that Parliament is seriously unrepresentative and will remain so until elections are replaced by random selection.

That seems to hold together logically, but surely something has gone wrong. Let us begin at a different point: If I am charged with a crime, I shall need a legal *representative*, someone learned in the law and skilled in courtroom advocacy: in short, someone *un*like me in certain striking respects. He is to represent me, not by resembling me but by defending my interests, by making as strong a case for me as he can, by doing for me, at my commission, something which I cannot do for myself. When a lawyer helps me make a will, he is my adviser, not my representative. When he writes a letter on my behalf or stands up in court and fights my battle, he is my representative. Another aspect of legal representation is that the lawyer is accountable and responsible to his client. He may know vastly more about the law than his client does and be generally a much more competent person, but the client can sack him. H Bedford's remarks on representation stress the element of *resemblance*; mine stress action at another's commission, on behalf and in the interests of that other, and with responsibility to that other. If we are talking about *parliamentary* representation, those surely are more significant than resemblance. Bedford is right in saying that we cannot expect a Parliament to be *vastly* superior, morally or intellectually, to the community from which it has been elected, but geniuses and altruists would not fail to represent us just because they are unlike us. They might do the job very well, though it is not unknown for geniuses and altruists to be ignorant and self-satisfied. Those defects would diminish their usefulness as representatives. Another former parliamentarian was not breaking new ground when he wrote:

> Australian Cabinets have been notable for an over-supply of lawyers, intellectuals and farmers, and an almost complete lack of men with experience in business, large scale organisation and administration, and technology. . . . The Labor Caucus is no longer a worker's caucus . . . the lawyers and doctors predominate . . . .
> . . . the best Labor leader is one who at some time in his life has been hungry. None of Labor's present leaders has ever been hungry.
>
> (McManus, 1977: pp. 176–177)

Let us suppose that Parliament etc. are so composed. If the writer is correct in evaluating that as a bad thing, that is not because they make Parliament a statistically inaccurate picture of the polity, but because they deprive Parliament of certain necessary (or at least highly desirable) kinds of *awareness*, so that there are windows on the world through which it sees only darkly if at all. If it is desirable that a Labor leader has experienced hunger, that is not for statistical reasons, but for reasons of empathy (12.43) (though some who have battled their way from poverty to the top have been harsher bosses than some who were born to the purple).

'Represent' is a *very* ambiguous word. The conventional signs on a map represent various features but, in most cases, they have no resemblance to those features. On the other hand, a representative sample of X shows you what X is like, and a representational portrait tries (more or less) to show you what the sitter looks like.

But ambiguity is not the only complicating factor. There are *criterial*[46] factors also; i.e., we may differ about what aspects of X, what features of the sitter's appearance and personality are significant. The Zville Vampires represent Zville in the League competition, and all loyal Zvillians hope they do it well, which does *not* mean that they want the Vampires to *resemble* the population. To call the Vampires a representative team is an invitation to the population to *identify with* the Vampires. But *identifying with* is itself a complicated and obscure notion (12.12–12.14). Suppose Tom is a Zvillian. Tom is being invited not *only* to support the Vampires. He is also being invited to experience the team's fortunes as if they were his own, but that vicariousness is not all, either. He is also being invited (and exhorted) to feel his relationship with the Vampires as part of his consciousness of being-a-Zvillian.

And the word also has its political uses which are related in a variety of ways to its non-political uses and can be expected to be no less complicated than they are! The political concept of representation draws on various aspects of the non-political concept to varying degrees. Not every political use of the word draws on the same aspects of the non-political concept. Hence, the political concept of representation is a volatile collection of fragments, an unstable and inconstant mixture. Any attempt to state '*the* political sense' of the word is (like the preceding and following paragraphs) an attempt to capture it and make it work for a particular political outlook.

J *Parliamentary representation: What is represented? How?*

My analogy of *legal representation* does, I think, bring to notice aspects (descriptive and prescriptive) of parliamentary representation which Bedford's stress on resembling (or sampling) obscures, but it *is* an analogy. For one thing, there can be no doubt about *what* my legal representative represents: he represents me, a natural person, an individual, a spatio-temporally continuous psycho-material object, with 'a local habitation and a name'. Parliamentary representing is not so clear a relation. There is a phrase 'my local Member', but its referent is not 'mine' in that he represents *me*; he is 'mine' by virtue of my membership of an entity which he does represent. If Harry is the member for Zville and I am a citizen living in Zville, Harry is my local Member. So it is his representation of Zville which is primary. But what is this Zville? It has few of the metaphysical attributes which I just now claimed (uncontroversially) for myself. It does, of course, occupy a certain area of the earth's surface. It can be outlined on a map. One can tell where one is in it and where one is out. One can walk across it or around its borders, etc.

But if we cling to those pieces of solidity, the essential Zville eludes our grasp, because the electoral Division of Zville is not just a piece of land, but a *social object* (2.2): it 'contains or involves a number of human beings'. It *is* (in some very unclear way) the human beings who live on that piece of land. Now, there are various interesting ontological problems about social objects: Just what does it mean to assert that they exist? Does 'exist' there have the same sense as it has in 'Harry exists'? Etc., etc. This is not the place to explore those problems. Our bother about Zville is less an ontological one than a psychological one. Like you, I am a member of various social objects: country, state, town, suburb, street, etc. Each of those is an ontologically problematical entity, but (to me, anyway) my suburb, or Newcastle, or even Australia has a *prima facie* solidity which my electoral division,[47] the Division of Shortland, lacks. What *is* it? And what is *my membership* of it? The second question might be more illuminating than the first. The legal foundation of my membership is my being an Australian citizen living within certain boundaries. Since I am over eighteen, that membership confers the right and duty[48] of casting a vote when the representative is chosen.

Is that all? In strict law, that *is* all, but convention and custom add something more. If I have some sort of bother with a Government department and need help or redress, then I have an entitlement to bother my local Member about it, stronger than my entitlement to bother other Members. He has a corresponding duty to treat my concern seriously. There are similar entitlements and duties with respect to political issues. These entitlements belong not only to individual electors, but also to groups of electors. If some issue especially affects the electorate or parts of it (if, e.g., it concerns a new airport to be built within it), then the Member has similar obligations to take the matter seriously.

These are entitlements which exist by convention. It is important to notice that, even by convention, there is no general obligation on the Member to do more than listen. Of course, if he never takes action on behalf of an elector, he is not doing his job, but he is not obliged to do as the electors wish in every case. Further, if the Member's legal and conventional duties are all (or mostly) duties of *representing his electorate in the Parliament*, then representation requires him to take an interest in matters which are of no special relevance to his electorate and electors. Both of these matters are addressed in Burke's 'Speech to the Electors of Bristol':

> Parliament is not a *congress* of ambassadors from different and hostile interests, which interests each must maintain, as an agent and advocate, against other agents and advocates; but Parliament is a *deliberative* assembly of *one* nation, with *one* interest, that of the whole – where not local purposes, not local prejudices, ought to guide, but the general good, resulting from the general reason of the whole. You choose a member, indeed; but when you have chosen him, he is not a member of Bristol, but he is a member of *Parliament*.
>
> (Burke, 1975: p. 158)

There we have *both* the assertion that the Member has to consider more than his constituency and the assertion that he is not obliged to act solely as the electors wish. The circumstances, however, required that the second should be stressed:

> . . . it ought to be the happiness and glory of a representative to live in the strictest union, the closest correspondence, and the most unreserved communication with his constituents. Their wishes ought to have great weight with him; their opinions high respect; their business unremitted attention. It is his duty to sacrifice his repose, his pleasure, his satisfactions, to theirs, – and above all, ever, and in all cases, to prefer their interest to his own.
>
> But his unbiased opinion, his mature judgment, his enlightened conscience, he ought not to sacrifice to you, to any man, or to any set of men living.
>
> (ibid., p. 157)

What are we to make of this? Is Burke being high-handed, or honest and conscientious, or both? We want our Member to be honest. We want him to be responsive to our wishes: two aspirations, which (logically speaking) need not conflict, but, as a matter of fact, they are bound to conflict in practice. These days, almost always, the person we elect is a party-member and is elected largely because of his party. That adds a further possibility of conflict. Once again, we see that politics is, to a large extent, a matter of reasonable demands which do not add up (cf. 4.8). In 1953, the then-dominant liberal wing of the United Party in the Transvaal succeeded in imposing on all candidates a pledge that, should they win and then leave the Party, they would resign their seats. Six years later, three of those Transvaal liberals left the United Party to join four other MPs in the new Progressive Party. They did not resign their seats, saying that 'that would leave the people who hold and support our views voiceless in the supreme legislature' and that the United Party had 'deviate[d] substantially from the policy it proclaimed at the time the undertaking was given' (Strangwayes-Booth, 1976: pp. 80–81, 164–165). I think that they were probably justified, but the reasoning has the funny smell which all reasoning has when it enables the reasoner to cancel a promise and hang on to what he has got. It might be rash to say that *no* reasoning from 'the' principle of representation *ever* yields an uncontroversial conclusion, but I cannot, just now, think of any. The trouble is that there is nothing '*the*' about 'the principle' (see *TP* 5.30). I am not falling into evasive emotivism ('means different things to different people' FULL STOP). I am pointing to an area of enormous and important complication which needs to be given a more thorough investigation than is possible here. On the occasional (though not rare) duty of a government to act unpopularly and to break promises, see 8.10, 9.25. For *will of the people*, see 10.43–10.46.

Though representation is a problematical thing, it is only in terms of it that we can give any felt reality to the modern electoral district; i.e., to feel that one is a resident of such and such a street or such and such a suburb seems, as it were, natural, but our membership of an electoral district can be given flesh and blood only in terms of our entitlements *vis-à-vis* our Member. Electoral districts are not *just* products of human decision and convention. They are quite directly artificial, called into being at the word of Parliament and similarly annihilable. That frequently means that an electorate is not the kind of object that could have an opinion or an interest even in the (obscure) way that a suburb or a street might. We want the Member to represent his district (so we want it to be representable). We want also the overall election result to correspond (broadly) with the opinion of the electorate at large; hence we want electorates to be equal in size – yet another example of intrinsically reasonable demands which, in combination, do not add up (cf. Burke, 1968: p. 315).

Earlier, I quoted Randolph Bedford. He also remarked that 'Little newspaper men . . . know that there is not any closed season for politicians' (1976: p. 180). It may well be that one of the unacknowledged functions of the politician is to represent the electorate rather as the scapegoat[49] represented the Children of Israel.

K *Representation: delegates and trustees*

The distinction which Burke is drawing (J above) is sometimes said to be one between the *representative* and the *delegate*. It would be clearer to treat *representative* as a genus of which *delegate* and *trustee* are two species. Each represents a body of people, but the delegate is closely bound by the instructions of those he represents and has little scope for initiative. The trustee, on the other hand, while ultimately responsible to those he represents and having a duty to defend their interests, is not bound by their instructions and *must* exercise initiative. Delegation and trusteeship are important elements in any concept of parliamentary or democratic representation. They can (but do not always) clash with each other and it is probable that there is no way of removing the possibility of clash. A politician who attempts to achieve a compromise between the two roles is sometimes called a *politico* (Jackson, 1993: p. 39; Emy, 1974: pp. 455–499), though the term has a less technical and more general use as well (4.11). The notion of trustee used here is derived from, but not identical with the legal notion, for which see Mozley & Whiteley, 1977; Osborn, 1976.

Suggested Reading

Burke, 1975: pp. 156–158; Scruton, 1983: pp. 400–401; Barker, 1951: ch. v.

L *Representation and democracy*

It has generally been agreed that, except in very small collectives, democratic government (8.18–8.27) necessarily involves representation so that, if Xland is a modern polity, 'Xland is a democracy' implies 'Xland is a representative democracy'. There have always been some who dissented, e.g., Rousseau and anarchists, but, for the most part, dissent has been negligible. In the late 1960s, however, it became so noisy that it could not be ignored. The New Left of the time (11.11B), especially in universities, told us that 'representative democracy' is a self-contradictory fraud, that the whole point of True Democracy is *participation* by all those likely to be affected by the decisions to be made,[50] so that only *participatory* (or *simple*, or *direct*) democracy would do. That was the only way in which People Could Be in Control Of Their Own Lives. This movement ran out of steam some time in the 1970s, but, before that happened, many people made interesting, if disillusioning discoveries, e.g.:

> that much collective decision-making is both time-consuming and unexciting and that involvement in it (surprise!) reduces the time available for other activities;
> that, though mass-meetings and assemblies of everyone are splendidly exciting, they are not really the best forums for 'discussion in depth';
> that, even at such assemblies, the participation of most is severely limited; i.e., not everyone can speak, let alone have a significant effect on the decision taken;
> that there could still be winners and losers;

that, if representative institutions alienated people from control over their own lives, participatory ones were no better.

Not much has been heard of participatory democracy in recent years, so that, for many ageing academics, reading the last few pages of Pitkin, 1989, has been a nostalgic, bittersweet experience, like hearing again a long-forgotten hit tune. (See also 8.28, *industrial democracy* and Munro-Clark, 1992.)

Suggested reading on representation

Pitkin, 1989, is indispensable. J. S. Mill's *Considerations on Representative Government* (1861) and Burke's 'Speech to the Electors of Bristol' (1774) are classical texts. On proportional representation (advocated by Mill), see J. F. H. Wright, 1980 (which deals with other matters as well) and Hermens, 1938. Pitkin, 1967, and Birch, 1964 and 1972, are important books. If Griffiths & Wollheim, 1960 is not a classic, it should be. See also de Grazia, 1968; Sartori, 1968(b); Janda, 1968; Fairlie, 1968: chs iii–v; Cassen, 1967; G. C. Lewis, 1898: ch. xii. Anyone with a serious interest in the topic should work carefully through *OED*'s entries for 'represent' and its cognates.

3 The *polis* and the political
OR
Has politics *got* a nature?

ANCIENT AND MODERN

3.1 *Polis*

Our words 'politics', etc. are derived from *polis* (plural, *poleis*), the word the ancient Greeks applied to the independent political entities to which they belonged, e.g., Athens, Sparta, Thebes, Corinth, etc. Although Greeks were very proudly conscious of being Greek (and not 'barbarian'), there was no such thing as *Greek* citizenship. The customary translation 'city-state' is misleading partly because it has too urban a sound (and because it can make people think of Singapore). Each *polis* had (and had to have) a relatively large rural territory and population. Further, one of the meanings of our word 'state' is *a specialised, permanent and largely professional governing and administrative body*. There was very little corresponding to this in the *polis*. Athenian governance (2.7B), in particular, was amateur to a degree startling to the modern reader. '*Polis*' could readily be used to refer to the *citizen body*. Our word 'state' is not like that. The *poleis* varied in size, but none was large by our standards. There were two on the small island of Rhodes, fifty in Crete. Athens, a very large *polis*, had a territory of 1,000 square miles, much smaller than some Australian electoral districts. Its peak population was no more than 275,000, of whom only 40,000 were citizens. There is a tendency, even amongst scholars, to confuse the *polis* with a romanticised picture of Athenian democracy at its best. Authoritarian Sparta was no less a *polis* and Athens was not always a democracy. When it was, it was not always at its best.

Suggested reading

Crick, 1973: ch. iii; Finley, 1971: ch. iv; Jouvenel, 1961; Kitto, 1951: chs v, ix; Devambez *et al.*, 1970: pp. 107–109; Laslett, 1956(b); Maddox, 1974; Warner, 1944.

'TRUE' POLITICS

3.2　When we are told that there is no water on Mars, we know what is meant. It is an assertion of fact like any other, except to the extent that the ordinary person cannot check it for himself. When we hear someone say that there are no honest men in Canberra, we know that we are hearing irritable hyperbole. When Socrates says that he, like everyone else, knows nothing, or the Prophet Isaiah tells us that 'all our righteousnesses are as filthy rags', we know that we are hearing not just hyperbole but also a reference to ideal standards, and that the remarks are not refuted by the undoubted existence of decent people or our tolerable certainty about how many beans make five. Other odd remarks, such as 'A good man cannot be harmed' or St Augustine's 'Love God, and do whatever you like' are best treated in the same way.[1]

3.3　What are we to make of the assertion that politics no longer exists? People do say it.[2] When we look or listen more closely, we sometimes find such phrases as 'as politics was conceived in the age of Pericles'. That might, at first, seem to draw the paradoxical sting. There are vast differences between the affairs of something like ancient Athens and something like modern Greece, and, if we were to go into those differences at length, we should not only have a better understanding of both kinds of society but of the concept of politics as well. But we soon find that that is not the drift of these writers. We find them talking of 'true politics', of its absence in the modern world, of whether 'the recovery of politics' is possible. They tell us that *the political* has been replaced by *the social*, that politics and the economy are mutually irrelevant, and that society is a comparatively modern invention.

　　What have we here? Something in cipher, perhaps? It may all be true. The trouble is that the politics I am interested in is the sort of politics talked about in daily newspapers, and economic matters (i.e., basic material needs) are intimately connected with it, prosaic as such things may seem to some writers. Perhaps it is not 'true' politics. Nevertheless, I find it interesting and worth investigating. It may not be 'true', but it is certainly *real*, sometimes far too real for comfort. Perhaps *true politics* is like *real tennis*, which is

> A game in which a ball is struck with a racket and driven to and fro by two players in an enclosed oblong court; . . . having an enclosed corridor on one of the long sides roofed over by a penthouse.
>
> *(OED)*

That is not what is played at Wimbledon, but the Wimbledon game is no fantasy and a perfectly legitimate object of interest.

POLITICS AND THE POLITICAL: SOME DEFINERS

3.4　We possess the concept of politics as surely and as securely as St Augustine possessed the concept of time (1.14), but, if we try to answer the question, 'What is politics?', we are likely to find ourselves in his predicament of knowing, yet not knowing. Politics is not so fundamental a notion as time, but it is well worth investigating. If we can bring our implicit knowledge of it to the surface and critically systematise it, we may have begun to get a better understanding of ourselves and our social world.

3.5   The intellect desires to know. That appetite is as primary as our appetite to eat and as little in need of justification. But giving an account of the concept of politics seems to have been of some practical importance as well. People have quarrelled fiercely over whether things are or are not political. Sometimes whether one has or has not involved oneself in politics is, quite literally, a matter of life and death. Hence it is worth asking 'Are there criteria for distinguishing decisively what is political from what is not? Are there things that are essentially and inevitably political and things which are essentially non-political?' Another reason why we should bother about 'politics' and 'political' is that many clever people have tried to answer the question 'What is politics?' and have come up with disconcertingly different results. We should treat that as an incitement, rather than a discouragement.

3.6   I have argued that definitions are not as important as many think (1.3–1.9), but if one does define, the definition must *fit*. It must be neither 'too narrow' nor 'too broad'. Socrates would insist that it include every possible instance of the *definiendum* and exclude every possible non-instance. As a concession to the untidiness of the world, less rigoristic critics would allow a few *borderline cases*, but there must be no more than a *very* few. It is not satisfactory to define the political as 'whatever concerns the state' (Raphael, 1976: pp. 27–32). As J. D. B. Miller points out, when a stamp is bought from the Post Office, neither the customer nor the postal clerk is thereby involved in politics (1965: p. 13). Another point is that one of the functions of the state is *law*, which concerns *all* sorts of things. It tells us how to make a will and not to shoplift; it regulates the flow of traffic and imposes taxes; it tells us how to interpret insurance policies and not to spit on the pavement. All these, therefore, 'concern the state', but not all are political. Any of them can *become* political or *raise political issues*. Ordinarily, they do not: ordinarily if you spit or refrain from spitting on the pavement, your action or self-restraint is thoroughly apolitical. If someone started an agitation for stricter or more liberal laws about spitting on the pavement (SOP), then, until the matter were resolved, there would be *a political issue* about SOP. If we organised a National Day of SOP as a demonstration in favour of more funds for higher education and cultural activities, then SOP would, for one spectacular day, become *a political act*, but that status would be short-lived.

3.7   So Raphael's definition of the political is too broad. It is also too narrow. In a then non-independent developing country, I knew people who regularly stole from a certain supermarket, because (they said) they disapproved of the way its owner-company treated its workers and of its influence on the economy of the country. It makes perfect sense to say that those shoplifters were trying to offer a *political justification* of their behaviour, but it involves no direct reference to *the government* or *the state* at all. It concerns the *use of economic power.* Raphael does attempt to meet objections that his account is too narrow, though not that one. The objections he imagines are these (1976: pp. 29–30):

(i) Stateless societies have politics.
(ii) Social units which are not states (e.g., churches and universities) have their own politics.

To the first objection, Raphael replies that the problems of political philosophy arise only in more sophisticated societies which usually have states. That, if true (and is it?), affirms a necessary condition for the existence of political philosophy, not for the existence of politics. (There was no one to bother about geological problems in the Jurassic, either.) On the second objection, Raphael says that, very often, members of a church or university who use the word 'politics' about its affairs do so pejoratively and are complaining about something they regard as inappropriate in church or university affairs. This, he says, is evidence of a metaphorical use of the term 'parasitic on the normal use [i.e., "the political is whatever concerns the state"]' (pp. 27–32).

3.8 Perhaps people often talk that way. It does not follow that church or university politics is any the less 'real politics'. In my experience, people just as often talk of church or university politics with no pejorative intent at all (though most would insist that it be 'kept in its place', i.e., in the place of something ancillary). I am quite happy to agree that, in our concept of politics, the politics of states (see 2.6) holds a certain primacy or centrality, so that the words 'politics' and 'political', if unqualified, normally suggest the politics of a state. But that is as far as I will go. The activities of a Bigman of the Papua New Guinean Highlands[3] or of an academic trying to gather support for a proposal he is putting to his Faculty Board are so analogous to the activities of parliamentarians, parliamentary candidates and parties that it is absurdly arbitrary to say that such people are not involved in politics – not 'primary' or 'central' politics, but politics nonetheless. Trying to see how this 'non-primary' or 'non-central' politics is related to 'primary' or 'central' politics might be very illuminating.

3.9 I have referred already to J. D. B. Miller's *The Nature of Politics.* A book with such a title might be expected to contain some positive statements about what politics is. It does: a few too many, perhaps. At pp. 14–15, Miller says that the essence of politics is conflict, that political activity is that which[1] is intended to bring about change in the face of possible resistance or resist a proposed change, and that the harder people contend over policy and position, the more political the situation is. Bertrand de Jouvenel says much the same in three words: 'Politics is conflict' (1963: p. 189). He says that the largest part of governmental activity is 'de-politised' because it does not involve conflict. Miller agrees (op. cit.: p. 20). This implies that (A) all conflict is political, and (B) everything political involves conflict. A is false. There can be conflict between neighbours over noise or the activities of dogs. Is B true? Miller's remarks about *policy* seem to suggest that it is not:

Politics is about policy, first and foremost; and policy is a matter of either the desire for change or the desire to protect something against change.

(1965: p. 14)

Not all such matters *need* involve conflict. Jouvenel also departs from B:

. . . politics occur whenever a project requires the support of other wills – to the extent to which its author sets out to rally those wills. . . . Any action tending to rally wills is, in kind, a political action.

(1957: p. 17)

Apart from these issues of consistency, are we not getting too far away from the ordinary concept of politics if we leave out *all* reference to government? Miller seems to think so (op. cit.: p. 14). Similarly, Jouvenel says:

The use of the word 'politic'[5] designates not a thing, but the relations of anything with government. . . . There is no natural affinity between the word[s] 'politics' and . . . 'meat', but they come together as soon as it is proposed that the government do anything about meat.

(1957: p. 15)

So if politics has an 'essence' (Jouvenel and Miller seem sure that it does), that essence cannot be conflict and nothing else.

3.10   There are certain free and breezy spirits who say, in effect, 'Ordinary concept of politics be damned!' Bernard Crick (1977, 1982) and A. J. M. Milne use the word 'politics' to mean what simpler folk might call 'liberal politics' or 'politics of an open or relatively open society':

. . . the concept of politics . . . embraces everything . . . relevant to implementing the representative principle and the principle of constitutional opposition . . . .

A logical consequence is that there can be no politics properly so called[6] unless the form of government is representative . . . .

(Milne, 1972: pp. 47–49)

Milne quite cheerfully accepts the proposition that Lenin, before and after the Revolution, was a thoroughly apolitical person. This is not as *totally* perverse as it might seem (see Scruton, 1983: p. 361), but it *is* perverse. We can make use of it in our clarification, but only if we refuse to be content with it.

3.11   Raphael defined the political as whatever concerns the state. Barry Hindess and Kate Millett ask us (almost) to forget about the state or at least to push it well away from the centre of our concerns. Hindess distinguishes two notions of the political. In normal, everyday usage, 'politics is to do with the activities of governments or political parties, or somewhat more generally, with the sorts of issue that political parties concern themselves with'. He contrasts this with 'a broader conception in which politics pertains to the social structuring of power and its uses'. The difference, he says, is not merely verbal: 'The broader one's conception of politics, the more aspects of society become (potentially) open to question. . . . If management–worker relationships are conceived of as political, then they are open to dispute and to change.' The normal, everyday use tends to favour the status quo and to restrict legitimate action to parties and the organs of government (Hindess, 1971: pp. 14–16).

3.12   Millett is concerned with the relationship between the sexes and whether it can 'be viewed in a political light at all' (1972: pp. 23–24). In her text,[7] she explicitly presents two definitions of the political. One, which she rejects, defines it in terms of:

> that relatively narrow and exclusive world of meetings, chairmen and parties. (C)

She prefers to say that:

> The term 'politics' shall refer to power-structured relationships, arrangements whereby one group of persons is controlled by another. (D)

But having declared what the term 'politics' shall refer to in her book, she goes straight on, 'By way of parenthesis' to talk about *an ideal politics* which 'might be conceived of as the arrangement of human life on agreeable and rational principles from whence the entire notion of power *over* others should be banished' (E). What can the word 'politics' mean here? It fits neither C nor D. The only sense I can make of it is to see C and D not as definitions, but as descriptions of *aspects of* (undefined) politics.

3.13   Both writers link politics with power. That is, I would say, a logical link, part of the meaning of the word (though since the concept of power (see 2.14–2.15) is itself very obscure, it may not be as immediately helpful as they think). Hindess also links *X's being political* with *X's being open to question*. That is not a logical link, but a (or an alleged) moral link. Elizabeth I, James I, Franco and Stalin were four very different rulers, but each would have agreed that politics pertains to the social structuring of power and that it has a much wider scope than that given by those conceptions which Hindess and Millett regard as normal but narrow. They would have gone on to say that *therefore* the right to question political arrangements is very limited indeed. James, in his own way, spoke for them all (and for many a senior university administrator):

> That which concerns the mysterie of the Kings power, is not lawfull to be disputed; for that is to wade into the weaknesse of Princes, and to take away the mysticall reuerence, that belongs vnto them that sit in the Throne of God. . . .
>
> It is Athiesme and blasphemie to dispute what God can doe; good Christians content themselues with his will reuealed in his word, so, it is presumption and high contempt in a Subject, to dispute what a King can doe, or say that a King cannot doe this, or that; but rest in that which is the Kings reuealed will in his Law.
>
> (Speech in Star Chamber, 20 June 1616, James I, 1965: p. 327)

Hindess and I would dissent heartily, but that is because our moral views differ from James's. It is not a disagreement on a piece of logic.

3.14   Millett's remarks about politics and power are (or can be) illuminating. They can help us to see the familiar in a new light, but they do not add up to a satisfactory definition. Very often the situation which we call *typically political* is the sort of situation in which it is not true that one group is controller and the other is controlled. Very often, each group imposes some form of control or constraint on the other, because, for practical purposes, they are evenly matched. In Australia, relations between governments and trade unions have often been like that.[8] Sometimes even those with a little power have found it possible to resist those with greater power successfully.

3.15   Hindess does not make this mistake. His phrase 'the social structuring of power and its uses' allows for a great deal of tug-o'-warring, but, even then, his 'broad definition' is illuminating and helpful *as a hint, not* as a definition. If we accepted it as a definition, we would have great difficulty in distinguishing politics from anything else. What is there that is not relevant *in some way* to the social structuring of power and its uses? (Cf. Stassinopoulos, 1974: pp. 151–152.) Suppose there are snails in your garden. If they eat the vegetables, you will become more dependent on the shops and the commercial growers – clearly relevant to the social structuring of power and its uses. If you decide to do something about the snails, that will involve taking time off from reading newspapers, watching current affairs programmes, and training for The Revolution. You will also have to buy some stuff to sprinkle on the snails, thus giving a little more profit to ICI or some similar gang of capitalistic bloodsuckers. And, as we see you pottering about your snail-ridden or snail-free garden, do we say, 'Ah, political activist at work'? Not unless we are in the grip of very unplausible theory.

3.16   In this section, I have considered various remarks about politics and rejected them as definitions. It is both more charitable and more profitable to treat them NOT as definitions, but as *insights into, glimpses of* the nature of politics. Indeed, I would say a word in heavily qualified praise of the pseudo-definitions offered by Millett and Hindess. As definitions, they are weak and tremble on the brink of grandly bombinating emptiness, but they have a merit which is absent from the useful, but more conventional formulas of Jouvenel, Raphael and J. D. B. Miller. These point (reasonably enough) to competition, conflict and the activities of governments and politicians. Thus, they draw our attention to the overt and public. They might give us the impression that where there is no open conflict, no public fuss-and-bother, no organised dissent, there is nothing political. We should remember that much-quoted scrap of dialogue between Watson and Holmes:

'Is there any other point to which you would wish to draw my attention?'
'To the curious incident of the dog in the night-time.'
'The dog did nothing in the night-time.'

'That was the curious incident,' remarked Sherlock Holmes.

(Doyle, 1950: p. 28)

What is publicly most agreed on, what seems least likely to be challenged, most likely to 'go without saying' may be of immense political significance. Hindess and Millett draw our attention to that, even if they point to it through a glass darkly. (See Pitkin, 1967: pp. 10–11, 25.)

3.17   If we treat the various failed definitions as insights into, glimpses of the nature of politics, we get this:

Politics concerns:
(i)   the state
(ii)   government, the way in which the collective affairs of a collective are managed
(iii) disagreement or conflict
(iv)   policy
(v)   the rallying of support
(vi)   the social structure of power and its uses etc., etc., etc.

Notice that there is no 'is that which' between 'Politics' and 'concerns' and that the instantiation of the political does not require that anything have all these characteristics. Notice also the 'etc., etc., etc.'

ENCOUNTERING EXAMPLES

3.18   What the definers do, it seems, is to walk up to the noun 'politics' and demand, 'What do you name?' (or even declare, 'I shall tell you what you jolly well ought to name'). That is a time-honoured way of doing things, but its results are hardly encouraging. A bit of active listening to how people use the adjective 'political' may be more helpful. It may give us new items to add to our list (3.17). During the Vietnamese War, people who talked of a *political solution* usually had in mind a solution reached by negotiation, so I shall add:

(vii)   the seeking for consensus; negotiation; the making of compromise.

Someone I know complains of people 'behaving politically' or 'getting political' when they are being very competitive: determined to win arguments or to 'top' the other's stories, anxious to be number one, playing one-upmanship, etc. This speech-habit is (1) a figure of speech, and (2) an eccentric one at that, but it is readily understandable and picks out what most will recognise as salient aspects of politics, so I shall add to the list:

(viii)   competition, including competition for office.

(viii) is closely related to, but not identical with, (v) and (iii). We shall notice more of these criss-crossings as we go along.

3.19   The presence of *any* of these characteristics (i)–(viii) *can tend* to justify us in saying 'There's something political', 'That's an instance of politics', or the like: 'can tend to', *not* 'will always'. I am not saying that any one of these characteristics is sufficient to make whatever has it political, any more than I am saying that the conjunction of all the characteristics is necessary to make a thing political. We have here *a* (not *the*) list of political or politics-making characteristics. It is not a definition, stating that something is political if and only if it has characteristics (i)–(viii) or (i)–(n). Only a concept which is *definite* can be so defined (i.e., definite in having clear boundaries). Our concept of politics is not like that and I see no reason for forcing it to be. See Wittgenstein, *Philosophical Investigations* pt I §§69–71 (1958(a): pp. 33–34).

3.20   If the concept of politics is as I have suggested, then there may be things which are political in one respect, but not in another. It is possible also that there are things such that it is desirable (or inevitable) that they be political in one respect and highly undesirable that they be political in another. That may help sort out some disputes about playing sport with teams from reprehensibly governed countries or about the political 'neutrality' or 'involvement' of churches, charities, universities, public servants, armies, etc. It is quite possible, however, that this sorting-out may clarify issues, but not resolve the dispute. The dispute may survive the clarification, or even blaze the fiercer because of it.

3.21   I have said that we need to listen. We especially need to listen to examples in which 'political' seems both to fit and not to fit. The year 1980 was the year of the Moscow Olympics. It was also the year in which the Red Army marched into Afghanistan. That gave rise to much controversy over the desirability and possible 'politicalness' of participation in the Games. I heard and read statement F many times, statement G only once:

> Politics and sport cannot be separated in the case of the Moscow Olympics, because, in the USSR, virtually everything, and certainly everything public, is political. (F)

> The Moscow Olympics will be completely non-political, because the Soviet Government has completely banished politics from the everyday life of the Soviet citizen. (G)

On the face of it, F and G are incompatible (contrariety: see TP 10.4), but their meanings are not given by their face value. Indeed, I believe that both were true, but that is irrelevant to our concerns. What matters is their compatibility. F makes a familiar point: In pre-*glasnost* USSR, there was almost always a 'correct', official line on everything: a symphony could be counter-revolutionary, an abstract painting seditious, a biological theory deviationist. Public events, especially large-scale ones, were controlled by the State or Government and manipulated to serve its ends. The Games would be political, the speaker says, because of an unusually strong and pervasive influence of State and Government, i.e., the political-making characteristics he has in mind are (i), (ii) and (vi) (3.17).

3.22   The G-speaker denies none of this. Implicitly, he asserts it. Both F and G assert that the USSR was totalitarian (see 2.16B), but the G-speaker wants to draw attention to the absence of public dispute, debate, competition, support-seeking by rivals, noticeable aspects of politics in our society; i.e., aspects (v) and (viii), so G is not as silly as it may look, though it does have a paradoxical air. That could be helpful, because paradox is often a matter of being off-centre: if there is a centre, there should be some possibility of making my account of the political more systematic and shapely, less messy, but, pretty obviously, the concept will not turn out to have the sort of unity which Socrates taught us to look for (see 1.3–1.9 and *TP* 1.14).

3.23   Am I saying that 'political' is ambiguous? No. Things are more complicated than that. If a word is usefully said to be ambiguous, that implies that it has at least two clearly distinguishable senses (see *TP* 2.7; Flew, 1975: pp. 70–72). A lecturer might say 'Every student is expected to have read that book', and a little later say of the same students and the same book, 'I expect a few of them haven't read it.' Since 'expect' has both descriptive and pre-scriptive senses (*TP* 5.12A), there need be no inconsistency. But 'political' is not like that. There is an absence of the clearly distinguishable senses. Perhaps 'political' is a little like such words as 'intelligent', 'clever', etc. The statements 'Tom is intelligent' and 'Tom is a fool' may look incompatible, but both might be true, provided that each concerns a different aspect of Tom (e.g., how he copes with symbolic logic as compared with how he copes with money, or vice versa). There is no question of separate senses of 'intelligent' and 'fool', merely of different aspects from which Tom can be assessed.

3.24   'Political' is not so much ambiguous as *plurisignative* (to borrow and, in some respects, modify a notion of Philip Wheelwright, 1954: pp. 60–75, 100–117). 'Ambiguity,' Wheelwright says, 'implies an "either–or" relation, pluri-signation a "both–and".' (In Flew's Trafalgar example (1975: p. 72), 'expect' is used plurisignatively.) I want to say that 'intelligent', 'political' and 'non-political' are plurisignative in that they can be *either* either–or *or* both–and. There is a range of respects in virtue of which the word can be applied and/or denied to the same thing. Sometimes, however, applying the word in virtue of only one aspect, and in spite of a large number of contra-indicative aspects, has an air of paradox. If someone is superlatively good at only one kind of performance, it is not false, but a little eccentric to say that he is *clever*, or *intelligent*, or *adroit*, etc. Hence the somewhat odd sound of statement G.

3.25   A few years ago, I had to attend a meeting of a certain hobby group. I was not a member and though the hobby is one I regard benevolently, I do not find it very exciting. Even if I had been interested in it, the meeting may not have greatly interested me, as it was a business meeting with minutes, business arising, correspondence, etc. But there I was. I could not get up and go, so I was faced with a choice: either to become bored and irritable or to *make* it interesting. I decided to do the latter by playing anthropologist; i.e., by observing what was going on and seeing how it resembled and differed from other meetings I had been to. The important thing in any such investigation is to 'get yourself a problem', otherwise observation becomes unfocused and disorderly. I soon had a problem.

3.26   It was this: I remembered a remark of Michael Oakeshott: 'Politics I take to be the activity of attending to the general arrangements of a set of people whom chance or choice have brought together' (1962: p. 112).[9] That had seemed to me to be a plausible statement about the nature of (though not a definition of) politics, but here was a meeting, the whole purpose of which was to attend to the collective arrangements of a set of associated people, and I felt a certain oddness about saying that what was going on was politics. So, while watching and listening, I tried to work out why I felt that, and what, if anything, is wrong with Formula H. One noticeable thing was that the atmosphere was very relaxed but, at the same time, formal. The chairman ran things efficiently and more or less according to the standard manuals, but I missed that curious compound of tension and boredom that characterises many meetings. That, on its own, however, seemed insufficient as an explanation of my feeling that the word 'politics' did not fit this meeting with entire comfort. What produced the relaxed attitude? It was not that there was no disagreement. People were expressing different preferences about where to go for the next field trip and so on, but there was something about the quality of those disagreements. They were conflicts only in the barest sense of that word. The decisive thing was that there was no *disagreement on policy*. Any disagreement was on the *implementation* of policy. Policy was a datum, so much so that no one thought of it as policy. There were no observable differences about the point or purpose of the club. Such disagreements as there were raised no conflicts over principle.

3.27   Another reason for finding the word 'politics' uncomfortable was the absence of competitiveness. If people disagreed over where to go for the next field trip, then *that* and that alone was what they were disagreeing about. *There* was a difference from typically political arguments, i.e., public dispute between politicians. The ostensible topic might be almost anything (unemployment, tariffs, education, health services . . .), and it is nonetheless a real topic for being ostensible, but whatever the ostensible topic, there is also, explicitly or implicitly, another: whether the Ins should be in or the Outs should be in. There was no such issue involved in the few disagreements expressed at the hobby club meeting. In more obviously political situations, participants often have to say to themselves: 'In itself, this isn't a bad proposal. Indeed, *in itself*, it's very good, but how would adopting it affect the balance of power and influence in the group?'

3.28   Those, it seemed to me, were the reasons why I felt uncomfortable about saying that observing the meeting was observing something political. They are, however, reasons NOT for saying that the club had *no* politics, but for saying that it had *minimal* politics. As a set of people associated together, it attended to its general arrangements (aspects (i) and (ii)), so it had its politics, but those politics were very different from the politics of the polity. The very absence of competition (aspect viii) heavily emphasises competition as a characteristic element of politics. In a similar negative way, emphasis is given to aspects (iii) and (iv). The example suggests a ninth item for our list of characteristics. I also add a tenth, though it has no special relevance to that example:

(ix) Typically, political disagreement, whatever else it is about, is also, explicitly or implicitly, about *who* should be in office or have power and how governance should be conducted, not only with respect to the obvious, overt issue under dispute, but more generally as well.
(x) The politics of a collective, being concerned with the governance of that collective, thereby concerns the relations of that collective with other collectives outside it, with law and order and the management of internal conflict, and the allocation of resources within the collective.

3.29 I am not proposing the hobby club as an ideal model of how politics should be. It was not only small; it was also narrowly based on one activity which all members shared and enjoyed. A group of the same number of residents of a street would embrace and deal with a wider range of interests and opinions and with conflicts from which the hobby club was free. The cut-and-thrust and bludgeoning of Parliament would be totally out of place in that club, but its placidity and harmony could be transplanted to Parliament only at the cost of tyranny. A polity cannot be 'one, big, happy family' in the cliché sense (and neither, I think, can one, big, happy family: cf. 10.14–10.15). And what is wrong with Oakeshott's Formula H (3.26)? Nothing, except that it completely fails to capture the flavour of the word 'political' (and by 'flavour', I do not mean only 'emotive tone'. The formula completely overlooks quite a few key factual expectations).

DRAWING THE MAP

3.30 I have assembled a list of ten political-making characteristics. It looks and is messy, but it can be tidied up. A glance reveals two major themes: governance and policy on the one hand and the activity of the politician on the other. Despite people like Kate Millett, I am quite sure that *primarily* the concept of the political refers to the polity, so that its applicability to the governance and internal affairs of other groups depends on certain significant resemblances between them and the polity. I shall use the word 'quasi-polis' to refer to the polity and other groups.[10] Hanna Pitkin compares the concept of representation to 'a rather convoluted, three-dimensional structure in the middle of a dark enclosure'. Political theorists take flashbulb photographs of it from various angles, each of them claiming that his photograph shows the whole structure. The task of the analyst is to fit them together (1967: pp. 10–11). The concept of politics is something like that. The most notable difference is the presence of those two major themes. That suggests a different metaphor. The concept of politics is like a globe with two poles, the North Pole being the governance of a Quasi-Polis,[11] the South Pole being the Politician.

3.31 Saying *what* a polity is and *what* a politician is are both pieces of hard and controversial work, but there is no great difficulty in arriving at a list of agreed examples of both: on the one hand, Australia, Austria, Mexico, Tuvalu, etc.; on the other hand a list of members of parliaments and other legislative bodies (see 4.1–4.3). So our two poles, Quasi-Polis and Politician, can each be explicated in quasi-ostensive fashion. Not every facet of a politician's life will be equally relevant to our conceptual investigation of the political, or will every aspect of a polity:

- 'Lo, a politician,' says someone brandishing a photograph of a rural MP looking respectfully at a Hereford with a ribbon round its neck. That does not tell us much about politicians and politics, but goes on to tell us what it exemplifies about what rural voters require of their MPs and why a prudent MP fulfils those expectations – then you are talking about politicians and their vocational activities, about politicians as such.
- Talking about Australia in terms of its location and rainfall tells us little about politics and the polity, but go on to relate what you have said to strategic and economic conditions – those facts about Australia are facts which its governing apparatus needs to take cognisance of in its work of governance. They are facts about a polity as such.

3.32   But is there still a problem about the Northern Hemisphere? Are we to say that everything connected with governance is political? The point is this: intuitively, it seems reasonable to say, 'If you want to know what the political is, go and look at the polity and its governance.' When we do, we find such things as legislation, resource-allocation, policy-making, etc. Those ring true as political, but we find also things which do not: e.g., people and computers sending out notices about the renewal of driving licences. Perhaps we can say something by means of (admittedly imperfect) analogy: the typist who types the manuscript of a novel is not *engaged in* literary activity, though he/she is *doing something ancillary* to literary activity. Similarly, those sending out driving licences are doing something ancillary to the governance of the polity, i.e., to things of the kinds mentioned in (ii) and (x) on the list of political-making characteristics. If someone says: 'But does that make what they are doing ancillary to politics? Answer "Yes" or "No"', my reply is 'I'll do nothing of the kind. I *have* answered and given the most precise answer I believe possible. You are being tiresome.'

3.33   The following formula (Formula α) sums up what I think I have found by looking at the Northern Hemisphere of the political, the one whose pole is the Quasi-Polis and its governance:

Something is political if it is directly related to the governance of the polity (i.e., to the making and administration of public policy). By this criterion, the degree of political significance of something is *normally* and *primarily* a matter of its closeness or relevance to the making (rather than to the execution) of public policy. (When speaking analogously of collectives other than polities, for 'polity' and 'public', read 'collective'.)

But we are not out of the wood yet. Consider the story of the F111 bomber, which went on for a considerable time in the latter half of the 1960s. Would Australia withdraw from the contract to purchase (and so lose a lot of money)? Would Australia honour the contract (and so run the risk of losing a lot of money)? Some time before the final decision, the Minister of Supply said, 'When a decision is made, it will not be a political decision.'

Alter Ego: What? A decision to be made by Cabinet? And involving a lot of public money? And concerning defence, one of the primary functions of government? Not a political decision? Nonsense!

Ego: You are right to some extent. Because of the considerations which you mention, it couldn't avoid being political. That's a matter of logic, but the Minister wasn't denying that. He meant that the decision would be made on cost-effectiveness criteria and that the effectiveness would concern defence. He was *denying* that the criterion would be 'What will be more likely to help the Government in its continual battle with the Opposition?'

Alter Ego: Is the word 'political' ambiguous then?

Ego: No. See earlier remarks about plurisignation and aspects (3.23–3.24). The whole phrase 'political decision' is, however, ambiguous because it has at least two distinct senses: (i) *decision made by a holder of political office*, and (ii) *decision influenced by political considerations*. Notice that the first of those 'politicals' is 'Northern' and the second is 'Southern'. It's because of considerations like these that we need to move to the South Pole, the Politician.

3.34   On the basis of Formula α, we can say:

If you submit an honest taxation return, your action has some political significance. The same is true if you engage in a tax fiddle. But in neither case would your action be *political*, as would submitting a blank return with a letter saying that you were doing it in protest at what the Government was doing or not doing about something. That would be political action and *might be* action of very great political significance.

Formula α carried us some distance, but, as the F111 example showed, it will not carry us all the way. If we treat it as giving *the* analysis of *the* concept of the political, we collide headlong with perfectly intelligible, possibly true English statements. When the Minister gave his assurance of the non-politicalness of the decision on the F111, many said, 'If you believe that, you'll believe anything', but that scornful incredulity is clear evidence that he had said something intelligible.

3.35   Formula β summarises the topography of the Southern Hemisphere of the political:

Politics is something which people called 'politicians' vocationally do and concern themselves with. To involve oneself in such activities and concerns is to involve oneself in politics. What is relevant to those activities, concerns and objects of concern is of political relevance or significance.

That formula makes it highly improbable that there is a 'common core' to the political. If politicians' vocational concerns and activities are heterogeneous, there could be a multiplicity of criteria for the political. *Beginning* with the politician does not commit us to *staying* with him. We can speak of politics wherever we find the same sorts of concerns and activities. Similarly, we can speak of the politics of collectives which are not polities or which are acephalous.

3.36   '. . . is political' is at least sometimes a *relational* predicate. A thing can be political not because of its intrinsic nature, but because of its relation to the activity of the politician or of the Government, a relation which might be temporary, so that a thing might be political at one time and not at another:

> The greatest political achievement of the Tudor monarchy was the Book of Common Prayer, but now that religious observance does not normally threaten the order of the polity, the churches can be left to write their own prayer books.
>
> (Webb, 1960: p. 13)

Such a matter no longer creates (or seems likely to create) significant problems for the peace, order and good government of the polity, neither is it an issue on which politicians have to or find it useful to take a stand. At the same time, it *may* well be something on which a government and/or its civil service still needs to have *some* policy, even though there is no longer controversy about it. It is worth remembering that, as late as 1928, the British Parliament did *not* allow the Church of England to write its own prayer-book, and that, in the 1970s, some manufacturer of journalistic beat-ups was able to create a brief stir by asking what would happen if Prince Charles wanted to marry a Catholic princess. Sleeping dogs wake, and so, sometimes, do sleeping dogmas. Thus, it is quite clear that anyone who declares, in a 'universal' tone of voice that religion can have nothing to do with politics is talking rubbish, and that someone who substitutes 'sport' for 'religion' is doing nothing better.

3.37   Now, it seems, I can draw my map of the political. Which of the political-making characteristics (3.17, 3.18, 3.28) are closest to the North Pole, i.e., the Quasi-Polis and its governance? Imagine a polity like the hobby club (a logical possibility: *TP* 3.12). It would have its collective affairs ((ii), (x)), which would need to be looked after and probably a group whose special job it is to look after them ((i)). That group would have to administer policy ((iv)), even though that policy would be a non-controversial datum. There would not be much conflict, but there would be some disagreement, so (iii) goes into the Northern Hemisphere, but close to the Equator. There would be little or no call for (v), but much for (vii). (vi), like (v), straddles the line. Such a polity would, we have supposed, have its rulers and legislators, but we would hesitate to call them politicians. That polity would lack what politicians would contribute to it, but it would also lack what would make politicians necessary. A prankish radio newsreader once inserted this sentence in a weather report: 'There was no weather at Coonabarabran yesterday.' 'Xland has no politics' is similar (though not as funny).

3.38   We can approach the matter from a quite different angle. From time to time, in various countries, bands of armed men in uniform seize control, announce a ban on 'political activity' and throw the politicians into gaol. What are they trying to exclude? Elements (viii) and (ix), I think. They are trying to diminish (iii). They may or may not go in for (vii), but, if they do, it gets absorbed into (ii) and (x), rather as it is in our very different hobby-club polity. There was little need for (v) in that polity, but, in the military-ruled polity, (v) is most important, so it also is absorbed into (ii) and (x). In such a polity, (v) and (vii) are governmental monopolies, becoming less strict only as the military rulers voluntarily loosen or involuntarily lose their grip. So (v) and (vii) are possible elements in the Quasi-Polis hemisphere, but indispensable elements in the Politician hemisphere. We get, I think, a map something like this:

QUASI-POLIS & ITS GOVERNANCE

(i), (ii), (x)

(iv), (vii)

(iii)

---------- (v), (vi) ----------

(vii)

(viii), (ix)

POLITICIAN

3.39   The concept of the political has many facets, but any unpacking of it must keep in mind its two major facets: the affairs of the quasi-polis and what politicians vocationally do. Something may be political by virtue of having all these characteristics, or by virtue of only some. When the only political-making characteristics which something has are those closest to either the North Pole or the South Pole, it *may* be misleading to say simply that the thing is political or of political significance. When all the political-making characteristics are near the North Pole, it may be clearer to say 'administrative' rather than 'political'. When all the political-making characteristics are those closest to the South Pole, it may be appropriate to put the word 'politics' in scare-quotes (*TP* 1.6B); hence, the insufficiency (though, if treated carefully, it can be illuminating) of Jouvenel's remark: 'Conduct which . . . causes men to perform whatever is necessary to the realisation of the prime mover's object, is "political" conduct and "political" action is action which inclines to his will the wills of others' (1957: p. 16). Those double inverted commas imply not that the 'is' should be 'is not', but that it needs careful and explicit qualification. On *politicking*, see 4.3, 4.16.

3.40   What I have been trying to do is to bring out the *complexity* of the concept of the political, and, at the same time, to bring out such *order* as there is in it. It is not a neat and simple order. Most accounts of *the political* fail because they concentrate on too few facets (sometimes only one) of a many-faceted concept. If my account succeeds, it does so by taking cognisance of that many-facetedness. I said 'that many-facetedness', not 'those many facets'. I do not claim that my account lists all the facets of the political. It lists those I have been able to think of. It trails off into the distance with a row of dots or an 'etc., etc.' That is one of its merits. Unlike a formal definition, it does not bring things to an end, merely to a tidier beginning. It conforms to the Austinian principle: 'Neither a be-all nor an end-all be' (Austin, 1979(a): p. 271). If you were expecting a formal definition, a little bottle of attar of politics, you will be disappointed, but, if so, you had to be disappointed, because there is no such thing. I do not claim for my account that it will solve or dissolve all – or even most – disagreements over whether the word 'political' is rightly applied. That is because such disagreements are often conflicts over principle or deeply entrenched interests (see *TP* 2.11). I hope, however, that my account may help towards a clearer view of what those conflicts *are*. A dispute over the 'politicalness' or otherwise of playing rugby against the Springboks is *not* like William James's one about the squirrel (1.17). See S. Harris, 1972.

3.41   My account would also enable us to recognise, without any sense of strain, the political significance of many phenomena which are not readily or normally recognised as political. At the same time, it should preserve us from thinking that all activities are political activities – a view which, despite its modishness, is fundamentally both absurd and totalitarian. It *may* be that everything has a political aspect, but, if so, the political aspect of most things must be pretty negligible, so negligible that only very special circumstances would make it worth talking about.[12] Nevertheless, a *médécin sans frontières* may find himself *un politique malgré lui*.

3.42   The most important logical consequence of my account is that, while there are things which are essentially political and things which are not essentially political, there are no things which are essentially non-political. (To put the matter in Platonic jargon: There is no Form of the non-political and no Form necessarily departs when the Form of the political approaches (cf. *Phaedo* 103B–106E: Plato, 1961: pp. 84–88).) For that reason, we should scrutinise very carefully demands that churches or universities or scientific bodies or charities[13] or . . . should not 'meddle in politics'. It would, I think, at least in present circumstances, be quite inappropriate for (e.g.) the Australian Academy of Science or the Diocese of Newcastle to issue how-to-vote cards, but there can be no *absolute* bar on any organisation or person involving itself in political matters. The reason is that anything whatsoever can become political. Governments and political parties *make* things political. They must not be allowed to make criticism of themselves essentially improper. ('Non-political' sometimes does duty for 'politically neutral'. That can be very misleading. See 11.12F.)

3.43   Another consequence of my account of the political is that a people might have politics without having anything like 'our' *concept* of politics. That should surprise no one. The prevailing 'Indo-European' concept of religion is probably centred on such things as *worship* and *sacred books*. Those are usually quite alien to the social life of animist peoples, but we can, nevertheless, recognise religious aspects of their lives.

3.44   The concept of politics (like other concepts) is not an idea in the head nor is it an elusive essence which underlies our talk of politics or which we try, with greater or less success, to reach and grasp in our political talk or in our talk about that talk. The concept of politics is what can be done intelligibly with words like 'politics', 'political', 'politician' (see Geach, 1957: ch. v). Let no one say 'Is that all?' Investigating it is quite enough to keep anyone busy.

DEFENDING THE METHOD

3.45   I have based my account of the political on (1) the collective affairs of the polity and (2) the vocational activities of politicians. It might be objected that this gets us nowhere because it is circular: 'If we refer to the vocational activities of the politician, we are assuming that we already know what the political is. The same is true if we refer to the collective affairs of the polity. What, after all, is a polity but a *political* society?' My answer to that objection is: 'Of course it's circular. It has to be. Of course we already know (implicitly) what politics is. It is pointless to pretend that we do not' (1.10–1.14).

3.46   If a heuristic pretence is needed, let us not fool ourselves by adopting the self-delusions of the respectable theory of definition. Let us pretend that we are strangers in a strange land, Yland. We can speak the Ylandic language fairly well, but not as well as the Ylanders. One of the things that puzzles us is talk about Xics and Xical things. When we ask our Ylandic friends to explain it, their answers are not always very helpful. We notice, however, that it often involves people known as Xicians. We get a list of such people. 'But,' our Ylandic friends say, 'not everything an Xician does is Xical and sometimes non-Xicians do Xical things. An Xician does Xical things as an occupation.' So, accompanied by some Ylanders, we set about observing the Xicians:

'Is that Xical behaviour?'
'No.'
'Is that?'
'Yes.'
'Is that?'
'Well . . . up to a point.'

And slowly we build up a picture of what Xical behaviour is, what an Xical issue is, what Xics is, etc. If we can do this in Yland about Xics and the Xical, why can we not do it in our own society about politics and the political? The journey is circular, but that is nothing to object to. In a circular journey, we might learn a lot, and even (if we are lucky)

> ... arrive where we started,
> And know the place for the first time.
>   (T. S. Eliot, *Four Quartets*
>   (1974(a): p. 222)

Suggested reading

Archer & Maddox, 1976; Connolly, 1983: ch. i; Hindess, 1971: pp. 14–18; Jouvenel, 1957: ch. i, 1963: chs i–iii; Clarke, 1988; W. J. M. Mackenzie, 1978: pp. 106–110; E. F. Miller, 1980; J. D. B. Miller, 1965: chs i–ii; Millett, 1972: ch. ii; Webb, 1960; M. Weber, 1948(b).

For references on the public service (i.e., civil service) and politics, see 2.13A.

4 Politicians, politicking, leaders, leading, etc.

POLITICIAN: SPECIMENS OF THE GENUS

4.1 The three cognate words 'politics', 'political', 'politician' are equally familiar, but the third is easiest to grasp, which is why I have treated it as a *primitive* (i.e., undefined) term in my attempt to explicate the concept of the political (3.30–3.38). A word which can be used to identify a person in terms of what s/he does for a living (or habitually and publicly) has the concreteness which arises from the existence of a set of agreed examples. Bertrand Russell's 'definition' of philosophy, 'what philosophers do', is a joke, but it can be a starting point for an investigation of the nature of philosophy. Two members of the Australian Association of Philosophy might disagree fiercely about *what philosophy* is, but it is guineas to gooseberries that each will agree that *the other is a philosopher*. They would have no difficulty, either, in drawing up an agreed list of philosophers, though each might blackball a few of the other's nominations. (See *TP* 2.10B.)

4.2 In a similar way, we would have no difficulty in drawing up an agreed list of politicians. Most would be parliamentarians and other elected members of legislatures. To them, we can add directly elected heads of state who are not legislators, but have a highly active constitutional role, e.g., American and French Presidents (unlike, e.g., the Irish President whose powers are not unlike those of a British monarch). I am not saying that *only* these are politicians, but that these are the examples everyone would agree on. They are clear and uncontroversial instantiations of the concept of politician, i.e., *paradigms* (*TP* 5.11). Are parliamentary candidates or candidates for pre-selection politicians? Perhaps and perhaps not, but there can be no 'perhaps-ing' about those who get elected. We might wonder a little about US Secretaries of State, of the Treasury, of Health, Education and Welfare, etc. They are not elected, but their appointments must be confirmed by the US Senate. Their position is, in some ways (though not in all)[1] analogous to that of Ministers in the Westminster system, but they do not have to have the crowd-pleasing qualities so helpful to the candidate for election. We might wonder whether Dr Kissinger was a politician. We need not wonder about Senator Kennedy. In Australia and the UK, trade unions are not merely politically *significant*. Some of them are affiliated to Labo(u)r parties and many union officials are powerful figures in those parties. Are those officials politicians? Was Mr R. J. Hawke, President of the Australian Council of Trade Unions, a politician? We might feel uncertain, but no one would doubt that, when Mr R. J. Hawke, MP, made his maiden speech, the world (or some of it) heard the words of a politician.

4.3 Visiting a certain Australian university, I asked one of its academics, 'What's your Vice-Chancellor like?' 'A politician,' the academic replied with a certain edge to his voice. I think I know what was meant. We could argue until the cows came home over whether that reply was literal, metaphorical, analogical, or even something else.[2] But if we saw that V-C talking to the Premier, we would have no hesitation about agreeing that that conversation involved at least one politician. My point is this: it does not matter whether elected members of legislatures and certain heads of state are the only politicians or the only 'real' politicians (whatever that might mean). The usefulness of the agreed list is that it is a list of people who, undoubtedly, are engaged in politics. That enables us to ask 'What is it that they are engaged in?' and to arrive at some kind of answer. Then, we can look at those whom we excluded from the list, not to see whether they 'really are' politicians, but to see how they are related to that in which the paradigm politicians are engaged. The role of some of them in it may be greater than the roles of some of the paradigms.

THE EXISTENCE OF POLITICS AND THE EXISTENCE OF POLITICIANS

4.4 If you give yourself a solid diet of sixteenth- and seventeenth-century political writing, you may find a still, small voice murmuring to you thus: 'These people have no idea of politics. When politics happened in their time, it was always a dubious business, always at least on the brink of sedition and treason. Even Locke (liberal culture-hero and Man Friday to the leading Whig of his day) gives no theoretical place to any political activity except ruling and resistance, yet there is much more to politics than that (i.e., the whole 'South' of the concept: see 3.30–3.38).' But another still, small voice might be saying: 'The very existence of the *Book of Homilies*[3] is of great political significance (cf. 3.36). Some of its contents are highly and directly political (e.g., "An Exhortacion to Obedience"). Some are only of remote and indirect (if any) political significance (e.g., "Against Whoredom and Adulterie"). Others, though not directly political, are of clear and strong political significance (e.g., "Against Strife and Contencion"). It follows that there was politics in Tudor and Jacobean times.'

4.5 Each still, small voice has a point and the points are reconcilable. The second talks about the governance of the polity. The first talks about the politics of physically peaceful conflict, the politics of legitimate, open opposition between interests, between principles, between 'visions', between power-seekers, the kind of politics which sees conflict as a permanent and not necessarily evil condition, the politics in which being 'agin the government' is nowhere near a hanging offence and can be so respectable as to be uninteresting (i.e., 'Cricko-Milnian' politics: see 3.10). 'Loyal Opposition' and 'His Majesty's Opposition' were originally paradoxical jokes, labels for something new, strange and not quite believable. In Tudor and Stuart times, 'South-Polar' politics, even when not uncomfortably close to illegality, was usually (in one sense of that versatile word) *private.*[4] Though intimately connected with the polity (i.e., the *res publica*: see 2.9C (ii)), most of *that* politics never saw the light of day. Even in our day, there is much in politics (whether of a university department or of international relations), and much politicking (4.16) which is not publicised. Indeed, most of the operations of the 'operator' are performed discreetly, but though there is no reason for the fly-on-the-wall to complain of boredom, the politics of a modern liberal polity involves *publicity* to an extent which would have startled James I (3.13) or even John Locke.

4.6 It is this politics of public, peaceful conflict which Milne and Crick are thinking of when they deny the existence of politics in Czarist or Bolshevik Russia. That kind of conflict is an important element in *our* concept of politics and also (for most of us) an important element in our notion of a tolerably livable-in society. But it is a bad mistake to talk as if this were the only (or the only *real*) politics there is. If one sets out to answer the question 'What is xics? What makes a thing xical?' and if, at the end of the day, one has a theory which implies that a large number of things which almost everyone calls 'xical' are non-xical, then one should say not, 'Lo! I have made a discovery!', but 'Something's gone wrong. I'd better go back and check.' An important rule of investigative procedure: 'Do not shout "Eureka!" when you have achieved no more than the loss of the soap.' Milne and Crick have, however, pointed to a very important difference in kind between regimes. We can accommodate their insight with little damage to ordinary language by agreeing that the activity of the *politician* is possible only to the extent that open competition and opposition are possible and legitimate. Thus Elizabeth I and Burghley, Lenin and Parvus, with their respective opponents, were up to their necks in politics, were political figures, leaders, activists, but were not politicians in the primary late twentieth-century use of that term.

'POLITICIAN': THE FLAVOUR OF THE WORD

> To his good friends, thus wide I'll ope my arms
> And like the kind life-rendering *politician*,
> Repast them with my blood.
> > *Hamlet* Act IV scene v
> > (My italics. That is the Folio version.
> > Most editors follow the
> > Second Quarto and substitute 'pelican'.)

4.7   For some centuries, the word 'politician' led a double life. On the one hand, it meant something like *political theorist*. That was what Puttenham meant when he said (1589) that 'Poets were the first lawmakers . . . and the first politiciens' (quoted, *OED*). When Hobbes wrote (1651) of 'the Venom of Heathen politicians', he was condemning the corrupting effects of reading Plato, Aristotle and Cicero. When Madison (1787) dismissed the 'theoretic politicians, who have patronised [direct democracy]', he meant Rousseau and his lot. On the other hand, 'politician' could mean either a vocational practitioner of politics or *someone very like one*. That use, while not inevitably pejorative, did have an odd smell, as it does now. The Folio misprint would not be even slightly funny if it did not. Indeed, all authentic Shakespearian uses of it are pejorative, e.g.:

> Why, look you, I am whipp'd and scourg'd with rods,
> Nettled, and stung with pismires when I hear
> Of this vile politician, Bolingbroke.
> > *I Henry IV* Act I sc. iii

> Get thee glass-eyes, and like a scurvy politician, seem
> to see the things thou dost not.
> > *Lear* Act IV sc. vi

(For other references, see Cowden-Clarke, 1881: p. 583 or Bartlett, 1956: p. 1190.)

If I am right, that was before the emergence of politicians in the modern sense, but they were about in the time of Adam Smith (1723–90), who wrote of 'that insidious and crafty animal, vulgarly called a statesman or politician' (quoted, *SOED*), and, of course, even today, the word is not without a slightly odd smell.

4.8   Part of the reason can be found in Shakespeare's writings: the connection between being a politician and being *politic* (cf. 4.3). 'Politic', as describing a human agent, is not ambiguous in meaning but ambivalent in tone (cf. 3.23). Like 'shrewd' (especially in current Australian speech), it can commend for sagacity or condemn for cunning (and, sometimes though not always, whether one praises for sagacity or condemns for cunning may be less a matter of morality than a matter of interest or personal liking disguised as a matter of morality). 'Am I politic? Am I subtle? Am I a Machiavel?' asks Mine Host of the Garter in *Merry Wives* (Act III sc. ii). To be politic is often to appear to be what one is not:

> These are the City gates, the gates of Roan,
> Through which our policy must make a breach.
> Take heed, be wary how you place your words,
> Talk like the vulgar sort of market men . . . .

So says 'Joan LaPuzell' (*I Henry VI* Act III sc. ii), using 'policy' as the (now thoroughly obsolete) substantive form of 'politic'.[5] 'Policy' can also be grey, unpleasant, contrary to the warmer feelings. 'That were some love, but little policy,' says Northumberland (*Richard II* Act V sc. i). Though a nasty man, he happens (on that occasion) to be right. Politicians must compromise and calculate. In a forgotten (but still worth reading) novel of Nigel Balchin (1949: pp. 86–91), a Cabinet Minister agrees that people are fundamentally decent, just and peaceful and want decency, justice and peace, but, he says, they want them on their own terms which do not add up:

> . . . decency and justice without interference with their liberty to do as they like . . . peace without risks . . . . How to do less work and have more money. How to spend more, reduce taxation, and balance the budget. How to be strong if there's a war but not to prepare for it, mention it, or even think about it beforehand.

The politicians who survive, he says, are those 'who've spent a lifetime learning to compromise between a set of demands that are all very reasonable but . . . don't add up'. In May 1982, the UK Government's policy on the Falklands had enthusiastic popular support to an extent unknown since the end of the War in Europe, perhaps since 1940. That was confirmed by public opinion polls which showed also that 60 per cent of British adults thought that liberating the Falklands should not cost a single British life (*CT* 1982(a), (b)). The Voice of the People (10.21–10.28) speaks to Government: 'We are with you all the way, and, if anything goes wrong, you are utter villains and we will not forgive you.' (Which goes to show that a logically odd utterance can be entirely non-ambiguous.)

4.9 Politics 'selects for' certain traits of personality: energy, ambition, confidence, competitiveness, combativeness, the capacity to give and take hard knocks, the kind of self-control that permits manifestation of intense emotion only when it is useful. None of these traits is, in itself, a fault, but they are dispositions towards certain vices as well as towards certain virtues. Political life provides a climate in which both the virtues and the vices can develop, but it is the vices that are more noticeable (see 9.31–9.44 on *corruption*). They can be damaging and they are almost always absurd. But their possibility is an integral part of the working of any relatively free political system. Political life attracts those for whom that life presents what Catholic moralists call 'occasions of sin' (see Kreyche, 1967; Klueg, 1967). Plato, tired of the wranglings in the Assembly, the plots and stratagems and failures of Athenian politics, suggested what might sound like a neat solution. Only those without political ambition should go into politics:

> Good people won't want to govern, either for money or for honour . . . so compulsion will be necessary, with a penalty if they refuse to take office. . . . The heaviest penalty is being ruled by someone worse than yourself. That's why decent people take office . . . . In a community of good men, the competition to be out of office would probably be as fierce as the competition to be in office in our community. They would know that the

true ruler pursues his subjects' interests, not his own, so every sensible person would want someone else to do the job.

> (*Republic* 347B–D. For another version,
> see, e.g., Plato, 1974: pp. 89–90)

That is all very well, but, as Dorothy Emmet sensibly remarks, Plato 'went too far, since most things are better done by those who enjoy doing them' (1966: p. 210 n.). To be without propensity to the vices of the politician is to be without propensity to political competence, let alone excellence. That is particularly so for those who aspire to lead. Trollope's Plantagenet Palliser, Duke of Omnium, is certainly a nice man, but I doubt whether someone so self-effacing and self-doubting could, even when Dukes were Dukes, rise to the heights at which Trollope has placed him.[6] Such a man in power could be far more dangerous than a tough professional with more than a faint smell of Tammany about him. Eric Ambler's Deltchev is also a nice man, and it is his specific, self-doubting niceness which betrays his people to their enemies. A sense of duty *alone* is *morally* insufficient for taking on a complicated and exacting way of life. Of William Neal Gillies, Premier of Queensland for eight months in 1925, it has been said that:

> The very qualities which had won [him] the leadership – his personal kindness, his freedom from spleen, his ability to co-operate with all factions – did not fit him for the position with credit to himself or advantage to the [Labor] party at that difficult period of industrial unrest.
>
> (K. Kennedy, 1990: p. 359)

Of a better-known Premier, it has been said that:

> . . . one thing which no one would dispute . . . is that she is completely a politician: a fighter for causes, a constant manoeuvrer for advantage, a blood-and-guts performer whenever she's under attack and often when she's not.
>
> (Young & Sloman, 1986: p. 51)

4.10   Of course, one must remember that not all politicians are leaders and also that it does not follow that leaders should be totally lacking in kindness and bubbling over with spleen. Still, such cases do remind us that even non-violent politics can be very harsh, very grim. The qualities which make for political success may exclude lovability. See 9.19–9.30.

The politics of the politician is a morally perilous business, but a business necessary for and inseparable from a free society. To say that politicians need constant scrutiny and criticism is one thing. To damn the whole lot of them with one all-embracing sneer is quite another, for what is to replace them? The elect of God? Experts who need seek no support because they Know they are right and because 'none can call their power to account'? Those with a Correct

Understanding of the Movement of World History (and a secret police to help them)? Give me the politicians any day, even the more sordid and venal of them.

Suggested reading

Bay, 1975; Cranston, 1977; Crossman, 1958: pp. 3–88; Fairlie, 1968: chs i, ii; Howson, 1984; J. D. B. Miller, 1960; Minogue, 1972; Schumpeter, 1954: chs xxi–xxii; J. Walter, 1979; M. Weber, 1948(b).

POLITICO, POLLY, ETC.

4.11 There is no one word to refer to politicians, political partisans and those with strong political interests. The narrator of Joyce Cary's *Not Honour More* sometimes calls them 'politicos'. (The word has also been given a more restricted technical meaning: see 2.17K.) Here are some of the other things he calls them:

> Bugs in the wallpaper, bunkumboys, diddlers, fakers, gas experts, gas squirt and clack merchants, grabbers, hot air politicocks, jabber boys, jabberwocks, plan merchants, politikites, rats in the sewer, swindle cookers, talky boys, tapeworms.

In Australia, politicians are sometimes referred to as *pollies*.

STATESMAN[7]

4.12 In 1880, within twenty-four hours of each other, W. E. Gladstone told a young man that 'Statesmanship is the noblest way to serve mankind' and John Bright declared that 'If the people knew what sort of men statesmen were, they would rise and hang the lot of them' (M. Creighton, 1956: p. 342). Today, those of Bright's opinion would say 'politicians' and a modern Gladstone would say 'a career in politics'. If you call the average MP 'a statesman', he will (granted sanity on both sides) know that you are pulling his leg.[8] In other words, 'statesman' was once a polite substitute for 'politician' but it is more than that now: it is *honorific*. Statesmanship is what politicians are called on to aspire to or display: 'If Mr Z were a statesman and not a mere politician, he would take the brave and intelligent course of . . .', etc., etc., etc. A smart-alec definition says that 'A statesman is a successful politician who is dead.' According to Harold Macmillan, 'When you're abroad you're a statesman; when you are at home you're just a politician' (Cohen & Cohen, 1971: p. 146). But 'statesman' is not merely a cheer-word. People are given the title because, in their day, they had an apparently unique capacity to deal successfully with a great national crisis. Two standard examples are Winston Churchill and

Abraham Lincoln. They are absolutely conclusive evidence for the thesis that the statesman is not something totally distinct from the politician. As J. D. B. Miller says of them, 'Few men have been so consistently accused of being shameless politicians right up to . . .their supreme moment' (1960: p. 12). (Australian readers will relish the title of Townsend, 1983.) See 5.41–5.45.

Suggested reading

J. D. B. Miller, 1960; Fairlie, 1968: ch. ii; Sperber & Trittschuh, 1964: p. 329.

LEADER, LEADERSHIP

4.13   *SOED* does not get beyond 'one who/that which leads' in its explication of the concept of leadership. That fails to capture the flavour of condemnations of individual politicians or governments for lack of leadership, or assertions that Australia (or somewhere else) Needs a Leader. Accusations that a party leader's or a government's leadership is defective are usually intended to suggest at least some of the following: dithering and indecisiveness, a lack of initiative, a lack of self-confidence, disunity in the party and lack of followers' confidence, an incoherence of policy, a reluctance to tackle hard issues. Frequently, the demand for leadership is a demand that a government should have a definite, systematic policy and not simply react in an *ad hoc* fashion to events or to pressure (even popular pressure). One Opposition attack on a Premier contrasted 'the leadership and long-term decision making' for which 'the community [2.12] is looking to the Government' with 'the short-term populist [see 8.30–8.40] approach to pump-prime the economy' (Koch, 1990).
4.14   These are faults in someone's leadership *of a party and/or a government*. Leadership *of a nation* is quite a different kettle of fish. A free polity needs *a government*. It does not need *a leader*, except in times of very great emergency (2.7, 2.4, 5.43–5.47). Frequently, the perfectly reasonable demand that a government or its head should lack the faults listed above gets mixed up with a demand that he should give his compatriots 'inspiration', 'a sense of purpose', 'a vision for the future'. That is either mere waffle or something much more sinister: a hankering for The True Leader who will have the Wisdom and Courage to sweep away all the untidy complexity of politics as it is, so that we can be Uplifted, Saved and Unanimous, free from all uncertainty and controversy (see 2.16B). We should never forget that the German word for 'leader' is 'Führer'. On war and political leadership, see 5.41–5.45.

Suggested reading

IM, 1991; Legge, 1973; Lucy, 1979. See also 2.14H, 2.15F, 4.10.

LEGISLATING AND RULING

4.15   Many people seem to regard the words 'legislator' and 'law-maker' as more dignified substitutes for 'parliamentarian' and 'politician'. Because these are seen as more dignified terms, they are seen as more complimentary and, therefore, more reproachful when reproach is needed: 'Law-making's a great thing and it's what they SHOULD be doing, but . . . .' Our newspapers use the words 'legislator' or 'law-maker' as elegant variants for 'MP'. Where the London *Daily Telegraph*, a right-wing paper, talks of 'Tory MPs', the *Newcastle Herald* talks of 'lawmakers of Britain's ruling Conservative Party' (23 April 1985: p. 11). More forgivably, the papers also use 'legislator' or 'law-maker' as a comprehensive term to cover the members of parliaments and of analogous assemblies that are not quite parliaments, such as the United States Congress. But then they go and call the Supreme Soviet 'the Russian parliament', when, until its second-last gasp, it was more like the Edinburgh Festival Tattoo, only not so much fun. Quite apart from these vagaries, it is also true that some of our parliamentary bodies have the word 'legislative' as part of their names and a great deal of parliamentary proceedings is debate on proposed legislation.

There is, then, a belief, and some evidence to encourage it, that the whole point of politics is law-making and that someone who aspires to be a politician aspires to make laws. As I said in the previous chapter, law *and policy* (the two are not the same) are products of politics and it would be a bad mistake to see them as mere by-products. Even so, it would be the wildest of mistakes to think that a politician's working hours (which, incidentally, are almost all his hours) are devoted to the production of laws in the way that a potter's working hours are devoted to the production of pots. To call a politician a *legislator* or *law-maker* is to adopt a way of talk which suggests that his professional skill is to be measured by the number and quality of the pieces of legislation he produces. Perhaps that puts it too individualistically, since few politicians can be seen as individual producers. I'll try again: to call a politician a legislator is to adopt a way of talk, suggesting that his professional skill is to be measured by his contribution to the production of pieces of legislation. It is to suggest that his professional work is analogous to that of a member of a continuing team of craftsmen who produce a series of objects to which each member contributes – Rolls-Royces, cathedrals, films, drainage systems, whatever.

But that is unrealistic. It may, however, suggest why some very bright lawyers, brimming with good ideas for legal change, have failed disastrously as politicians. Such a politician will see politics and parliamentary life as a series of legislative tasks: modernise the bastardy laws. That's done. Now to the Criminal Code. Big job that, but after it, we can get down to defamation and the laws governing insurance policies. And the competitive strife, the point-scoring, the electors who demand his presence at various social functions and bore him to tears with their half-baked notions and their problems and the Branches which demand to be cosseted – all of that he sees as distraction from his tasks. And, unless he changes his ways, all that distraction will take its revenge and dump him very hard. His mistake is to see himself primarily as a maker and hardly at all as a doer, as a performer with an *un*finished and unfinish*able* job (cf. 4.8).

To call a politician a *ruler* is, of course, very misleading. It calls up archaic pictures of Good King Wenceslaus or Bad King Herod, people possessed in their own right of immense authority and/or power, whereas politicians – even the most powerful – seem much more enmeshed in rules and procedures, can be effective only with the co-operation which arises from compromise, and need to keep a hundred different powerful interests onside or not too belligerently offside.[9] Richard Nixon seems to have thought of himself as a ruler and look what happened to him.

All that is true but, if we can delouse 'ruler' of its Good King and Bad King associations, we can use it to get a clearer picture of politicians. Many people whom we normally would not call rulers *do* exercise rule, authority, control. Consider a self-employed tradesman whose business is large enough to employ others, but small enough for him to be still a tradesman himself. He is a man in authority (2.15) over his employees, and, if he is a sensible man, he will want that authority to be underpinned by their unforced consent and loyalty and not merely be a matter of legal right and economic power. He has to be able to deal with his employees, to establish the appropriate mixture of friendliness and distance. He must know when to request and when to give orders. He must have some comprehension of the immense range of styles which the expression 'to give orders' covers and he must have the discernment to use the right style at the right time. ('To give orders', considered in isolation, usually seems to suggest a brass-throated sergeant-major, but that is misleading.) This employer-tradesman will receive his money for the performance of a succession of jobs (possibly even the making of a succession of objects, i.e., a succession of mutually resembling but discrete tasks). But the 'man-management' aspect of his work cannot be accurately represented in that way. Like felicity-according-to-Hobbes, it is a matter of 'continuall prospering' (*Leviathan* ch. vi. 1968: p. 129), certainly not goal-less or aimless, but lacking an achievable goal *which terminates it*. It is a coping, maintaining, keeping-things-going activity, which is not to say that it is devoted to keeping things going precisely as they are. Indeed, the more innovative our self-employed tradesman is, the more care he must devote to keeping things going.

The politician does not 'rule' as our self-employed tradesman does, but there is an important analogy between the two. Whether one considers the politician as a professional with his own interests to protect and a family to feed, or as a member of a team competing with other teams, or as a servant of the commonwealth, his work is primarily one of coping and maintaining and keeping things going – doing rather than making. Though rarely kingly, the politician is involved in activity which, though it has both *dux* and *rex* aspects, is much more *rex* than *dux*. (If that is unintelligible – and even if it is not – see Jouvenel, 1957: pp. 15–55.) A consequence of what I have been saying is that political agents of the following kinds are, if politicians, anomalous politicians (though not necessarily the worse for that): the reformer whose political activities are concentrated towards the achievement of one or several definite goals,[10] the revolutionary who aims to bring about a transforming event, senior politicians in time of war (especially total war) in so far as their energies are concentrated toward victory (see 5.41–5.45). For some remarks on political decision-making, see 9.25–9.28.

POLITICKING; PLAYING POLITICS; POLITICALLY MOTIVATED

4.16   *To politick* is to campaign politically, to attempt to rally support for one's own side and to diminish the support of the opposition, 'to practise manoeuvre, management and persuasion' (Fairlie, 1968: p. 16). Persuasion-by-argument comes into it, but so does persuasion-by-the-doing-of-favours and -by-reminder-of-past-favours-done. It frequently involves public campaigning, but it also involves less public and even secret murmuring, dealing, squaring and buttering-up, i.e., *intrigue*. (See.3.7–3.8. For an elegant picture of this, see Cornford, 1953: pp. 22–23.) Politicking involves the practice of 'policy' in the Elizabethan sense (4.8). Politicking can involve the championing of causes less because of their merits than for tactical reasons. That is an unavoidable part of the practice of politics, but gives it a certain ingloriousness. The word is also applied to intrigue in collectives other than the polity. ('It is familiar in every hierarchy, where the jockeying for tenure, prestige, and of course money sees the dull and the crass show a talent for self-advertisement' (Freeling, 1988: p. 245).) Despite the ingloriousness, all statesmen (4.12) politick.

4.17   '*Playing politics*' is a pejorative phrase, often used to accuse someone of politicking in an irresponsible fashion: raising issues or taking action *merely* for political advantage, regardless of their merits (e.g.: 'They make fanciful charges against the prime minister which suggest they are playing juvenile politics rather than arguing about a serious issue' (H. Young, 1991)). Sometimes, the suggestion is that the person accused is acting *regardless of any adverse consequences of his actions in raising the issues*, especially, sometimes, adverse consequences for those whose cause is ostensibly being championed:

> How can I meet with him when he's going to play politics? . . . He wants to confect some basis for an early election or something. You shouldn't play politics with people's interests like that.
>
> (R. J. Hawke. Quoted, A. Buckley, 1984)

> Mr [X] . . . asserted that the hospital was playing politics in not allowing an outside chiropractor to treat his son . . . who has been unconscious for four months.
>
> (Barrass, 1982)

At its least derogatory, 'playing politics' imputes an inappropriate influence of 'southern hemisphere' political considerations on 'northern hemisphere' matters (3.39).The phrase, however, is often used simply as a missile. As 'I am firm, you are hard to persuade, he is as stubborn as a mule,' so is 'I campaign, you politick, he plays politics.' Some people are able to make the phrase 'a carefully organised campaign' sound like an accusation of some vile crime.

Suggested reading

Jouvenel, 1963: pts III and IV; Laver, 1979; J. Coleman, 1972; Bailey, 1969; Pfeffer, 1992.

4.18 Politically motivated

Literally, anyone who does anything in the hope of achieving a political outcome is politically motivated, but the phrase is frequently intended to imply that someone is *politicking* reprehensibly or *playing politics* (4.17). Some-times, the only argument raised against a proposal is the assertion that it is 'politically motivated'. That, even if true, is not necessarily an absolute, knock-down refutation.

4.19 RESPONSIBLE BEHAVIOUR, RESPONSIVENESS; HUMILIATING BACKDOWNS, CAVE-INS, ETC.

In 4.8, I quote the Balchin dialogue in which politics is said to be a matter of compromise between demands which 'just don't add up'. It is not only policy demands that are mutually incompatible. Demands as to political behaviour can be just as odd. We agree that the Government should be responsive to public opinion and that it should not be so stubborn that it sticks with a policy merely because it has made that policy. That would be irrational. The rational person is prepared to revise his opinions and decisions and does not ignore new arguments and facts that have newly come to light. That is how the rational person behaves and it is how the rational government behaves, too. Quite so. You and I agree and so do all the best newspapers. Then the Government announces a policy and controversy erupts. Not just the Opposi-tion, but also the media and various experts and organisations and lots and lots of ordinary folk say that it just will not do. There are petitions and protest rallies and the backbench is mutinous. 'Oh, all right, then,' says the Govern-ment. 'We won't do it,' or 'We'll do only half of it,' or 'We'll do it, but in a very different way.'

And what happens then? Do we say that the Government has acted in a rational fashion? Do we pat it on the back for being responsive to popular opinion? No, we do not. The media begin chanting 'Yah boo! You backed down! You caved in!' And we all start muttering about a lack of decisive leadership or a 'leadership vacuum' (whatever that might be).[11] That sort of thing must soften the blow of losing an election. But even the Opposition is not free from mutually incompatible demands. You and I and the best newspapers all agree that the Opposition ought not oppose for opposition's sake alone. And when the Opposition shows any signs of thinking so too, we say that they are weak as water and that the Government is running rings round them.

In politics, failure is inevitable, though, of course, some kinds of failure are worse than others. For some remarks on the ambiguity of 'responsible', see Parker, 1976; Thynne & Goldring, 1981.

5 Loyalties and unities

ON BEING AN X FIRST AND A Y SECOND

5.1 In February 1979, Anastasio Somoza, the dictatorial Nicaraguan President, was overthrown militarily by the Sandinista National Liberation Front (FSLN), whose leader, Daniel Ortega, became President. Eleven years later, there was a presidential election in which, to everyone's surprise, Ortega was defeated by Violeta Chamorro. The Reuters dispatch said that, amongst the problems which Mrs Chamorro would face, was an army 'raised to be fiercely loyal to' the FSLN. It 'is officially known as the "Popular Sandinista Army" and its officer corps is drawn entirely from party ranks and owes its loyalty to the party first and the nation second' (Debusman, 1990: pp. 1–3).

5.2 Those remarks are relatively unproblematical. The questions worrying the author are 'How will the Army behave? Whom will it obey?' The liberal-democratic norm is that the army of Vland takes its orders, ultimately, from the Vlandic Government *of the day*. The Government is treated as legitimate, as representing (2.17) the polity, so long as those orders fall within certain moral and legal restrictions. The Government is expected not to use the army to advance the interests of the party in power and to harass its political opponents, but to use it in defence of the people and territory of Vland. That is the cash-value of 'An army owes its loyalty to the nation first.' In the liberal-democratic view, a party, as such, is merely *une partie*, i.e., a mere part, a mere portion, and also just one party to an at least two-sided dispute (5.34–5.39). Legitimacy is a matter of recognising those moral and legal restrictions and of coming to power in the constitutionally appropriate way. The FSLN had come to power in the only way any opponent of Somoza could, i.e., militarily. As a revolutionary movement, it claimed (with some justification) to represent the nation against Somoza. If one uses 'party' in its liberal-democratic sense, the FSLN had claimed to be not a mere *party* but a *national movement*. The worry in February 1990 was whether it and its members could make the attitudinal transition to being a mere party, in particular whether the army could see itself as an arm of the Government of the day, rather than as part of a national movement. That is the cash value of worries whether that army would put its loyalty to the nation before its loyalty to 'the party' (i.e., the FSLN). Thus, Debusman's remarks are relatively unproblematical.[1]

5.3   Not all uses of the notion of being an X first and a Y second are quite so reasonable or quite so clear. In the 1970s, an academic from Papua New Guinea (PNG) visited Irianjaya (i.e., 'West Papua', the western half of the 'Big Island' of New Guinea, formerly Dutch territory, now Indonesian). He noticed that all or virtually all positions of responsibility were held by people from other parts of Indonesia, so he asked a senior official (a Javanese) what plans the Government had for *localisation*. The word was an unfamiliar one to the official. The academic explained that it was the word used in PNG for the process of training indigenous people to replace expatriates in positions of responsibility. 'But that does not arise here,' said the official. 'We are all equally Indonesians.' So the Irianjayans were Indonesians first and Irianjayans second and, therefore, there could be no complaint if they were dominated by people from other provinces of Indonesia.

5.4   In 1981, the Queensland State Government proposed to set up a corporation to buy shares in companies threatened by takeover from outside the State. This was denounced in a newspaper editorial, headed 'Queenslanders are Australians first' (*The Australian*, 1981):

It is easy to understand the resentment of Queenslanders to the State's resources being exploited by others . . . .

It is every person's right to protect that which is his own . . . .

'But,' it continued sternly, 'that doesn't mean creating a fortress mentality and environment.' It did not tell us what it *did mean* (in terms of political action), but simply rejected the notion that a State could have interests which clashed with and needed protection from those of another State. Such a notion was said to be *unhealthy, insular and xenophobic, paranoid*, and *bordering on the ridiculous* ('bordering on' is nicely anti-climactic). The nearest thing to an argument for this was the title and the last sonorous paragraph:

Queensland is, after all, part of Australia, part of something much bigger and bountiful. 'Stateism' is fine when it's confined to cricket, football and so on. But God forbid the day should arrive when a citizen of this country is not Australian first.

5.5   I find it not (*prima facie*) unreasonable for Queenslanders or anyone else to worry if they see trade and industry in their part of the country coming substantially under the control of people in other parts of the country. They may fear that such economic power might be used in ways not to their benefit. They may also fear that their State could become a kind of outer suburb to the more populous and more wealthy parts of the country. Whether they have reason for those fears is another matter. What they should do about them is another again. But to tell them that it is very naughty to have those fears because they should be Australians First sounds like the blarney of a confidence trickster or the bland words of the Indonesian proconsul. If we worried about

*power over the Australian economy passing to the Japanese, The Asahi
Shimbun* or something might well remind us that Australians are human
beings first and Australians second. Perhaps *The Australian*'s editorialist
would find that reassuring.

5.6   The idea that the wider group-membership must always be given
preference over the narrower is deeply rooted. Perhaps it seems like a logical
axiom. A. J. M. Milne writes:

> Can a community hold together in the face of internal moral diversity? Isn't
> this likely to have a socially disintegrating effect? Not necessarily. It may be
> due to religious differences which are accepted as part of a way of life in
> which religious freedom and mutual toleration are basic principles . . . . But
> if [it] is not to have a disintegrating effect, it must be contained within a
> wider moral framework which is generally accepted . . . . Primary loyalty
> must be to the community, not to particular groups or classes within it. The
> ideas, beliefs and values which the members share must be more important
> to them than those which divide them.
>
> (1972: pp. 37–38)

> . . . if a community is to hold together, its members must want to live
> together despite their differences, and must be able and willing to maintain
> institutions and practices through which they can do so. Primary loyalty
> must be to the community, not to particular groups, classes, or . . .voluntary
> associations within it.
>
> (ibid.: p. 41)

5.7   Broadly speaking, the editorialist and Milne are in agreement, and I suspect
that, to most people, what they say seems obvious, or, at least, orthodox: the onus
of proof would be held to rest on someone disagreeing with, rather than on
someone maintaining this view of loyalties and duties. But is it so obvious that the
larger group, or even the polity as a whole *must* have priority in *all possible*
circumstances? If the Government wants to sacrifice your children to Moloch, are
you morally bound to acquiesce, even if most of your fellow citizens are
enthusiastic Molocholators? But, if you do not acquiesce, are you not, in at least
one respect, putting your loyalty to your family ahead of your loyalty to the
polity? Milne softens things a little by talking about 'mutual tolerance', but that is
to say less than enough. He talks about the necessity for people to want to live
together despite their differences, which is better. He talks about the need for
people to be able and willing to maintain institutions making that living together
possible, which is even better still, but that in no way supports the demands which
he makes at the end of each extract. Mutual tolerance (10.31 n.) might begin with
not making those demands. It is important that there be an institutionalised *tact*
which prevents things from coming to the sort of crunch in which people have to
decide 'what they are first'. The demand that Vlandic Callathumpians be Vlanders
first and Callathumpians second may well be a demand that they be unsatisfactory
Callathumpians or even no Callathumpians at all. That demand *could* be a
reasonable one: if, say, Callathumpianism required its adherents to behave

like the Thagi, those devotees of Kali to whom we owe our word 'thug'. But Milne talks as if it MUST be a reasonable demand *whatever* Callathumpian dogma and morals are like, and where in that are 'religious freedom and mutual tolerance'? A demand of that kind might have a much more 'socially disintegrating effect' than Callathumpian unwillingness to say without qualification that their status as Vlanders comes before their status as Callathumpians. Given that people do disagree, and that they disagree on matters they regard as fundamental, the best Milne's prescription can give us is (in Milton's words) 'the forced and outward union of cold, and neutral, and inwardly divided minds' (*Areopagitica*, Milton, 1951: p. 43).

5.8   And is it a reasonable demand that the Callathumpians should regard what separates them from their fellow Vlanders as less important than what they share with them? The Callathumpians may believe that they are in possession of a unique revelation from God, a revelation which their fellow Vlanders reject. It is hardly even coherent, let alone reasonable, to ask them to treat such a difference as relatively unimportant. What one can ask is that the Callathumpians see the differences as less significant *politically* than those things they share with other Vlanders, but that is something that the Callathumpians *cannot do on their own*. Non-Callathumpian Vlanders and the Vlandic Government need to be doing it, too.

5.9   Milne's remarks, taken literally, would rule out all recognition of conscientious objection to military service or to anything else. I doubt if he wants that, but it is by no means clear what he does want. Milne taught for many years at Queen's University, Belfast. If he thought of Northern Irish affairs when writing the words quoted, he probably saw himself as saying something which both tribes of the Six Counties should take into account. But the minority would reject it *in toto*, since they do not see Northern Ireland as a community to which anyone should belong. The majority would see it as a truistic description of what they do all the time.[2]

5.10   Let us return to Vland. If the Callathumpians went about saying *explicitly* (though perhaps *covertly*) 'We are Callathumpians first. We are Vlanders second,' the other Vlanders would be quite entitled to worry – to suspect that, at the least, Callathumpians, given the chance, would look after one another nepotistically at the expense of everyone else.[3] That would show, not just the 'unhealthiness' of Callathumpian attitudes, but also that questions of the shape 'Are you a X first or a Y first?' are unhealthy. They seem to demand that either Xness or Yness be utterly subjected to the other. The question may be asked with less tyrannical intent, but, in that case, the questioner has used the wrong words.

5.11   'Are you an X first or a Y first?' should always be answered with other questions:

What are you after?
What (in some detail) am I being asked to choose between?
What impact do you see a choice as having on what I have to do or believe?

Loyalty is a complex concept and raises more problems than can be dealt with here. Those who wish to pursue it further should take a good hard look at the relevant entries in *OED* and may find E. R. Emmet (1968: pp. 75–80) helpful. It is, of course, not a purely political concept (see Fletcher, 1993) and is related to such matters as friendship and love (see, e.g., C. S. Lewis, 1963). Pettit (1988) and Sabini & Silver (1989) are relevant to that relationship and also to the question whether loyalty is reconcilable with the impartiality which seems essential to morality (9.1–9.18). Loyalty is connected with problems of *political obligation* (see *TP* 9.11B and references therefrom; see also Allen, 1989; Minogue, 1987; Nathanson, 1989 and 1990) and with the virtue which the Romans valued as *pietas* (*OED*: 'pietas', 'piety I 3,4'; *OxLD*, 'pietas'; Currie, 1973: pp. 16–23; R. D. Williams, 1977; B. Byron, 1972).[4] But loyalty need not always be virtuous (2.13B, 9.31–9.44; Shernock, 1990; Ewin, 1990). Whether loyalty is applicable to modern employer–employee relations is discussed in Grosman, 1989. This raises a question relevant to political obligation: What is the relation between *loyalty* (to a person, cause, social object) and *fidelity to a contract*? The two are not identical and some would say that, in some respects, they are not even compatible. In Australia, it is sometimes alleged that the word 'loyalty' has been 'hi-jacked' by imperialists, anglophiles and similar villains (Alomes, 1988: index; Raymond Evans, 1987; Grant, 1972; W. J. Hudson, 1989; Ward, 1970). For some discussion of what it is possible to be loyal to, see Seddon, 1973.

NATIONAL UNITY

> One is one and all alone and ever more shall be so.
>
> Old song

5.12   Unity is not a simple notion. Even the *Shorter Oxford* takes quite a while to tell us about it, identifying eight main uses of the word, several of which branch out into subvarieties. Follow 'unity' through Roget's *Thesaurus*, and, if you have done it with care and attention, you have made a long and arduous (though enjoyable) journey. 'But we're concerned with *national* unity, aren't we – with "unity" in a socio-political sense. Doesn't that narrow things down?' No. The socio-political flavouring adds further complexity.

5.13   Thomas Hobbes is one of the great simplifiers. His philosophy is, of course, a complex and sophisticated structure, but he does have a way of dismissing complexities and diversities as flimflam or flummery. He is a 'Nothing-but' man. Hobbes's opinion is that social unity, conceptually at least, is a rather simple thing:

> A Multitude of men are made *One* Person, when they are by one man, or one Person, Represented . . . . For it is the *Unity* of the Representer, not the *Unity* of the Represented, that maketh the Person *One* . . . . And Unity, cannot otherwise be understood in Multitude.
>
> (*Leviathan* ch. xvi, 1991: p. 114; see also 4.22–4.25)

That is not an argument for monarchy. Hobbes's sovereign can be a body of rulers or even the entire citizen-body assembled as a decision-making body (*à la* Athens). The point is that it is the *one* set of authoritative decisions, the one *will* which confers unity on the multitude. That is not just an isolated statement of a preference or a prejudice, but rests on complex psychological and linguistic doctrines. One of these doctrines is Hobbes's demand for mathematical precision in language and his rejection of all ambiguity and 'open texture'[5] as dangerous. We can imagine him saying: '"Unity" means "oneness" and only a single thing can be one.' But we can accept that proposition without accepting either Hobbes's linguistic doctrines or the conclusions which he draws from them.

5.14 It is simply false that 'Here is one society' *means* 'Here is a group which obeys one leader or one government.' The criteria for oneness are more complicated than that. It is not that 'one' is ambiguous or even that it becomes ambiguous once it moves outside the realm of pure mathematics. 'One' is *indeterminate*, rather than ambiguous. The indeterminacy is directly related to the indeterminacy of the word 'thing', which in turn has much to do with the complexity of human beings and of the world they live in. This indeterminacy is brought out very neatly by some of those odd questions which J. L. Austin used to throw at people:

> Why is it absurd to say that I did exactly (or even approximately) ninety-seven things yesterday?

> How many things are there in this room?

5.15 It *may* be that one would not identify a group as a *polity* (2.5) unless it had a set of co-operating decision-making organs which were largely effective throughout the group, but that is a matter of the definition of those terms. We *might* accept it as a necessary condition for the existence of a *polity* (or, etc.)[6] without accepting that either *total submission to* or *total authorisation of* a sovereign (or a government) is either necessary or sufficient to make a multitude into a polity.[7] But Hobbes's thesis includes much more than polities. He says that '*Unity*, cannot otherwise be understood in Multitude', a term wide enough to cover *any* kind of collection of people, and the assertion is quite unequivocally universal. Hobbes asserts his thesis as a necessary truth, but it is not true, either as a matter of logic or as a matter of fact. Even if we took unity of governance as a decisive and defining characteristic for polities, that would not commit us to the view that governance is the only politically significant aspect of a polity, neither would it commit us to the view that a polity (i.e., political society) is, considered as a society, nothing but a *political* society.

5.16

1 Canada
2 Belgium
3 Sri Lanka
4 Lebanon

Each of these has a government unique to it, claiming supreme legal authority over the relevant territory. By the criteria of international law, each is to be counted as one whole thing. By Hobbist criteria, each of the first two is certainly to be counted as one whole thing. If the *claim* rather than the *effectiveness* of the claim is what counts, the same is true of no. 3 and of no. 4. But there are good reasons, reasons of great socio-political significance, why we would not predicate oneness of any of those four polities without some sort of qualification. And the 'nations' (7.1–7.12) internal to those polities do not derive their existence from having a legal or illegal quasi-sovereign or quasi-government of their own. Any such quasi-government is parasitic on the existence of the 'nation', rather than the other way round. Without Tamils, there can be no Tamil Tigers or Tamil United Liberation Front. (And one government did not give Lebanon social unity, neither did social unity collapse because of the collapse of the Government.)

5 Wales
6 Ireland (minus six counties in the north-east)
7 Lithuania

By Hobbist (and many other) criteria, each of these, for at least a sizeable part of its history, could not be counted as one distinct whole thing. But, at the same time, there are reasons why we *would* predicate certain kinds of distinct-whole-oneness of them. The inclusion of Canada and Belgium in the first of those lists shows that their kind of *lack of oneness* need not entail an ineffective, merely (or almost merely) self-styled government, helplessly presiding over a chaos of individuals or groups. Their kind of *lack of oneness* is quite compatible with the existence of a by-and-large effective government in a country whose inhabitants belong to different and easily distinguishable cultural groups, and are very conscious of belonging to those groups, so that that diversity colours the political life of the country.

5.17   If we can for present purposes pin the word 'political' down as meaning 'directly concerned with the governance of a polity', then we can say that Hobbes's criterion for social unity is exclusively *political* (or, perhaps, *juridical*). That criterion is the unity of will of the representer. Hobbes makes little allowance for any of the phenomena which we lump under the headings 'custom' and 'culture'. So far as he recognises these things at all, there is more than a suggestion that they are impediments to the polity.[8] It seems that the activity of the Sovereign and that alone is the corporate life of the polity and every legitimate activity within the polity has its being from the sovereign, but that is to oversimplify and distort. Societies or communities are more than solely political or juridical bodies. To understand them that way is to *mis*understand them. Even their political life arises from and presupposes social interaction of kinds which cannot be called 'political' – at least, not without further explanation. (They are interactions which are not political *per se*. See 3.41–3.42.)

5.18   Hobbes offers us a recipe for social unity, something with a high place on most people's scales of political values, but *his* social unity may not be the social unity *we value and want*. Hobbes sees *any* conflict as being inimical to society, *conceptually* inimical, not just *factually* inimical. The distinction can be explicated by analogy:

> The presence of a bacillus of type X in my body is inimical to my health. (S)
> The presence of illness in my body is inimical to my health. (T)

If S is true, it is true empirically, not by logical necessity (*TP* 3.5, 3.8). It can be denied without self-contradiction, unlike T, which is true by virtue of the concepts of illness and health. To the extent that I am ill, to that extent I am not healthy. That is not a proposition that needs confirmation by pathological investigation. Hobbes treats the relationship of conflict to social breakdown as being like the relationship of illness to the breakdown of health, not just as being like the relationship of the presence of bacillus X to the breakdown of health. Such a view involves disregard for many relevant facts and a radical and arbitrary redefinition of terms. Even construing the relationship of conflict to social breakdown on the analogy of the presence of bacillus X to the breakdown of health is inadequate. Austin Duncan-Jones once remarked that 'Societies can stand a good deal of "chaos"' (1958: p. 256). He is right, though it is as well to remember that there are limits to the chaos which they can stand. It is one of Hobbes's merits that he reminds us of that, even if he overdoes it.

5.19   Hobbes, like most political philosophers, prescribes away in a largely timeless tone of voice. That is not entirely illusory; his philosophy is not *merely* a disguised reaction to the events of his time, but it *is, in part*, such a reaction, and it is useful to ask 'What is worrying him? What does he see us as needing to be *saved* from?' Hobbes was born in the reign of the first Elizabeth (prematurely – so he says – because his mother was frightened by the Armada) and died six years before the death of Charles II: ninety years of very troubled English history. There was much to worry Hobbes. It is a mistake to see the Civil War and Commonwealth period as being *merely* a time of conflict between Royalists and Parliamentarians. It was a time of multiple conflict. As Christopher Hill shows us, the phrase 'the world turned upside down' was on many people's lips (see, e.g., C. Hill, 1958, 1975). It was a time when, to many people, almost anything seemed possible. One could react to that with enthusiasm or with fear. Even Hobbes had some occasional modestly Utopian hopes (*Leviathan* ch. xxxi, 1991: p. 254), but, for the most part, he was *worried*. The fragmentation of authority and of the realm seemed a real possibility. Not only were there many prophets claiming the special inspiration of God. There were even those who claimed *to be* God. It required no very neurotic imagination to see this chaos of conflicting certainties becoming a physical chaos. The *war* which worried Hobbes was not the sort of thing that went on at Edge Hill and Marston Moor. That had an order about it. It had an end and, when it was ended, everyone knew who had won. Hobbes's state of war is a state of utter chaos and frustration in which there is no order and no victory. It is not surprising that he saw unity as all-important and saw it as a unity of will, a central authority which must animate the whole realm – a unity and a will which are utterly singular.

5.20 For present purposes, it is sufficient to deny that there *is* a need for the complete constancy that Hobbes demands. The evidence is the continued, relatively peaceful existence of polities lacking that constancy. Obviously, there must be *some* sharing of values among the group. Without it, there would be not only continual conflict, but also mutual total incomprehension (10.20). We can, however, get along together while disagreeing fairly furiously (cf. Lucas, 1967: pp. 1–17). Unity can be compatible with diversity and even with conflict. Again: 'Societies can stand a good deal of "chaos".' But, if we look on Hobbes's remarks on value terms and the diversity and mutability of the passions as *a theorised picture* of an England infested by prophets, projectors and dogmatists, and inhabited also by bewildered bystanders, tugged this way and that by contrary messages, *then* it all becomes much more plausible, and the proposition that social unity can be the product only of one sovereign will, absolutely authorised, would be convincing – if we did not know from experience that it is false. Putting Hobbes's argument on unity in its historical context reveals both its strengths and its limitations (and might make us a little suspicious of any 'timeless' arguments on such matters). This thing, unity, is beginning to look rather heterogeneous.

5.21 'Monolithic unity.' Outside mathematics, *the monolith* is the most striking example of unity (or of one kind of it). Literally, or at least etymologically, a pebble is a monolith (*monos lithos* = 'one – or a single – stone'), but we reserve the word for stones whose singleness is remarkable: Egyptian obelisks, mysterious standing stones in Britain and France put up God-knows-when by God-knows-who for God-knows-what purpose, boulders of the kind plentiful in the New England district of New South Wales. What is striking about the monolith is its unity (i.e., its oneness) combined with its bulk: its huge, unbroken continuity, its uniformity ('unimaterity' would be the better word, but it has no recognised existence). The unity of a monolith is striking. So thoroughly single and unimaterial a thing can be contrasted with a Gothic cathedral, e.g. Chartres, full of diversity and difference. But isn't Chartres striking for its unity, too? A rather different kind of unity, a very different kind of unity. (And the several monoliths of Stonehenge make a unity also.)

5.22 Outside mathematics, when we predicate unity of something, it is *usually* something which, in certain striking respects, is not a unity. (The monolith is not just a striking paradigm. It is also a striking exception.) The thing is diverse, heterogeneous, a plurality, perhaps even discordant, but we insist (often with justification) that it is *really* a unity. (There are plenty of artistic examples. Plenty of socio-political examples, too.) Similarly, things for which we desire or recommend unity are typically not merely lacking in unity *now*, but are also things which, in certain striking respects, can *never* be unities (or units), even if they eventually approximate to, even if they eventually fully realise, what we desire or recommend. The monolith is a unity, but the predicate '. . . is united' does not fit it comfortably. Only pluralities can be united in the sense of 'go through a process which unites them' and the sense of '. . . is united' which ascribes a state (i.e. condition) applies primarily to pluralities also. ('. . . is united' applies to the whole because the relational predicate '. . . is united with . . .' applies to each of the elements.)

5.23　If we are asked for 'the opposite of' the word 'unity', we are likely to say 'disunity', and, by so doing, step firmly into quicksand. It is not so much that the answer is *false*. The trouble is that both it and the question which evokes it are grossly misleading. There can be more than one opposite to a word and there is more than one kind of verbal opposition (see *TP* 10.1B). As well as that, 'unity' is a very general word which can do duty for a variety of slightly less general words such as those in the first column below:

(i)	Singleness	Plurality
(ii)	Homogeneity	Heterogeneity
		Diversity, Difference
(iii)	Unanimity	Dissent
		Disagreement
(iv)	Harmony	Discord
		Conflict
(v)	Systematic connection	Hodgepodge
(vi)	Coherence	Separateness
	Cohesion	Distinction
		Division
		Chaos
(vii)	Singleness	Division

5.24　The first column lists words for (as it were) species of unity. The second column lists *contrasters* (1.5 n.) to those words. It is by no means clear to me that each of those contrasters is a word for a species of *disunity*, though each is a word indicating that some species of unity is, to some degree, lacking. From (iii) down, it makes *somewhat* better sense to talk of species of disunity, but, even then, it is by no means clear to me that each of those disunities must be a *bad thing*. It is even less clear to me that all socio-political instances of them are bad things which we should aspire to abolish or suppress. One danger with talk about *national unity* is that it may (consciously or unconsciously) take just one species of unity (and perhaps an inappropriate one) as the example to be aspired after (see, e.g., 5.41–5.44). Another danger is that national-unity-talk may simply meander from one species to another in a quite uncritical, though ideologically (*TP* 7.2D) self-interest-serving fashion. The point of all that is NOT that 'unity' can mean so many different things that the phrase 'national unity' means nothing at all, but that different aspirations and ideals can animate talk of national unity. We need to know what is *worrying* the person who calls for national unity and what he wants us to do (cf. 5.11, 5.19–5.20).

5.25　The slogan for National Day in Papua New Guinea during the 1970s was 'Bung wantaim–Ahebou–Unite'. (Three ways of saying the same thing. The first two are, respectively, Tok Pisin and Hiri Motu.) I was told one year that the people planning the celebrations had thought of adopting a new slogan: 'Yumi wanlain' (roughly: 'We are one family') or 'Yumi wanpis' ('We are one' – 'one piece' – 'all of a piece'), but had decided that the imperative mood was more suitable than the indicative. What was a Papua New Guinean being told to do? More or less, to be conscious that there exists a social object (2.2), Papua New Guinea, to which he belongs, together with people from the other end of the country and even hereditary enemies from the other side of the creek. (Cf. the quite low-key and unexcited fashion in which Australians in the eastern States have no difficulty in thinking of people in Perth as fellow citizens.)[9] But there was no point in telling Papua New Guineans to be homogeneous. They could not be 'wanpis' in that sense: 'seven hundred languages', differences in culture, in physical appearance, loyalties to kinship and language groups, hostilities, etc. The concept of *Papua New Guinea* is itself of exotic origin and in need of domestication. That 'Bung wantaim' type of call for national unity is only one such call. Others may be based on an already firmly established sense of common citizenship, for co-operation to meet a crisis. There can also be calls to widen habitual loyalties, to widen the circles of loyalties. (For *nation*, see 7.1–7.16.)

5.26   Here are some other slogans of unity:

(i)   *Faciam eos in gentem unam.*
      (I shall make them one people.)
(ii) *E pluribus unum.*
      (Out of many, one.)
(iii) *Bhinneka Tunggal Ika.*
      (They are many. They are one.)
(iv) *Wanpela pipal. Wanpela nem. Wanpela kantri.*
      (One people. One name. One country.)
(v)   *Ein Volk. Ein Reich. Ein Führer.*
      (One people. One polity. One leader.)

Slogan (i) was inscribed on a coin (known as the *unite*) issued soon after the Crowns of Scotland and England were united in the person of James I. It is a quotation from Ezekiel (xxxvii. 22). Seen in its original context, it suggests that very high claims were being made for James. (The same chapter of Ezekiel pretty clearly influenced the imagery of Hobbes, also someone given to making high claims.) But the immediate reference is to the uniting of distinct political entities. The same can be said of slogan (ii), the motto on the Great Seal of the United States, which later acquired a new significance with polyglot immigration. (See 12.44, *melting-pot*.)

5.27   Probably we are meant to interpret those slogans as asserting the persistence of plurality within unity. The same could be said of (iii), the national motto of Indonesia. The language is Sanskrit, and I am told that the phrase originally referred to the unity of the many Hindu gods in Brahma.

Indonesia is, of course, a predominantly (though rather idiosyncratically) Muslim country with a Hindu past, so the very act of choosing such a motto has a complicated symbolic significance of its own. Slogans (iv) (a Pangu Party slogan from Papua New Guinea) and (v) (a Nazi slogan) might at first seem disconcertingly similar, but the most likely explanation of the similarity is that both are echoes of St Paul: 'one Lord, one faith, one baptism' (Ephesians iv. 5). Despite the similarity, the two slogans are diametrically opposed, since the unity for which the Pangu slogan calls is a unity of inclusion, whereas the Nazi slogan calls for a unity based on exclusion. Again, the point is that calls for unity can be calls for very different things. (Co-operation is a form of unity and so is unanimity, but, as political ideals, they are very different.) Some pleas for unity can be very like the proposals for nuclear freezes made by whichever Great Power happened to be ahead at the moment. (A *New Yorker* cartoon of the Vietnam years showed a General shouting: 'We could have a viable democracy here tomorrow if only those damned dissenters would shut up.')

5.28   The organismic image (i.e., 'body politic' and the like) has appealed to many people as a way of representing the unity-in-diversity which characterises polities and other social objects. It can illuminate, but its weakness is that it can suggest that all dissent, all conflict is pathological. That notion, persisted in consistently, leads to idealising the kind of co-ordination which has given the German word *Gleichschaltung* such a sinister ring (2.16C). Hence the importance of recognising an image as an image and *expecting* it to break down. Hence also the importance of not letting one's thinking be dominated by *just one* paradigm of unity:

> A main cause of philosophical disease – a one-sided diet: one nourishes one's thinking with only one kind of example.
>
> (Wittgenstein, *PI* pt I §593, 1958(a): p. 155)

It is one of the virtues of the kind of philosophy called 'linguistic' that it encourages the bringing to the surface of paradigms and pictures and opposes the tendency to overlook diversities for the sake of theoretical orderliness.

5.29   Basically, *unity* is related to the word 'unit'. X is a unity IFF (i.e. if and only if) it is one thing, but the criteria for 'oneness' will differ according to the kind of thing X is, and, even then, X may be a unity in one respect and not a unity in some other respect.

Unity can be predicated of something *on the basis* of uniformity.

Unity can be predicated of something *on the basis* of consistency. (And there is more than one kind of consistency, too!)

Unity can be predicated of something *on the basis* of homogeneity.

Unity can be predicated of something *on the basis* of harmony.

Unity can be predicated of something *on the basis* of co-ordinated action of elements.

ET CETERA, ET CETERA, ET CETERA.

5.30   And consider the diverse things that can come under the heading 'co-ordinated action of elements', e.g.:

A group singing a simple song
A group singing a madrigal
Soldiers on parade
Soldiers on patrol
A *corps de ballet*
A co-operative investigation
People going about a common task
People going about their several tasks and not getting in one another's way
A chess game played by evenly matched expert players
The co-ordination within each pair in a doubles tennis match
The competitive co-ordination, inside a framework of rules, between the two
   pairs
A controversy in which all the participants stick to the point and observe the
   decencies of debate.

Looking at that list, we see different types of co-ordination. They differ in complexity, in the types of authority involved, in the degree of initiative allowed to elements, in the degree of co-operation, in the degree of uniformity of action. One of the morals of that is that appeals for *national unity* should be closely scrutinised before we start cheering. Just what *kind* of unity are we being asked to support? Another moral is that accusations of creating *national disunity* should also be closely scrutinised. Just what are we being asked to condemn as *disunity*? Some people are inclined to see disagreement, dissent, diversity in world-view as disunity. To identify unity with homogeneity and to try to impose homogeneity by suppressing or ignoring diversity is a good way of creating disunity (i.e., strife and the alienation of minorities). But, of course, the determined advocate of unity-by-suppression will see that as yet more evidence that diversity is wicked and dissent is treasonous. Pleas for unity can be pleas for reconciliation or at least the acceptance of 'Queensberry rules' governing controversy and conflict (10.13). But pleas for unity can also be the very reverse of that: they can be attempts to raise intolerance and bigotry to the status of unchallengeable first principle (cf. 5.27).

5.31   The problem of *social unity and diversity* stands to socio-political thinking as the problem of universals (*TP* 1.10A) stands to metaphysics. Each is a (almost *the*) central and persistent problem of the intellectual enterprise in which it occurs (and each, of course, is an attempt to deal coherently with an interplay of unity and diversity: cf. 2.9C). The practical problem of social unity and diversity is always with us and we deal with it, on that level, with varying degrees of success (see the newspapers, etc.). On the theoretical level, the problem cannot be ignored and shows no sign of ceasing to be a problem. Contemporary (and earlier) political science and political philosophy have failed to cope with it satisfactorily. We are still a little like the pre-Socratic

Greeks in their attempts to explain the nature of things. As they lurched from monism to extreme pluralism (*TP* 7.10B), so do we. On the one hand, we have people who talk as if there were (or as if there should be) really nothing but unity in a society and as if diversity were really illusory, merely superficial, or perhaps, a collection of pathological growths which need to be removed. On the other hand, we have those who talk as if there were nothing but diversity and as if any appearance of unity were merely illusory. A strong tradition in Australian political science and political philosophy upholds this latter view (6.18). It is all very much like Parmenides versus Herakleitos – and both are wrong. There are also radical dualists such as those Marxists who assure us that, always and everywhere, there is a clash between two parties and only two parties. That, too, is political superstition.

5.32 'Wouldn't it be nice if we had a *definition*, a *formula*, a *theory* or even just one *image* which would give a succinct, illuminating and complete account of that interplay of unity and diversity?' I am by no means sure that it *would* be nice. But, however that may be, I have no such definition, formula, image, theory, and neither, I think, has anyone else. Until one is found, the best we can do is to multiply pictures and endeavour to keep them *all* in mind – and also to distrust deeply anyone who professes to have such a definition, formula, image or theory.

5.33 As noticed above, the slogans quoted in 5.26 have a rather religious flavour. There are two obvious hypotheses which might be advanced to account for this. One is that, if a society has sacred books and a religious vocabulary, then, if a member of that society is deeply impressed by something or wants to sound impressive, he will tend to echo that vocabulary, even if the object of his wonder is something he regards as quite secular. The other explanation is by Machiavelli out of Charles L. Stevenson (see Urmson, 1968): that the devisers of such slogans wish to annex the emotive tone of religious language for their own socio-political purposes. I have no doubt whatsoever that there is some truth in both those hypotheses. There is a third possibility which is less obvious but worth considering: that social unity in diversity is something so important, yet so difficult to conceptualise (as is shown by the largely unsuccessful efforts of philosophers and sociologists), that it constitutes a *mystery* in something like the theological sense of that word. But, having said that, I am hit by the fear that I might seem to be saying 'search no more'. I am most definitely not. The recognition that social unity is a (kind of) mystery should be seen as a stimulus to further investigation. See also 5.41–5.45 (*war and unity*), 10.11–10.42 (*consensus*), especially 10.18. For 'One nation', see 7.19.

Suggested reading

Carling, 1991; Gellner, 1987: chs ii, iii; Lukes, 1977: ch. iii; McKenzie & Silver, 1968: ch. ii, pp. 179–181; Milne, 1972; Stretton, 1969: ch. x; H. W. Morgan,

1971; Richler, 1991; McRae, 1974; Lijphart, 1977; Barry, 1975; Shils, 1975: pp. 3–16, 48–90.

PARTY AND FACTION

5.34

> Here lies our good Edmund, whose genius was such,
> We scarcely can praise it, or blame it too much;
> Who born for the Universe, narrow'd his mind,
> And to party gave up what was meant for mankind.
> > Oliver Goldsmith (1728–1774)
> > 'Retaliation: A Poem' (1906: p. 88)

Party is a body of men united, for promoting by their joint endeavours the national interest, upon some particular principle in which they are all agreed. (Edmund Burke (1729–1796) *Thoughts on the Cause of the Present Discontents*

(1852: p. 170; 1975: p. 113))

Goldsmith's lines are a mild example of the disapproving tone in which the word 'party' was often pronounced in the eighteenth century. Party was regarded as something which distracted the attention of public men from the general interest, and the words 'faction' and 'party' were often used interchangeably. Burke, however, believed that 'Party divisions, whether on the whole operating for good or evil, are things inseparable from free government' (1852: p. 7). He distinguished *party* from *faction*, using the latter word to refer to combinations of purely selfish or subversive or illegal motivation. The Court of George III was, he believed, such a faction (1852: p. 173; 1975: pp. 117–118). Burke was by no means naive and he knew perfectly well that the 'definition' of *party* quoted above is normative, i.e., stating an ideal, rather than stating those properties which every party exhibited all the time. His definition has been ridiculed by some of those who reject the concept of the general or national interest (e.g., Schumpeter, 1954: p. 283; see also 6.17–6.29), but that definition does recognise the *contestability* (6.22; *TP* 8.10B; see also Connolly, 1983: ch. i) of the concept, implying clearly that there can be different conceptions of what the general/national interest is. In a country with relatively free institutions, parties are distinguished from *pressure* (or advocacy) *groups* by the fact that they seek to exert influence or power over policy by gaining elective office.

5.35   The word 'faction' is still heard, sometimes with the full pejorative fury of its eighteenth-century use, but it is also used more neutrally for a *grouping within a larger grouping*; hence 'faction' is sometimes used *in contrast* to 'party'. Scruton says that a faction 'is identified by perceived common purpose rather than by rules of membership' (1983: p. 165). Frequently, that is so, but, in recent years, the word has been applied to quite formally organised groupings within the Australian Labor Party. It is used rather similarly in anglophone discussion of the internal affairs of the Israeli Likud and Japanese Liberal Democratic parties.

5.36 Burke speaks of *party divisions*. He would have regarded the phrase 'one-party state' as a linguistic monstrosity, which it is (see also 2.16B, 5.2). The party of a single-party state is not a contender for government, but an instrument of government, or, rather, its own central apparatus is usually the effective government. (The Royal Family of Kuwait could call itself a party if it wanted to.) Even so, one-party states vary greatly. Socio-political life in one-party Tanzania was vastly different from socio-political life in one-party China or in Nazi Germany. The parties of multi-party systems also differ greatly. Parties *tend to* proliferate in systems which use proportional representation. There is more of *a tendency to* two-party polarisation in other systems, but please note those italics. In 'Westminster' polities, i.e., polities in which the Government requires the confidence of Parliament, party discipline will tend to be stronger than polities like the United States, in which the 'Executive Branch' is separated from the Legislative. The Australian Labor Party and the Indian Congress Party can each be described as 'a collection of factions', but the ALP is a far more stable collection than the ICP. Etc., etc.

Suggested reading

Scruton, 1983: pp. 164, 345–346; R. Smith, 1993(b); *PPW*, 1988; Burke, 1852: pp. 167–174, 1975: pp. 109–119, 1960: pp. 132–138; Needler, 1991: chs vi, ix; Jaensch, 1983; Jupp, 1982; Warhurst, 1986. For some remarks on party names, see 7.20, 11.9–11.11.

5.37 In Australia, intra-party conflict is frequently much more bitter than conflict between the parties. This is particularly true of the Labor Party (ALP), though the conservative parties also have their moments (see, e.g., Reid, 1972). One true believer rang a newspaper to clear things up:

> Let's get the ALP factions clearly defined. Right-wingers are mostly Liberal infiltrators and DLP[10] sneakers. Centre-Leftists are reformists, doing all right for themselves out of capitalism and scared of change. And Left-wingers still hold for real Labor principles regardless of gaining power, prepared to hold fast while capitalism wrecks itself.
>
> (Simons, 1985)

But another observer has said, 'If you like, call the Montagues *The Right* and the Capulets *The Left* and say that Mercutio represents *The Centre*. In ALP politics, "Right", "Left" and "Centre" have as much and as little meaning as football colours.' An experienced insider confirms this view: '. . . you learn in ALP factional politics . . . that there are no permanent relationships, only permanent interests . . . [and] that matters of principle are not the basis of separation, but it is usually personal hatred and animosity' (R. Cavalier, reported by Steketee, 1981).[11] There is hyperbole on both sides. For some vivid pictures of life inside the ALP, see Cumming, 1991; *QPD*, 1967; *VPD*, 1956; Murray, 1970; Parkin & Warhurst, 1983. For more on *left, right* and *centre*, see 11.11–11.12.

PATRIOTISM, JINGOISM, CHAUVINISM

5.38   Everyone knows Samuel Johnson's apophthegm, 'Patriotism is the last refuge of a scoundrel.' Johnson was given to uttering neatly turned, dogmatic wisecracks in the presence of James Boswell, who was given to writing them down. This particular one was 'uttered in a strong determined tone' on 7 April 1775. Boswell characterises it as 'an apophthegm at which many will start' (i.e., which will startle many), and adds 'But let it be considered, that he did not mean a real and generous love of our country, but that pretended patriotism, which so many, in all ages and countries, have made a cloak for self-interest' (1980: p. 615), which is more than likely. In other words, Johnson was not affirming 'If someone professes patriotism, he is a scoundrel seeking his last resort' but 'If someone is a scoundrel seeking his last resort, he will profess patriotism.'[12] (The one does not imply the other. See *TP* 6.18–6.19.) Even so interpreted, the assertion is a hyperbole, other resorts often being available to the scoundrel (e.g., collaboration with the invader or departure to foreign countries with which his own has no extradition treaty). Patriotism, like other loves, can be counterfeited or pathological. To condemn it holus-bolus on those grounds condemns all other loves as well. Jean-Jacques Rousseau condemned 'those so-called cosmopolitans who . . . boast of loving the whole world so as to have the right to love no one at all'.[13] Patriotism also can be used as such an excuse, but does not have to be. Edmund Burke agrees, to some extent, with Rousseau on this matter (but on few others):

> To be attached to the subdivision, to love the little platoon we belong to in society, is the first principle (the germ as it were) of public affections. It is the first link in the series by which we proceed towards a love to our country and to mankind.
>
> ('Reflections' (1968: p. 135))

> We begin our public affections in our families. No cold relation is a zealous citizen . . . . The love to the whole is not extinguished by this subordinate partiality. Perhaps it is a sort of elemental training to . . . higher and more large regards . . . .
>
> (ibid.: pp. 314–315)

On this view, patriotism is (as it were) a *theorem* rather than an *axiom*. (See Mary Gilmore's poem 'Nationality' (1954: p. 2).) This needs to be distinguished from the view that country should be valued merely as a container of more basically valued things. See also 7.17–7.18. Jingoes and chauvinists (old sense: see 5.40) are patriots, but it is not the case that all patriots are (still less, must be) jingoes or chauvinists. *OED* records the word 'patrioteer', a term of reproach for those whose patriotism is uncritical, unduly ostentatious, or insincere. For *war and unity*, see 5.41–5.45. For suggestions on reading, see 5.11.

Orwell suggests the following distinction:

> Patriotism is 'devotion to a particular place and . . . way of life which one believes to be the best in the world but has no wish to force upon other people . . . . Nationalism, on the other hand, is inseparable from the desire for . . . more power and more prestige . . . for the nation or other unit in which [the nationalist] has chosen to sink his own individuality'.
>
> (1970(c): p. 411)

Some such distinction needs to be drawn, but it would be clearer to say *aggressive chauvinism* (5.40), rather than *nationalism*, leaving the latter word for movements and sentiments stressing the distinctiveness and urging the independence of nations (especially as Orwell – perceptively – says 'nation or other unit'). For *nation* and *nationalism*, see 7.1–7.16.

Suggested reading

Orwell, 1970(a), (b), (c), (d): indexes, 'nationalism', 'patriotism'; C. S. Lewis, 1963: pp. 25–32.

5.39 Jingoism

> We don't want to fight,
> But (by Jingo!) if we do –
> We've got the ships. We've got the men.
> We've got the money too.

That is the refrain of an English music-hall song of the late 1870s, supporting Disraeli's bellicose policy towards Russia. Hence, a jingo is a bellicose or aggressive patriot. He may also be a warmonger. On the other hand, he may really mean that first line. See *OED*; Brewer, 1970: p. 588; Sperber & Trittschuh, 1964: pp. 221–222. See also 5.43–5.47.

5.40 Chauvinism

Nicolas Chauvin, one of Napoleon's soldiers, was utterly devoted to the Emperor and his expansionist policies. While Napoleon reigned, Chauvin was greatly admired. After Waterloo, he became a figure of fun. A chauvinist regards his own nation, its people and its practices as superior to all others. He may also (though need not) believe that his nation deserves to be supreme over all others. 'Chauvinist' is a near-synonym of 'jingo', but a *pacifist chauvinist* is a logical possibility; a *pacifist jingo* is not. To use 'chauvinism' *merely* as a disparaging substitute for 'patriotism' is like using 'sentimentality' as a disparaging substitute for 'affection' or 'compassion'.

More generally an Xian chauvinist is an X who believes uncritically and bigotedly that Xs are superior to all non-Xs. He may also believe that Xs should be supreme over all non-Xs, hence 'male chauvinist'. But it would be a pity if the meaning of 'chauvinist' were narrowed to 'male supremacist' or widened to 'prejudiced'. (Both tendencies are there. Both are verbicidal (12.13).)

Suggested reading

OED; Brewer, 1970: p. 215; Scruton, 1983: pp. 59–60.

WAR AND UNITY

5.41

> We discover the reality of the community in our inner consciousness, as well as in the world of external fact. The incorporation of our Ego in a social Being of a higher order is a matter of our own inner life . . . . If we derive from our internal experience a certainty of the reality of our ego, this . . . extends to the fact of our being a part-unity within the higher life-unities. It is true that we cannot discover these higher life-unities themselves within our consciousness . . . . Indirectly, however, we can deduce, from the effects of communities upon us, the conclusion that social Wholes are of a corporeal-spiritual nature . . . . In our ordinary daily life any effort of attentive introspection will suffice to convince us of the existence of these spiritual forces. But there are times when the spirit of the community reveals itself to us with an elemental power, in an almost visible shape, filling and mastering our inward being to such an extent that we are hardly any longer conscious of our individual existence, as such. Here, in Berlin, in the Unter den Linden, I lived through such an hour of consecration on the 15th of July, in the year 1870.
>
> (Gierke, 1957: pp. lxviii–lxix)

The speaker is Otto von Gierke and his deeply spiritual experience was the outbreak of the Franco-Prussian War. But a very different man, C. H. Rolph (English, anti-militaristic, humanitarian and *New Statesman*ly socialist) wrote this of the effect of Churchill's 'finest hour' speech of 4 June 1940:

> There was something in the air that no one had ever known before, an atmosphere in the streets, trains, buses, pubs, restaurants, offices. Men who, to my knowledge, had always detested each other were united in a surge of righteousness that they barely understood, even if they later came to see it as self-preservation disguised as brotherhood.
>
> (1987: p. 92)

Even J. D. B. Miller, who declares that 'in its most usual employment in politics, the general interest is a fake' (1965: p. 59: see 6.17–6.29), regards Britain in 1940 as displaying 'obvious and virtually unanimous agreement over ends and means' which he regards as a sufficient condition for the 'existence of a general interest' (ibid.: pp. 54–55). There are at least three important points there and Miller has got them all wrong. There was no doubt *virtual* unanimity on the need to prevent invasion and, without doubt, no sane person in the blitzed towns found the bombing any better than troublesome. But we must not slur the word 'virtual'[14] (*TP* 1.1B (iii)). Neither must we forget that many people (whose opinion of Hitler and the 'Narzees' was no more favourable than Churchill's) had to be coerced into doing what the Government believed necessary. And, as every volume of war memoirs and war history has made clear, there was anything but unanimity on means amongst the politicians and the generals. In his superb book, *Living through the Blitz*, Tom Harrisson says:

> For better or for worse, we can only insist that *every* generalization about forty million Britons is almost endlessly subject to qualification. At no time in the Second World War . . . were British civilians united on anything, though they might be ready to appear so in public on certain issues.
>
> (1978: p. 17)

Harrisson sees his task as the amendment of popular legend. That carries its own dangers of overstatement, but Constantine Fitzgibbon, who paints a more conventional picture of 'the finest hour', speaks of 'the invincible stupidity and frivolity of a large portion of the public' and says that 'To instruct . . . [many Londoners] even in the basic rudiments of self-protection was not easy' (1974: p. 43).

5.42   Setting aside those qualifications, it is true that a great crisis, especially an external threat, can lead to great feelings of solidarity and to prodigies of co-operative effort. Some will look back nostalgically to that (or to a greatly exaggerated version of it) and regard the co-ordination of action, and the subordination of all or almost all other interests to the achievement of one supreme aim as the only satisfactory state of affairs. And it is the way of some politicians and groups to want to prolong such solidarity and co-ordination after the emergency has ceased. '"If only we could recapture that war-time spirit" – how often has one heard this cry of the politically incompetent, from the time of the Persian War to the present day' (Dowling, 1960(b): p. 7). And the politically astute sometimes find that cry useful.

5.43   An Australian Deputy Prime Minister, engaged in the fraternal task of undermining his leader, declared that Australia had never had 'a real leader with the capacity to inspire the public with a vision for the future'.[15] His examples of Real Leaders were Washington, Lincoln and F. D. Roosevelt, a choice probably influenced more by postage-stamps and propaganda than by any serious study of history. It is significant, however, that all three were heads of government in times of major war, as was John Curtin,[16] whom he patronisingly conceded to be 'a trier'. In such times, it is possible for some to see a head of government as transcending the ordinary divisions of politics, as ceasing to be a mere politician and becoming 'One Man . . . symbolic of his Native Land'.[17] Such things never last for long and are rarely as fully instantiated, as 'pure' as nostalgic recollection and sheer ballyhoo make them. In short, what we have here is an instance of weariness with the conflicts and compromises and only partial successes of ordinary pluralistic politics. This solemn, stirring 'visionary' stuff is mere dictatorial day-dreaming.

5.44   And it is thoroughly unhistorical. As a *military* leader during the first American civil war, Washington certainly inspired his own, ultimately victorious faction. His election to the Presidency was unopposed and as nearly unanimous as any decision at that level can be, but, once normal political life set in, he became a figure of controversy, accused of various sins, including treasonable Anglophilia, ungrateful Francophobia, and the desire to found a Royal Dynasty of Washingtons. Bruce Felknor begins his book, *Dirty Politics*, with the sentence, 'in the beginning, American Presidential politics was pure and simple' (1975: p. 17). He means *scarcely beyond the first instant*. Lincoln, in his lifetime, inspired more dislike and even hatred than 'vision'. In 1860, he became President on less than 50 per cent of the popular vote. The secession of the Confederate states did not mean that all his enemies were on the other military side. In the North, he was hated by sympathisers with the South, by the war-weary, by those more fire-eatingly pro-Union than himself. In the election of 1864, with only the Union states voting, he scored 55 per cent, after a deplorably scurrilous campaign in which neither side was guiltless. (See ibid.: pp. 23–24.) Death restored Washington to the Pantheon. It needed a particularly dramatic death to admit Lincoln to it for the first time. Roosevelt, never quite the hero at home that he was abroad, died in office, which did wonders for his reputation. These secular deifications recall Edmund Clerihew Bentley's tribute to Clive of India:

> What I like about Clive
> Is that he is no longer alive.
> There's a great deal to be said
> For being dead.
>
> (1981: p. 30)

In the British election campaign of 1945, Churchill tried very hard to maintain and capture wartime solidarity and to render it partisan. He failed spectacularly.[18] The (war-time) National Government, its disappearance after the defeat of Germany, and the decisive electoral defeat of the Conservatives accurately reflected changes in British social life as a whole. Impressive as wartime solidarity is, it is not something that, in peacetime, is either possible or desirable, and the yearnings some politicians have for a 'Visionary' role of 'Real Leadership' are as sensible and as worthy of encouragement as the wish of the lover in an old Scots song:

I wish my love were in a mire
That I might pu' her out again.
(Quoted, Burns [1883]: p. 416)

Cf. 12.36.

5.45 In English-speaking countries, appeals to the general interest and the manipulation of symbols of national unity tend to be more associated with the conservative parties than with their more radical opponents. This, however, is far from universal, as recent events (and non-events) in Australia have shown (see 10.33–10.42). For French appeals to maintain the solidarity of the Resistance, see Werth, 1965: pp. 168–179, 186–233. This is particularly interesting in that it indicates that the desire to prolong war-time solidarity was not, in the immediate post-Liberation period, an exclusively Gaullist one, and that the different branches of the Resistance had very different ideas on what that solidarity would be. For some Indonesian views on the 'Continuous Revolution', see Feith, 1962: pp. 578–608; J. J. Fox *et al.*, 1980: pp. 557–709; Lane, 1991; Ricklefs, 1981: pp. 225–279. (I seem to remember a statement made by Sukarno in 1965 that a revolution had no need of an independent press, but I cannot cite the source.)

6   Interests

THE NASOPERSONISTS

6.1   According to psychological egoism (*TP* 7.15D, 5.20), every human agent is always, unavoidably, incurably and utterly self-interested. On examination, the theory says no more than 'All voluntary action is action done with the intent of bringing about what the agent intends it to bring about', an empty tautology (*TP* 3.7, 5.6–5.7), casting light only on the capacity of people to fool themselves, yet, for many, it seems The Truth. Psychological egoism is not improved if we modulate it into a doctrine about groups, rather than individuals. Consider, for instance, this assertion:

> The only consistent way to treat interests is subjectively. The interests of a group are what its members *think* they are, and if a number of people organize to persuade the Government that we should all be made to wear cardboard noses and big, black spectacles we can only assume that they expect this to further their interests. Any other approach involves us in deciding what the group's 'real' interests are, and this decision will vary according to the observer making it.
>
> (Westerway, 1963: p. 121)

It would be unfair to take Mr Westerway completely literally. Consider this example:

> Group Primus is a group of people associated together for the purpose of making money. That is what its members think is the interest of the group, and, therefore, it is the interest of the group.
>
> The members of Group Primus believe that they will make a lot of money if they invest most of their capital in Wildcat NL; therefore, they think that that is in the interest of the group; therefore, according to Westerway taken literally, investing most of Group Primus's capital in Wildcat NL is in the interest of the group.
>
> Unknown to the members of Group Primus, Wildcat NL is on the verge of collapse. Its liabilities exceed its assets tenfold and the directors are already on their way to Bolivia. Therefore, according to Westerway taken literally, it is in the interests of Group Primus to make an investment that

will lose most of their capital (while, at the same time, it is in their interests to make money).

Can Westerway really mean that? He does assert that the interests of a group are what its members think they are, but perhaps we should interpret him as talking, not about means, but about ends, goals, aims-and-objects. The means/end contrast (2.14F) is more complex than many people think, but (at least for the present) let's not worry about that. Let's just assume that Westerway is talking about ends, goals, aims-and-objects and see what that implies.

6.2 Suppose that there is such a group as the one he imagines in his second sentence. We can call them *the nasopersonists.*[1] The following conversation might happen between Mr Recto (a follower of Westerway) and Mr Verso (neither political scientist, philosopher, nor sociologist, but something less sophisticated, like a process-worker or a brain surgeon):

Mr Verso: Why do the nasopersonists want the Government to make us wear those things?

Mr Recto: Because they expect that to further their interests.

Mr Verso: Oh, they'll make money out of it, will they?

Mr Recto: I don't know about that.

Mr Verso: Well, have *they* got faces which would look better behind cardboard noses and big black spectacles?

Mr Recto: I don't know about that.

Mr Verso: Then what do you mean when you say that the nasopersonists want us to wear those things because that will further their own interests?

Mr Recto: It's quite simple, really. Any group which wants anything wants it because it believes it will further its interests. That's true of all groups, the Red Cross, the sugar lobby, trade unions, the Racing Commission Agents' Association, the Immigration Reform Group, the NSW Council of Churches, the Australian Federation of Sun Clubs[2] – any group at all.

Mr Verso: Do they all want the same things?

Mr Recto: No, but they all try to further their interests.

Mr Verso: What are their interests?

Mr Recto: Whatever it is that they try to further.

Mr Verso: Thanks, mate. I feel so enlightened that I could be physically ill.

6.3 In other words, Westerway asserts that *the purpose of groups which try to influence the decisions of public officials is the furtherance of their interests.* That sounds like a serious assertion, suggesting a front-page headline:

NASOPERSONISTS UNMASKED!

But, on examination, it turns out that it means that *the purpose of groups which try to influence the decisions of public officials is the furtherance of the purpose for which they try to influence the decisions of public officials.* True,

true, only too true, and far too true to be good. Deciding on its truth-value is certainly not a 'decision [which] will vary according to the observer making it'. It is every bit as bad as psychological egoism. In fact, it *is* psychological egoism transposed into a corporate key.

6.4   That tautological pseudo-thesis has nothing to do with Westerway's assertion that 'the only consistent way to treat interests is subjectively',[3] though he seems to think it has. I am not sure what role 'consistent' has in that sentence. 'Deciding what [a] . . . group's "real" interests are' may be a perilous business, but I cannot see that it *must* involve inconsistency, i.e., self-contradiction. I hope Westerway is not using 'consistent' as a stylish substitute for 'appropriate' or 'OK'. Perhaps he means, not that any non-subjective treatment of interests will be *internally* inconsistent, but that different people's non-subjective treatments of interests might be inconsistent with one another. That would be a terrible thing, wouldn't it? And one difficult for us to cope with, since disagreement is so very rare in our experience. *Let us leave this matter of 'consistency'*.

6.5   Westerway explicates his recommendation that interests should be treated subjectively by going on to say: 'The interests of a group are what its members *think* they are' (his emphasis). Let x, y and z be what the members of group A believe are their interests. What, on Westerway's thesis, do the members of group A believe about x, y and z when they believe that x, y and z are their interests? It seems to follow that they believe that they believe that x, y and z are their interests. But that will not do. What the members of group A believe about x, y and z is that the adequate protection, or the furtherance, or the achievement of x, y and z would in some specifiable ways, be *a good thing*. Westerway's purpose is to tell us about the operations of certain pressure groups, what they want and how they set about getting it, and he can certainly do that while treating their interests subjectively, but he really should not say that that is the *only* appropriate way to treat interests. J. D. B. Miller says that it would be *presumptuous* to say that people can be mistaken about their interests (1965: p. 42). Westerway warns us that it could be controversial. We should try not to be presumptuous, but we should try also to be sensible. One *can* be wrong about one's real interests. Neither Miller's moralism, nor Westerway's shudder quotes, nor the fear of controversy should frighten us into denying that only too familiar fact.

INTEREST, NEEDING, WANTING

6.6   *SOED* lists eight different (though related) uses of the word 'interest' and notes its derivation from Latin *interest* meaning 'It is important', 'It makes a difference'. Perhaps that can be our starting-point and we can say:

> Something, α, is in the interests of a group or individual person, X, if it is important to (or: for) X.[4]

A statement of the form 'α is important to (for) X' is open to at least two interpretations:

α is *objectively* important to (for) X.
α is *subjectively* important to (for) X.

Indeed, since the two possibilities are not mutually exclusive, it is open to a third interpretation also:

α is *both objectively and subjectively* important to (for) X.

6.7   An example may make things clearer. The example will need to involve:

(i)   a group of which we are not members (we do not want to be distracted by our disagreements over coal-loaders or airport noise, etc.);
(ii) a proposed course of action which we would agree is important to (for)/in the interests of that group;
(iii) but which many members of the group do not want in the least.

Zland[5] is a tropical, developing country in which malaria is a problem. The Zlandic Department of Health employs 'spraying teams' which are sent into towns and villages in malarial parts of the country. I expect that we all agree that it is important for the inhabitants (in their interests) to minimise their chances of getting malaria. We may not all be willing to say the same about spraying, but, for the sake of argument, let us assume that we are. I am assuming then that we agree that it is in the interests of the inhabitants of any malaria-prone village to avoid the disease and, hence, to have their village sprayed. The villagers, however, may take a different view. They may object to having a lot of strangers trampling round the village, getting in everyone's way, ordering people about, and making a nasty smell. They may object so much that they are prepared to offer violent resistance. By and large, people resort to violence only when something important to (for) them is at issue, so we have to say that it is of importance to (for) them *not* to have their village sprayed. But we have already said that it is important to (for) the villagers to *have* their village sprayed. Do we want to withdraw that statement? We do not. We know what causes malaria, what malaria does to people, and how to reduce the chances of infection. So we have two true propositions:

It is important to (for) the villagers to have their village sprayed.
It is important to (for) the villagers NOT to have their village sprayed.

Since both are true, the conflict must be *mere* appearance, and we need a distinction:

There are two ways in which we can talk of something, α, being of importance to (for) X:
Talking of α being of importance to (for) X in a sense which commits us to the view that α affects X's well-being.

Talking of α being of importance to (for) X in a sense which commits us to the view that, in X's opinion, α affects X's well-being.

We can call these, respectively, *the **objective** sense* and *the **subjective** sense*. It follows that there are two senses in which something can be said to be in X's interests and that we can speak of *X's **objective** interests* and of *X's **subjective** interests*. When we attribute subjective interests to X, we are putting the stress on X, the *subject*, and on X's *attitudes* to the object. When we attribute *objective* interests to X, we are putting the stress on the *object* and on *its* relation to the subject X. So here the subjective/objective distinction is more than a solemn noise (a comparatively rare occurrence: see *TP* 8.1B). Notice that the distinction is not mutually exclusive. Another village might greet the spraying team with 'And about time, too!' (It *may* be true that 'important to' fits the subjective sense of 'interest' better than it fits the objective sense, while 'important for' is more at home with the objective sense than with the subjective. But I suspect that ordinary usage is wobbly on this point.)

6.8   Groups and individuals can choose to strive only for what *seems to them* to be important for them, to be 'worth their strife'. That is so whether the seeming is enlightened or misguided. Nevertheless, the objective sense has a primacy over the subjective. Having one's well-being affected (or being *objectively concerned*) is primary: thinking that one's well-being is affected (or being *subjectively concerned*) is logically consequent on that possibility. If we did not believe it possible to be objectively concerned, we would never be subjectively concerned. Further, if we can be objectively concerned and if we are fallible, then our subjective concern is likely to be, at times, mistaken. Everyone knows that, of course, but there are those who forget it when they put pen to paper. A brand of radial tyres used to be advertised with the slogan 'They mightn't be what yer want, but they're certainly what yer need' – a text worth meditating on. From this primacy of objective concern as an element in the concept of interest, it follows that the concept of interest is *need-regarding*, rather than *want-regarding*, or rather, that when it is *want-regarding*, that want-regardingness is dependent on *need-regardingness* (see Barry, 1965: ch. x), so interest-talk is to be analysed into need-talk. Want-talk can come into it, but no translation of interest-talk can be accurate if it is a translation into *pure* want-talk.

6.9   'α is in X's interests' implies 'X needs α'. But, on its own, 'X needs α' is incomplete and obscure. It needs, as it were, a special footnote on how to interpret 'need'. (Context and shared experience may, of course, render explicit footnoting superfluous, as with the tyre advertisement. In *this* society, even non-car-drivers know enough about skids and about what tyres are for. But there are dozens of cases which *would* need footnoting.) There is an *endorsing* use of 'need' such that if we say that X needs α, we are committing ourselves *not quite* to the evaluation that X *ought* to get α, but certainly to the evaluation[6] *that it would be a good thing if X got α*; e.g.:

'The country needs rain.'

'A sick person needs medical attention.'
'X needs money.'

But consider:

'X wants to shoot me but he needs a gun.'
'A blackmailer needs damaging information.'
'A bankrobber needs a good getaway car.'

These are not bizarre assertions, but we are not saying that it would be a good thing if X got a gun, etc. (which *would* be bizarre); i.e., the word 'need' here is being used in a *non-endorsing* sense. Even when 'need' is used in an endorsing sense, 'X needs α' never tells the whole story. It is elliptical and needs to be expanded into one of the following:

'X needs α if he is to get β.'
'X needs α if he is to become a.'
'X, as a b-type person, needs α.'[7]

Context, shared assumptions, common knowledge may tacitly fill the gaps, but, one way or another, they have to be filled. We never *just* need anything.[8] This applies to the endorsing use of 'need' as well. We need α if we are to get β, which, in some aspect or other, is some kind of good. We need α if we are to avoid γ, which, in some aspect or other, is an evil of some kind (cf. Hobbes on *appetites* and *aversions*, *Leviathan* ch. vi). More generally: if you need α, you need it under some aspect of yourself: You need α by virtue of being an a-type person or a b-type person, where those types are tied to possible objects of striving or avoidance, of 'appetite' or 'aversion'.

'X as a b-type person needs α.'

Replace 'a b-type person' by a role-term and α will be (or should be) something which enables X to continue to perform that role well or effectively, WHATEVER THAT ROLE MAY BE: poet, plumber, burglar, blackmailer – which again indicates that 'need' is not always used endorsingly.

6.10   What X needs as an a-type person may be in conflict with what he needs as a b-type person, so there may be a clash of needs and a clash of interests *internal to* an individual person. X is a smoker and smoking is bad for X's health, so X needs to give up smoking, and it is in X's interests to give up smoking. On the other hand, the same X is going on a journey and amongst the things he will *need* to take with him are tobacco, a pipe and matches. Otherwise, he will feel uncomfortable, become irritable, have difficulty in concentrating and in relaxing. So it is in X's interests that there be an adequate supply of tobacco, etc., available to him. Notice, again, that one can ascribe needs and interests in a non- or not thoroughly endorsing fashion. The example also makes the point that one can, without self-contradiction, ascribe contrary needs and interests to the one person. The objective/subjective distinction (see 6.7) may, in some cases, be applied to such troublesome ascriptions and draw their paradoxical sting. But that will not work in all cases. The smoker X may recognise his own need to give up smoking, and may recognise that that is in his interests, while at the same time needing a smoke and recognising that it is in his interests that there be an adequate supply of tobacco available to him. And a humane anti-smoker may recognise these as at least temporary needs and interests of X, before he can be given adequate therapy or be locked in a padded cell where his withdrawal symptoms will have less destructive effects than they would elsewhere. If there is any logical absurdity here, it is in *the attitudes of X*, not *in the description of him* (cf. 10.22). The following points are worth noticing:

> There are cases in which one can, without inconsistency (though with necessary restrictions), endorse conflicting needs.
>
> It is possible for the interests of even one person to conflict.
>
> In such cases as that of the smoker, X, one feels an impulse to talk of X's *real* or *true* or *best* interests. (If X smokes in an ill-ventilated room in the presence of non-smokers, he is *being selfish*. But he cannot be selfish unless he is pursuing his own interests to the unjustifiable detriment of the interests of others; *ergo*, it is in his interests to smoke, even though it is not in his real, true, or best interests.)
>
> X himself may talk that way and not necessarily because he has been browbeaten into it.

Hence again, the radical incompleteness of locutions of the form 'X needs α' and 'α is in X's interests'. It is not merely that a person who makes an assertion of that type has not told us the full story: the trouble may well be that we do not know what story he wants to tell. When he gives *reasons*, then we begin to know in what respect he believes α to be in X's interests or in what capacity of X, X needs α. We can then begin assessing and evaluating the assertion, making such judgements as:

whether α is a need of X;
whether it is an important need of X;
whether it is a legitimate need;
how it fits in or fails to fit in with the needs of others;
whether it is the sort of need which X should be allowed to seek to fill without
    obstruction;
whether it is the sort of need which others (or the Government) should fill for
    him or help him fill;
etc., etc., etc.

In that respect, interest-talk is atypical. With most statements, meaning and support are distinct. If you say 'X is a burglar', I know what you mean, even if I do not know how you would support that statement. If you say something of the form, 'X needs α' or 'α is in the interests of X', the reasons you give are related to your statements not *only* as *support* but *also* as *explication*. Another important feature of interest-talk brought out by this approach is the possibility of conflict, not just between different people, but also within the one person. Because the same person has many different capacities and characteristics, his interests may clash with one another. The melancholic 'I' of A. E. Housman's poem 'The Welsh Marches' (1939: pp. 44–45) is an extreme case, but he is an extreme case of something which most of us are acquainted with in the closest way possible. Within a human individuality, there is never complete unity (cf. 10.22–10.28).

6.11   People have interests only because of their characteristics and capacities, and the fact of human diversity is quite well known. Nevertheless, I think we can assume that there are certain 'goods' the possession of which can be regarded, other things being equal, as in the interests of each individual person. These 'goods' would be such things as health, food, money, shelter, rest, safety, contentment, knowledge, affection. There are some interests you have by virtue of being the possessor of (e.g.) a human digestive system. And it is in the light of considerations of that kind that I say that there are certain goods, the possession of which is a good for anyone. That is a 'so far as it goes' or 'other things being equal' statement. I am not saying that these are goods without restriction, or that it will always be in a person's interests to maximise these goods for himself, or that it would never be sensible or morally right to treat something else as more important. What I *am* saying is that, taking a large number of people over a large range of times and places, these 'goods' will normally be in the interests of most people. We can say that these 'goods' will normally be in a person's interests, considering him as a person who is statistically normal in certain widely recognisable respects. And I am saying also that the denial that having one of these 'goods' is in some individual's interests always requires special justification. The onus of proof falls on the person who *makes* that denial.

6.12   To say 'X needs α' (or 'I need α') is a larger claim than 'X wants α' (or 'I want α') and has a stronger chance of being controversial. The distinction between *wanting* and *needing* is as indispensable as the distinction between *knowledge* and *opinion*, which it resembles in some respects. As 'know' is not merely an emphatic substitute for 'believe', so also 'need' is not merely an emphatic substitute for 'want'. 'I know that p' is a more contestable claim than 'I believe that p'. 'I need α' is a more contestable claim than 'I want α'. It is possible to examine contestable claims rationally, whatever 'value-free' social scientists may say to the contrary (see, e.g., 6.1 above). 'It is essentially presumptuous', says J. D. B. Miller, 'for any one person to tell another that he knows for certain what is his interest' (1965: p. 42). Often, yes, but sometimes not. What worries writers like Miller, I think, is the possibility of authoritarianism, of unrestrained paternalism.[9] Those are things we should resist, but not at the cost of endorsing the rampant falsehood that everyone (e.g., I) is always right about what is in his interest. (That pretence is unlikely to be effective. The price of liberty is neither self-deceit nor stipulative definition, but eternal vigilance.) Even the concept of *need* has, in recent years, come under fire from certain right-wing writers who regard the *want/need* distinction as authoritarian. See, e.g., some of the contributions to Fitzgerald, 1977. The distinction between *knowledge* and *opinion* is often attacked by neo-Marxists. The underlying logic (or illogic) of the attacks is the same.

RELATIONS AND SAKES

6.13   *SOED*'s eight definitions of the noun 'interest' can be condensed as follows:

1 The relation of being directly concerned in something by having a right or claim to it, or a share in it.
2 The relation of being concerned in respect of advantage or detriment.
3 A thing in which one has an interest or concern.
4 (i)   A business, cause or principle, in which a number of persons are interested.
   (ii)   The party interested or having a common interest.
5 Self-interest, i.e., one's personal profit, benefit, or advantage.
6 Influence with a body or persons.
7 (i)   The feeling of one who is concerned in something.
   (ii)   The state of feeling proper to such a relation.
   (iii) A feeling of concern for or curiosity about a thing.
8 The fact or quality of mattering.

Two main themes run through these definitions: a reference to advantage or detriment (discussed in the previous section) and *relation*. Basically and primarily, interest should be thought of as *a relation* rather than as *a substance* or *quasi-substance*. That gives strong support to the following linguistic point:

> The use of the word 'interest' as part of an adverbial or adjectival phrase is primary. Its uses as an independent substantive are parasitic on its uses as part of an adverbial or adjectival phrase.

It is the fact that something is advantageous or disadvantageous for someone that puts him in the relevant relation to it. A group which is an interest in *SOED*'s sense 4 (another non-primary sense) is so because of a shared relation to some real or apparent source of advantage or detriment. Such a group may be an *interest group* in the technical sense of *a group which actively and in an organised way seeks to further its interests by influencing public opinion and/ or government* (see Scruton, 1983: p. 329). The relation, however, is primary.

6.14   J. D. B. Miller begins his discussion of the concept of the general interest thus:

> Is there a General Interest?
>   In considering whether such a thing as a (or the) general interest exists, I shall start by stating as fully and fairly as I can the case for thinking that it

does. The conclusion that there is a general interest can be approached by a number of different routes.

(1965: p. 52)

Implicit in that, there is an assumption about the way in which substantival expressions (i.e., nouns and noun-phrases) work in discourse. Many substantival expressions are expressions which refer directly to various things or states of affairs or profess to refer directly to various things or states of affairs.[10] Thus, these are both substantival expressions:

'The Lord Mayor of Newcastle' (i)
'The Emperor of Newcastle' (ii)

There is something to which (i) refers. There is nothing to which (ii) refers. But the statement 'The Emperor of Newcastle is fond of fish' presupposes the existence of something (a person) corresponding to (referred to by) phrase (ii). So, if we are investigating the truth of affirmative, categorical statements about The Lord Mayor of Newcastle or The Emperor of Newcastle (statements which ascribe events or characteristics to the Lord Mayor of Newcastle or the Emperor of Newcastle), we must first satisfy ourselves whether there exists something corresponding to (referred to by) phrase (i) or phrase (ii). The existence of The Emperor of Newcastle is a necessary condition for the truth[11] of the statement 'The Emperor of Newcastle is fond of fish.'

6.15   *On the face of it*, it may *seem* reasonable to assume that:

Where 'X' is a substantival expression, affirmative categorical statements apparently about X are not true unless there exists at least one referent for 'X'.

That may seem reasonable, but it is not true. While most substantival expressions function like that, some do not, e.g., 'public danger' and 'sake'. In the traditional classification of 'parts of speech', the word 'sake' is a noun, a substantive. In modern English, however, it never functions as what *OED* calls 'an independent substantive' but always as part of an adjectival or adverbial phrase. Consider this little dialogue:

Festle: I'm doing this for Fred's sake.
Fose: But has Fred got a sake? Do sakes exist?
Festle: The whole collection of Fred's needs constitutes Fred's sake.

Fose's questions and Festle's reply are quite mad. The word 'sake' does not function like that: it is always part of an adjectival or adverbial phrase, never an independent substantive. So we can discuss whether or not it is true that Festle was doing something for Fred's sake without presupposing that there exists a thing, namely a sake, which Fred has. Or consider the expression 'to the public danger'. Our deep-thinking friend, Mr Fose, has been driving his car at 90 m.p.h along the Industrial Highway, zigzagging from left to right as he does so. A motorcycle policeman finally brings him to a halt.

'Well,' says Mr Fose, 'what seems to be the trouble, Constable?'

'You were driving to the public danger,' says the policeman.

'Where is the public danger?' demands Mr Fose. 'Has the public got a danger? Can it have a danger which is not actually endangering it at that moment? Is it not a fact that no more than a minority of the public were endangered by my driving?'

At that point, I hope the constable puts the handcuffs on Mr Fose and charges him with everything he can think of. The phrase 'to the public danger' does not presuppose that there exists a thing, namely, a danger, which the public has. What it does presuppose is that it is possible to act in a way which might harm anyone who happened to be there. (Cf. 10.10.)

6.16   In political talk (as distinct from talk about political talk), the expression 'the general interest' most often occurs, not as an independent substantive, but as part of the adjectival or adverbial phrases, 'in the general interest', 'not in the general interest', 'against the general interest'. In other words, general-interest-talk does not presuppose the existence of a thing, called 'the general interest'. What general-interest-talk is about is the tendency of policies or actions, just as the policeman was talking about the *tendency* of Fose's driving, not presupposing the existence of some mysterious thing called 'the public danger'. It follows that Miller's questions 'Is there a general interest?', 'Does a general interest exist?' are the wrong questions to ask. The question should be: 'Are there (*or*: Can there be) policies which are in or against the general interest?' Putting the question like that does not remove the main problem: whether general-interest-talk is appropriate in a situation where there is either unawareness or conflict. But it will help us avoid some pseudo-problems and pseudo-solutions. Miller, for instance, argues first that no one can have an interest which he is not aware of and that 'Interests are those forces in society which actively resort to political means in order to improve or defend their positions one against the other' (1965: p. 39). Then he declares that 'a general interest' can exist in Xland only if every or almost every Xlander agrees in wanting some proposal to be put into effect. He maintains (reasonably enough) that this is rarely found, and therefore (less reasonably) consigns the concept to the dustbin of political theory. That takes a whole chapter and it has very little relevance to what speakers of the language do with the expressions 'interest' and 'general interest'.

INTERESTS AND THE GENERAL INTEREST

6.17   *Common good, General interest, Public interest, Interest of the community as a whole*: these are familiar concepts in political argument. They do not add up to four different concepts, neither are they just the one concept under four different names. They overlap a great deal. In the discourse of politics, they are contrasted with *special interest, sectional interest, vested interest, self-interest, selfish interest,* etc. (again, neither five different concepts nor just one under different names). Politicians and governments are often called upon (particularly by writers of newspaper editorials) *to put the general interest first* and are often accused of favouring sectional interests. The accusations reach their height in Ambrose Bierce's 'definition' of *politics*:

> *Politics, n.* A strife of interests masquerading as a contest of principles. The conduct of public affairs for private advantage.
>
> (Bierce, 1971: p. 248)

Many political theorists and philosophers and many 'non-theoretical' people would say that Bierce and the editorialists are complaining of the inevitable: that there is (perhaps even *can be*) no general interest or common good, that all interests are incurably and necessarily sectional (or even incurably and necessarily individual). Some of these attacks rest on some version of *psychological egoism* (6.1). Those which do not rest on it often gain assent because of it, but, as I argued in *TP* 7.16D, 5.21, psychological egoism is an utterly bogus doctrine. It may, however, be true that there are anti-general-interest theories which do not depend logically on psychological egoism, individual or corporate. Certainly, there are proponents of such views who would indignantly repudiate any connection between their opinions and psychological egoism.

6.18   In Australia, the rejection of general-interest-thinking has had powerful support from very able members of Sydney University's Departments of Philosophy and Government. The original influence was Professor John Anderson, with a lesser role being played by such American political scientists as A. F. Bentley and D. B. Truman.[12] For many Sydney intellectuals, this rejection of *common good*, etc. is no mere thesis which they happen to assent to, but an article of faith, part of their culture. In argument with the unenlightened (and sometimes even with one another), members of the tribe say: 'But you're taking a *Common Good* view!', rather in the tone of a seventeenth-century Calvinist who has detected Arminian tendencies. Whether *common good, general interest, public interest, interests of the community* are one concept, four concepts or any number of concepts, the old Sydney orthodoxy sees them as simply bits of deceiving rhetoric, Which Must Be Exposed As The Frauds They Are. The view transcends ordinary political divisions and is as dear to some members of the Association for Cultural Freedom as it is to the 'critical drinkers', 'pessimistic anarchists', and 'anarcho-Marxists' of the Libertarian Society (on whom, see Docker, 1972).

6.19   Pretty obviously, there is *something* in this view. Some groups, some individuals have a way of treating Common Good or General Interest as an all-powerful fifth ace which they whip from their sleeves to trump all opposition. And, somehow or other, it just turns out that what is in the Common Good or the General Interest returns a tidy profit to the group which invokes it. One does not have to be a cynic or an Andersonian to appreciate what the Longman Cheshire *Dictionary of Australian Politics* has to say about *public interest*:

public interest   The common weal or collective interest of a state or nation. The public interest can never be precisely measured, but it is a useful operational concept for government in justifying unpopular actions.

(Boyce *et al.*, 1980: p. 216)

But, admitting all that, I want to argue that there is something to be said *in favour* of the concept. *Abusus non tollit usum* ('Misuse does not cancel the possibility of legitimate use'). The undoubted existence of medical and pharmaceutical quacks does not deprive the expression 'This mixture will do you good' of all legitimate use. There may be legitimate uses for such phrases as 'general interest'.

6.20   The standard Andersonian or Andersonoid attack regards the existence of conflict as proof positive of the bogusness of general-interest-talk, but if general-interest-talk is in logical trouble, so too is much individual-interest-talk which often seems to presuppose conflict. 'It would be in your own interest to work hard' would, typically, be said to someone whose active concerns appeared to run in quite other directions. And it is not just second- and third-person individual-interest-talk which can presuppose conflict. 'I can see that it would be in my own interest to xify' sounds as if it would be said with a weary sigh, followed perhaps by a gritting of the teeth as the speaker addresses himself to a task to which he is not at all inclined (or by guilt-ridden *akrasia*: TP 9.6A). Conscious inclination may be the very thing which is missing and realised by the speakers to be missing in situations where people talk about things being in the interests of someone or of some collectivity. We do not normally say to ourselves: 'I will eat because it is in my interests to do so,' even though eating is (typically, anyway) in our interests. We are much more likely to say: 'I'm hungry and I'd like such-and-such.' Interest-talk about food is in place when we are dieting, when our favourite food is bad for us, when, for some reason, we need to eat something unpalatable, when we are devoid of appetite but need to eat, etc. (and, of course, when someone is coming between ourselves and our nourishment). Once again, interest-talk seems to presuppose conflict.

6.21   Let us look at some general-interest-talk.

Dictionary of examples
S   This policy is in the general interest.
T   This spray will exterminate the mosquitoes.
Q   But do you think it's good?

Asserting S is not usually (perhaps never or never *quite*) like asserting T. In asserting T, you are making a prediction about a matter of fact which people might *in principle* value in different ways. I emphasise 'in principle', because, as a matter of obvious fact, hostility to mosquitoes is widespread, almost universal, but someone who held that all life is equally sacred would have to disapprove of their extermination. Certainly, as a response to T, Q might be surprising, but it is intelligible. It is, of course, perfectly intelligible and

unsurprising when it is part of an enquiry as to whether the spray can have
undesirable side-effects. But Q can also make clear, if surprising, sense as a
response to T, if the enquirer uses it to call in question the goodness of
mosquito-extermination *in itself*.

6.22 I very much doubt whether Q, as a response to S, makes the same sort of
sense.[13] At least, that is so within most imaginable moral outlooks. Nietzsche
and the Marquis de Sade might well say that, if a thing is in the general
interest, that makes it very bad indeed, but we need not worry about that (or
need worry about it only to the extent of trying to keep such people out of any
kind of power). So, setting aside anti-humanitarian ratbaggery, the predicate
'. . . is in the general interest' is *defeasibly endorsing*. *Defeasibly* because one
can, without inconsistency and without committing oneself to some anti-
humanitarian outlook, concede that X is in the general interest but oppose it
on grounds of justice, etc. (On *defeasibility*, see 5.34 above and *TP* 9.12.) It
follows that the application of the predicate '. . . is in the general interest' is
always *in principle* contestable. That is only partly because of the defeasibility.
The main reason is the *endorsingness*. What one thinks to be in the general
interest depends on other notions one has of what kinds of things are more or
less valuable or disvaluable. And those assumptions need to be brought out into
the open, not for the sake of 'unmasking' them, but for the sake of
understanding them (see Gallie, 1964: ch. viii; *TP* 8.10B). '. . . is in the general
interest' is a 'conclusiony' predicate, not a 'premissy' one (cf. 6.10 above). So: if
an economist says of something or other that it will increase employment by n
per cent, a really *thorough* non-economist like me would be well-advised to say
'Oh, really?' and wait for other economists to come into the argument, hoping
against hope for some enlightenment. *But*, if an economist says that something or other *will be in the general interest*, someone like me would be well
advised to start asking questions right away, because, *up to a point*, that is a
matter on which there are no experts.[14]

6.23 There is a remark familiar to anyone who has moved in Sydney
intellectual circles: 'Anyone who says that something is in the general interest
is only trying to get his own values accepted.' The considerations raised above
indicate that this remark has *some* basis, but only some. A person who says
that Nazism is evil or that cancer is an illness is 'only trying to get his own
values accepted', too. But I cannot see that that is a ground for dismissing his
judgement. A person who says that we need rain, or that grass is green, or that
aspirin relieves headaches is 'only trying to get his own *opinions* accepted'. But
that does not imply that those opinions are *objectionable*, only that they *may*
be *contestable*. (On the folly of a promiscuous use of the phrase 'So *you* say',
see Geach, 1976: pp. 17–18.) In his essay, 'Utilitarianism', John Anderson
wrote:

> . . . the function of the legislator . . . cannot be conceived as that of a
> universal calculator or seeker of 'general welfare' . . . . there is no general
> interest, and . . . the legislator is simply a person who has certain demands

of his own and certain special ways of getting them satisfied; in particular, that of annexing . . . penalties to any opposition to his demands. The people legislated for may of course resist the imposition of these penalties; and the intelligent legislator will try to calculate what resistance he will meet with and whether it will be so great as to defeat his proposals. This is a calculation of the same type as that which arises in any attempt to meet difficulties and satisfy demands. It may quite well be in the legislator's 'interest', i.e., it may advance his schemes, to put about the notion of public welfare and the supposition that he is acting with that object in view; he may even put it in that way to himself, but it is not so.

(Anderson, 1962: p. 231)

Anderson no doubt took himself to be doing a bit of *unmasking*, 'but it is not so'. The important point he makes is that legislators are fallible and not always disinterested (*TP* 82), so that a legislator's notions of what is in the general interest or for the public good should be scrutinised. The rest seems to depend on the dreary truism that a legislator's demands are his demands (cf. 6.1). The *content* of the demands and the *character* of the legislator's 'certain special ways of getting them satisfied' do really matter. Being ruled by Roosevelt or Attlee or Menzies was quite markedly different from being ruled by Hitler or Amin. Bernard Crick defines *autocracy* thus:

Autocracy . . . [is] the form of government which attempts to solve the basic problem of the adjustment of order to diversity by the enforcement of one of the diverse interests as the only ideology to be tolerated and sponsored . . . . Autocracy was and is often as frightening in its powerlessness and inefficiency as . . . in its arbitrariness and unchallengeability. No one can rival the autocrat, but the autocrat can be hideously ineffectual.

(1973: p. 53)

If Anderson is right, all systems of government are like that. They are not. Anderson, therefore, is wrong.

6.24   '. . . in the general interest' might sometimes mean '. . . in the interest of every member considered as an individual' or '. . . in the interest of every group considered as a particular group', but there is no reason why it must always have such a meaning. To say that something is in the general interest can be to say that it is something which, so far as it goes, makes the collective, in some respect, a good collective, or at least a better one than it would otherwise be. Which collective would be a better collective?

One in which 80 per cent of the members have three full meals a day and 20 per cent have half a meal a day,

OR

One in which 100 per cent have two full meals a day?

I would have no hesitation in saying: 'Other things being equal, the second.' And I would say that any move in that direction by the first would, other things being equal, be in the general interest even though, in certain obvious respects, it would adversely affect the interests of the majority. It is a matter of *value* of course, but so what? (On this reckoning, justice is an element in general interest, which may, therefore, be at odds with general welfare.)

6.25 The concept of general interest could also be approached by way of Vinson and Homel's 'indicators of community well-being', most of which concern *ill-being* (1976: p. 7): They include such things as perinatal mortality, pedestrian injuries and deaths, admissions to mental hospitals, unemployment, court appearances and convictions, suicides, divorces, child care-and-protection orders, etc. Should one call these *indicators of* community *well-being* or *indicators of the well-being* of individuals in the community? In a community with a high (i.e., bad) score on these indicators, even members not directly involved (i.e., those who do not contribute to the disturbing statistics – well-adjusted political scientists and the like) *may* find themselves discommoded by the effects. Such people would regard it as not at all the place to live. But, quite apart from such considerations of 'enlightened self-interest', does it not make sense to say that that community is in a bad way, that it is analogous to a sick human being? While it is more difficult to state the 'aims and objects' of a polity, a town or a suburb than it is to state those of a Bantam Breeders' Association or even of a university department (2.4), is it really so difficult always to tell when a polity, town or suburb is not going well? Edmund Burke, in one of his many moments of hyperbole, said that 'the state' (i.e., the polity) 'is a partnership in all science; a partnership in all art; a partnership in every virtue, and in all perfection' (Burke, 1968: p. 194). For 'is', read 'ought to be'. Concede that every polity that has been, is, or will be falls sadly short of that ideal. Then, why not say that, to the extent that a polity falls short of the ideal, it is not satisfactory? And, if saying that is not too bad, what is wrong with saying that any member of the society, whether or not he is a beneficiary, *ought to* regard changes in the direction of the ideal as, other things being equal, *in the general interest*? No doubt, to think this way is to think in terms of your interest *as a member of the collective*. But that interest is hardly individual in the egoistic or egocentric sense. (It is not even comparable to your interest as a shareholder in BHP, if that is what you are.) And the actualisation of that interest might require action contrary to your interests as an individual. Obviously, this notion of general interest is very heavily laden with moral judgements, and, equally obviously, general-interest-talk of this kind may involve us in controversies over particular cases, or even (even!) over what ends should be pursued, but it is none the worse for that. (See Aristotle, *Nicomachean Ethics* bk I ch. iii, 1976: pp. 64–66).) Talk about what is in the general interest of a collective can presuppose such contestable standards as:

> its survival as a collective (Does its survival matter?)
> its survival as a collective of a certain kind (But of what kind?) or as a collective with certain definite activities (But which of its actual or possible activities?)[15]

the furtherance of its aims (But what *are* its aims? And is there an agreed order in which they can be ranked? And what methods of furtherance are appropriate to its aims?)

ET CETERA, ET CETERA, ET CETERA.

So, '. . . in the general interest' is one of those 'essentially contestable expressions' (6.22), and it is as well that there be some contesting of them. Unanimity in such matters can be a blinding, distorting, corrupting thing.

6.26   There is yet another angle from which it can be said that to act in the general interest may require acting against the interests of some or even all of its present members. And this applies *especially* to polities. Like the previously discussed notion of general interest, this one arises from considering a polity as an environment for people to live in. But it lays particular stress on the concept of a polity as something not confined to the present instant or even to the whole lifetimes of those who are members at any particular instant. This is to see a polity as (in a weird bit of modern jargon) *a four-dimensional spacetime worm*, or (in Edmund Burke's more pleasant phrasing) as 'a contract between those who are living, those who are dead, and those who are to be born' (Burke, 1968: pp. 194–195). From that point of view, it would make perfect sense to say 'Such-and-such is in the general interest even though it imposes considerable restrictions on what some or all present members may do in pursuit of some of their own interests' (cf. 8.10–8.11).

6.27   '. . . in pursuit of some of their own interests' – their own interests *as what?* As statistically normal people, as individual people with inclinations hither and thither. The felt and acknowledged interests of sane human beings include their own comfort and well-being, but they also go wider. R. M. Hare concedes that dead people have no desires or inclinations, but points out that nearly all of us

> have many and frequently very strong desires whose objects are states of affairs after our death . . . . If the average Englishman were asked, for example, whether it would be all the same to him if his wife were to commit suttee after his death, he would certainly protest very strongly and, if there were any signs of his wife wishing to do so, would do his utmost to dissuade her. He would not be moved at all by the argument that, since he would be dead at the time, it could not matter to him.
>
> (1963: pp. 133–134)

If so (and I think it is so), action on behalf of future members which adversely affects the more obvious interests of present members may yet be action advancing other interests of those present members, and there is nothing tyrannous or presumptuous in saying that sometimes members may be *required* to prefer some of those other interests to their more obvious interests. Many philosophers take too narrow a view of the actual and possible interests of human beings. (See Routley & Routley, 1980: pp. 250–259.)

6.28   So far, I have been trying to sketch circumstances which would make it perfectly intelligible and true to say:

> In the general interest of the polity, this and that are required which will be adverse to you and her and him who are members of the polity.

Such a notion of general interest presupposes that 'the lines of life lead *outward*' (Midgley, 1979: p. 355) and that *some measure* of non-egoism is both desirable and possible. It does not presuppose that people either are *or should be* completely altruistic, neither does it presuppose the unanimity or near-unanimity which Anderson, Miller and others think all notions of general interest presuppose. At the same time, I think I have shown that such a notion of general interest is not self-contradictory. The following argument (trotted out by Baker as if it were absolutely conclusive) simply misses the point:

> if supporting (or opposing) interest or measure X is really in the general interest or the interest of us all, then to ask us to support X is to ask us to support what we already support. But, of course, appeals to 'the welfare of the community', 'the interests of all Australians' and so on, are notoriously made precisely when there is a patent conflict between the advancement of interest X and the advancement of some other interest Y, and an effort is being made to induce supporters of Y to change and support X.
>
> (Baker, 1979: p. 21)

John Anderson demands 'Nothing short of a rejection of this imaginary "common good" (something that satisfies every interest and every person)' (Anderson, 1962: p. 191). By all means, let us reject *that*. But there is absolutely no reason for believing that all talk about *common good* and *general interest* presupposes anything so absurd. The notion of general interest or common good which I have been unpacking (and I see no reason for thinking that it is some idiosyncratic production of my own) does not imply that there is anything which satisfies every interest and every person. To say that something is in the general interest is not necessarily even to say that every interest and every person *ought to be* satisfied by it. To say that something is in the general interest is to say that it ought to be *acceptable* to *every relevant* interest and *every relevant* person (which does not imply that no one may legitimately campaign to reverse it). And a judgement of that kind is as fallible as any other and more contestable than most. At the same time, the making of such judgements is indispensable. The alternative is a sort of political tribalism in which one recognises only one's political allies as fully one's concitizens (or even conspecifics) except to the extent that such recognition is tactically required.

6.29   There is one point, however, which must be granted to Anderson, Baker, Miller, *et al.* We frequently appeal to general (or common) interest as we might appeal to 'The Dictionary', to *Gregory's Guide*, to Wisden, to Hoyle, to a bus timetable, to the result of a calculation as arrived at by use of a clever machine; i.e., we appeal to general (or common) interest as to an authority which all concerned recognise as an authority. Sometimes this is quite untroublesome:

> In a block of flats with only one washing machine, it is, in the long run, in the interests of all the residents that there be a laundry-roster, rather than a free-for-all.

> The passenger in the stern of a rowing boat who tries to get every comfort and every interesting conversationist down his end really is endangering everyone including himself.

> It is in the interests of the team for Tom to turn out for training at 6.00 a.m., even though this has its inconveniences for him. If he prefers to avoid the inconveniences, let him leave the team.

In all these cases, to appeal to the general (or common) interest involves appealing to norms of morality and/or prudence so basic that only a psychopath or a philosopher would question them, but appeals to the general interest of a polity may lack this commonsensicality. There are often different conceptions of what would be a good condition for the polity to be in, along with different notions of what is possible, what methods are legitimate, and what costs are acceptable. Consequently, it may be naive to expect an appeal to the general interest to settle the controversy, in the way in which 'Think of your mates' might appeal to footballer Tom's better nature and rouse him from his bed. That is no reason why such appeals should not be made nor is it a reason for rejecting them as bogus.

Suggested reading

Scruton, 1983: pp. 229–230; Barry, 1965: ch. x; 1967(a), (b); Downie, 1972; Midgley, 1979: chs v, vi, pp. 351–363; Benn, 1960; Miller, 1965: chs ii–vi; Feinberg, 1977; M. James, 1981; Elster & Riemer, 1991. See also n. 12 above (Anderson, Baker, Dowling).

VESTED INTEREST

6.30   In 1988, the then Australian Minister for the Environment, Senator Richardson, gave a speech to a conference of conservationists. Amongst other things, he told them that

> You will always have the advantage that you fight for your cause from a position of sincerity and no vested self interest. When a timber or a mining company comes to me they are obviously arguing from a position of vested interest and no amount of corporate money spent on advertising and lobbying can overcome that difference. There are values that are more important, every time, than money.

> (Quoted, H. M. Morgan, 1989: p. 15)

Notice that the Senator says 'vested interest'. The phrase definitely has a sinister sound, as it did in a statement by a New South Wales minister:

'Many vested interests have opposed the scheme, not the least of whom are estate agents from Nelson Bay,' Mr Stewart said.

(*NH*, 1985)

6.31   As Alice might have said, 'Sinisterer and sinisterer.'[16] But what does it mean? How does a vested interest differ from a non-vested one? Why is being vested such a nasty thing for an interest to be? *SOED* has two entries for 'vested'. One concerns robes, etc. The other is:

Established, secured, or settled in the hands of or definitely assigned to a certain possessor; *esp.* with *right* or *interest*.

That is illustrated with a quotation from Blackstone's *Commentaries on the Laws of England*:

V. remainders . . . are where the estate is invariably fixed, to remain to a determinate person, after the particular estate is spent.

One of *SOED*'s entries for 'vest' (verb) is:

To become vested *in* a person; to descend or devolve *upon* a person as possessor.

The illustration is 'The property vests in the official receiver *qua* trustee.' It is, in other words, a lawyers' technical term, as is confirmed by consulting a few law dictionaries (e.g., Mozley & Whiteley, 1977: pp. 350–351; *APD*, 1981: p. 501; Osborn, 1976: p. 341).

6.32   None of this explains why the phrase 'vested interest' so frequently has such a sinister ring, why '. . . has a vested interest in . . .' can sound so much worse than '. . . has an interest in . . .'. In fact, in common talk (include polly-talk), 'vested' does not mean a thing. It is just a bit of murky colouring, forgivable, perhaps, but certainly in need of forgiveness.[17] The Senator's remarks about the comparative credibility of the conservationists and the industrialists are quite silly. Anyone who 'goes public' in a big way for some cause or proposition has an interest in its success. An interest of that kind can have as distorting effects on perceptions and presentations as can a financial interest. Sincerity is no guarantee of truth. Having a financial interest is no guarantee of insincerity or unscrupulosity. Senator Richardson presumably knew that and probably acted on it, but the prospect of loud and prolonged applause was just too much for him. Buttering-up audiences (what Papua New Guineans call *greasing*)[18] is an unavoidable part of the politician's job. But it can be overdone. Great dollops of grease are nauseating.

7 Nation

> *Fluellen*: Captain Macmorris, I think, look you under your correc-
> tion, there is not many of your nation . . .
>
> *Macmorris*: Of my nation? What ish my Nation? Ish a villain, and a
> bastard and a knave, and a rascal. What ish my Nation?
> Who talks of my Nation?
>
> (Henry V Act III scene 2)

'INTER*NATIONAL*' AND '*NATIONALISM*'

7.1 What is a nation? What does the word 'nation' mean? One meaning is
sketched fairly well by John Stuart Mill in chapter xvi of his *Considerations on
Representative Government* (1861):

> A portion of mankind may be said to constitute a Nationality if they are
> united among themselves by common sympathies which do not exist
> between them and any others – which make them co-operate with each
> other more willingly than with other people, desire to be under the same
> government, and desire that it should be government by themselves or a
> portion of themselves exclusively. This feeling of nationality may have
> been generated by various causes. Sometimes it is the effect of identity of
> race and descent. Community of language, and community of religion,
> greatly contribute to it. Geographical limits are one of its causes. But the
> strongest of all is identity of political antecedents; the possession of a
> national history, and consequent community of recollections; collective
> pride and humiliation, pleasure and regret, connected with the same
> incidents in the past. None of these circumstances, however, are either
> indispensable, or necessarily sufficient by themselves . . . . Yet in general
> the national feeling is proportionally weakened by the failure of any of the
> causes which contribute to it.
>
> (1972: pp. 359–360)

That gives an adequate sketch of one meaning of the word (and it is much
better than Mill's historical predictions in the same chapter), but it is far from
the whole story.

7.2 Nation-talk is odd. Even 'nation-state', which is used as a quasi-technical term, is far from unambiguous. Sometimes, it seems to mean something whose boundaries are (exactly or roughly) coterminous with a nation in the John-Stuart-Millish sense of the word. Sometimes, it seems to mean a *sovereign* state (i.e., a state which recognises no legal superior to itself (2.6, 2.10)), regardless of its internal cultural structure. Thus, Fox and Fox, in an encyclopedia article on *international politics*, tell us that:

> The modern nation-state began to emerge in the fifteenth century with the division of Europe into units whose monarchs recognized no superior authority.
>
> (Fox & Fox, 1968: p. 52)

'Nation-state' there means the same as 'sovereign state'. Hans Kohn, on the other hand, in the same encyclopedia's article on *nationalism*, says:

> Nationalism centers the supreme loyalty of the overwhelming majority of the people upon the nation-state, either existing or desired. The nation-state is regarded not only as the ideal, 'natural,' or 'normal' form of political organization but also as the indispensable framework for all social, cultural, and economic activities. Yet nationalism and the nation-state are comparatively recent historical developments.
>
> Unknown before the eighteenth century, when it originated in north-western Europe and northern America, nationalism spread with ever-growing rapidity over all the earth.
>
> (Kohn, 1968: p. 63)

The dates differ by three hundred years. In principle, the divergence could be argued away. Kohn does not explicitly say that nationalism and the nation-state began together, and it is logically possible that nation-states emerged before nationalism, but that seems rather implausible. Further, some other remarks of Kohn suggest that he is neither agreeing nor disagreeing with the Foxes but talking about something else:

> Nationalism has from the beginning been a politically revolutionary movement. It has tried to transform or overthrow the 'legitimate' governments of the past whose claim to authority was based upon divine ordination or hereditary rights. It wished to establish totally new political entities: states coextensive with ethnic or linguistic frontiers.
>
> (ibid.: p. 64)

That does sound more like things which happened in the eighteenth century and after than things which happened in the previous three centuries, so it would seem that the nation-state of which Kohn speaks is a different kind of thing from the nation-state of which Fox and Fox speak; i.e, the expression 'nation-state' is ambiguous.

7.3 Scruton says that the 'emergence [of the nation-state] from the various international jurisdictions of Europe has been regarded as one of the major facts of modern political history' (Scruton, 1983: p. 313). And rightly so regarded, whichever sense of 'nation-state' is intended. (Scruton seems to incline towards the Fox sense rather than the Kohn sense.) It needs to be recognised, however, that the development of some nation-states from the fifteenth to the seventeenth centuries involved not only emergence from wider groupings, but also centralisation and the submergence of smaller political entities. The newly emerged nation-state of France involved the absorption of Bretons and Provençaux (who still feel rather different). England and Scotland were sufficiently disrespectful of future definition-makers as to put themselves under one king in 1603. In 1707, their Parliaments were united. Ireland was absorbed (much less willingly and must less justifiably) in 1801, just when, according to Kohn, nationalism was spreading 'with ever-growing rapidity over all the earth'. How perverse of history! European trade and empire-building were also spreading with ever-growing rapidity over all the earth.[1]

7.4 It begins to look as if the meaning of 'nation' as in 'inter*nation*al' is different from *and clearer* than that of 'nation' as in '*nation*alism'. There are the usual difficulties of definition, of course. If we really do not know what 'nation' as in 'international' means, would we be very much helped by a definition in which the words 'sovereign' and/or 'independent' occur? Nevertheless, 'nation' as in 'international' can be pinned down in the quasi-ostensive fashion used to pin down 'polity'(2.5):

> A nation is the sort of thing that can be represented at the United Nations. It can be a party to treaties. Legally, it is not a dependent part of any other such thing. It has a flag and an anthem, issues postage-stamps, etc.

7.5 There are anomalous cases which help make things clearer. The Byelorussian and the Ukrainian Soviet Socialist Republics became members of the United Nations, even though they did not conform to the specifications given above. Legally, they were parts of the Soviet Union, originally given membership of the United Nations as a mild counterweight to Western preponderance. Despite some appearances (e.g., flags and titles), the effect was simply that the USSR had three votes in the Assembly, and that was not a merely *de facto* matter. It was *de jure*. The Byelorussian and Ukrainian SSRs were not even nominally independent. Although their names appeared in the list of member-nations of the UN, it was perfectly reasonable to say 'They are not *really nations* as the other members are.' (On 'really', see *TP* 1.16.) Let us call what we are talking about now 'International Affairs nationhood' or 'IA nationhood' for short. IA nationhood seems logically independent of *nationality* as sketched by Mill or the sort of nationhood (whatever it may be) which Kohn has in mind, though there can be all sorts of *factual* relations between the two. Certain kinds and degrees of internal lack of unity, of cultural or communal disharmony can lead to the disappearance of an IA nation (e.g., the Federation of Rhodesia and Nyasaland in the early 1960s, Yugoslavia in the 1990s), to its radical transformation as an IA nation (e.g., Pakistan in 1971), or to its virtual nullity as an IA nation, even though key formal legalities persist. Lebanon in the 1980s was an example of that last type. It had its seat in the Assembly of the United Nations and printed its stamps, but, having no effective government, it was not a participant in most of the ordinary business of international affairs. But all that does not alter the main point. 'Xland is an IA nation' or even 'Xland is an effective IA nation, a non-nullity' does not imply anything very precise about its internal composition or structure.

7.6 There can, however, be links of aspiration between the concepts of IA nationhood and nationalism. Xland is legally part of Yland, but there are Xlanders who want Xland to be independent, to be the kind of entity which (typically) is represented at the United Nations, i.e., a nation in the sense talked of above. Those Xlanders are styled Xlandic *Nationalists*. But is this as much of a link as it may look? We are calling them 'Nationalists' for IA reasons. It is the wish for independence from *Yland*, for IA nationhood, which is decisive for our application of the expression 'Xlandic Nationalists'. Obviously (unless they are quite mad), they believe that Xland is or can be cohesive enough to survive as an IA nation, but that does not imply that Xland satisfies the Mill criteria to a very high degree. Those who sought Belgian independence in the early 1830s were aware of the internal diversity of Belgium as well as of the factors making it one entity and giving it separate interests and 'identity' from the interests and 'identity' of the Dutch Netherlands. (The use of the word 'identity' here is unsatisfactory, but all I mean is that Belgium was *a very significantly other thing*. See also 12.1–12.41; 5.12–5.33.)

7.7 IA nationhood ('nation' as in 'international') is relatively untroublesome. There are some other relatively untroublesome uses, those which involve a contrast between what is *national* and what is *regional, local*, etc. In Britain, the *national newspapers* are those which circulate throughout Britain and their 'coverage' and style reflect that fact. They are contrasted with *regional* newspapers and *local* newspapers, circulated within and written and published for more limited areas. The one Australian national daily, *The Australian*, has a section headed 'National weather', which gives reports and forecasts more comprehensive and detailed than those given in other papers circulating principally within one town or state. And, of course, within a federation, 'national' is sometimes used as a substitute for 'federal'.

7.8 But the plot must thicken. I must say something about *'nation' as in 'nationalism'*. Earlier, I imagined someone saying of the Byelorussian and Ukrainian SSRs: 'They are not really nations as the other members are.' Someone else might respond to that remark with 'Not nations in *that* sense, no, but nations in another sense.' Arguments for this will invoke various cultural distinctnesses (language, customs, religious tradition, etc.), and also the fact that Byelorussians and Ukrainians think of themselves as Byelorussians or Ukrainians, giving that description a certain kind of priority, which the description 'South Australian' or 'Queenslander' almost always lacks. Similarly, the Xlandic Nationalists, almost certainly, will insist that they are nationalists not only in that they want Xland to have the status of IA nationhood but also in that they recognise and participate in an existing distinctness in Xland, i.e., various important interests and cultural features, which make the propositions 'Xland is part of Yland' and 'Xlanders are a species of Ylander' inappropriate, even if, as a matter of constitutional and international law, they happen to be true. And there may be Xlanders who say 'Of course, we're not Ylanders. We are a nation, but we don't need independence. We're better off as we are.' The Xlandic Nationalists will not like that, but they would be wrong if they said that it was self-contradictory. Those Xlanders who say 'We're better off as we are' might also say 'We're nationalists too, but we're not separatists. We're nationalists with a little "n".' ('Nationalism' is beginning to sound slippery.)

7.9   My Xland/Yland example fits certain kinds of 'nationalism' (or, to avoid that troublesome word, *separatism, independencism*). It calls to mind relations between Belgium and the United Kingdom of the Netherlands from the Congress of Vienna (1815) to the 1830s. It calls to mind also relations between various bits (past and present) of a rather better known United Kingdom. Xland/Yland fits those examples well enough. It fits less well many of the 'nationalisms' (i.e., separatisms, 'independencisms') which we have seen in the forty years since the Second World War. The relation between Belgium and the United Kingdom of the Netherlands was very different from that between Belgium and the Congo, and I am not thinking primarily of the fact that any oppression suffered by the Belgians before their independence was infinitely trifling compared with Belgian oppression in the Congo. For present purposes, the significant thing is that the Congo was a Belgian artefact.

7.10   Post-1945 nationalisms could be clear and confident in their external, IA aspect: Get the foreigners out. In their internal aspect, they have often been whistling in the dark. In the 1970s, the PNG politician, Albert Maori Kiki, was fond of saying, 'Why be afraid of independence? We were independent for centuries before the white men came', which was clever, but hardly accurate. A Papua New Guinean nation, people or polity had *not* existed for centuries. What was there when the white man came was a vast collection of groups, some of them remarkably dissimilar, none of them aware of anything corresponding to Papua New Guinea, most of them aware of no wider world than an immediate neighbourhood, partly populated by hereditary enemies, and sometimes of unknown, remote places from which trade goods came. As I said earlier (5.25), the concept of Papua New Guinea is one of thoroughly foreign origin, perhaps the most thoroughly alien of all the concepts and institutions brought in with colonialism. In 1972 at the University of PNG, someone wrote on a wall: 'National Unity Is A Colonialist Plot.' There was some truth in that. The Gorton, McMahon and Whitlam Governments were committed to what E. P. Wolfers called 'a policy of Unite and Quit', as distinct from Divide and Rule. The contrast with, e.g., Ireland is enormous. The concept of Ireland was not an exotic one, even when Ireland was a collection of clans and kingdoms. And, for many centuries, someone from one end of

Ireland had no difficulty with the proposition that someone from the other end of the country was his compatriot. This sense of Irishness was not always a separatism, but it was something to which separatists could appeal, and, more important, it was something which could survive the achievement of independence for the counties which became the Irish Free State and, later, the Irish Republic.[2]

7.11   The concept of nation in its internal aspect is both woolly and slippery, as is shown by the bad prose-poetry often talked by nationalistic activists. Even academic scholars of nationalism can go on in the same sonorous, obfuscating fashion (see, e.g., Kohn, 1968). Sometimes, the bad prose-poetry happens because the nationalists have much to hide. 'Xland must be free from Ylandic rule!' say the Xlandic Nationalists. 'Xland is culturally a different entity from Yland. The Xlandic people must have their own identity and must pursue their own destiny!' And substantial non-Xlandic minorities within Xland are simply treated as invisible, as nonentities. The Hungarian rising of 1848–1849, led by Lajos Kossuth, failed, largely because its notions of Hungarian nationality were considerably narrower than its notions of Hungarian territory and because the non-Magyar minorities preferred the Austrian devil they knew to the Hungarian devil which they also knew. That did not prevent English liberals and Irish nationalists from regarding Kossuth as a great apostle of liberty. As Sir Ivor Jennings has said, 'On the surface it seemed reasonable: let the people decide. It was in fact ridiculous because the people cannot decide until someone decides who are the people' (quoted, Rustow, 1968: p. 11; see also 8.1–8.16).[3] According to the UN declaration on decolonisation, 'All peoples have the right to self-determination' (article 2). For what that can amount to in practice, ask the West Papuans and the East Timorese.

7.12   There can then be falsehood, self-contradiction and brutal dishonesty at the base of European nationalisms. The vocabulary can be used, not to fit the facts, but to disguise them. If that can be so in Europe, it is much more likely to be so in Africa, not because of any European superiority, but because the IA nations of Africa are, for the most part, successors of colonial territories whose size and shape depended on the ambitions and success of the colonising countries. All boundaries are, to at least some extent, historical accidents, but historical accidents several hundred years old have a way of becoming natural features. The boundaries of African territories were not allowed to mature. It may be that the vocabulary of *nation* and *nationalism* is ill suited to some political realities. It may also be that that is quite irremediable (and far from *merely* verbal: see *TP* 2.11).

THE NATION AS UNACKNOWLEDGED EMPIRE

> 'I reduce God to the attribute of nationality?' Shatov cried. 'On the contrary, I raise the people to God. And indeed has it ever been otherwise?'
>
> (Dostoyevsky, *The Devils* pt II ch. i, 1953: p. 257)

7.13   I remarked earlier (7.3) that the emergence of older IA nation-states such as France involved not merely detachment from rambling medieval groupings but also the political (usually not the cultural) submergence of smaller political entities. Most movements known as *nationalisms* have demanded that the boundaries of some nation *à la* Mill should be the boundaries of an IA nation. That has been the justification used in fixing the borders of the IA nations which emerged on the break-up of the Ottoman and Habsburg Empires, and it is something we are seeing now with the break-up of the Soviet Empire. The idea of *national self-determination* attained something like Scriptural status in the 'Fourteen Points' of Woodrow Wilson:

> IX. A readjustment of the frontiers of Italy should be effected along clearly recognizable lines of nationality.
> X. The peoples of Austria-Hungary, whose place among the nations we wish to see safeguarded and assured, should be accorded the freest opportunity of autonomous development.
> XI. Rumania, Serbia, and Montenegro should be evacuated; occupied territories restored; Serbia accorded free and secure access to the sea; and the relations of the several Balkan States to one another determined by friendly counsel along historically established lines of allegiance and nationality; and international guarantees of the political and economic independence and territorial integrity of the several Balkan States should be entered into.
> XII. The Turkish portions of the present Ottoman Empire should be assured a secure sovereignty, but the other nationalities which are now under Turkish rule should be assured an undoubted security of life and an absolutely unmolested opportunity of autonomous development . . . .
> XIII. An independent Polish State should be erected which should include the territories inhabited by indisputably Polish populations, which should be assured a free and secure access to the sea, and whose political and economic independence and territorial integrity should be guaranteed by international covenant.

> (Hofstadter, 1969: pp. 225–226)

7.14   It sounds very nice, but it could not work. The new Uland must be culturally and demographically Ulandic. That was the principle on which its legitimacy was to rest, but it was rarely possible to draw a line which gave both Ulanders and Vlanders complete self-determination. It was not a matter of individuals or families finding themselves on the 'wrong' side of the border. It was large portions: whole villages, whole towns, large areas of countryside. (See Jouvenel, 1963: pp. 208–210 on the case of Upper Silesia.) Virtually every Uland had a Vlandic minority, condemned to be logically impossible. Usually, their status was worse than it had been under the old empire. Then, they were merely subjects, just one of the peoples over whom the Emperor or the Sultan ruled, but now the appetite for national self-determination had been raised to a sacred principle. That appetite had been provoked, titillated, stimulated to a frenzy - and precisely because of self-determination, they were sentenced to be an anomalous foreign element in the towns and countrysides where their ancestors had lived for centuries or to be driven into exile.[4] Each of the new nation-states was, in fact, a little, unacknowledged empire. Jouvenel remarks,

> Eduard Benes was a man of the highest moral character, he invoked self-determination to obtain the setting up of Czechoslovakia; he did not like it when Sudeten and Slovakian leaders invoked it to obtain their independence from Prague. Neither did I like it . . . .
>
> (1963: p. 210)

As Benedict Anderson says, 'the "nation" proved an invention on which it was impossible to secure a patent. It became available for pirating by widely different, and sometimes unexpected hands' (1983: p. 66).

There were also the provisions that Thisland and Thatland should have access to the sea. It is hard to believe that even Woodrow Wilson could have been so self-deceiving as not to be quite consciously aware that, in practice, that would mean giving Thisland and Thatland unwilling colonies of ethnic Otherlanders – all in the sacred name of Self-determination and Nationality. 7.15   And, in 1989, the whole thing started all over again with the dismantling of the Soviet Empire and the re-Balkanisation of the Balkans. Gorbachev seems to have been a second Woodrow Wilson – a well-meaning maker of utter disaster. 'The devil can quote Scripture for his purpose.' Hitler and his supporters could invoke national self-determination when it suited them – very effectively, too. In 1990, the broadcaster, Alistair Cooke, quoted someone as having 'said the unsayable': 'There's one thing can be said for empires: they usually stopped the natives from killing one another.' To liberate is to set free; it is also to let loose. We once heard much of *captive nations*. Perhaps some are better kept under lock and key. That is an appalling thing to say, but it is provoked by appalling deeds and tendencies. See, e.g., Hockenos, 1991. The word 'nationalism' can be a euphemism for '*xenophobia*' or '*racism*' (and still refer to a nationalism). John Stuart Mill says:

> One hardly knows what any division of the human race should be free to do if not to determine with which of the various collective bodies of human beings they choose to associate themselves . . . . Free institutions are next to impossible in a country made up of different nationalities.
>
> (1972: p. 361)

The former Yugoslavia in 1993 gives that remark a point of which Mill was unaware. Cf. 2.9F.

The main conceptual point of those historical remarks is that the concept of nation-as-in-'nationalism' is frequently sunk in a mire of self-contradiction, lies and ethnic hostility. That does not lessen its political potency. At the same time, mere respect for truth requires that one recognises that there *are* nations in that sense. Mere respect for justice may require one to approve of some nationalisms, and also to hope that some can be cooled down.

7.16 There is another point: Ylandic rule over Xland may be oppressive because of Ylandic harshness or greed or arrogance or ignorance, and so, of course, may Ylandic rule over Ylanders. It *may* be that foreign rule is more likely to have those faults than non-foreign, but, once self-determination becomes a Principle, it begins to suggest that foreign rule is oppressive because foreign, and not because of anything that it does or does not do. 'Ylandic rule over Xland is oppressive' becomes, for some Xlanders, as axiomatic, as unshakeable as 'Triangles have three sides'. It needs only a small group of them to take this view. Once they begin acting accordingly, Ylandic rule will tend to become oppressive in an ordinary, non-axiomatic sense. As Burke said, 'Kings will be tyrants from policy, when subjects are rebels from principle.'[5] Some nationalist groups have deliberately provoked retaliation which will fall not on them but on their less committed compatriots, because that is a useful recruiting technique. They 'bring out the inherent oppression of the system' as one might bring out the inherent unworkability of a car by putting sugar in the tank. As one of Graham Greene's characters says, 'you have to be prepared in these days for criminals – everywhere. They call it having ideals' (1950: p. 50). All too frequently, the people whom the patriot (or patrioteer (5.38)) loves do not yet exist. Those that do are mere raw material out of which he hopes to fashion a suitable object of his love. The same is often true of The Workers, beloved by other high-principled activists. See Plamenatz, 1960.

NATION AND COUNTRY

7.17 What is the relation between these two concepts? We can, of course, set aside 'country' = 'rural area' as a mere harmless homonym, but, even when we have done that, it seems that the two concepts are not identical.[6] Consider this example:

> If a European migrant to Australia says 'I have lived in this country for twenty years,' then we know what he means. If he says 'I have lived in this nation for twenty years,' then too, we are in no doubt about what he means, but we know also that his English is not yet perfect.

It is easy enough to spot the mistake and correct it. It is much less easy to cite a rule to back the correction. One is tempted to say '"Nation" is not a geographical word, so a nation is not the kind of thing one *can* live in', but then one notices those uses talked of in 7.7 which *do* make 'nation' a geographical word.

7.18 'A swagman or hitchhiker – even the average first-class tourist – might travel all over the country. Only a politician or an ad-man would travel all over the nation.'

The suggestion is that 'nation' is an oratorical word, used for making large claims (perhaps invoking patriotic (5.38) values). Pursuing that line, one might explain away 'national newspaper' (7.7) as a ballyhoo-laden self-description which certain newspapers have been allowed to get away with.

'National weather' *perhaps* invokes the same ballyhoo (but certainly occupies less space than the more idiomatic 'weather across the country'). There is something in that, I suspect, but we would be wrong if we went on to say that 'country' is a *merely* geographical term, or that, whether it is merely geographical or not, it is, in comparison with 'nation', an uncoloured, tame, unexciting word.

That will not do. When an English-speaking person is in a patriotic mood, isn't it the word 'country' that he is more likely to use than the word 'nation'?

'I vow to thee my country, all earthly things above . . .'
'My country, 'tis of thee . . .'
'Though friends may desert me and kindred disown,
My country will never do that'[7]

Or is that true of only certain kinds of patriot? Is there a different kind that goes on about *national identity* (12.26–12.37) and is less inclined to use the word 'country'? I do not know.

I find myself unable to express the relation between 'nation' and 'country' in any kind of formula. Someone, of course, might say that it is all quite simple: '"Nation" is abstract. "Country" is concrete.' I feel tempted to agree, but then it occurs to me to ask 'What does that mean?', and I have to answer that I do not know, and I doubt whether he does, either. (See *TP* 1.11.) See also 5.38–5.40 (*patriotism, chauvinism, jingoism*).

'TWO NATIONS', 'ONE NATION'

7.19   These phrases have their origin in Disraeli's novel, *Sybil*:

'Well, society may be in its infancy,' said Egremont, . . . 'but, say what you like, our Queen reigns over the greatest nation that ever existed.'

'Which nation?' asked the younger stranger, 'for she reigns over two. . . . Two nations; between whom there is no intercourse and no sympathy; who are as ignorant of each other's habits, thoughts, and feelings, as if they were dwellers in different zones, or inhabitants of different planets; who are formed by a different breeding, are fed by a different food, are ordered by different manners, and are not governed by the same laws.'

'You speak of –' said Egremont, hesitatingly.

'THE RICH AND THE POOR.'

(Bk I ch. v. 1927: pp. 76–77)

The phrase is related to one in another of Disraeli's novels: 'A sound Conservative government . . . I understand: Tory men and Whig measures' (II vi, 1911: p. 85). The need for policies aimed at creating or maintaining 'One Nation' has been a catchcry of various kinds of Tory Reformer, and was an important part of the thinking of Tories (such as Macmillan, Butler and Hailsham) who supported the Welfare State, economic planning and a regulatory role for government in commerce and industry (thus putting themselves well to the left of the Australian Labor Party under its present management). But Lady Thatcher, the leader of a very different, *laissez-fairiste*, kind of conservatism (11.9A (ii), 10A), has also used the slogan:

> I am much nearer to creating one nation than Labour will ever be . . . . [S]ocialism is two nations, the privileged rulers and everybody else. What I am desperately trying to do is create one nation, with everyone being a man of property, or having the opportunity to be a man of property.
>
> (*SMH*, 6 April 1988)

She may well have done for 'one nation' what Chamberlain did for 'peace in our time', but, four years later, an Australian Labor Prime Minster, defying augury, chose the phrase as a title for his economic policy.[8] Clearly, it still has magical properties.

CONCLUSION

7.20   'Nation' is incurably ambiguous. There are uses of 'national' which mean merely *polity-wide as distinct from something pertaining to a more restricted area of the polity*: 'national newspaper', 'national weather report', etc. This use seems unloaded with doctrine or ideology – or at least not necessarily loaded with doctrine or ideology. Sometimes it is loaded with self-congratulation. Whether a newspaper is national in the sense spoken of in 7.7 is a mere matter of fact, but, when a newspaper calls itself *a national daily*, it wants to impress us with its grandeur. That use of 'national' is more or less innocuous, as are various close-to-meaningless uses: e.g., as a name for a pub, or as in 'ABC Radio National', or as in the name of New Zealand's National Party (but not in the name of the South African Nationalist Party or that of the National Party of Australia. The point of the latter name is: 'We are no longer just a Country Party.' The former proclaimed the nasty ideal of a white, Afrikaner nation). The 'polity-wide' sense of 'national' takes a controversial turn when the contrast of whole with part is no longer (or not only) geographical, but a contrast of allegedly national interests with allegedly special interests (6.1–6.29). (The old Australian Nationalist Party which existed from the Hughes split until the Lyons split was making that dubious claim, and *just* that claim. There was nothing anti-imperial about the old Nats.)

7.21   There is an odd ambiguity in the term 'nation-state' (7.2–7.3) and, in practice, it may be impossible to discern whether someone is talking of IA-sense nationhood or of nationhood-as-in-nationalism ('cultural' nationhood). One may even be unsure about one's own intentions in the matter. It is possible to use 'nation' in its cultural sense without endorsing either a particular separatism or a general, prescriptive, Woodrow-Wilsonian doctrine of national self-determination. The possibilities for confusion are enormous. There can be dispute over whether something should be a nation in the IA sense (7.7), but there is no necessary tie between that sense and any ideology or contentious doctrine. It is the first word in the title of the United Nations that is embarrassing, not the second. '. . . is a Nation' in the IA sense predicates a legal status which is tolerably well defined. Dispute over whether something is (as distinct from *should be*) an IA nation is possible but, up till now, very exceptional. In 1991, certain doubts were raised when the Federated States of Micronesia applied to join the United Nations. Perhaps, in the future, similar doubts may be raised about members of the European Community. The complexities are most unlikely to be 'merely linguistic'.

Suggested reading

Ritter, 1986: pp. 285–299; Scruton, 1983: pp. 101–102 ('Country'), 312–316 ('Nation', etc.), 440–442 ('Sovereign', etc.); R. Williams, 1983: pp. 81–82, 213–215; Fox & Fox, 1968; B. Anderson, 1983; Farrar, 1989; N. Harris, 1992; Jouvenel, 1963: pp. 204–212; Hobsbawm, 1990; Plamenatz, 1960; Kamenka, 1973; Kedourie, 1961; Kohn, 1973; Mill, 1972, *Representative Government*: ch. xvi; Calwell, 1963: ch. i; P. Morgan, 1980; Rustow, 1968; Cobban, 1969; Mackenzie, 1978; Post, 1973; Shafer, 1955; Snyder, 1990; Vogler, 1985.

8   The people, democracy, populism

THE PEOPLE

> By the waters of Babylon I heard
> That art was for the people; but they meant
> That art should sweeten to the people's mouth
> The droppings from the perch of government.
> James McAuley (1971: p. 29)

8.1   *OED*'s discussion of the word 'people' and its cognates is well worth a close look. (It covers, in the second edition, nine and a half closely packed folio columns, providing sufficient evidence that 'people' is a very complicated word. It may even leave the reader with the feeling that it is an astonishing thing that we can do anything so complicated as speaking our own language.) For present purposes, we can select just a few of the many uses listed. *OED*'s sense 1 is

> 1. A body of persons composing a community, tribe, race, or nation;
> = Folk I. Sometimes viewed as a unity, sometimes as a collective of number.

In this sense, the word 'people' can take the plural form 'peoples', though, for some centuries, writers considered 'peoples' not entirely respectable. I do not know why. Anthropologists frequently use the phrase 'a people' in a sense corresponding to *OED*'s sense 1. They use it in a way which tends to suggest a high degree of homogeneity and (at least until recently) self-containedness. In this sense, it is natural to speak of the Mdelpa, the Arapesh, the Tolai as *peoples*; it strains the phrase if we call the totality of Papua New Guinea Highlanders *a people*; we strain it to breaking point if we apply it to the totality of Papua New Guineans. It may be that, even when applied to 'an anthropologist's people', the phrase 'a people' suggests more homogeneity and self-containedness than may be there.

8.2   A people in this sense is not necessarily the kind of thing recognised as *a nation* in international law. The word 'nation' in the definition has the sense of 'culture-group'.[1] In this sense, the Jews, the Kurds, the Armenians, the Macedonians are each *a people* (or *a nation*), even though each is far larger and more diffuse than 'an anthropologist's people' and even though none of those groups has a common citizenship. Similarly, one might speak of the Scottish people or the Welsh people – or the English people?

8.3 Is something funny happening here? 'The English people' does sound decidedly odd, if said in the same breath as 'The Jews, the Kurds, the Armenians, the Macedonians are each a people.' Why is that? Perhaps it is because it seems to attribute to the totality of the English a homogeneity and a 'sharp-edgedness' which that totality no longer has (or, according to Defoe (1975(b)), ever had). And do the Kurds, the Armenians, the Macedonians have that homogeneity, that sharp-edgedness? Well, I don't really know, do you? It may simply be that we find it easier to think of those groups as homogeneous and sharp-edged because we do not know a great deal about them, whereas we just know too much about the English to think of them in that way. ('I'm giving a course on contemporary English philosophy,' someone said to me once. 'You know: Wittgenstein, Waismann, Popper, Körner, and so on.') It is certainly possible to be both a Jew and English.[2] It may well be possible to be English and a Kurd or an Armenian or a Macedonian. Salman Rushdie is frequently characterised as a *British* writer. It will not be long before the less comprehensive adjective 'English' is applied to him, but I cannot help wondering how wholeheartedly and by how many, and whether the same adjective will be applied to or accepted by the generality of non-white immigrants and their descendants. Even a controversial novelist with a price on his head can have privileges which bus conductors and the unemployed lack. But, setting that aside, Rushdie's Englishness could be perfectly compatible with a persistent Muslim-Indianness.

8.4 'The Scottish people' and 'The Welsh people' do not sound as odd as 'The English people'. Are the Scots and the Welsh more homogeneous, more sharp-edged than the English? Probably, though Glasgow and Cardiff are not much less cosmopolitan than London. Perhaps something else is coming in here. The Scots and the Welsh, *vis-à-vis* the English, are not subjected, nor exactly subordinate, but they are not dominant. They are less numerous than the English and (broadly) less affluent. The Welsh were once a conquered people. Scotland is a more complicated case (see Mackenzie, 1978: pp. 170–172), but it has never been the senior partner, even under the Stuarts. When the French think of the United Kingdom, they are far more likely to think of it as 'Angleterre' than as 'Grande Bretagne' or as 'Le Royaume Uni'. (I suspect that the last two expressions are ones which members of the French foreign service have to be *taught*.) It may be that it is this sort of thing, this suggestion of an unfortunate history, that makes it easier for us to accept the phrases 'the Scottish people' and 'the Welsh people'. That, of course, does not come into *OED*'s sense 1 of 'people', which is perfectly legitimate. Different senses of 'people' do tend to flavour one another.

8.5 One of *OED*'s examples for sense 1 is an instance of this phenomenon:

> 1835 Lytton *Rienzi* II. vi. Rienzi addressed the Populace, whom he had suddenly elevated into a People.
>
> [Lytton, 1911: p. 132]

At first sight, this might seem ironical, but it is not. Cola di Rienzo (i.e., Rienzi) had 'convened the Romans to provide for the safety of Rome', and (according to Lytton) this had evoked a response such that they were no longer *just* a populace, no longer *just* the collection of inhabitants of Rome.[3] His point seems to be that they were transformed into something like *a nation* in the sense of the first two syllables of 'nationalism': a group with an 'identity' (12.1–12.37) and a 'destiny' of its own, and a 'will' which must be carried into action, a super-tribe, even a super-individual. ('Nation' in 'nationalism' does not always have all of that as its meaning, but there is often a tendency for it to go that way.)[4] That is saying *much* more than *OED*'s definition of sense 1 says. Perhaps the example was chosen injudiciously by *OED*, but it is a good example of one kind of use of 'a People'.

8.6   Let us get our feet back on the ground, familiar ground, Mayfield[5] to be precise. Mayfield has people, i.e., there are people who live in Mayfield. One can call them the people of Mayfield if one likes (though it sounds a little melodramatic), but only a Napoleon of Notting Hill[6] would call them *a people* in the 'Rienzi' sense. When I say 'Mayfield has people, i.e., there are people who live in Mayfield', what sense has the word 'people'? A familiar sense: *OED*'s sense 6 which tends to melt into *OED*'s sense 2:

6. Men or women indefinitely; men and women; persons, folk.

2. The persons belonging to a place, or constituting a particular concourse, congregation, company, or class.

'People' here does not take a plural. It *is* plural. 'People' in this sense is often used as a *substitute* for 'human beings': 'There were six people waiting for a taxi' is good English; 'There were six human beings waiting for a taxi' is merely quaint. Do we say that 'people' so used is a *synonym* for 'human beings'? If we do, we may be in trouble, because there is a popular tendency to think of 'people' as the plural of 'person'[7] and there is no self-contradiction in the notion of a non-human person or (perhaps) in that of a human non-person. That complexity is waiting to trip us up in controversy over such matters as abortion, foetal experimentation and euthanasia (See *TP* 1.24).

8.7   A further use of 'people' makes it synonymous with certain uses of French *on* ('On dit que . . .') and English 'they' ('They say that a mild winter means a bad summer for bushfires'). 'People' here does not mean *all the people there are*, or *all the people there are in some given region*, or even *most of the people there are* or *most of the people there are in a given region*. If people say that p, then p is a *common* opinion, one *often* met with (see *OED* 'People' sense 7).

8.8   There is also 'people' in the sense of *the rest* relative to some institution, group or office-holder:

The Government and the people
The priest and the people (e.g. in some liturgical texts, setting out who says what when; cf. *OED* 'People' 4.b)

Parliament and the people
The politicians and the people
The banks and the people

'People' in this sense is usually treated as plural. *The people* here is or are *the rest*, often (but not perhaps inevitably) the subordinate rest or the less privileged or (in some way) dependent rest.[8] Notice that a locution of the form 'the Qs and the people' does not rule out the possibility that some or all of the Qs may also be members of the people. The legislators make the laws which bind the people. Thus, the legislators have a privileged position, but each of them is a member of the people bound by the laws. There *can* be a *tendency* for this sense of 'people' to merge with 'people' in the 8.6 sense. We need, nevertheless, to remember that these are different senses of the word.

8.9 In a complex, modern, western society, 'the people' in 'the Qs and the people' sense has a varying membership. As different substitutions are made for 'Q', a given individual will find himself sometimes a Q, sometimes one of the people. Thus, in such a society, this sense of 'the people' will tend to become interchangeable with 'the public'. 'The public' denotes no logical (or social) class in the way that 'the rich' or 'the semi-skilled' does.[9] Armed with a reader's ticket, you legitimately march past a sign saying 'The public are not admitted to this library', but your reader's ticket avails you nothing when you meet a similar sign in a different building. In a more rigidly stratified society, 'the people' in 'the Qs and the people' sense may have a less varying membership and, in that case, the confluence with 'the public' will not occur. Even in a complex, modern, western society, there *may* be a large class whose members are quasi-permanently 'the rest' with respect to holders of power, influence, wealth, purchasing-power, privilege and prestige. In such a case we have a *people* in *OED*'s sense 4:

4.a. The common people, the commonalty; the mass of the community as distinguished from the nobility and ruling or official classes. Const. as *pl*. Cf. *man of the people . . . .*

Things are getting a little sticky and ideological. (See *TP* 7.2D.) If someone said 'But, in modern Australia, there is no people in this sense of a commonalty,'[10] I would suspect him of trying to trick us into thinking that there are no substantial inequalities or deprivations (which, of course, there are). All the same, in a society in which such things as education, high purchasing-power, *politesse*, privilege and prestige are not concentrated in the same hands, talk of *the people* (in this 'commonalty' sense) becomes rather tricky. One of *OED*'s examples concerns Paul Robeson: 'everywhere he met with the people'. One would assume that, offered a choice between the company of unskilled workers and that of senior lecturers in philosophy, he would choose the former. That is a legitimate way of talk. Senior lecturers in philosophy have many privileges which unskilled workers lack and there is a certain (rather ambivalent) prestige attached to their work which is not attached to that of unskilled workers. (See 11.14B.) But some unskilled workers (e.g., at the Sydney oil terminals) have much higher incomes than most senior lecturers. It may be that certain highly questionable assumptions are built into (or, at least, closely associated with) some applications of the word 'people' in this 'commonalty' sense. (Quite apart from overlooking the shabby genteel and *les nouveaux pauvres*, it may suggest more uniformity than there is amongst the less privileged.) See Needler, 1991: ch. viii.

8.10   Senses of 'the people' or of 'people' vary in their comprehensiveness. If an anthropologist goes to study *the Xish people* (8.1) and there are Xish hereditary chiefs, he does not ignore them and their families. But, quite clearly, the chiefs and their families are not members of the Xish people in the sense discussed in *OED*'s sense 4. Or take its sense 8:

> *Politics*. The whole body of enfranchised or qualified citizens, considered as the source of power; esp. in a democratic state, the electorate.[11]

In Xland, an Xlandic millionaire is as much a member of that body as any other Xlander, but to proclaim him, therefore, *a true man of the people* would be a *non sequitur*. Where a word expands and contracts in this fashion, there are many opportunities for sliding from one sense to the other without noticing it (or doing it intentionally, but hoping that the audience won't notice it).[12] A piece of discourse involving the word 'people' used that way would have only a surface, merely rhetorical coherence. Even worse dangers appear when we consider that a concept like *the people of Australia* is *open, four-dimensional*, not limited to the present (cf. 6.26–6.27). Someone charged with the responsibility of caring for his or her family will, at least at some stages, have to take into account the interests of possible future members of the family. Similarly, those charged with legislating and making policy for the people of Australia (in the sense discussed in 8.6) have to take into account the *certainty* that what they do will affect the interests of Australians yet unborn; i.e., the membership of the people of Australia is not limited to those Australian people (human beings) living at any particular tick of the clock (or on any particular polling day). There is also the possible clash between short-term sentiment or demand and long-term interest. Because of these factors even the most democratically minded government might find that, if it is to do its duty, it must sometimes do the unpopular thing and hope that, before next election, it can persuade enough voters that it is right. See 2.17J–K (*representation*).

8.11   All that is true and unavoidable. But there is a danger that politicians (by psychological necessity, not the most self-doubting variety of human being) may move from the quite possible truth that they sometimes know better to the megalomaniacal falsehood that they always know best. Similarly, it is possible that a politician (or a political theorist) can confuse the truth that *the people of his polity* is not identical with the totality of citizens at any particular tick of the clock with the megalomaniacal falsehood that the people is quite distinct from that totality and something with which he has a uniquely intimate relationship:

Only one body is supreme in Queensland – the people. Parliament, government and the executive are merely instruments of the people and accountable to them.

(Johannes Bjelke-Petersen[13] in 1978)

Over and above parties, confessions and classes we have set the German people, and it is only as a people, not as a group of individuals or parties, that it can survive. Above all, we have worked out in Germany a single will . . . he who represents this will should be respected in his will.

(Adolf Hitler in 1937)

(Both quoted, D. McM. Wells, 1980)

I am quite sure that those two remarks are sincere. Others may question that with respect to one or both of them, but there is a remark of Eamon De Valera which is so naive and so vulnerable that it cannot be other than sincere:

I have been brought up amongst the Irish people . . . I have not lived solely amongst the intellectuals . . .; therefore . . . whenever I wanted to know what the Irish people wanted, I had only to examine my own heart and it told me straight off what the Irish people wanted.

(Quoted, Longford & O'Neill, 1974: p. 176)

Here we have three very similar utterances by three very different political leaders. Each asserts the supremacy and sovereignty of the people. Each declares his own subservience to the people. And, in each case, this is an expression of supreme *self*-assurance, suggesting that the speaker has little to learn from anyone in particular. De Gaulle also had a habit of communing with an entity named 'France', over the heads of Frenchmen and Frenchwomen. I am not, of course, suggesting that all four are tarred with the same brush. Even De Gaulle, even Bjelke-Petersen accepted in principle that they could legitimately lose office, which makes them very different from Hitler. De Valera never doubted the legitimate precariousness of a leader's position. The only conclusion I would draw from these specimens of people-talk is that people-talk may not always be what it seems. It is available to politicians, vastly different in personality and political orientation, and, for all its humble sound, it can be the expression of a self-confidence so strong that it verges on, or even tumbles into, the hubristic or the insane.

8.12   There are various societies described by anthropologists in which the legitimate king or chief is the man who could hold the emblems of authority with appropriate dignity. He might have had to use force to get hold of them, but, usually, it would not have been worth his while to do so unless the incumbent was someone whose grip – metaphorically, literally, or both – was slipping. In some societies, the transfer of authority could be managed by a private payment and a public mock battle, but the general principle was the same: he who could hold the emblems with appropriate dignity was the legitimate chief (cf. Mair, 1962: pp. 115–119). Some political language is emblematic in a similar fashion. It is utilisable in various different political causes and all or almost all political groups seek to make it their own. Its use may invoke honoured and semi-unquestionable assumptions held by almost all people in the relevant society. Its use may also invoke a variety of more controversial assumptions, some of them mutually incompatible. The phrase 'the people' is one such bit of political language.[14]

8.13   Commonly, it is used with *sanctifying* intent. One can scorn and condemn large sections of the population. One can condemn *Society*. One can even rebuke *The Community* for its apathy. (See 2.12B.) All those actions are safe, but one had better not say a word against *The People*. 'The people', says Jean-Jacques Rousseau, 'is never corrupted, but it is often deceived, and that is when it seems to will something bad' (*Social Contract* bk II ch. iii. Rousseau, 1972: p. 127; 1973: pp. 184–185; cf. 8.32). It would be very difficult for anyone (especially a politician) to reject publicly that solemn piece of doubletalk, without laying himself open to allegations of elitism, authoritarianism, even Fascism. Aristotle mentions an oath taken by certain Greek supporters of oligarchy:

> I will be an enemy to the people, and will devise all the harm against them which I can.
>
> (Aristotle, *Politics* bk III ch. ix, 1941: pp. 1250–1251; 1981: p. 331)

That robust old spirit is dead, whether 'people' has its all-inclusive Rousseauesque sense or whether it means (as it did for the oligarchs) the commonalty (8.9). Even then, expressing it openly was hardly prudent. Aristotle advised that, for the sake of social tranquillity, oligarchs 'should always appear to speak on behalf of the people . . . [and] their assumptions and their ostensible conduct should be the opposite of [the oath quoted]. They should declare on oath that "I will do no wrong to the people"' (ibid.). The advice has been heeded. These days, politicians and political enthusiasts always claim to have the people's interests at heart. It would be a mistake to write this off as mere pretence. (It may well be much more dangerous than that.) I am quite sure that few politicians, whatever their affiliation, ever make pronouncements about The People without feeling Very Sincere.

8.14   As we have seen (8.11), sincere people-talk is not an inevitable sign of democratic or freedom-favouring sentiments (and sincere democratic sentiments are not always freedom-favouring: see 8.23). Revolutionary movements speak of *the people*; nationalist movements speak of the *Xish people*, but it would be naive to draw the conclusion that all who speak that way are ready to be responsive to public opinion or accountable to an electorate. Such movements are often paternalistic: they believe that they know what the people want and need better than other members of the public. What they sincerely call 'the demands of the people' may be merely the demands which they believe the people would make if they were properly enlightened. The Three Tailors of Tooley Street addressed Parliament in a petition beginning 'We, the people of England' (Brewer, 1970: p. 1059). They would have been less of a joke if they had planted car-bombs. Sometimes, this revolutionary paternalism goes along with a cold-blooded 'futurism' (7.16). Even when movements do not adopt policies of that kind, the connection between people-talk and democracy can be obscure; e.g.:

> The Fenian tradition of Irish revolt was by no means obviously democratic. No doubt there was some rather vague conception of a democratic régime to be established, once Ireland was free. But Irish freedom came a long way before everything . . . . And it came to be assumed that it must, in fact, be achieved by a heroic minority whatever the majority attitude. The men of 1916 would never have struck their immortal and triumphal blow for freedom if they had waited for a majority verdict.
>
> (Longford & O'Neill, 1974: p. 466)[15]

One of those men of 1916, the Socialist, James Connolly, said, 'Ireland, as distinct from her people, means nothing to me' (ibid.: p. 238). I am quite sure he meant it, but I am by no means sure that I know what he meant. Even De Valera's notion of democracy was (shall we say?) somewhat pragmatic. Despite his ability to know what the Irish people wanted by pure cardiac introspection, he also said that 'The people have no right to do wrong' and 'Republicans maintain that there are rights which may be maintained by force by an armed minority, even against a majority' (quoted, U. O'Connor, 1967: p. 166). That was in the months between the Anglo-Irish Treaty and the outbreak of the Civil War. In the late 1930s, after De Valera had (quite legally) become Prime Minister, Oliver St John Gogarty wrote angrily of 'the little yellow leprechaun . . .who now persecute[s] the Irish people in the name of The Irish People' (1937: p. 17).

8.15 Language used to sanctify can be used also to curse and excommunicate. In Northern Ireland, mutually (and blood-thirstily) opposed enthusiasts make assertions about the opinions, aspirations, etc. of 'The People of Ireland' or 'The People of Ulster' – assertions which, if true, would not need to be made, or not in *that* tone of voice, anyway. 'The people of Ireland (or Ulster) want what I want and, therefore, there are many people born and bred and living in Ireland (or Ulster) who are ready to kill or die in order to prevent what I want from coming to pass.' Even De Valera – a Republican very different from those now violently active – could say (commenting on the arrival of American troops in Northern Ireland in 1942):

> no matter what troops occupy the Six Counties, the Irish people's claim for the union of the whole national territory and for supreme jurisdiction over it, will remain unabated.
>
> (Longford & O'Neill, 1974: p. 398)

From a purely logical (though not a moral) point of view, De Valera's error is less 'forgivable' than that of the Northern terrorists, for those on each side regard the other part of the population merely as enemy aliens. De Valera, however, was always insistent that the Unionists of the North are as Irish as he was.[16] The terrorists are more consistent, but such consistency is no kind of moral virtue.

8.16   That misuse of 'the people' is dazzlingly dishonest and/or stupid. There are more subtle misuses, one involving 'the people' in its *set-complemental* sense (8.8). The expression 'the people' is familiar in various contrasts. One of these is 'the government and the people'. That is legitimate enough, though loose. What is not legitimate is to conclude that everything wrested from or relinquished by the Government thereby goes to the people. *The people* and *The Government* are not two individuals or even two institutions, between whom all goods are divided. Similar tricks can be played with 'the state and the people' or 'the state and the individual' (e.g., J. M. Fraser, 1981). I have seen a letter-to-the-editor in which the 'privatisation' of government enterprises was characterised as giving 'the State's usurped power back to the people where it belongs' (Sherrard, 1985). This implies that, if the Government sells Telecom to Mr Mandragon the millionaire, Mr Mandragon is The People (or *The Individual* (I have often wondered who *that* is): see Mabbott, 1947: ch. viii). On the other hand, certain kinds of socialists (11.9F) talk as if *state ownership* were identical with *ownership by the people*. The right-wing sophistry that *the state* and *the people* exhaust all possibilities is evenly matched by the left-wing sophistry that that is true of *the capitalists* and *the people*. For *the will of the people*, see 10.43–10.46.

8.17   'The people' is one of the trickiest and most dangerous of all political phrases. It is also indispensable. That being so, no occurrence of it ought ever be taken for granted or allowed to pass without examination.

Suggested reading

Bell & Willett, 1988; Carew Hunt, 1957: pp. 113–117, 121–131; Priestland, 1988; Scruton, 1983: p. 350.

DEMOCRACY AND THE KRATIC ERROR

8.18   It is not news that the words 'democracy', 'democratic', 'democrat' are both ambiguous and vague, that they have 'emotive force' and all the rest of it. As Hobbes might say, many apply the word 'democratic' to any socio-political thing *liked*, merely because they like it (*Leviathan* ch. xix). What is undemocratic is the socio-political *misliked*. *The Newcastle Herald*, for instance, has condemned the Bank Holiday and state honours which carry titles as 'undemocratic'.[17] This kind of talk has nothing to recommend it. A notion which embraces equality, modernity, justice, and anything else which seems desirable is too vague to be useful. Let us agree that the word 'democracy' refers to *a system (or certain systems) of government and decision-making*. Even that leaves us with considerable problems. There is still the close association between democracy and (as Crick says) All Things Bright and Beautiful. Everyone, I suppose, believes that democracy can be attacked or endangered. Indeed, many people seem to believe that democracy is almost always endangered, that, all over the place, there are anti-democratic individuals, organisations, institutions, practices. The word, however, has become so much a hip-hip-hooray word that many would regard it as inconceivable that anyone would come out and say 'I am against democracy'. I recall a student who argued quite passionately that the democracy of ancient Athens had to be a *false* democracy. The reasoning went something like this:

> Democracy is a good thing.
> Socrates is a good thing.
> Socrates criticises Athenian democracy.

Therefore,

> the Athenian so-called democracy which Socrates criticises must be only so-called.

The argument would have amazed Socrates, who believed that Athenian democracy was a badly flawed system, precisely because it was democratic.[18] Plato developed the criticisms into wholesale condemnations.

8.19   Even before the Second World War, 'democracy' and its cognates could be used in startling ways, provoking T. S. Eliot to say 'Totalitarianism [2.16B] can retain the terms "freedom" and "democracy" and give them its own meaning.' One self-professed British Fascist and admirer of Hitler declared himself 'a firm believer in the democracy of Mazzini, because he places duty to the nation before individual rights'. 'From my point of view,' said Eliot, '. . . [he] has as good a title to call himself a 'believer in democracy' as anyone else' (Eliot, 1939: p. 69). Since that war, the word 'democracy' has taken on all the colours of the rainbow: 'People's Democracies' in which dissent is a crime against the state, 'Democratic Kampuchea' which conducted a campaign of something like genocide against its own people, and (for a worrying while in the 1960s) a neo-Nazi party in Germany called (what else?) *the National Democratic Party*.[19] And midst this tumult, we can hear from far and near, voices proclaiming True Democracy and telling us to beware of fraudulent misrepresentations. But that, too, is a game for any number of players and there is no clear rule which decides the winner. Bernard Crick describes the situation with characteristic cheeky neatness:

> Democracy is perhaps the most promiscuous word in the world of public affairs. She is everybody's mistress and yet somehow retains her magic even when a lover sees that her favours are being, in his light, illicitly shared by many another.

(1982: p. 56)

8.20   But despite this Babel of usages, there seems to be at least one common feature: etymology, *demos* = 'people',[20] *kratia* = 'rule'. To many, this has seemed something solid, a spar we can grasp, a piece of ground on which we can stand. Unfortunately, it is not as solid as it may look. He who professes commitment to democracy usually believes that it is necessary to represent the system of institutions which he supports as something which can, with some plausibility, be described as *rule by the people*. Such a professed democrat tends to see himself as someone who has answered the question: 'Who should rule?' by: 'The people should rule.' This kind of outlook creates a tendency to see (or to present) issues in terms of 'Whose opinions, interests, moral judgements should be decisive? The people's or those of some other group?' And, it seems, the democrat must answer 'The people's and no one else's'. Thus, on this view, the basic political question was formulated by Humpty Dumpty in *Through the Looking Glass*:

'The question is which is to be the master – That is all.'

And that *is* all – or so it seems to many democrats when they are thinking abstractly about politics – except to invent institutions which will enable the people's opinion to be heard and to be effective. That goes along with a widespread view that can be styled *simple democratism*: 'If there is not unanimity amongst the people, the majority must prevail; If the people cannot all meet in the Athenian agora or the Anglo-Saxon folkmoot, then they must choose representatives; The sole task of the representatives is to carry out the wishes of all the people, if that is possible, or of the majority if it is not. In practice, it is the will of the majority.' I have often been told that 'Democracy means that whatever the majority wants must prevail and it is the duty of the minority to shut up and obey.' It is further held that this is the only legitimate way of managing collective affairs, and that adherence to it is the criterion for distinguishing the friends of freedom from the friends of tyranny, the political sheep from the political goats.

8.21   Unfortunately, this way of thinking is not so plain, so clear, so intelligible, so self-evidently satisfactory as it might appear to many. The proposition that the task of legislature and government is the purely *executive* one of carrying into effect an already existing public opinion assumes that, on every issue requiring governmental or legislative decision, there is such an already existing public opinion. And that seems unlikely.[21] In addition, the concept of *the people* is itself rather slippery (see 8.1–8.17). Is the people one class amongst others in the community, so that democracy is rule by that class (or members of it) to the exclusion of all other classes? That was how the Greeks thought of it and it was that notion of democracy which so worried the American Whigs and was a nagging anxiety for many supporters of electoral reform in England (see, e.g., Mill's *Representative Government* and 8.25 below). Most of the democrats we are likely to meet take a more inclusive view of the people. They prefer to think of *the Xlandic people* as *the Xlandic citizenry*: 'all of us'. But that, however sincere and well-meant, leaves us with many problems and can end up no less exclusive than the Greek notion. Naive talk of 'the will of the people' implies an exaggerated view of the possibility, desirability and necessity of social solidarity, and that can lead to ways of talk and thought which excommunicate whole sectors of the citizenry from The People. In really pathological, tyrannical cases, such ways of talk are deliberate attempts to outlaw dissenters, to exclude them from consideration, not merely as members of the people, but even from consideration as *people*: hence, the paradoxical-sounding but all-too-genuine possibilities of *authoritarian democracy* and *totalitarian democracy* (see, e.g., T. S. Eliot, 1939: pp. 19–20, 69; Jouvenel, 1952: ch. xiv; Talmon, 1970). Hence also, Democratic Kampuchea. As long ago as 1798, John Adams told the citizens of Westmoreland County, Virginia, that

> The declaration that our People are hostile to a government made by themselves, for themselves, and conducted by themselves, is an insult.
>
> (Quoted, B. Stevenson, n.d.: p. 431)

No doubt he Meant Well, but his assertion implies that to call a government 'democratic' is to place it beyond opposition. By implication, he endorses that important (but not often acknowledged) principle of so many new democracies of the late twentieth century: 'One man, one vote, once only.'[22]

8.22 Talk of 'true democracy' and 'false democracy' is often an attempt to exorcise that kind of embarrassment. The word 'populist' has been used in similar fashion: when a leader obviously has a great deal of support despite the fact that you disapprove of him, you might call him *a populist*, a word which seems to have acquired of late a very derogatory tone and saves you from the embarrassment of having to say 'democratic but tyrannical' or 'democratic but dotty' (8.30–8.37). But such moves are desperate attempts to save an untenable theory.[23] They are also evidence that most simple democrats are far too sane and decent to be consistent. Simple democratism emphasises the 'Who' of decision-making to the total neglect of the 'What' (see Jouvenel, 1957: introd. and *passim*). Whatever he might *say* in his more theoretical moments, a sane simple democrat cannot consistently hold to that view. That is especially so if he is serious about his commitment to freedom. Indeed, its pro-freedom element condemns simple democratism to inconsistency and preserves it from beastliness. (There should be a special day, once a year, set apart for the celebration of beneficent and sane self-contradictions.)

8.23 Democracy can be oppressive, dictatorial, tyrannical, but that is not the most piquant of its paradoxes. The decisions of a sovereign *demos* may, in content, be *anti-democratic*. The *demos* may decide to hand over power to a tyrant, a monarch, an aristocracy or what it wills. There is nothing logically impossible about such a decision. Indeed, such decisions have been made. Their possibility involves a democrat of the the-people-should-rule variety in a self-contradiction:

Let a decision of the type just spoken of be styled 'D-type'. Let the proposition that *the people should rule and the people's will should prevail in all circumstances* be styled 'E'. Since D-type decisions are possible, a democrat who asserts E is involved in a self-contradiction.

That paradox concerns decisions about constitutional law. There is another paradox for the simple democrat:

> Someone who is a democrat will (obviously) prefer democracy, but he will also have preferences about other matters which can come under governmental or legislative consideration. (If he had not, he would be very odd.)
> Suppose he supports proposal F.
> Then he wants proposal F to be carried into effect.
> But, being a democrat, he also wants whatever proposal receives the support of the people (i.e., usually, of a majority of them) to be carried into effect.
> If the people reject proposal F and accept proposal G instead, then he both wants proposal F to be carried into effect and wants it to be rejected; and he both wants proposal G to be rejected and wants it to be carried into effect.

(See Popper, 1966: ch. vii and notes thereon; Wollheim, 1962; Barry, 1979; Fishkin, 1979.)

8.24   It is important to notice that these paradoxes afflict not only democracy, but also *every other* political attitude which treats 'Who should rule?' as the basic political question. But they are not inescapable paradoxes. We can *avoid* the first paradox by refusing to accept 'Who should rule?' as the fundamental political question. We can *dissolve* the second paradox if we distinguish *questions concerning the quality of proposals from questions concerning the method of deciding between differing proposals*:

> One can, without self-contradiction, say that policy F is superior to policy G and should be adopted for reasons R, S and T, but that we should abide by policy G because it has been adopted by method M which we support for reasons U, V and W.

One can even, without self-contradiction, say that policy Q is so morally monstrous that we will not abide by it, despite the fact that it was adopted by means of a method which we usually support. (One would hope, of course, that the need for taking such an attitude would not arise.)

8.25   But where does that leave me with respect to democracy and democratic theory? I have rejected the view which I have labelled 'simple democratism'. Does that involve the rejection either of democratic institutions or of democratic values? It does not. There are political attitudes which can plausibly be called 'democratic' but do not involve treating 'Who should rule?' as the basic political question. When the Practical Men of the 1880s said that the labouring classes were unfit to govern, Lord Acton replied:

> Every class is unfit to govern. The law of liberty tends to abolish the reign

of race over race, of faith over faith, of class over class. It is not the realisation of a political ideal: it is the discharge of a moral obligation.[24]

Splendid as that quotation is, it does become rather woolly – the very finest Merino, but wool nonetheless. How does 'the law of liberty' do this (and do it not once and for all, but continually)? The answer lies in the existence and working of socio-political institutions: not The Answer in the sense of a removal of the problem, but a necessary condition for its satisfactory management. Freedom is not a static property (like having a high IQ), but a continual activity in the face of opposing tendencies (like living intelligently). Sir Karl Popper, for instance, says that the question we should ask is not 'Who should rule?' but 'How can we so organise political institutions that bad or incompetent rulers can be prevented from doing too much damage?' I agree with Popper on that and I also agree with him that a satisfactory answer to that question must include reference to some institutions of the type usually called 'democratic' (e.g., free and fair elections and a party-system which facilitates dissent and peaceful competition). But that does not imply that *all* institutions (even all political institutions) should be democratic in the sense that positions in them are elective or that decisions by them are reached by popular vote. The Popperish doctrine is one of checks-and-balances, which aligns it with conventional and traditional liberalism (11.10). What might seem rather unconventional and untraditional is the frank avowal that we need checks and balances to restrain King Demos himself from folly and tyranny (i.e., 'from doing too much damage').

8.26 Actually, it is not as unfamiliar an idea as it might look. John Stuart Mill is a culture-hero of liberal theory, and the need to guard against the fallibility and peccability of King Demos is one of his central ideas.[25] But what about liberal practice? The same thing can be found there, too. When constitutions (or parts of them deemed especially important) are 'entrenched', i.e., made more difficult to amend than most law, that is (at least partly) an attempt to stop King Demos from acting too hastily. Even many people who profess simple democracy, who use 'undemocratic' exclusively as a term of condemnation, and who would be shocked and angry if it were applied to them, are at times willing to make King Demos a constitutional monarch, not an absolute emperor whose every word is law (cf. Sitwell, 1949). Even *The Newcastle Herald* (whose ardent democratism I have noted in 8.18) has recommended a four-year parliament (rather than three-year) on the ground that electoral considerations can be too much of a distraction from the task of government, especially in economic matters. This is a radical departure from simple democratism. The Chartists wanted annual parliaments to ensure the absolute sovereignty of the people. In the frenzied late 1960s, Anthony Wedgwood Benn and others dreamt of an electronic utopia in which people, having viewed the evening news on television, would press various buttons and a computer in Whitehall (or Canberra) would print out the instructions to be followed by Parliament and Government. Indeed, under such a regime,

Parliament would wither away as redundant. The will (or rather, the impulses) of the people would rule. (I doubt that even *your* impulses are much more reliable than mine. (See Bosanquet, 1923: pp. 111–112).) See also 10.43–10.46.

8.27   We must reject the question 'Who should rule?' Although it is possible to support certain institutions usually called *democratic* without involving oneself in those paradoxes, it is nevertheless true that much discourse in which the word 'democracy' occurs plunges into them, head over heels. The Humpty-Dumptyan thesis that the basic political question is 'Who should rule? Who is to be the master?' is a deep-rooted part of political folklore. Since that thesis *inevitably* involves its proponents in logical confusion, it *must* be wrong (*modus tollens*: see TP 6.16). For that reason, I call the thesis *the kratic error*. The word 'democracy', it seems to me, should be reserved for a range of *methods* of decision-making. If there is a kratic error, there is also a *demotic error*, which is committed by those who forget or underemphasise the point that democracy *is* concerned with ruling, with governing, not just with expression of opinion or with presenting an accurate picture of popular opinion. One of the fathers of Australian Federation[26] said that Parliament should be 'the mirror of the nation's mind'. If that is literally so, Parliament is superfluous, unless the suggestion is that the nation cannot know what its mind is like unless it looks at Parliament. Even then, a mere reflection would be little better than a map on the scale 1:1. Neither is it true that Parliament should be an *epitome* of the nation's mind, reproducing in little all its important thoughts. The nation's mind contains even more conflicts than yours or mine (10.21–10.31). The point of Parliament is to resolve (or even override) those conflicts which need resolving (or overriding) so that things can be done and so that people can have reasonable expectations of a secure life. (For *representation and democracy*, see 2.17.)

Suggested reading

Bullock, 1988(a); Scruton, 1983: pp. 115–118; Barry, 1979; Burnheim, 1985; Carew Hunt, 1957: pp. 7–10, 53–56, 113–117, 124–127; Crick, 1982: ch. iii; Dahl, 1979, 1989; Fishkin, 1979; Hanson, 1989; G. C. Lewis, 1898: ch. ix; Lively, 1975; Lucas, 1976; McCoy & Playford, 1967; Macpherson, 1973, 1977; Maddox, 1986; Pateman, 1970; Percy, 1954; Popper, 1966: ch. vii; R. Robinson, 1964: pp. 228–253; Singer, 1973(a); Srzednicki, 1987; Wollheim, 1962.

For *the referendum* and democracy, see Bogdanor, 1981; Braham & Burton, 1975; Munro-Clark, 1992: pp. 37–68.

INDUSTRIAL DEMOCRACY

8.28   Herbert Kaufman (1968: p. 66) contrasts *the industrial democracies* with *the undeveloped countries* and *the industrialised dictatorships*; i.e., he uses the term to mean *industrialised democratic polity*. In the same encyclo-pedia, however, Sartori (1968(a): p. 114) uses it to mean *the application of democratic ideas on decision-making and management to industry*, a sense which is rarely used in the plural. It is Sartori's sense with which I am concerned here.

The detection of that ambiguity does not render the term crystal-clear, since 'industrial democracy' embodies most of the slipperiness of its second word (8.18–8.19). Broadly speaking, demands for industrial democracy are demands that the workers in an enterprise or an industry should have some share in its management or control. Note that word 'some', a perfectly ordinary, quite clear little word, which ranges in its meaning from the smallest particle of something to its totality (*TP* 6.29A (vi)). Hence, a distinction is drawn between *participation* and *control*. But the question still remains 'How much control?' And control over what, the whole productive and distributive process, or something less? How should *control* be exercised? By mass meetings of all, each to count as one and none for more than one,[27] or representative institutions? Who is to count as a worker? What weight is to be given to expertise? to consumer or public interest? Etc., etc. (Hence the sceptical epigram 'We participate, you participate, THEY control.')

These remarks are not intended as a rubbishing of industrial-democracy-talk. They are intended to show that, if all you know about Mr X is that he is a sincere believer in industrial democracy, X remains an unknown quantity. See 2.17L.

Suggested reading

Marsh, 1979: pp. 147–148 and references therefrom; Scruton, 1983: pp. 220–221; French & Saward, 1983: pp. 146–147; Balfour, 1973; Broekmeyer, 1970; *CW*, 1944: ch. vi; Chamberlain, 1967; Derrick & Phipps, 1969; J. Elliott, 1978; Emery & Thorsrud, 1969; Hackney, 1958; John XXIII, 1962; Radice, 1974; Tabb & Goldfarb, 1970; Wolin, 1961: ch. x.

DEMAGOGUE, DEMAGOGUERY

8.29 Originally and literally, the Greek word *demagogos* meant *a leader of the people as distinct from other sections of the polis* (8.9, 3.1); i.e. (usually), a leader of the less privileged or plebeian many as distinct from the wealthy or aristocratic few. The word, however, acquired a derogatory meaning: the power-hungry egomaniac, the unscrupulous manipulator, the irresponsible ranting fanatic, the crowd-captivating confidence trickster. Greek politics was a *vocal* business, and the connection with *oratory* was part of the word's neutral meaning. In the derogatory meaning, the connection is with oratory which appeals to irrational motives and urges irrational action. (The use of such methods is *demagoguery*.) Some English writers of the seventeenth and eighteenth centuries used 'demagogue' neutrally, but that is long obsolete. In contemporary English, the word is always derogatory. Its career is like that of 'sophist' (TP 7.3C). There are two very different reasons for this development:

1 Some of those to whom the word can be applied in its neutral sense exercise their leadership in a way that deserves the derogatory sense. Crooks and crackpots dragged the word down.
2 The other reason is upper-class propaganda, the pretence that the opposition is always led by crooks or crackpots and that there would never be serious unrest if it were not for '*trouble-makers*'.

Two of Sperber and Trittschuh's examples (1964: pp. 116–117) are worth meditating on:

> There are as many and as dangerous aristocratical demagogues as there are democratical.
>
> (John Adams, 1808)

> I had begun to suspect that, whenever a man in public life was called a demagogue, there was something good in him, something dangerous to the system. And that since the plutogogues[28] could not fasten any crime on him they fell back on the all-sufficient charge that he was a demagogue.
>
> (Lincoln Steffens, 1934)

We need a word to refer to the sort of leader whose oratorical powers create a huge popular following, who (like Cola di Rienzo: see 8.5) seems to be able to turn a huge multitude of individuals into a united quasi-kin-group. The non-derogatory sense (even if it could be revived) does not say enough. The derogatory sense says too much. We need a word which will simply describe such people. There are not a great many of them, but they are immensely various: e.g., Rienzo, Hitler, Yeltsin, three men with very little in common except for their capacity to move crowds and create an enthusiastic following and for their dependence on that capacity. 'Charismatic leader' will not do. It lacks the necessary connection with oratory and wide popularity. Apart from that, it is far too messy. Even Max Weber, who introduced the term, used it confusedly. Later social theorists and political commentators have made 'charisma' mean something like 'glamour' or 'socio-political oomph'.[29] (See Howard, 1980: ch. iii; Shils, 1975: pp. 256–275; B. R. Wilson, 1975.) As for 'populist', that word is in an even worse mess (8.30–8.40).

Suggested reading

OED 'Demagogue'; Scruton, 1983: pp. 115, 58; Sperber & Trittschuh, 1964: pp. 116–117; Andreski, 1968(b); Bell, 1988(b); B. R. Wilson, 1975; T. Wolfe, 1987.

POPULISM

(i) 'Populism' as the self-chosen name of a party or movement

8.30 The Russian *Narodniks* (*narod* = 'the common people') were intellectuals who believed that the Russian peasants possessed a vast fund of wisdom and virtue and could be the makers of a revolution which would transform Russia into a classless society, without the need of going through the 'stage' of capitalism. The principal Narodnik writers were Alexander Herzen and Michael Bakunin. In the summer of 1873, hundreds of Narodnik students descended upon the peasants, telling them that they were the salt of the earth and the hope of Russia, and urging them to (largely peaceful) revolution. The peasants were not impressed and reported them to the police. This failure was one of the things that convinced Lenin that revolution had to be the work of a comparatively small, tightly organised and violent group, a 'vanguard of the people', rather than the people at large (see 8.14, 11.14B). 'Narodnik' is often translated as 'populist' (see Worsley, 1969: p. 219).

8.31 In 1891, an American organisation called 'The People's Party' changed its name to 'Populist' for the very practical reason that you can call someone 'a Republican' or 'a Democrat' but you cannot call him 'a People's' (Sperber & Trittschuh, 1964: p. 331). The Narodniks saw *the people* as a group distinct from themselves that needed just a little prompting from outside. The American Populists definitely saw themselves as members of *the people*, those who were not being served by the established parties and were being exploited by monopolies. Theirs was basically a rural party, though attempts were made (on both sides) to establish links with trade unions. The Populists' policies on electoral procedures were aimed at giving the electors a stronger and more direct role in government. They included the direct, popular election of Senators (then chosen by State legislatures) and of the President, votes for women, the use of primary elections for party nominations, and the referendum and initiative. Their economic policies included state ownership of railways, a graduated income tax, controls on interest rates, a currency not tied to the gold standard ('fiat money'), the breaking up of monopolies, stricter controls on banking, government loans and other assistance to farmers, and an eight-hour day for industrial workers. Although the Populist Party did not survive the 1890s, most of its electoral proposals have been adopted.[30] Even many of their economic proposals became part of government policy (especially under F. D. Roosevelt's New Deal), though it would be a mistake to ascribe all (or even most) of that to Populist Party influence.

(ii) Populism as an American tradition

8.32 American historians talk about a *populist tradition*. This seems to be related not so much to the policies of the Populist Party as to a world-view which went along with, or seems to have gone along with, or is alleged by someone or other to have gone along with those policies. One of these elements is a particular notion of the people as a homogeneous and righteous body as contrasted with its exploiters and oppressors. One convention of the party declared that 'A majority of the people can never be corruptly influenced' (quoted Hicks, 1968: p. 15; cf. 8.13, 8.21). Another Populist manifesto declared that

> there are but two sides in the conflict that is being waged in this country today. On the one side are the allied hosts of monopolies, the money power, great trusts and railroad corporations, who seek the enactment of laws to benefit them and impoverish the people. On the other are the farmers, laborers, merchants, and all other people who produce wealth and bear the burdens of taxation . . . . Between these two there is no middle ground.
>
> (Quoted, Hofstadter, 1968: p. 60)

This is a rather simple view of socio-economic conflict and suggests that the solutions must be simple. There is also a tremendous emphasis on America as 'the last, best hope', an ideal picture of it as a land of liberty, equality and prosperity. The ideal is seen as something from which America has sadly receded, under the influence of 'the money power' and other oppressors, but also as something which will be attained if, but only if, the people have the power. (See also 2.14G (*the powerful and the powerless*).)

8.33   I am not sure what emphasis should be placed on these and other 'theoretical' or 'ideological' assertions[31] of the Populists. I have no doubt that virtually all Populists believed them and believed also that they provided a justification for their practical proposals, but the practical proposals were primary. Theodore Saloutos says:

> The Populists drafted various documents and resolutions that were geared to immediate action. Like most Americans, they were long on action and short on theory, but they knew what they were after.
>
> (Saloutos, 1968(b): p. 113)

The Populists, like other politicians, were voluble, and there is a vast amount of primary literature, some of it 'theoretical' or 'ideological'. Various historians have put in a thumb here and a thumb there and pulled out plums of diverse kinds. On the basis of these discoveries, some have argued that the Populist tradition is basically humanitarian, liberal, reformist. Others have argued that it is basically authoritarian, intolerant and even paranoid. Edward Shils alleged that the Populist tradition 'is so powerful that it influences reactionaries like [Senator Joseph] McCarthy and left-wing radicals and great upperclass personalities like Franklin Roosevelt' (quoted, Woodward, 1968: p. 81). To me, a non-American non-historian, the only significant feature shared by Roosevelt and McCarthy is that they were both American politicians who professed to respect the people and to champion its interests. All American (and most non-American) politicians sometimes make noises like some of the noises made by the Populist Party. So?

(iii) 'Populism' as a combination technical-term/term-of-abuse in the writings of political scientists

8.34 A politician may be popular (in an uncomplicated, ordinary sense of that word (8.10 n.)), yet authoritarian, intolerant and no meticulous observer of the decencies of debate or the rules of the game. He may also have quite a lot of nice things to say about The People (see 8.11). Of one such, it has been said:

> Bjelke-Petersen is a leader of a classically populist kind, orchestrating the supposed grievances of 'the people', identifying the will of 'the people' with morality and justice (and putting it above other social standards and mechanisms), and insisting on a direct relationship between people and government, largely independent of institutions and their petty constraints.
>
> (Walter & Dickie, 1985: p. 38)

The term has been applied also to Perón of Argentina,[32] to various unpleasant governors in the southern USA during the controversies over 'integration' in the 1950s and 1960s, to people like Mayor Daley of Chicago and even to Hitler. I am tempted to say that calling someone *a populist* in this sense is only a posh, social (pseudo-)scientific way of saying that he is a successful demagogue (8.29) who deserves to be thoroughly disapproved of. That, however, would be far too swift. There *is* a syndrome of argument and rhetoric (*TP* 8.4) which is being referred to. The word here *could* have a clear sense, were it not for the other uses and for the fact that, used in this sense, it is definitely derogatory. I too am against most political figures who are populist in this sense, but I do not see why I must be committed by definition to disapprove of all of them. There are definitely snobbish overtones to this use of 'populist' – a rapid writing-off of both 'the populist' and his following as *canaille*, 'peasants' in the slang sense. A replacement word is urgently needed: 'populite'? 'authoritarian democratist'? Perhaps we just have to say 'populist in the sense that he talks a great deal about the people and uses that talk as a justification for illiberal and/ or unconstitutional action'.

8.35 'Populist' in something like this sense can be used (quite dishonestly) to avoid collision with the Principle that Democracy means All Things Bright and Beautiful (8.18). If we disapprove of the way Xlanders use their votes, we can say 'in Xland, they do not have democracy. They have (ugh!) Populism.' But it would still be imprudent to say, straight-out, 'The Xlandic people are wrong' (8.13).

(iv) 'Populist' in contemporary Australian political discourse

8.36 'Populist' is a very fashionable word in Australia just now. Some use it because they regard it merely as a sophisticated substitute for 'popular':

> ... twice elected to the Supreme Soviet by populist vote.
>
> (D. Evans, 1991)

Her populist support was no match for the . . . cabal of the armed forces, the fundamentalist Muslim groups . . .[etc.]

(Loudon & Pillai, 1990)

. . . governments noted more for their populist appeal than for responsible policies.

(*SMH*, 1991(a))

The third of those quotations may not be quite as silly as the others. There is one current Australian use of the word which appears to mean something like 'playing to the gallery', 'taking an easy, short-term line which solves nothing and avoids hard but necessary decisions' (this also links it with *demagoguery* in the disparaging sense (8.29, 8.34)):[33]

Mr Howard's speech was political rather than economic in substance. It made few attacks on the Budget apart from a populist comment that taxes should have been reduced . . . .

(*NH*, 1988)

Calling for a reduction in immigration intake now is short-sighted and populist. It might be popular with the mob but doesn't do anything for the nation's economic interest.

(Norington, 1991. The words are those of the Secretary of the Labor Council of NSW, not of Coriolanus)

There, the word seems to be saying something. Sometimes, however, it seems no more than a vague term of abuse, e.g.:

. . . it is probably asking too much to expect populist politicians . . .to have the subtlety or wisdom to understand that any society which . . .[etc., etc., etc.]

(Burton, 1991)

Using the word 'populist' in these senses (or non-senses) is best avoided as a noisy nuisance.

(v) Concluding remarks

8.37   The hardliners' anti-Gorbachev coup collapsed on 23 August 1991. That afternoon, I listened to a radio discussion between Sovietologists. One said that he did not have a high opinion of Mr Yeltsin: 'I think he's really just a populist with no very clear idea of where he's going.' A few hours later, I heard a television pundit contrast Mr Gorbachev and Mr Yeltsin as 'the party-man and the populist'.

8.38   One man, one word, two meanings. The second speaker seems to be making the point that, whereas Mr Gorbachev owed his position and his legitimacy at least partly to his position in the Party, Mr Yeltsin had left that Party and was reliant entirely on the electorate. There may also be a *class* element: Mr Gorbachev is a rather *bourgeois* Communist, and Mr Yeltsin has a quite different style (see 8.9 and its quotation from *OED*). That is evaluatively neutral. There is no contradiction in adding either 'therefore, hooray for Yeltsin' or 'therefore, hooray for Gorbachev'. The radio pundit's remark is, however, distinctly derogatory. He seems to be saying that Yeltsin is good at creating a following and a bonny fighter, but not good at either making or executing policy; i.e., in the terminology of 3.30–3.40, his political skills belong to the 'south' of the concept of politics rather than to its 'north'. I do not think that the pundit is saying that Yeltsin is a crowd-pleasing chooser of soft options (8.36), but he may be.

8.39   Peter Wiles says that populism is 'a syndrome, not a doctrine' (1969: pp. 166–179). It is much worse than that: it isn't an *it* at all. The concept is fractured into little bits, some of which have little if any connection with the others. Perhaps it would be better if the word vanished altogether, except as the name of two long-dead political organisations, one Russian, the other American. Unfortunately, it is not going to do that in a hurry.

8.40   A rare non-pejorative use of 'populist' occurs in Gyford & Haseler, 1971. They distinguish two strands in modern democratic socialism (11.9F): *liberal-progressivism* (concerned with 'permissive legislation, the arts, higher education and technical efficiency') and *Labour-populism* (concerned with 'housing, employment and the cost of living'). They argue that, in the British Labour Party in the 1960s and early 1970s, the former strand received too much emphasis, the latter too little. Crosland agrees with them, but finds the terminology embarrassing (1974: ch. iv).

Suggested reading

Jaensch & Teichmann, 1988: pp. 160–161; Ryan, 1988(b); Scruton, 1983: pp. 363, 312; Sperber & Trittschuh, 1964: pp. 331, 312; Saloutos, 1968(a); Ionescu & Gellner, 1969; Walter, 1990.

9   Morality and politics

MORALITY

9.1   Like the word 'politics', 'moral',[1] 'morally' and 'morality' are part of our ordinary vocabulary, perfectly familiar, but very difficult to unpack. Indeed, explicating 'moral', etc. is even harder than explicating 'politics'. We are inclined to say things like 'Morality is concerned with what is right and wrong, with what is good and bad.' True. But it is not concerned with right and wrong ways of using a shovel or a soup-spoon, or with good and bad omelettes or poems. Moral standards, judgements, problems, reasoning, etc. are to be distinguished from standards, judgements, problems, reasoning, etc. which are (e.g.) aesthetic or technical. Moral rules are to be distinguished from rules of etiquette, grammar, etc.

9.2   So moral rightness or wrongness, goodness or badness are a special type of rightness, wrongness, goodness, badness. What distinguishes them from other types? There we stick again. Someone might say 'rightness or wrongness of *conduct*, goodness or badness of *character*'. But that is not as helpful as it might sound. If 'conduct' means *human action*, then etiquette and grammar are also concerned with conduct. If 'character' means *personality* or *the kind of person someone is*, then just about anything gets in: the kind of person who enjoys travel, the kind of person who falls asleep in front of the television.

'No, no, I mean conduct and character in a different sense.'

Well, *what* sense? I suspect that it is a *moral* sense, which does not help us. Definitions of the moral in terms of conduct and character (great favourites of dictionaries) seem to work only because words like 'conduct' and 'character' tend to have 'moral' built into them: human action and personality *seen from a moral point of view*.

9.3   The problem is, of course, *not* that we do not know the meaning of 'moral'. If someone says, 'It's true that So-and-so was a very cruel man, but he was not immoral,' and someone else replies, 'You've got a very narrow notion of morality,' we understand what is being said (1.14).

Primus writes a poem. Secundus reads it and says, 'I find your poem morally objectionable.' 'Why?' Primus demands. Secundus replies, 'It lacks rhythm and

the vocabulary fails to fit together with either itself or the theme.' Primus
concludes that he is playing the fool or that he does not know English very
well. Tertius wonders whether what Secundus is trying to do in a very clumsy
way is to accuse Primus of laziness, of falling short of the effort required of a
poet, of (perhaps) treating his audience contemptuously. That would make the
accusation intelligible, though it would still be clumsy.

That connects morality with *ideals* (the sort of effort that befits a poet) and
with *attitudes to others*.

9.4 If I were to say: 'I've got a moral problem on my hands. I want to buy a
car and I don't know what kind of car to buy,' you would at first wonder
whether I am crazy. Then, perhaps, you might come to the conclusion that I
want to know what kind of car is safest, least wasteful of precious resources,
least polluting to the atmosphere. I might also, you think (and you are being
very charitable), want to know how to avoid unnecessary ostentation and how
best to spend the money which is not merely my own but also my family's.
Apart from those considerations of safety, the use of resources and avoidance
of arrogant display, the problem of what kind of car to buy is not, cannot be a
moral problem. We all know that.

9.5 Notice again a tie-up to ideals of the sort of person worth aspiring to be,
another tie-up to possible effects on others, to the use of things we hold in
common, and to loyalties to others. Those seem to be important features of
what we regard as of moral significance. I am not saying that all of those
features are always present when we regard something as of moral significance, or that they are the only factors making for moral significance. I do say
that *each* of them is *a* feature which makes for moral significance.

9.6 Another frequent feature of the moral seems to be that it is of overriding
importance. If Primus says something like 'Of course, it's morally wrong but
that doesn't matter,' he has made a rather puzzling utterance. Secundus might
be inclined to explain it away by making guesses at 'what he really means'.
'What he really means', Secundus says, 'is that it is against some *conventional*
moral rule, but that he rejects that conventional moral rule. He doesn't really
mean that what he is talking about is morally wrong. That's not the moral
judgement he's *really* making. The moral judgement he's really making is that
whatever it is is morally permissible.'

9.7 I am by no means sure that Secundus is right (though he would be
supported by many moral philosophers), but, however that may be, the
example indicates that, normally, to say that something is morally wrong is to
say that there are reasons against doing it which override any reasons for
doing it, whatever kinds of reason those other reasons might be: reasons
concerned with prudence, profit, pleasure, etc. What is morally right is what
befits a human being to try to do or be. That is not an endorsement of any
particular morality, but an attempt to bring out what is meant by saying that
something is morally right. At the same time, this notion of the overridingness
of moral reasons does not rule out the possibility that the moral reasons for
doing something may still not make it the most attractive of available things to

do. Moral reasons are often in competition with other reasons and they do not invariably win, even when they are recognised as moral reasons. Moral ideals, then, are ideals that we can fall short of. While the morally good and the morally right are what befits a human being to try to do or be, moral considerations can clash with inclination, advantage, interest, though some would want to say not with long-run or 'deep' inclination, advantage, interest (cf. McCabe, 1979).

9.8   Much is written and said of the 'diversity of morals' amongst different societies, classes, periods, but it is important to notice that there are also great similarities. Truth-telling, for instance. There are differences about how widely the obligation to tell the truth extends (about everything? or only about some things? to everyone? or only to some people?), but it is hard to imagine a language in which the word corresponding to 'liar' is a mere neutral word of description, like 'farmer' or 'redhead'. The keeping of faith (i.e., fidelity to promises, and the like) is another common element. Societies may differ on the depth and breadth of this obligation. Perhaps some may hold up as a model a person who is prepared to risk his life in order to keep something roughly equivalent to a dinner engagement, while, in other societies, such a person would be regarded as a neurotic, misguided ass. Some societies may regard treachery to foreigners as quite permissible. Others may not – indeed, do not. But it is difficult to imagine a morality which did not make some sort of fuss about the keeping of faith.

9.9   Much has been said about diversity of sexual morality. *Some* of the things said owe more to the overheated imaginations of western observers than to careful observation (see, e.g., Freeman, 1983). But, whatever the differences, most moral codes agree in treating sex as something particularly likely to raise moral problems, partly, perhaps, because it is seen as related in some way to the need to keep faith with other people. A distinguished biologist, the late Bede Morris, made dizzy by the moral and social problems arising from genetic engineering, declared that we could solve the problems by 'divorcing the procreative act from religious and moral and ethical considerations' (Merson *et al.*, 1982), i.e., if we can persuade ourselves that it is utterly trivial, we won't be troubled by any problems about it. Clever.

9.10   Again, notions of kinship vary from society to society, but it is probably only in our own time that substantial numbers of people have declared kinship to be of no moral significance at all. Another area which has always and everywhere been treated as of moral significance is the taking and preserving of human life. That is not to say that all societies take the same view on it, but it is always something hedged about by rules and treated as of great importance. And, certainly, amongst ourselves, even though we may disagree about what the word 'moral' means and about what is morally right and wrong, there is agreement that that is an area of moral significance.

> 'Which is the more effective weapon for killing the enemy: the FN rifle or the good old .303?'
> 'Should we be killing the enemy at all?'

If anyone says that he does not understand what is meant by saying that the second of these is a moral question and that the first is not, then he is simply not telling the truth about himself.

9.11 Another feature of the authentically moral is a certain kind of *impartiality*, perhaps *universalisability*, if not that, then *generalisability* (see *TP* 9.5). If Primus says that it is morally all right for him to xify, then he is committed to saying that it is morally all right for anyone to xify or give some good reason why. As Antony Flew says, 'Everyone knows why we impugn the sincerity of the selective moralist; or, better, "moralist".' Flew's example is someone who professes strong moral disapproval of the use of poison gas, but only when used by forces which he does not favour. When those he favours use it, he says nothing (Flew, 1975: p. 81). We are entitled to suspect that that person is using the language of moral judgement, not to make moral judgements, but as a weapon.

9.12 We must, however, distinguish 'authentically moral' from 'morally good' or 'morally correct'. One can recognise an attitude, or a principle, or a judgement as authentically moral without having to approve of it or agree with it. 'Be kind to members of your own clan but to no one else.' That would be an expression of an authentically moral attitude, but not one which I would accept. Moral attitudes and moral judgements can be immoral. It is also possible that we might need to say that at least some inauthentic moralities are nevertheless moralities. Flew's selective moralist, let us suppose, is *not* pretending: he really does run his life on the principle that there is one set of moral rules and values for himself and those he likes and a quite different set for everyone else. Clearly, he is sunk deep in a mire of bad faith (*TP* 9.6E), but, since that is what he lives by, it is his morality. (See Stevenson's *Kidnapped* ch. xviii.)

9.13 Any morality is concerned with the taking and preserving of human life, with sex, with promising, with property, with the infliction and the relief of pain, because these are important matters for the lives of human beings. Moral judgements on these topics differ, but they are, typically, central parts of the subject matter of morality. Morality, then, concerns matters which are serious or seen as serious (a deliberately cagey formulation). It would seem that there are some matters which a morality must deal with. Are there any matters which a morality *cannot* deal with? Consider:

One should never step on the lines on a pavement; it is important to walk inside the squares. (A)
It is not right to wear brightly coloured clothes. (B)[2]
Always squeeze the toothpaste from the bottom of the tube. (C)

Could these be moral judgements? They do (do they not?) look rather different from 'Thou shalt not kill' or 'Do not break your promises', or even, 'Be loyal to your clan and hate its enemies'. Those concern matters basic to morality, part of the stuff of which morality is made. I think we would be baffled if someone said that A, B and C are amongst his moral *principles*. If something is a principle, it is something basic and it scarcely seems possible that anyone could regard these as basic.

9.14   Could they be moral judgements of a less basic kind? We can begin to make sense of C as a moral judgement if it is related to consideration for others, to the proper use of resources, to the avoidance of self-indulgent and slovenly habits. That is to relate it to matters which seem more obviously moral. We may not *accept* it or we may still say that it is too trivial to be worth making so much fuss about, but when it is tied up to considerations of those kinds, then it begins to make sense as a moral judgement. We can say much the same of B. Taken on its own, it looks like an overblown or overgrown expression of taste. It is one thing to dislike brightly coloured clothes. It is quite another, one might say, to declare that it is not *right* to wear brightly coloured clothes. What on earth could someone who says such a thing be thinking of?

He might say: 'Wearing brightly coloured clothes is ostentatious. People who do it are pushing themselves forward too much and it's something which can lead to destructive competition.' To me, that would seem unduly severe, but I would be able to make sense of it as a moral judgement.

The affirmer of B might take a different line, defending it by talking about worldly vanity. In that case, what he says makes sense as a moral judgement derived from a certain kind of religious outlook. Again, we may not agree with what he says, but we can make sense of it and we can make sense of the claim that he has made a moral judgement.

9.15   But what of A? Here, I can imagine nothing which would make the judgement intelligible. But suppose that we see the person who says this trying conscientiously to act consistently with it, trying to persuade other people to do the same, thinking he deserves to be blamed if he fails to keep within the squares, refusing to give up his policy because it would be convenient for him to do so. There he is, very tired, out in the rain, and with a blister on his foot, but on he goes, avoiding the lines. 'Well, what else can I do?' he says. 'It's a matter of principle.' (Cf. Foot & Harrison, 1954: pp. 104–105.)

This is weird. I would be inclined to say that he is rationalising a neurotic compulsion by treating it *as if* it were a moral judgement. I can make no sense of *it* as a moral judgement. I have no difficulty with the proposition that he is making it as a moral judgement.

9.16   Suppose it was not just a unique individual who affirmed A. Suppose we found a whole community of A-affirmers. They praise people who stay within the squares. They disapprove of people who step on the lines. If someone steps on a line, he feels guilty about it and tries to conceal the fact. They encourage their children to walk within the squares and rebuke them when they do not. They tell stories about heroes and heroines who stayed within the squares despite great inducements to walk on the lines. They also snigger over stories about people who shamelessly walk on the lines.

'Curiouser and curiouser.' All we could say is that here is something we cannot understand, but the reason for that is that these people treat something utterly trivial as if it were a matter of great moral significance.

9.17   My point is that there is a core of topics which we can expect to be central to any moral outlook. But a morality is not just a collection of views about certain areas of activity. It is also a way of thinking and feeling and striving, and it is quite possible that some people may have moral opinions which some others not merely dissent from but also find unintelligible. One can, however, find a view unintelligible while still recognising it as a genuinely moral view. In other words, moralities have both a characteristic *content* and a characteristic *form* (i.e., a morality treats certain topics with a particular kind of concern or emphasis), and it is not impossible that a judgement or attitude may have the characteristic form, but lack characteristic content.

9.18   That, at the moment, is my answer to the questions, 'What is morality', 'What does the word "moral" mean?' It is not a neat answer, not a definition as many people think of definitions, i.e., crisp, authoritative, definitive formulas, settling all questions about the application of the terms, once and for all. But no definition of that kind is available for these terms – or for many of the other terms we use in our attempts to make sense of the world and of ourselves. Explicating such terms is a matter of charting their contours, of 'mapping' them. And one of the advantages of such chartings is that, unlike definitions, they do not even look as if they are the absolute last word on their topic. They encourage further investigation and positively cry out for development and amendment (1.3–1.9).

Suggested reading

Frankena, 1973: chs i, iv–vi; Frankena & Granrose, 1974: pp. 1–37; G. J. Warnock, 1967, 1971: ch. v; B. Williams, 1976: pp. 52–95; Baier, 1965; Foot & Harrison, 1954; McCabe, 1979; Singer, 1973(b); Wallace & Walker, 1970.

MORALISTS AND MORALISM

9.19   In a strictly neutral sense, a moralist is a student of morals, perhaps a moral philosopher or a moral theologian. Perhaps it *suggests* someone largely concerned with what is sometimes called 'practical ethics' or 'applied ethics' and particular cases of conscience (*TP* 9.7B), but that is not a *necessary* feature of those called *moralists* in this neutral sense. Sir Basil Willey's book, *The English Moralists*, contains chapters on such philosophers as Hobbes, Locke, the Cambridge Platonists, and the third Earl of Shaftesbury. It contains also chapters on Sir Thomas Browne and Joseph Addison, who are not usually thought of as philosophers, but they do have a serious concern with problems concerning human conduct, its rightness and wrongness, goodness and badness.[3]

9.20   But, although such people can be called *moralists*, one would not call what they do *moralism*. They do moral philosophy, or moral theory, or moral thinking.[4] The word 'moralist' in that sense is not correlative with 'moralism'. 'Moralism' can sometimes mean *the habit or practice of emphasising moral considerations*, and that sense does seem to have a sense of 'moralist' as a correlative. In this sense, a moralist is one who, while not rejecting as unimportant considerations of pleasure, profit and efficiency, will nevertheless be inclined to ask, 'But is it right, is it just, is it consonant with human dignity, etc.?' Socrates's insistence that inflicting injustice is a much worse misfortune than suffering it is a pure and extreme example of this. ('Extreme' need not be a boo-word. See 11.12A.) *But do we use the words 'moralism' and 'moralist' about such a person if we both agree with him and do not find him a bit of a nuisance?* Perhaps, yes, but there can be a funny smell about it.

9.21   'Moralism' and 'moralist' can also be connected with the notion of *the moral of a story*. Aesop's and La Fontaine's fables are little stories, ending with a general principle about conduct. The moralist, in this sense, is the person who *draws lessons* from events and experiences. He is inclined to say 'That just shows that we should always . . .' or 'That just shows that we should never . . .' Not necessarily a bad habit, *but if he does it too often and aloud, he may well become a self-righteous bore* (see TP 9.6C). That sort of association can give a word a pejorative flavour. A person might also be called a moralist or moralistic on the ground that his moral judgements are too hasty or too simple. He overlooks the complexity of things. Perhaps he is unduly sententious, making insufficient allowance for human shortcomings. Perhaps he assumes that, in any situation of difficulty, there must be one and only one blameworthy party. Perhaps he too facilely divides the world into sheep and goats, into the forces of light and the forces of darkness. Perhaps he is unduly critical of others, insufficiently critical of himself. Perhaps, even, he is a conscious or unconscious crook, like Flew's man with the selective views on poison gas (9.11).

9.22   I am suggesting that the words 'moralism', 'moralist', and (especially) 'moralistic' (see TP 7.1B) are often 'dirt-is-matter-in-the-wrong-place' words (cf. 2.16A (i)). They often suggest an inappropriate, disproportionate, unseasonable, or mistaken application of moral categories, so that, when people tell us that they are against moralism in politics or in foreign affairs, they may not be telling us as much as they think they are. One should not use the derogatory label 'moralistic' *merely* because one disagrees with the views so labelled (or finds them inconvenient). That reduces the word to a mere grunt. To use the word pejoratively of *all* moral views is to make a moral judgement against *all* moral judgements, which is self-refuting. (See TP 9.2, 3.1.)

Suggested reading

Acheson, 1958(b); Berlin, 1969: especially pp. xxvii–xxxiii; Lefever, 1972(b); Midgley, 1981: ch. vii; Schlesinger, 1972.

MORALITY AND POLITICS

> Occasionally, Parliament, like the rest of our lives, even to our eating and apparel could hardly go on if our imaginations were too active about processes.
>
> (George Eliot, *Middlemarch* ch. li, 1965: p. 544)

9.23 The Tough-Minded of the Political Science Departments and of journalism vary between saying that moral judgement has no rightful place in *their* kind of study of politics and saying that moral judgement has no rightful place in *anyone's* study of politics because it has no rightful place in politics.[5] Henry Mayer, for instance, declared, on various occasions, that politics is an *autonomous and amoral* activity, so that (I suppose) making moral judgements about political action is a kind of category mistake, a bit like criticising an Australian Rules player for being offside (TP 3.4B). But *the moral* is not a department of life: it is a way of viewing life, so the thesis that morality is irrelevant to politics (or to anything else) is simply incoherent. It would be one thing to say that *a certain kind* of morality is out of place in, or cannot cope with a certain kind of human situation or department of life. It is quite another to say that there is a certain kind of human situation or department of life about which no moral judgements can be made.

9.24 Apart from that conceptual matter, Mayer's dictum has consequences that seem intuitively unacceptable. Why should politicians be immune from moral assessment? Are we to say that no moral judgement can be made about the involvement of politicians in the shenanigans which preoccupy investigative reporters and Royal Commissions? A boys-will-be-boys attitude to expense-account rorting and casino-protection is, I think, quite misguided, but it is a tolerable attitude. Would it be tolerable to take that attitude to the activities of Pol Pot and Hitler? Behaviourists (*TP* 7.11) have been accused of 'feigning anaesthesia'. Tough-minded refusal to judge such matters would be feigning psychopathy. And if politicians are to have this immunity, why can it not be claimed by every other occupational group? By butchers, bakers, candlestick-makers, orthopaedic surgeons, bankers, burglars, etc.? Business, as they say, is business.

9.25 But perhaps we should treat Mayer's remark not so much as a thesis to be critically considered, but more as a moan of discomfort, an expression of a sense that there is something morally *odd* about politics. According to some paradigms of rationality, political decision-making is an absurd and irrational business, absurd and irrational in ways which make it morally questionable. It is often performed under conditions which restrict the availability of information. Circumstances frequently demand decisions which disrupt carefully thought-out plans (and plans which, moreover, the government may have promised to implement). Political decision-makers can rarely decide on something simply because it seems best to them. Not only do the constraints referred to above get in the way, but there is also the need to have support, hence decision-making involves taking into account the demands and interests and wishes and habits of groups in the country, in the government, in the administration. Not all those demands, etc. will be right and reasonable and it will not always be possible to reject them on those grounds alone. In such cases, this will detract from the rightness and reasonableness of the decision and the processes by which it is reached. How annoying and disappointing it is for technical experts (who, of course, *know* what is *the* right thing to do) when they make carefully reasoned recommendations which the politicians mutilate or reject on the frivolous ground that all hell would break loose if they were implemented.[6] Experts frequently complain that politicians are too short-term in their thinking. Politicians frequently complain that experts are too narrowly focused. Quite often, both are right.

9.26   And, quite apart from any effect on the intrinsic quality of the decisions, this need for support and conciliation means that the politician, in all he says and does, including his participation in decision-making, is constantly looking over his shoulder, judging possibilities at least partly in terms of what other people will think, say and do. Thus, he is not *autonomous* in the way in which we are often told human beings should be.[7] That 'other-directedness' is connected with the fact that politics (at least in countries like our own) is a highly competitive activity of which decision-making is only a part. As a result, the making of important political decisions gets entangled with these competitive considerations. And political decisions, characteristically made in conditions of distraction and lack of certainty, affect the lives, liberties and estates of large numbers of people. Thus, to the extent that political decision-making involves 'playing politics' (4.17), it involves playing politics with human lives and human welfare. Politicians, by their voluntarily chosen profession, must, at least some of the time, 'play politics'. Quite apart from that, they are, by that profession, involved in making decisions on matters of great human importance without full assurance that those decisions will turn out well, sometimes without any such assurance.

9.27   Those are all reasons why my account of political decision-making might seem to support the proposition that politics is an irrational and morally questionable activity. On the matter of certainty, I agree with Aristotle:

> . . . the same degree of precision is not to be expected in all discussions, any more than in all the products of handicraft . . . . it is a mark of an educated mind never to expect more precision in the treatment of any subject than the nature of that subject permits . . . .
>
> (*Nicomachean Ethics* bk I ch. iii, 1976: pp. 64–65)

No more precision and no more certainty than the nature of the case admits, but no less either, especially in important matters such as those dealt with in political decision-making. And when all the precision and certainty that the nature of the case allows has been obtained and a decision has to be made, then there will still be uncertainty and sometimes the possibility of disastrous error, so the politician, having done all that, is still an unprofitable servant. See Jouvenel, 1963: pts iv, vi; Joll, 1979.

9.28 But that, qualitatively speaking, is the epistemological condition common to us all, though there are obvious quantitative differences. As imperfect and dangerous decision-maker, the politician is oneself writ very large. To say of something 'and that is the best we/I can do' need not be complacent. It may well be said as a resigned or anguished recognition of the complexity of things and of one's own limitations. In one of his epigrammatic moments, Oakeshott remarks that 'to try to do something which is inherently impossible is always a corrupting enterprise' (1962: p. 115). An exaggeration, of course. It can be a duty to try to do the impossible and a disinclination to try can be very corrupting. But, certainly, thinking that the inherently impossible is something which is *someone else's* plain duty to perform can be very corrupting indeed – as can treating what is at best a purely ideal paradigm as if it were a practicable ideal. Politicians are condemned for the fact that they are no more infallible than anyone else. Shortcomings in political decision-making are ALL explained in terms of faults personal to the makers or species-specific to politicians. May it not be that some of those shortcomings are the results of limitations which politicians share with the rest of the human species? But that question is hardly ever asked. Indeed, it may be too painful for many people to consider. Asking it requires an acknowledgement of one's own metaphysical and moral insufficiencies, and there are whole industries devoted to making that seem 'morbid'. It is much more comfortable and much more fun to see the trouble as the special fault of someone else: in this case, the politician.

9.29 In assessing morally the actions of rulers or politicians, one should consider all the circumstances of the case, just as one should when assessing morally the actions of non-rulers or non-politicians. In both kinds of case, that kind of consideration *may sometimes* extenuate, even excuse action which, *prima facie*, seems evil. Given that a State is involved in relations with other States and that international law is not effective in the way that 'municipal' (i.e., internal) law normally is, given that any State severely limits 'self-help' by its subjects in the redress of wrongs, given the immensity of the interests a State is charged with protecting – given all these things, there must be some actions which would be immoral if undertaken by private persons but are not immoral if undertaken by public authority. For one private person to throw a tomato at another might be morally wrong, whereas a bombardment ordered by public authority might be morally right. The State can imprison malefactors, but if I were to try to do it, I would quite clearly be getting above myself. All that is true, but none of it implies that:

> A public act which inflicts loss, such as war, confiscation, the repudiation of a debt, is wholly different from murder or theft.
>
> (Bosanquet, 1923: p. 303)

The 'is' should be 'may be' (just as a 'private' act of killing will not be murder if done in necessary self-defence). Bosanquet talks at times as if the truth that a State *per se* cannot have certain human weaknesses ('selfishness and sensuality' (p. 300), 'private malice or cupidity' (p. 303)) means that its actions cannot be judged in *any* way like the way in which 'private acts' can be judged. Acton had replied to this before Bosanquet said it:

> In public life, the domain of History, vice is less than crime. Active, transitive sins count for more than others.
>   The greatest crime is Homicide. The accomplice is no better than the assassin; the theorist is worse.

(Acton, 1956: p. 340)

See also *TP* 7.2D (*ideology*).

Suggested reading

Acheson, 1958(a), (b); Acton, 1956: pp. 328–345; Benn, 1983; Bosanquet, 1923: pp. xlvii–xliv, ch. xi; Bose, 1977: ch. xiii; Cranston, 1968: pp. 1–21; Hampshire, 1978; Held *et al.*, 1972, 1974; Jouvenel, 1963: pts iv, vi; Lefever, 1972(a); Parekh & Berki, 1972; Pettman, 1979; Weber, 1948(b).

REALPOLITIK: MACHTPOLITIK

9.30   The word '*Realpolitik*' (German) is usually not translated. If it were, the translation would be 'reality-politics (*or* -policy)'. It can mean:

> A politics or policy free from illusion or obsession. Wishful thinking is not allowed to distort the vision of how things actually are or can be made to be. Possible consequences are carefully considered. Costs are carefully counted before action.

It can also mean:

> A politics or policy free from moral restraints, seeking only power and valuing anything else only if it is a means to power.

Scruton would like to restrict the word '*Realpolitik*' to the former and call the latter 'power-politics' (German: *Machtpolitik*).[8] I agree entirely, but when he and I agree on that point, we are not saying something parallel to these:

> Z: Don't say that a whale is a big fish. It's a different kind of thing from a fish (i.e., 'You've got the classification wrong').

It would be *something* like Z only if the classification of the whale were a matter of controversy, especially a controversy about (e.g.) the basic principles of zoology, but that is not so. When we assert Z, we oppose nothing more than zoologico-linguistic ignorance or carelessness, not disagreement in principle. But when Scruton or I say that a reality-politics need not (or even, perhaps, must not) be a power-politics, we are not talking simply about words and classifications. The issue between us and our opponents is far more complicated and fundamental. For *power*, see 2.14–2.15. For relations between material and 'moral' force, see 10.1–10.10.

Suggested reading

Scruton, 1983: pp. 395, 367; D. C. Watt, 1988; Bullock, 1988(b); Wight, 1978. *OED* has some very interesting examples. For an interesting point about the limited prudence of *Machtpolitik*, see Orwell, 1970(c): p. 176.

CORRUPTION

> . . . a being, so brilliant yet so corrupt, which, like a rotten mackerel by moonlight, shines and stinks.
>
> (John Randolph of Roanoke on Henry Clay)
> (Quoted, Adams 1898: p. 286; J. F. Kennedy, 1957: p. 49)

9.31   The word 'corruption' has a physical sense as well as a moral sense. Indeed, the physical sense is primary or (at any rate) original. Thus *SOED*:

Corrupt (adjective) 1. Changed from the naturally sound condition; putrid, rotten or rotting; infected or defiled. 2. Adulterated; debased, as money.
Corrupt (verb) 1. (transitive) To turn from a sound into an unsound impure condition; to make rotten; to putrefy. 2. To infect, taint; to adulterate. 7. (verb intransitive) To become corrupt or putrid.
Corruption 1. The destruction or spoiling of anything, especially by disintegration or decomposition; putrefaction. 2. Infection, infected condition; also (figuratively) contagion, taint. 3. Decomposed or putrid matter; pus.

These uses are morally, though not evaluatively, neutral. This is a point at which the so-called 'dichotomy' of fact and value collapses (see *TP* 5.21, 9.4). *SOED* (quite correctly) marks almost all of them 'archaic' or 'obsolete'. We say that the tomato *is going bad* or has *gone bad* (or '*off*') not that it is corrupting or has become corrupt. We cannot, however, consign the physical senses to the archives and forget about them. The moral senses depend on them for some of their force; i.e., they involve metaphor and the metaphor is 'live', not merely etymological. The ideas which John Randolph of Roanoke yoked together are distinct from each other, but not mutually incongruous. He not merely imputes moral turpitude, but does so in a disgusted and even (intentionally) disgusting fashion. In these physical meanings, we can distinguish two strands of meaning:

Contagion, infection, contamination
Putridity, rottenness

Linked to both strands is the idea that

The putrid (or the rotten) can itself be a source of contagion and of further putridity or rottenness.

I have only ever met Randolph's remark as a quotation. While it is quite clear that he does not regard Henry Clay with unmixed admiration, his precise claim is uncertain. It may be only that he is alleging deep and extreme immorality; i.e., 'corruption' here may be *merely* a word of very intense moral condemnation. The words 'rotten' and 'putrid' are often used in that fashion. Randolph was a vituperative and muddle-headed speaker. Perhaps his words are mere invective. Even if so, the associations which I have just mentioned make it powerful and vivid.

9.32   There is a use of the verb 'to corrupt' such that:

If Primus corrupts Secundus, then Primus induces Secundus to become a morally worse person.

That is not a definition. It could only be part of one, since not just *any* moral deterioration is involved. To justify the use of the verb, either what Primus induces Secundus to do must be seriously wrong or Primus has some responsibility for a long-term deterioration of Secundus as moral judge and moral agent. (The disjunction is non-exclusive.) It is in this sense that Socrates was accused of *corrupting the young* or, as some might misleadingly say, 'of corruption', i.e., accused of *being a corrupter*, not necessarily of *being corrupt* himself. The victims have been *corrupted*; i.e., and are morally worse than they were. It does not follow that they have become *corrupt*. The metaphor here is less *putridity* than *contamination*.

9.33   The distinction is an important one, because, in the vocabulary of politics, this family of words has two quite distinct, yet easily confusible senses. 'Power', says Acton, 'tends to corrupt' (1956: p. 335). Loveday speaks of 'the anxiety [of nineteenth-century Labor men] . . . lest the representatives should become corrupted – declassed – by being in parliament and so cease to represent them faithfully' (1971: p. 5). Here, we have something like contamination-type corruption, i.e., the holders of power or the Labor MPs become morally worse than they were before, like the alleged victims of Socrates, though here there is no individual corruptor. They have been corrupted, but it does not follow that they have become corrupt. To speak of their *corruptedness* sounds clumsy, but it is preferable to talking of their *corruption*, because that leads to confusion with the other important political sense of 'corrupt'.

9.34   If we see a headline, 'Cabinet Minister Accused of Corruption', do we interpret that as meaning *merely* that someone has accused him of great wickedness, or do we have rather more precise expectations about the content of those expectations? Is Pol Pot corrupt? Was Hitler? – Or, rather, does the adjective fit them, as, according to some, it fits Sir Robert Askin, a former Premier of New South Wales, who, once he was safely dead, became (despite a lack of evidence) a byword for corruption? (Cf. 2.16A (ii).) What, in more precise terms, was Askin accused of? *Not*, it is important to note, of having blood on his hands. One author alleges that he accepted very large sums of money from illegal gambling interests in return for impunity and that he accepted $55,000 in return for a promise that a tax on bookmakers would not be increased (Hickie, 1985; Reading, 1989). It was alleged also that companies received very favourable (and profitable) treatment by the Government in return for share placements and other favours to Sir Robert and some colleagues. Another allegation concerned the sale of knighthoods.

9.35 One prominent feature of this is *the use of public office for private gain* in a manner specifically forbidden by the law (with good reason). That, perhaps, is something like (but not quite) a definition of *official corruption*, i.e., corrupt conduct by an office-holder as such. There are differences not merely in scale, but also in kind between types of official corruption. In some places, policemen have entered into arrangements to do something not in itself illegal, but exclusively favouring some particular persons; e.g., to inform a particular towtruck operator as soon as there is news of a traffic accident. A notification *per se* is neither illegal nor immoral. Here it is the arrangement and the acceptance of reward which constitute the offence. If the allegations against Sir Robert Askin are true, then he, in return for reward, became an accomplice to something which was 'intrinsically' and independently crime (i.e., the illegal gambling). Further, corruption on such a scale could hardly be a one-man business. Other Servants of the Crown were also drawn in (many without regret). Finally, while favouring one towtruck owner over another is unlikely in itself to be to the public detriment, similar favouritism to mining, development, or building companies could have highly detrimental effects. The kind of conduct attributed to Sir Robert Askin makes the system *go bad*; i.e., corrupts *it* (in something like the 'Socrates' sense, involving both *contamination* and *contagion*). This element of contamination would be there, even if Askin's conduct did not implicate other officials.

9.36 Why, though, has the word 'corruption' become attached to this kind (or these kinds) of official misconduct? Why are both Askin and his conduct styled 'corrupt'? Somewhere at the base of it, I think, is the wish to express disgust and *to inculcate a general attitude* of disgust for that kind of behaviour. Unless that attitude is kept fresh and lively, we may (and office-holders may) come to look on the behaviour as just-the-way-things-happen. In the nineteenth century, getting the speech-community to accept the application of the label 'corrupt practice' to what had been quite normal ways of winning votes was an important part of changing electoral procedures. Free drinks are attractive, as is (if you are a grocer) an exceptionally large order from a candidate with an assurance of future custom.[9] The attraction becomes less if we associate them with a bad smell and rottenness. (See G. Hughes, 1988: pp. 76–77.)

9.37 Perhaps there is also, in the 'Askin' sense of 'corruption', the idea of the *whited sepulchre*:[10] the exterior semblance of the dignity of office, and the association with socially valuable ends and activities, contrasted with a hidden badness which the semblance is used to foster and protect. To persuade an official to take a bribe is to corrupt him in a 'Socrates' sense, but it would have been nonetheless official corruption ('Askin corruption') even if the official required no persuasion; i.e., to involve oneself in official corruption is not necessarily to make anyone worse than he was, or to seduce anyone from his duty. He may be utterly and entirely seduced already. The 'rottenness' is the gravamen of the offence, not 'contamination'.

9.38   It is always important, in thinking about such matters as these, to have a vivid awareness of differences in scale or degree. Perhaps Alfred W. McCoy's 'five-stage model for both the scale and quality of police corruption' could be adapted and applied to political corruption:

(i)   So called 'honest graft': '. . . police . . . find ways of earning an informal bonus for the proper execution of their duties'; e.g. the towtruck matter (9.35).

(ii)   '. . . accepting bribes not to arrest an individual violator [of the law].'

(iii) '. . . an individual officer accepts regular retainers . . . not to investigate violations . . .'

(iv)   '. . . police officers using their position and authority to become criminal entrepreneurs.'

(v)   '. . . a syndication of all organized crime activity by a tightly-structured group of senior police officers.'

(McCoy, 1980: pp. 32–33)

9.39   The methodological morals I draw are these:

(i)   The importance of *finding examples* when one is explicating concepts. Despite anything that Socrates or Plato said, that is the way to begin. We need examples, many and various.

(ii)   The importance of looking for ambiguities in order not to be misled by them – in this case, the ambiguity between 'Socrates' corruption (9.32), 'Askin' corruption (9.35–9.37) and 'Randolph' corruption (9.31) (which, unless I have misinterpreted the quotation, makes 'corrupt' *merely* an emphatic term of disapproval).

'Political corruption' is not a synonym for 'political misbehaviour' or 'political immorality'. The mistake is an easy one to make, because it is a commonplace that involvement in politics, especially the possession of political power, can corrupt 'Socratically' (i.e., make people morally worse). Nevertheless, the distinction must be drawn. An aggressive, unjust war is a serious immorality: it is not an instance of corrupt conduct, as the taking of bribes (something less immoral) is. When Harrington said 'The corruption of Monarchy is call'd Tyranny' (quoted, *SOED*), he meant that tyranny is monarchy gone very bad, not monarchy gone corrupt *à la* Askin. To speak of *the corruption of the Church in the time of Alexander VI* is to speak primarily of *habitual and immense breach of duty*, of which bribery and venality were only a part. Carlyle, in a famous phrase, characterised Robespierre as 'the sea-green incorruptible' (*The French Revolution* pt II bk IV ch. iv, 1906: p. 16). It is not

self-contradictory to say that Robespierre was both mad and bad and that that phrase fits him very neatly. There are rottener things than corruption.
9.40   It is possible to characterise 'Askin' corruption in terms of a distinction between public and private roles. That, I think, would be quite appropriate, even perhaps inevitable if one is to understand the concept. But that gives rise to problems. The distinction itself is not entirely clear. That is not a reason for discarding it, but it does complicate the task. More important, it might not be easy to apply that distinction to every period and culture. The payment of *salaries* to officials is a modern invention. In the medieval and early modern periods, they were expected to recoup themselves out of the fees they collected. They were, so to speak, commission agents for the Exchequer. That considerably blurs the distinction between public and private, but those ages were not without a concept of political or official corruption. (Indeed 'cheat' derives from 'escheator', the title of a medieval official concerned in the assessment of property reverting to the Crown (G. Hughes, 1988: p. 87).) In the eighteenth century, the East India Company paid very low salaries to its 'servants', who were permitted and expected to trade on their own account. That was asking for trouble, especially in eighteenth-century India (see Chaudhuri, 1975). The precise line is hard to draw when that is the arrangement.
9.41   Again, there are present-day societies in which modern methods of government and administration (embodying a public/private distinction) sit uneasily with traditional notions. The Melanesian *bikman* (3.8) attracts and maintains his following by, amongst other methods, distributing largesse. When that is incorporated into modern political life, it can come perilously close to electoral bribery and peculation. Traditional morality may demand that anyone who has wealth and power under his control should use it to the advantage of his kin. Incautious compliance with that norm can also look like, or even become, plain roguery. There are governments which tacitly follow the salary policy of the East India Company. There, officials *must* take 'kickbacks' if they are to eat. Do we call them all corrupt? We *must* distinguish between the official who will do his job properly only if bribed and the official prepared to do his job improperly if bribed. While few of us would sing sad songs for Lockheed and Bofors,[11] it may be true that they were *both* sinned against *and* sinning. (See also 5.10.)
9.42   That is as far as I am prepared to carry cultural relativism on this topic. It is simply not true that 'we cannot judge' people in other cultures. We can and must. There is, of course, need to be careful about it, as there is in judging members of our own culture. The sale of medical degrees or the activity of a health inspector who will, for a bribe, certify contaminated food or pharmaceuticals as fit for consumption – activities of that kind are corrupt and wicked wherever they happen and we must not let the witchword 'ethnocentric' deter us from saying so. To say 'We cannot judge such things' is to make the very ethnocentric judgement that such things are bad for us, but may be good enough for the Indians (or whoever).
9.43   It is significant that McCoy (9.38) speaks of *stages*, not merely of *types*

of corruption, thus indicating the possibility of temporal and causal links between them. There are indeed various 'slippery slope', 'thin end of the wedge' problems about corruption (*TP* 9.5D). A Prime Minister who picks his own Cabinet will rarely be able to fill *every* position on best-man-or-woman-for-the-job criteria. There are factions, localities, and other interest groups to keep on side. Drawing the line between this and the corrupt use of patronage is no easy job, but it *must* be done. '[T]here is a vast grey area between behaviour which is clearly dishonest or illegal, and favours or promises which are a more normal part of political bargaining' (Boyce *et al.*, 1980: p. 41).[12] That grey area needs *unceasing* exploration and mapping. We might need to be very careful in formulating our questions. If we worry over whether a policeman should ever accept a free cup of coffee, are we asking 'Is *that* an instance of corruption?' or are we asking a question about building up a corruption-resistant frame of mind in policemen (not the same thing at all)?

9.44   Jeremy Bentham defines *corruption in government* as:

> Any state of things by which individual interest is put in a state of effectual opposition to the universal interest in such sort that by yielding to the seductions of the individual interest [an official] contributes to the sacrifice of the universal interest.
>
> (1973: p. 307)

That definition will work only if the concept of universal interest is acceptable. That is challenged by some writers (6.17–6.29).

I consulted six dictionaries of politics and found an entry for corruption in only one. Perhaps that proves that it is so rare a phenomenon as to be hardly worth talking about.

Suggested reading

WPLD, 1988: 'Corrupt', 'Corrupt practice', 'Deprave or corrupt'; Alatas, 1968; Bentham, 1962: see index; Crick, 1982; Friedrich, 1966; Grabovsky, 1989; Heidenheimer *et al.*, 1989; Lockard, 1973; McShea, 1978; Mill, 1963(b); Peters & Welch, 1978; Prasser *et al.*, 1990; Punch, 1985; Schumpeter, 1954: pt IV; Shumer, 1979; Steintrager, 1977: see index. *PSCC*, 1989 is a Golden Treasury of Political Scandal.

10 'States of mind' of the people and of similar entities

MORALE

10.1   As *OED* tells us, 'morale' in its current sense has been with us since 1831, but it was an elegant gallicism[1] until the 'first world war, when the quality denoted by the word was naturally much talked about' (Fowler, 1974: p. 370). What is 'the quality denoted by the word'? Fowler's off-the-cuff definition is 'state of discipline and spirit in armies and the like' (ibid.: p. 371). *OED* says the same at greater length.

10.2   Our word 'morale' is closely related to 'moral' in 'moral support' and 'moral victory' and to certain uses of the French adjective *moral(e)* which give trouble to anglophone translators of Jean-Jacques Rousseau. Rousseau frequently uses the expressions *'corps moral'* and *'personne morale'*. An unwary translator would English these as 'moral body' and 'moral person', but those 'literal translations' would be thorough *mis*translations. What Rousseau is getting at is *something like* the notion of *legal personality*.[2] Logically speaking, you cannot punch ICI on the nose or shake it by the hand, and the same goes for the University of Newcastle, but they can own property, sue and be sued, be parties to contracts and the like. They are not *natural* persons, but they are *legal* persons. Rousseau also tells us that part of the task of 'The Legislator' who brings the desirable society into existence is:

> substituer une existence partielle et morale à l'existence physique et indépendante que nous avons tous reçue de la nature.
>
> (Rousseau, 1972: p. 138)

The Everyman's Library version makes that into:

> substituting a partial and moral existence for the physical and independent existence nature has conferred on us all.
>
> (Rousseau, *Social Contract* bk II ch. vii, 1973: p. 194)

10.3   The member's status as an individual, *independent* entity ceases to be the most important thing about him. Instead, his new aspect as a *part of* a whole greater than himself, the Desirable Society, becomes his central and most significant characteristic. 'Moral' here contrasts with 'physical' and has the same, faintly mysterious sense it has in 'personne morale' and 'corps moral'. Brumfitt and Hall (Rousseau, 1973: p. 317) say that 'the English word "moral" is never used in this sense'. That is not so (though they seem to have *OED* on their side). If you give someone *moral support*, you do indeed give him support, but it is support which is quite unlike physical support: you encourage him by complimenting him, or cheering for him, or by sticking his picture on the wall. You do not give him guns, or troops, or all the money he needs: you do not run on to the field and physically assist him to tackle the opposing team. A *moral victory* is a genuine victory, but it may not improve your physical position. It may even leave you physically worse off. A moral X may be indeed an X, but an at least slightly odd X: while it is an X, it lacks the physical characteristics of a typical X, or it is something which (in certain important respects) is 'as good as an X', even if it is not an X (in certain other important respects). Bertrand de Jouvenel (or his translator) uses the word 'moral' in a sense like this and contrasts it with 'concrete' (1963: p. 63).[3] A more usual contraster is 'material' or 'physical':

> But the Soviets claim they are giving massive material and moral support to peace fighters in other countries and why disbelieve them?
>
> (Sir John Hackett. Reported, *DT*, 1982)

> . . . we managed to make little barricades on both sides, and set ourselves to hold them until dawn. Of course, these flimsy heaps of brushwood and broken stone were not a serious obstacle, but the moral effect of holding a fixed line is very great.
>
> (Alfred Duggan, 1951: p. 152)

The word 'physical' does not occur in that passage, but there is an obvious contrast with 'physical effect' (so obvious that I am tempted to say that the word is *morally present*).

10.4   A moral X in that sense is an X which to 'the eye of sense' may not look much like an X. Something like that is lurking in the concept of *morale*: When we talk of the *morale* of the troops, we are talking about something which may, as yet, be imperceptible to the casual observer. We are not talking about their physical condition, nor about their material equipment. We are talking about their enthusiasm, about their confidence, about whether they see their role as worthwhile and making sense, about their readiness to obey orders, their discipline, their capacity to endure hardship, about their *esprit de corps*. It is perhaps significant that we so often come back to *troops*.[4] The moral/physical (material) distinction is one which has impressed many writers on military matters. We find the substance of it in Xenophon:

> . . . not numbers or strength bring victory in war; but whichever army goes into battle stronger in soul, their enemies generally cannot withstand them.
>
> (*Anabasis* bk III ch. i, 1964: p. 64)

and in Napoleon: 'In the end the Spirit will always conquer the Sword.' We find the very words in another Napoleonic dictum: 'The moral is to the physical as three is to one'[5] (Richardson, 1978: p. 1). The great theorist of war, Carl von Clausewitz (1780–1831), wrote in the aftermath of Napoleon's striking victories and equally impressive defeat. He saw war as a contest between *wills*, 'a test of moral and physical forces by means of the latter'. Though he had a quite lively appreciation of the usefulness of physical force, he insisted on the supreme importance of what he called *moralische Grössen* (i.e., 'moral factors'):

> One might say that the physical [factors] seem little more than the wooden hilt, while the moral factors are the precious metal, the real weapon, the finely honed blade.

> (1976: p. 185)

The Duggan quotation (10.3) is from a historical novel. The speaker is Cerdic, founder of the Royal House of Wessex. I am sure it is no anachronism.

10.5 A contemporary American officer tries to pin the concept down thus:

> Either morale is a word of convenience, employed because it is easier to say than 'the body of thought of a person or persons, as to whether it disposes the thinker to high endeavor or towards failure,' or else it has no meaning. I prefer to think that it is the former because we then have something to go to work on.

> (Marshall, 1978: pp. 157–158)

As they say in the Australian Army, 'Fair enough' (though incomplete). Basically, 'morale' is a military word and its application to non-military groups involves analogy. Marshall (arguing a different point) insists on 'the single-ness of purpose of a military body': its 'interior economy and system of relationships are different from those within the civil body from which . . . [it] springs' (ibid.: pp. 166, 165). In other words, an army is a *team of action* (2.4), completely focused on one end: the deterrence or defeat of the enemy. Another peculiarity of an army is that, though it is a very large group, it is (even in a push-button age) dependent very much on the internal relations within very small groups. As a British medical General has written:

> in the last ditch . . . the soldier will be thinking more of his comrades in his section or platoon than of 'The Cause', Democracy, Queen and Country, or even of . . . the Regiment . . . . [I]t is with these men that a soldier's personal honour is most closely involved.

> (Richardson, 1978: p. 12)

'When the chips are down,' says an American Colonel, 'a man fights to help the man next to him' (Marshall, 1978: pp. 157–158).

10.6 There are non-military groups like that, and, in talk about them, the concept of morale can be applied without strain (e.g., ships' companies, sporting teams, research teams, hospital staffs). The polity as a whole, however, is not like that, although it can approximate to it in times of total war. It was one view of what total war would be like that led to an application of the term 'morale' to polities. In 1921, there appeared a book, *Il dominio dell'aria* by General Giulio Douhet. As its title suggests, this book is concerned with the role of 'airpower', primarily the bomber, in warfare. Douhet 'foresaw wars fought by droves of bombers which would render armies and navies redundant, aerial defences miserably ineffective', the object being to 'hammer the *nation* itself [as distinct from its armed forces] to give in' (Harrisson, 1978: pp. 21–22). Douhet's theory was adopted by all the major belligerents of 1939–1945. Cities were to be subjected to massive bombing and the expected consequence was the total breakdown of social and economic life, social chaos and despair on a comprehensive and hitherto unknown scale: mass panic, mindless destruction and interpersonal violence, uncontrollable mobs fleeing the cities. The result of this worse-than-Hobbist collapse would be that, whatever was happening in the field or on the ocean, the bombed nation would be forced to sue for peace, because, in certain vital respects, it was ceasing to exist. This collapse of social life was summed up in the phrase 'the destruction of civilian morale'. Quite obviously, this did not happen in Britain during the Blitz of 1940–1941, but that did not lead to any loss of faith in Douhet or to any misgivings concerning the usefulness of the concept of morale. Instead, British official opinion took the Blitz as showing that the *'ingrained* morale of the British nation' was very powerful stuff indeed. German morale ('presumably uningrained', says Harrisson) was still seen as fragile, provided that much more force was used against it (Harrisson, 1978: pp. 23, 301). The bombing of Germany did not produce social breakdown. Despite this double refutation of Douhet, the American bombing of North Vietnam was based on hypotheses of the Douhet kind, with no greater success.[6]

10.7   Despite the conviction that 'ingrained British morale' was a very high-quality, durable product, officialdom remained concerned about it. Tom Harrisson's team of do-it-yourself sociologists, Mass Observation, was recruited and at least three committees were set up:

> . . . high level interest in preserving and improving morale . . . increased and became more particular. Those few of us directly concerned with the study of the masses *en masse* found ourselves more and more engaged in assessments of morale. This in turn led . . . to increasing uncertainty regarding our terms of reference, terminology and the like. What were we trying to measure? And how were we to do it?
>
> Imagine a doctor – or even a psychiatrist – trying to diagnose a disease that had a name but no defined symptoms! This was our problem – and a ripe source of confusion.

(ibid.: pp. 284–285)

10.8   The committees, it seems, all disintegrated, achieving nothing. What went wrong? One factor seems to have been *oversimplification*, the assumption that there was a thing, namely *morale*, which went 'up and down with bombing, a sort of invisible cousin to medical shock' (ibid.: p. 287). This assumption led to the treatment of the phrase 'low morale' as a *diagnostic term* rather than as an (at best) *descriptive term*.[7] So there were all the conditions for the existence of what we have since learnt to call *a buzz-word*. Further, it was a buzz-word which tempted Cabinet Ministers and senior civil servants to locate the cause of problems in the population, rather than in deficiencies of administration, a temptation to which many succumbed:

> If things went badly, a supposed 'break' in morale could be blamed without facing up to the background factors which caused the break: resentment at patent unfairness, confusion, misunderstanding, cold weather, lack of entertainments, inadequate leadership, utter boredom, for example.

> (ibid.: p. 286)

10.9 Since Cabinet Ministers and senior civil servants set the agenda (figuratively at least, but often literally as well), it may have been difficult for the committees even to see (let alone follow) possible lines of enquiry which might lead to the conclusion that the questions they had been asked were misconceived. But there was more to it than that. Harrisson repeatedly complains that *morale* was *undefined*, that there was no way of *measuring* it, and that may have been the problem. I do not mean that useful things could have been said and done about morale if, but only if it were definable and measurable: What I mean is that that opinion may have doomed the committees to impotence.

10.10 For, after all, were Harrisson and his colleagues left as much in the dark as he says? Douhet had given them (not a definition but) a fair specification of what a *complete collapse of morale* would be like. While that does not answer the question 'What is this thing called "morale"?', it does enable the asking of such questions as 'How far away from such a disastrous state are we?', 'What factors might move us in that direction?', 'What factors might counteract such a move?' Harrisson complains that

> Morale could hardly bear close analysis. No one then around could come up with clear definitions, let alone clear programmes for dealing with the matter once it had been defined.

> (ibid.)

But there was a document (dated 1 October 1941) in which Stephen Taylor of the Ministry of Information analysed morale:

> ... the factors determining morale could usefully be divided into the material and the mental. The material factors were more important, and consisted of food; warmth; work; leisure, rest and sleep; a secure base; and safety and security for dependents. The mental factors were: belief that victory is possible; belief in equality of sacrifices; belief in the efficiency and integrity of leadership and belief that the war is a necessity and our cause just.

> (Addison, 1977: p. 185)

That document would have been available to most of the committees of confused people whose deliberations are scathingly reviewed by Harrisson, but it seems to have had no effect on them. That may well have been because it does not conform to everyone's idea of a definition.[8] It makes no attempt to pin down an elusive 'essence', nor does it identify *The Thing which the word 'morale' names*. What it does is to treat the word as a caption under which to assemble factors relevant to civilian confidence and willingness to participate in the war effort. That should have given the Practical Men something to get their teeth into. But no. Not for the first time, the Practical Men proved intransigently loyal to uncritical and unexamined theory. They wanted a definition or nothing, so they got (and apparently achieved) nothing. 'Much . . . strategic crudity', Harrisson says, 'stems back . . . to the presentation of the target as one vast, undefined, flat cake called morale' (1978: p. 330). But it was not the lack of a definition which did the damage; it was an unshakeable prejudice in favour of the wrong kind of conceptual *oneness*, which entailed a demand for definitions:

> O! *Plato*! thou art mighty yet!
> Thy spirit walks abroad and turns our swords
> in our own proper entrails.[9]

It is certainly naive to assume that, for every meaningful word, there is A THING corresponding to it, specifiable in a definition, and constituting (somehow) the *meaning* of the word. But it is no less naive to assume that, if it is impossible to find such a definable THING, then the word has no meaning. Indeed, it is precisely the same error,[10] but, expressed the second way, it sounds *so* much more scientific. The error is the 'Fido'-Fido theory of meaning (see Ryle, 1957): that if a substantival phrase can serve as the subject-term of true affirmative propositions, there must be something referred to by that phrase, something which has the same kind of unity as Fido has and the same (or at least a spiritually analogous form of the) solidity which Fido has (cf. 6.14–6.16). On the one hand, there are such things as Fido, a plum pudding, the Belvedere Apollo, and (if some religious opinions are correct) the Archangel Gabriel (I bring him in to indicate that the point I am trying to make does not depend on a distinction between the *material* and the *immaterial*). On the other hand, there are such things as politics, the team spirit (cf. Ryle, 1949: pp. 16–18), philosophy, the Baroque style of architecture, health, morale, public opinion, and public morality. Some would say that things of the first type are *concrete things* and things of the second type are *abstractions*, but that is not helpful (see *TP* 1.11–1.12). It merely sets us off in search of wildgoose essences. Cf. 6.15.

If Harrisson's account is correct, a theoretical error led not only to a waste of time and effort but also to such other practical inconveniences as the unnecessary destruction of cities and the burning alive of civilians and of airmen.

Suggested reading

Clausewitz *On War* bk III chs iii–v, 1976: pp. 184–189; A. L. Edwards, 1946; Harrisson, 1978: pp. 28–29, 75–76, 100–101, 227–232, 302–306, 330–331, 358–359; Turner, 1961: chs xiv, xix.

CONSENSUS

10.11   The word 'consensus' is ambiguous in at least three different ways. One of these is something like a process/product ambiguity (*TP* 4.3(ii)): 'consensus' can mean something which we *reach*: a conclusion or policy generally acceptable to the group (*product*); or it can mean the *process* by which that conclusion is reached: a discussion of options, involving nothing or little in the way of confrontation and competition, with the aim of producing such a 'product'. In a different sense, 'consensus' can mean a persistent spirit or climate of agreement in the group which makes such a 'process' and such a 'product' possible.

10.12   These differences need to be borne in mind, but there is another difference, which is even more important. The phrase 'indigenous animal' has *the same meaning* whatever kind of habitat you are talking about, but differences in habitat will make it *refer* to creatures of very different kinds (see *TP* 2.10). He who expects savannah creatures to be just like those of the rain-forest is in for a big surprise. Similarly, 'consensus' can refer to quite different kinds of thing depending on the kind of group you are talking about.

10.13   On the one hand, the word can be related to a small face-to-face group,[11] like-minded, at least to the extent that the members all agree (by and large) on the goals of the group. It is essential that the group come to a decision. It is important that the decision be one which every member will find acceptable, livable with. A board of examiners might well function like this; so might a medical team in, say, an intensive care unit. Another example could be a village (or its elders) in Africa or Melanesia. The essence of this kind of consensus is *talking till they all agree*. Something like this is at the heart of trial-by-jury as traditionally understood (and, perhaps, idealised). Those are small groups, but the word 'consensus' can also be connected with the proceedings of large groups or collocations of groups (e.g., a polity) which are not face-to-face groups and which lack the kind of initial like-mindedness or agreement on goals which the other type of group has. Consensus, in this kind of case, is an agreement on rules-of-the-game, on institutional means of reaching decisions (but see 10.19–10.20 for an important qualification). Consensus, in both cases, presupposes (at least initial) lack of agreement. It may take a great deal of talking before the village elders or the examiners reach a decision acceptable to all, but, in such a group, *the avoidance of conflict and of competition* are of great importance. If a decision is reached with anyone feeling like a loser, then the method has not worked in a fully satisfactory fashion. But large-group consensus <u>*presupposes*</u> *more fundamental conflict*. It

is the background against which conflict occurs (or conflict is the background from which consensus arises). It shapes conflict and competition so that they do not become conflagration, riot or civil war, but conflict and competition are 'what it is all about'. Large-group consensus provides means by which it can be decided who wins, who loses. The losers *have to* accept and live with the outcome, but they cannot be expected (or expect) to feel the same way about that decision as the members of a small *Gemeinschaft* (2.11) or *team of action* (2.4) would feel about a decision which they arrive at consensually (cf. 10.38).
10.14   The word 'consensus' is 'at home'[12] in both these settings, but the thing referred to is not precisely the same thing in both settings. The large-scale group (e.g., the polity) is not merely the small-scale group writ large, and the attempt to transplant the methods of one to the other can be ruinous or, at the very least, sadly disappointing. When a small university college becomes a large university, it does not only become larger: it also becomes more impersonal; its hierarchy is transformed from paternal squirocracy to cold bureaucracy (2.13).[13] To expect the institution to function as once it did, to expect relationships within it to be as once they were is to expose oneself to bitter disappointment. That can be bad enough, but there are worse possibilities. 'Party-spirit' within the small-scale group can be disastrous. Banning party-spirit from the large-scale group can be another name for tyranny or even totalitarianism (see 5.36, 2.16B). The skills of small-group consensus might even be a serious obstacle to the governance of a polity. In an article published in 1961, Dr Julius Nyerere (without doubt, one of the most admirable of our contemporaries) argued that Africans are natural democrats:

> A small village in which the villagers are equals who make their own laws and conduct their own affairs by free discussion is the nearest thing to pure democracy. . . .
>
> These three . . . I consider to be essential to democratic government: discussion, equality, and freedom – the last being implied by the other two. . . .
>
> The traditional African society . . . was a society of equals and it conducted its business through discussion. Recently I was reading a . . . book on Nyasaland by Mr. Clutton-Brock; in one passage he was describing the life of traditional Nyasa, and when he comes to the Elders he uses a very significant phrase: 'They talk till they agree.' . . . That gives you the very essence of traditional African democracy. It is rather a clumsy way of conducting affairs, especially in a world as impatient for results as this of the twentieth century, but discussion is one essential factor of any democracy; and the African is expert at it.
>
> If democracy, then, is a form of government freely established by the people themselves; and if its essentials are free discussion and equality, there is nothing in traditional African society which unfits the African for it. On the contrary, there is everything in his tradition which fits the African to be . . . a natural democrat.

(Excerpt in Burch, 1964: pp. 169–170)

Dr Nyerere finds the phrase 'They talk till they agree' very significant. I find it equally significant that it is *the Elders* who are said to do this, not the village population as a whole. But what is even more significant is that he and Clutton-Brock are talking about not polities, not even collectives on the scale of Australian municipalities or shires. The traditional African village is a small community whose members know one another, regard one another as (or virtually as) kindred, and (for the most part) have identical roles in a subsistence economy. In such a society, problems would tend to be predictable and policy would be a datum. 'Political' issues would merely be issues of implementation (cf. 3.26–3.29). Dr Nyerere says

> It is no use telling an Anglo-Saxon that when a village of a hundred people have sat and talked together until they agreed where a well should be dug they have practiced democracy.

> (ibid.: p. 170)

This Australian Anglo-Gael has no trouble with that as an example of *democracy*, but I dispute its relevance to the question of democracy *at the level of the polity*. No villager doubts that they need a well, and, even if they talk for days about where to dig it, the final decision need not matter very much. It is unlikely to bring economic ruin to some, wealth to others. It will force no families out of their homes, flood no one's pastures. Only ideological sentimentality would see this as a model for what can be done at the level of the polity.[14] No polity can have the solidarity of some villages (*some*, because we must avoid sentimentalising villages into paradises; some are infernal[15]) and it is worth pointing out that one of the sources of village solidarity can be the shared conviction of the villagers that they alone are The Real Human Beings and all others are 'flawed seconds', especially that lot on the other side of the creek with whom they fight an annual battle and to whom they recognise no obligations whatsoever. In a television series shown in Australia in 1988, Ali Mazrui blamed the former colonial rulers for the political troubles and disasters of African independence: the institutions imposed by the colonialists are based on conflict, whereas the traditional African way is to seek consensus, so it was inevitable that those imposed institutions would break down. Certainly, most of them have broken down, to a greater or lesser degree, but, if Professor Mazrui were right, consensus institutions would be taking their place. Military dictatorship is not a consensus institution, neither is torture or massacre, or virtually anything governmental which has happened in Uganda, Mazrui's own country, for the past twenty years. In many cases, independence has been much more destructive than colonisation.

10.15   To expect or require or even wish for village-consensus at polity level is chuckle-headed romanticism. It is also very dangerous and can lead to the proscription of dissent, of opposition, and of the articulation of interests. Even in a small group, a devotion to consensus and conciliation, a renunciation of confrontation can become dangerous. That attitude (even when sincere) can be used as a rationalisation for being *very* confrontationist and *very* pugnacious. 'Here am I, declaring allegiance to consensus, being as conciliatory as half a dozen archangels, and how do that lot react? They oppose me and question my motives, so they deserve as much pugnacity as I can muster.' I have noticed myself that a sincere attachment to rational discussion can be used as an excuse for irrational fury. The other person is being irrational, so one declares war. The ideal of consensus can also be used oppressively. A committee member may be in a minority of one. His colleagues may not be content to vote him down. They may say that voting is a harsh, confrontationist system. Consensus is the thing, so come on agree with us, and you'd better be sincere, too. And some people who go on like this have actually read Orwell's *Nineteen Eighty-Four*.

10.16   That is a bogus employment of the notion of consensus. Even when consensus is not bogus, it is often not quite what it seems. Notice that Dr Nyerere puts much stress on *equality*. Frequently, deciding by consensus is possible only because of the non-coercive dominance of a respected figure. This is brought out nicely by a hilarious passage in Longford and O'Neill's biography of Eamon de Valera, describing his style at cabinet meetings (1974: pp. 331–332). De Valera, it is said, 'did nothing to curtail discussion' and 'believed in letting every aspect of a question be aired'. His notion of collective responsibility ruled out decision by majority vote: 'the opposition of even one member . . . had to be taken seriously. A vote . . . could only make for division.' He preferred to hear the opinion of every minister and then to aim at consensus:

> He himself was adept at wearing down opposition for he could, and often did, argue interminably in favour of a certain course. If he failed to carry his cabinet with him on the first occasion, he would postpone the issue and raise it again and again until . . . he had reduced the opposition to at least a silent acceptance.

There *may* be nothing bogus about such consensus-seeking, but there is no doubt about *who is boss*. I myself was once a member of a committee which usually arrived at unanimous decisions *without any* 'wearing down' of opposition. I am quite sure that that would not have been so had its chairman not been the extraordinarily impressive person that he is. (He studies societies like those talked about by Dr Nyerere.)

10.17   So far, I have spoken of small-scale consensus and the folly of requiring something just like it, only bigger, at large-scale level. Requiring it at the level of the polity is, in a sense, an attempt to abolish politics (see 3.29–3.39). What of large-scale consensus, that agreement on rules-of-the-game, that sharing of values and beliefs, which is a background to and a limitation of political conflict? Is there such a thing? I am quite sure there is, but we must not exaggerate it. Especially, we must not see consensus as the only factor making for social cohesion. As P. H. Partridge has pointed out (1980: pp. 88–89), apathy and ignorance can be equally significant. In other words, it is fallacious to move from the apparent (or even real) existence of social cohesion to the conclusion that there is an exactly proportionate consensus. Sometimes apparent agreement may exist only because a question has not been raised in an urgent and noticeable fashion. The shoe has not yet pinched, but it may, and then the cry (and the pain) might astonish us. James Boswell held firm and favourable views on the feudal system:

> I argued warmly for the old feudal system. Sir Alexander opposed it, and talked of the pleasure of seeing all men free and independent.
> JOHNSON. 'I agree with Mr. Boswell that there must be a high satisfaction in being a feudal Lord; but we are to consider, that we ought not to wish to have a number of men unhappy for the satisfaction of one.'
> – I maintained that . . . the vassals or followers, were not unhappy; for that there was a reciprocal satisfaction between the Lord and them: he being kind in his authority over them; they being respectful and faithful to him.
> (Boswell, 1980: p. 482)

That conversation took place on Monday 6 April 1772. The French Revolution was only seventeen years away. Joyce Cary's character, Captain Jim Latter, says of England during the General Strike of 1926:

> The fact was people were getting rattled. The country looked calm enough
> . . . . But the general atmosphere was getting charged up all the time, and now it began to crackle . . . . A lot of minds were melting like neapolitan ices at a gymkhana when thunder's coming on, going soft at the edges and the colours running a bit. The white getting in the red, the red into the white, and the green all over the plate.
> (Cary, 1955: p. 146)

If it turns out that there is as much danger of a disastrous Greenhouse Effect as some say, any measures that can hope to deal with it will disrupt almost everything that we have come to take for granted. I wonder what that would do to the ice-cream of consensus.

10.18 But, setting such gloomy thoughts aside, what kind of ice-cream might it be? Perhaps an analogy from theory of meaning might help. According to a widely accepted view, if there is a concept of X, then there is a group of properties (a 'common core') which all and only instantiations of that concept share. In a very well-known passage of his *Philosophical Investigations* (§§65–67), Wittgenstein challenges this view:

> Consider for example the proceedings that we call 'games' . . . . What is common to them all? – Don't say: 'There *must* be something common' . . . but *look and see* whether there is . . . . For if you look at them you will not see something that is common to *all*, but similarities, relationships, and a whole series of them at that. To repeat: don't think, but look! . . .
> And the result of this examination is: we see a complicated network of

similarities overlapping and criss-crossing: sometimes overall similarities, sometimes similarities of detail . . . .

. . . we extend our concept . . . as in spinning a thread we twist fibre on fibre. And the strength of the thread does not reside in the fact that some one fibre runs through its whole length, but in the overlapping of many fibres.

But if someone wished to say: 'There is something common to all these constructions – namely the disjunction of all their common properties' – I should reply: Now you are only playing with words. One might as well say: 'Something runs through the whole thread – namely the continuous overlapping of those fibres'.

Wittgenstein, of course, was doing theory of meaning, not political philosophy, and, as theory of meaning, it is insufficient,[16] but might it not be a useful and revealing metaphor about that whatever-it-is we are grasping for when we use expressions like 'national unity', 'social fabric' and 'consensus'? I mean that the applicability of those expressions might depend not on there being a set of beliefs, values, rules to which all members of a polity (or even all law-abiding members of it) subscribe, but rather on the overlapping of diverse sets of beliefs, values, rules, etc.

10.19 Bernard Crick, ever the *enfant terrible*, declares that consensus on values is not amongst the conditions for the maintenance of a stable polity in which freedom is practised and protected (what he – provocatively – calls 'a political society': see 3.10 above) (1982: pp. 176–178, 200). Indeed, he goes even further and says that the absence of value-consensus is a necessary condition for such a polity, though he does not maintain this hard line consistently. He makes a distinction between a consensus on values and 'a pragmatic agreement . . . to do things politically' (in his sense of that adverb). I do not think that such a distinction can be maintained in the strict fashion in which Crick needs to maintain it.

10.20 It may well be true that the 'negotiators' at Panmunjom in Korea agree on nothing but rules of procedure, whereby, though they go no for'arder, they do not come to blows. But they meet in a very stylised environment. They never cross one another's paths in unpredictable or unexpected fashion. Those who live in ordinary social environments – or, to be more concrete, in Newcastle – find that their paths cross in all sorts of ways. For them, rules of procedure need to be so open-ended as to be not *merely* rules of procedure, i.e., some element of sharing of values is necessary. Another point is that in something like Newcastle, there is always the possibility of contagion of values: even insensibly, one person's or one group's attitudes spread to another. That sort of thing never happens in the hygienic atmosphere of Panmunjom. In a non-stylised social environment, an agreement on rules of procedure is a commitment to mutual tolerance (10.31, 5.7): it depends on and produces other kinds of agreement. Crick talks about *universal* consensus, but that is to push things too far. The sort of consensus which I sketch in 10.18 is not a set of principles on each of which there is universal agreement, but it is a consensus nonetheless, even a public morality.

CONSENSUS, PUBLIC OPINION/MORALITY ETC., AND FIDO

10.21 It is a mistake to insist that there can be a public morality in a polity only if there is a set of moral propositions on which virtually every member agrees. This is the same sort of mistake which has vitiated much talk about *morale*: the 'Fido'-Fido theory (10.9–10.10), a sure foundation for error and confusion, the mother and nurse of much muddle. In the present case, the muddle is muddled further by certain peculiarities about belief-predicates.

10.22 Ascribing a moral system, or a system of beliefs, or even a jumble of beliefs, to a society is, almost always, a complicated, slippery business. It is something easily done, but it is not easy to do it well. (Indeed, ascribing beliefs to an individual can be a tricky business, too.) T. S. Eliot, speaking in March 1939, denounced the totalitarian (2.16B) regimes of the time as 'pagan', adding:

> But it is as well to remember that the imposition of a pagan theory of the State does not necessarily mean a wholly pagan society. A compromise between the theory of the State and the tradition of society exists in Italy, a country which is still mainly agricultural and Catholic.
>
> (1939: p. 21)

'Mainly agricultural and Catholic' - yes, AND ALSO anticlerical, and pagan in a manner much older than Fascism with all sorts of practices and codes of honour, etc. which co-exist with Catholicism with which they are logically at variance. In saying that, I am not primarily thinking of *divisions within Italian society*: a Catholic division, an anticlerical division, etc. Those were and are there. But, primarily, I am saying that, if you took at random half a dozen of the rural Italians Eliot was referring to, you would probably find that each would hold some combination of those logically incompatible attitudes. And that is not a peculiarity of Italians or of rural people. Later, Eliot remarks:

> to answer fully the question 'What does *A* believe?' one must know enough about *A* to have some notion of the level on which he is capable of believing anything.
>
> (ibid.: p. 37)

I want to reverse the emphasis. Eliot is saying that A's capacity to believe things might be unsatisfactorily small. I am saying that A might be capable of believing *so much* that simple propositions about what A believes are, *at best*, misleading abridgements of the reality. The White Queen[17] sometimes managed to believe six impossible things before breakfast – an exceptional case, of course, but less exalted belief-systems sometimes show a remarkable degree of disharmony. It is rare that anyone is (e.g.) Presbyterian, or socialist, or liberal-minded, or old-fashioned about sex (or even: honest, or irritable, or kindly) in quite the same solid unequivocal, unwavering, univalent fashion that he is (e.g.) 5 feet 7 inches tall. Human beings (as thinkers, feelers, believers, wishers, desirers, etc.) are, in Jean-Paul Sartre's image, *viscous*, i.e., never completely graspable.[18] Logical incompatibility (*TP* 10.2) does not entail psychological incompatibility. There is no self-contradiction in the notion of a self-contradictory set of beliefs (cf. 6.10).

10.23   It follows that the account of belief as disposition to action (i.e., the theory which says that to believe that p is to have the disposition to act as if p), even if true, is less simple and less illuminating than it may look. The extent to which an agent's action as if p is evidence on which to base a prediction of no action by that agent as if notp will vary according to particular cases. *And that is so even if one sets aside all possibility of pretence.* R. M. Hare says that it is a person's actions that 'reveal in what principles of conduct he really believe[s]' (1952: p. 1). One problem with that forthright assertion is that a person's actions can present as inconsistent a picture as his words, or as his words and actions combined. Even where there is a striking dispositional disparity between profession and practice, what follows about the 'real' moral beliefs of the person involved? That question cannot be answered in the abstract. David Armstrong remarks:

> It is perhaps no accident that both Popper and Anderson preached the life of intellectual criticism so forcefully and effectively, yet were unwilling to see it applied in their immediate intellectual environment. (Others may recognise other examples.)
>
> (1983: p. 94)

(Cf. 6.10, 10.39.) Does one say that, therefore, Popper and Anderson 'don't/ didn't really believe in' the life of intellectual criticism? Not if one has a sanely scrupulous regard for truth (not to mention a moderate measure of common sense or fairness): 'the only thing to do, and that can easily be done is to set out the facts at length.'[19] One does that (and worries about the law of excluded middle later: see *TP* 6.27, 9.6).

10.24   If individual opinion and morality can be so complicated, so viscous, public opinion and morality are likely to be even more difficult to pin down. Rousseau (sometimes, anyway) seems to have believed that the differences, being 'pluses and minuses', would cancel out, leaving a coherent 'general will' (1973: p. 185: *Social Contract* bk II ch. iii). But that is simply a mixture of blind faith and false analogy, just another example of the effects of mathematical intoxication. One can, perhaps, protect such a *very* theoretical concept as Rousseau's concept of the *general will*[20] from error and oddity by writing in as many *ad hoc* defining features as one likes. And, from Rousseau's point of view, it does not matter in the least that that diminishes or destroys any possibility of the instantiation of the concept: 'Nothing is beautiful except the non-existent.'[21] Actual public opinion cannot be purified in the same way and may well be logically odd. That point is supported by some figures presented by Dr Paul R. Wilson. According to his survey, 65 per cent of the Queensland public and 64 per cent of the Australian public believe that, under some circumstances, abortion should be legal. According to the same survey, 66 per cent of each public believe that abortion should be legal if the mother's life is in danger (P. R. Wilson, 1971: p. 110). The cream of the joke (if one can call it that) is that Dr Wilson gives no sign whatsoever of noticing that there is anything odd about these figures. Consider also the very odd message which an opinion poll sent to the UK Government during the Falklands War (see 4.8). These examples of public confusion give no support whatever to the proposition that the people do not know what they want or think, and that therefore, there should be a Platonic Philosopher-King to do their wanting and thinking for them (he may be just as confused and, if more consistent, is likely to be much more dangerous). My point is simply that notions like public opinion are more obscure than they may look.

10.25 'What the people think', that which is identified as 'public opinion' may be merely the opinion of the majority – or even of a minority equipped with some form of power (the media, the more articulate, the better organised, etc.).[22] One frequently finds two opposed groups characterising each other dismissively as 'A Well-Organised And Highly Vocal Minority'. Usually, both are right in the characterisation, wrong in regarding it as an adequate reason for dismissal. Many statements about what 'the people' believe, want, etc. are attempts to deceive or are examples of self-deception (see 8.14–8.17). Tom Harrisson (1978: p. 27) says of the late 1930s:

> Well, in those pre-psephological days the noise of the general public, as interpreted by the media, could sound very different from the true, private, voice of the people, which might be saying the opposite – or nothing at all.

But, as Harrisson himself indicates, even in thoroughly psephological days such as ours, questions about public opinion may be less clear than crystal and 'the true, private, voice of the people' may be very hard to locate. Public opinion may be only what people are prepared to say in public: in Harrisson's phrase, 'What you'll say to a stranger' (ibid.: p. 314; see also pp. 331–332). What someone says to a stranger, to the boss, to friends, to spouse, to self at different times of the day, may *all* be significantly different, even to the point of incompatibility. Yet there need not be any insincerity involved: the varying 'expressions of opinion' may quite genuinely *be* that, i.e., may genuinely characterise him (and not merely fleetingly) as a thinking, feeling and (potentially or actually) *acting* person. The question 'But which of these is his *real* belief?' may rest on a misconception of the situation. Even the Recording Angel might not be able to answer it, except by reciting all the varying 'expressions of opinion'. (I am even more sceptical than Harrisson. He talks of 'the true, private, voice of the people'. I think it possible that what one says in private (one's *truly private* voice) may be no more (but no less) one's true voice than what one says in public.)

10.26   If what I have said so far is even approximately true, 'ascertaining the moral sense of the community'[23] may be a more difficult task than some have thought. Survey techniques have a long way to go before they will be a great deal of help. Frequently, questions are poorly phrased and cannot elicit an unambiguous response. (See, e.g., Sparkes, 1973.) Frequently, insufficient care is taken to minimise the tendency of observation to affect that which is being observed, i.e., 'the Hawthorne effect'[24] which can be quite transient, but *scripta manent* (i.e., written things last) and look so very solid when expressed as percentages. My own very small experience as an interviewer has made me think that a great many people are surprisingly *ready* to tell the truth about themselves and their attitudes to someone wearing a mantle of what looks like social-scientific authority, but that this *readiness* to tell the truth is not always matched by an *awareness of what the truth is*. If someone is asked 'How would you have voted if an election had been held last Saturday?', the question is clear and so will be the answer. But questions like 'Are you in favour of a broadly based consumption tax?', 'Are you in favour of non-European immigration?' are not concerned with an act at a specific time. They go far beyond the interview into a not entirely predictable future and may also concern areas of the answerer's psyche about which he is himself not entirely well-informed (cf. 12.4–12.6).

10.27   Too much survey-work is based on an unexamined, naive notion of how people think. It is simply *not* the case that everyone has one, coherent opinion on every matter of importance, nor is it the case that all who lack such an opinion can be accurately lumped under the bland heading 'No Opinion' or 'Don't Know'. People often have difficulty in saying what they believe, perhaps are not sure. I do not mean that they are primarily in a state of dubiety about *the proposition*; rather they can be in a state of dubiety or confusion about their own dispositions with regard to that proposition; e.g.: being racially or religiously tolerant while living in a middle-class suburb is fairly painless and costless, but things are different in Bogside and Brixton (or Walgett). A suburbanite may realise this and wonder about himself. But a survey demands a confident, clear answer *now*. A survey may represent our views, rather as some snapshots represent our appearance: yes, you did look like that at that particular split second, but you do not look like that at all (and perhaps, in a certain sense, never did, since at least some concepts of a person's appearance relate to 'presents' more 'specious' than are split seconds: see *TP* 8.18B). 'The camera cannot lie', but it can misrepresent and delude, and so can self-consciously and naively 'objective' methods of social investigation. Survey-methods have some role in 'ascertaining the moral sense of the community', but so has the pooled horse-sense of shrewd observers with their eyes and ears open.[25] And *they* can be wrong, too. See Bourdieu, 1979; Rowse, 1988.

10.28   I am not saying that each of us is locked up inside himself, unable to communicate with others, or (as a chronic state) facing enormous difficulties in communication. One hears that kind of glib semi-solipsistic scepticism (*TP* 7.3) quite often, and (ye gods!) its proponents expect one to hear, understand and sympathise. We do, in fact, manage to communicate our thoughts and feelings fairly well – in fact, sometimes more is communicated than the communicator is aware of or would like. The popular view is, in that respect, too sceptical. In another respect, it is not sceptical enough, because it tends to see 'The Individual' as being totally aware of his own beliefs and feelings. I am saying that one can be quite wrong about one's own beliefs and feelings, as well as about those of others. It is not 'communication' in which I see difficulties. The difficulties arise in interpreting the long-term 'characterological' significance of communications, whose intrinsic import may be as clear as crystal. The matters of 'expression', the 'presentation of self', and 'appearance and reality' as related to human character are fascinating, but I cannot, here, pursue them further.

10.29   In 10.10, I maintained that much thinking about *morale* – before, during and after the Second World War – has been vitiated by a fundamental error about *meaning*: the opinion that if a word has a meaning, there must be *a thing* named by that word, the 'Fido'-Fido theory. A tendency to the same error can often be found in discourse employing such concepts as *public opinion, public morality, consensus, community standards* (concepts which typically involve the attribution of beliefs or attitudes to large collectives of human beings). But I do not believe that that tendency to error is a good reason for rejecting all talk employing these concepts as confused. Indeed, I want to sketch a case in favour of a cautious and qualified concept of the public morality.

10.30   Law, by definition, is something imposed on those subject to it. But a respect for persons, a commitment to autonomy (9.26 n.) requires that, so far as possible, it should not be *pure* imposition: neither merely arbitrary (in a kind of 'O'Grady says' sense) nor yet that it should be something whose *rationalia* are unrelated to the wishes, acknowledged values, felt needs of those subject to it. Hence, there is an insistence that the morality embodied in the law should be *public*, not only in the (here tautologous) sense of being related to the governance of the *res publica* (2.9C (ii)), nor only in the (far from tautologous and very important) sense of being generally knowable and intelligible, but also in the sense of (in *some* genuine fashion) arising from the *populus* (8.10 n.). Hence, the important part played in political argument by such notions as *public opinion, community standards*, etc. Hence also, the insistence that a society must have a *common* or *public morality*. These ways of talk must not be dismissed. The aspirations they embody are too important for that, but they must not be swallowed whole either. Talk employing such concepts need not reflect a humane-liberal outlook, but what I have said in this paragraph may indicate reasons why some people of humane-liberal outlook (11.10) might be unwilling to do without them altogether.

10.31   In any society, there is a load of history, of social habits, of changes, and of conflicts, all of which needs to be *managed*. The attempt to cope with all this is *public morality*. Public morality is something which is never static, but always on the move (and usually at least slightly muddled). It is always in the making and never finally made. In a pluralist society (*TP* 7.10B), there is 'a constant testing of the bounds of tolerance'[26] in order to formulate something which can be said to be a consensus – but at best a temporary consensus, a settlement, not a solution (for this important distinction, see Jouvenel, 1963: pp. 204–212), at best something which might do very well for a while, but is always at least potentially challengeable. If law is not to be merely an alien imposition, it rests upon such a shaky, changeable, but real enough consensus. A reasonable social life involves *having regular expectations*, a general framework of regular expectations within which the surprises occur. Without such a framework (OR: to the extent that the framework is markedly diminished), social life is an alienating nightmare. That is not to say that the framework must be rigid and unchanging. Flexibility and adaptability are conditions of its being a framework of regular expectations. And, since human beings are poorly endowed with closed instincts (i.e., complex, unlearnt, inborn patterns of behaviour: see *TP* 1.13E), the expectations must be based upon custom, convention, and the like. The 'constant testing of the bounds of tolerance' of which I speak is not a competition in mutual outrageousness. What I mean is that social life involves the constant application (and, therefore, sometimes, *adjustment*) of rules and values to new situations. That would be so even if there were just one system of rules and values operant in the life of a society. As that is not the case – as we have a complicated network of overlaps, conflicts, things which are conflicts at one moment and mere differences of emphasis at another (and vice versa) – the bounds of tolerance, though rarely *fluid*, are continually being adjusted, re-drawn, 're-understood'. That *process* is consensus, public morality and public opinion (but note the *viscosity*; cf. 10.22).

10.32   What is the relation between *consensus* and *consent*? Consent, paradigmatically, is *an act, a conscious and deliberate act*.[27] There are less central instances which can be brought under the heading 'tacit consent' – a notion employed in various (and sometimes questionable) ways by many liberal thinkers (11.10). But consensus is a more complex and, to a large extent, a less (self-)conscious, less deliberate thing. It is a varying, bubbling collection of beliefs, aspirations, sentiments, affections, dislikes, prejudices, propensities, etc., etc. This notion of consensus may be enough to cope with some of the difficulties raised by Partridge (10.17). The Latin word, *sensus* has all the ambiguity of our word 'feeling'. That is an ambiguity which I have often cursed (see *TP* 5.23), but it may, in fact, for some areas of human life – socio-political, interpersonal, individual – provide us with the most precise and vivid picture possible. Consensus may be less something that is reached and more like a relationship which is maintained and needs continual maintenance. It may even be something like a non-stop football match which needs non-stop refereeing and St John's Ambulance work.

Suggested reading

Ryle, 1957, 1949: pp. 16–18, 1971: pp. 3–16, 164, 181; R. Williams, 1983: pp. 76–78; Dwyer, 1989: ch. iii; Emy, 1972; Shils, 1968; Lipsitz, 1968; Reilly, 1988(c); Scruton, 1983: pp. 88–89; Coombs, 1970; Cowen, 1977; Higley & Cushing, 1977; P. H. Partridge, 1971, 1980; Uhr, 1981, 1984.

AN EXAMPLE OF CONSENSUS-TALK: R. J. HAWKE, 1979–1985

De l'audace, encore de l'audace, et toujours de l'audace!

(Georges Jacques Danton)

10.33   On 3 February 1983, Mr W. J. Hayden announced his (not entirely voluntary) resignation from the federal parliamentary leadership of the Australian Labor Party (ALP). His successor, Mr R. J. Hawke, had been in Parliament for less than three years, but had had much experience of internal ALP politics and of negotiation and advocacy in trade-union matters. On the same day, the Liberal Prime Minister, Mr Malcolm Fraser, secured a dissolution of parliament. Labor won the election with a large majority and Mr Hawke became Prime Minister.[28]

10.34   The policy speeches of party-leaders (especially of Opposition leaders) frequently paint a picture of national *crisis*, i.e., a situation of both danger and opportunity for the polity (cf. Wolin, 1961: p. 239). They speak of being at the *crossroads*, at *a crucial moment in the nation's history*, of *a choice which will affect not only ourselves but our children and our children's children*, etc. (Cf. Pemberton & Davis, 1986: p. 57.) Leaders differ in the blatancy of their claims to saviourhood, but they all offer to deliver us from the danger and to guide us along the right path. Sometimes, they claim merely to be far better deliverers and guides than their opponents. Frequently, they depict their opponents as *part of* the danger. In 1983, Mr Hawke offered to deliver Australians not only from economic collapse (an issue which might bear only on the relative *competence* of the contending parties), but also from national disunity which he blamed on the Fraser Government. In his first press conference as ALP leader, he declared that 'Australians have been deliberately set against Australians and group against group.' He promised that an ALP Government would pursue 'national reconciliation' and 'be doing those things necessary to bring Australians together' (Kelly, 1984: p. 390). This was no new theme for Mr Hawke. Even before he entered Parliament (his ambitions were no secret), he declared:

Australia stands poised on the threshold of the 1980s more divided within itself, more uncertain of the future, more prone to internal conflict, than at any other period in its history.

(Hawke, 1979: p. 33)

10.35   The ALP's election slogan was 'Bob Hawke – Bringing Australia Together'. In his policy speech, he declared that the election was 'a fight for the future of Australia, for the true heart and soul of Australia' (Hawke, 1984: pp. 11–39). Significantly he encouraged a comparison of himself with John Curtin, a *war-time* Prime Minister (cf. 5.41–5.45). Again, he rejected 'the politics of division, the politics of confrontation'. He announced 'a commitment, which embraces every other undertaking . . . to reunite this great community of ours, to bring out the best that we are truly capable of, as a nation' (Kelly, 1984: pp. 395, 398, 406). It was recognised, however, that man does not live by high ideals alone and promises were made of tax-cuts and increased spending (ibid.: pp. 398, 401–402),[29] and, of course, of better 'management', but management was not stressed as much as in earlier and later campaigns.

10.36   These promises have often been called an attempt 'to seize the middle ground' (11.12D), but this consensus-unity talk (at least if taken quite literally) is better characterised as an attempt to seize the whole field, to rule the entire opposing team offside before it left the dressing-room. Mr Hawke's claim was not merely that the ALP better understood and could better represent the national interest. He claimed that the ALP was *the* party of the national interest (6.17–6.29) and that the governing Liberal and National Parties were antisocial forces, parties of faction (in the nasty sense: see 5.34–5.36). The ALP, on this claim, is not merely one amongst the parties and the best of them: it is The Party, with a monopoly on legitimacy (see 5.2). A few years previously, the ALP had adopted *the Australian flag* as its emblem, which was audacious enough, but Mr Hawke had gone much further. What was called 'The National Economic Summit Conference'[30] underlined the claim. It was held in the chamber of the House of Representatives. Invitations had gone out to a great variety of groups: trade unions, employer organisations, professional associations, welfare groups – but not to the Opposition parties. They were excluded from contributing to the national consensus, rejected, reprobate, excommunicated: *Anathemata sint*.

10.37   That is not only audacious. Taken literally, it is sinister: the Leader of the National Movement who alone can bring the nation together confers with the leaders of the corporations and treats the political opposition as irrelevant, with no contribution to make. That sounds disturbingly like Mussolini's Fascism (see, e.g., Burch, 1964; Lyttelton, 1975; Nolte, 1969; E. Weber, 1964). When a head of government goes on like this, can jackboots and compulsory castor-oil be far away?

10.38   Well, yes, they can, because Mr Hawke's remarks about consensus and national unity are not to be taken entirely literally. Many commentators have traced Mr Hawke's talk of consensus to his experience as an industrial negotiator.[31] That influence cannot be doubted, but there is one aspect of it which has not, I think, been sufficiently noticed. The connection is strongest at a point where it might seem to break down altogether. Pemberton and Davis note that Mr Hawke appeared to treat 'consensus' as far more than a temporary political war-cry and more as a condensation of a social philosophy. They say:

This is a long way from the work done by the word consensus in the language of European community, where the term is not the elevated concept that Hawke put forward, but is used to indicate a set of institutional and tacit transactions in politics between unions and employers.

(1986: p. 58)

True enough. Industrial relations are not a matter of putting an end to conflict and division, but rather of finding settlements for conflicts. Harmony and unity are neither restored nor created (though harmony may be approximated to). As Jouvenel says:

> The best settlement by compromise . . . will not cause that feeling of enjoyment which comes with the offering of the solution to a problem. The solution as it were dissolves the problem: it will never be a problem any more. The compromise settlement leaves the issue in being. It may be reopened at any time. [Cf. 10.13.]

(1963: p. 208)

Division persists and is incurable. Similarly, it would be futile to hope for an end to confrontation in industrial relations. Indeed, they frequently involve dramatic, public confrontation followed by cooler negotiation and discussion, which *may* end *that particular contention* for a while. That is *conciliation*, rather than *reconciliation*.

10.39 So, what happens to the analogy between politics and industrial relations? There is still one there, but it is not what, at first, it seemed. The significant analogy is not one which Mr Hawke *drew*, but one which he *performed*. One of the dramatics of industrial relations is the *ambit claim*, a demand which, taken literally, is unreasonable and known to be so by its maker. It sets a maximum, a 'circuit, compass, or circumference' (*SOED* on 'ambit') within which haggling and negotiation can proceed. Mr Hawke's talk of consensus was an ambit claim of that sort. He demanded everything, hoping to get something and knowing (even tacitly approving of the fact) that he would not be allowed to get away with what he seemed to want to do. He was *bargaining*, like an Indian in a market. Far from being a renunciation of pluralist politics, his talk of consensus and unity was an example of pluralist politics at its most melodramatic. The same is true of his descriptions of Australia as riven by conflict (10.34–10.35). Things were not too good, but those descriptions would be literally true of Northern Ireland, Lebanon, or Yugoslavia, and Australia in the 1980s was a long way from that. Mr Hawke's condemnation of 'the politics of confrontation' was itself a piece of confrontation: ordinary political posturing, aggressive, but quite un-Fascist. Even the 'Economic Summit' was just a dramatic piece of support-gathering, rather than a proto-Chamber of Corporations.[32] The jackboots and castor-oil were far, far away. Electoral discourse is a melodramatic, hyperbolical business and the Honourable Robert James Lee Hawke was a more than usually melodramatic and hyperbolical politician. (His love of consensus as an *idea* arises to some extent from his consciousness of his own pugnacity. Cf. 10.23. Anson, 1992, is a quasi-Freudian exploration of these matters.)

10.40   I have already drawn attention to the variety of kinds of thing referred to by 'consensus' (10.11 *et seq.*). That was a vital factor in Mr Hawke's use of the word. Nyerere's villagers, at their best, will come up with a decision which satisfies and pleases every one of them. Such a decision is *not* a compromise, something which those involved will accept as the best they can get, unsatisfactory though it may be, or even as the least of available evils. But what industrial negotiators achieve is almost always a compromise. The word 'consensus' can apply to both, enabling Mr Hawke to promise the latter while giving it much of the warm glow proper only to the former. (Hawkean consensus is discussed further in 10.42.)

Suggested reading

Hawke, 1979, 1984; Jouvenel, 1963: pp. 204–212; Kelly, 1984: chs xix–xxiv; Little, 1989; P. O'Brien, 1980; Pemberton & Davis, 1986.

ANOTHER EXAMPLE OF CONSENSUS-TALK: THE UK 1957–1985(?)

10.41

> Above all, I hope nobody's going to bring politics into this election. There are already signs of it. Let me warn them that if they do the British people will know what to do with them.
>
> ([Parody of Harold Wilson's election broadcasts]
> *Spectator*, 1966: p. 349)

(i) It would be a mistake to suggest that 'consensus' always evokes a warm glow. Sometimes, the reaction is closer to a yawn. The phrase 'consensus politics' has had two principal uses in UK political discourse. One describes the electoral and rhetorical style of Harold Wilson as Prime Minister. During the election campaign of 1966, Alan Watkins (1966: p. 348) wrote:

> Mr Wilson seems to have stumbled upon what is, for this country, an entirely new approach to politics: to describe it, 'the politics of consensus' seems as good a phrase as any . . . .
>
> Subject to certain exceptions (such as capital punishment, though not immigration), the approach consists in finding out what the public want, and then giving it to them . . . .
>
> Mr Wilson . . . is trying to appeal to everybody.
>
> . . . [His] proposals . . . are much more elusive [than those of Heath, the Tory leader], and hence it is much more difficult to become angry about them. It is only possible to become angry about Mr Wilson himself.

And, even though Wilson himself had thus 'personalised' things by substituting *himself* for policy, such anger could be easily made to seem mere spite, 'personal' in a sense which would 'write it off'. This, in one sense of the word, is *populism* (8.30–8.40).

Watkins remarks that 'the politics of consensus does not lead to anything very exciting or inspiring', but a more serious weakness is that it will work only so long as the public (largely) agrees that it is getting what it wants, and that is not likely to be so for long in a large, complex polity, especially one faced by grave economic problems (cf. 10.17).

(ii) This point becomes very clear if we consider the other UK use of the phrase 'consensus politics', viz., as a characterisation of mainstream Conservative and Labour policies from the mid-1950s to the end of the 1960s. There was, it seemed, a convergence. Both parties were committed to a mixed economy, the welfare state, selective intervention in industry. The Liberal Party was a very minor party, but two dead Liberals, Beveridge and Keynes, seemed to dominate the major parties. This was the era of Butskellism (a word derived from the names of two Chancellors of the Exchequer, R. A. Butler (Tory) and Hugh Gaitskell (Labour)). The term 'consensus politics' suggested two things: a consensus between the parties and a policy reflecting the opinions and aspirations of the people at large.

That was always hyperbole. There was still plenty of conflict and disagreement, and there were serious disturbances and unrest in the late 1960s, but the term 'consensus politics' did point to genuine differences between British politics of this period and those of the preceding and following decades. Not everyone rejoiced in this. To some, it seemed unadventurous, complacent, unthinking, unprincipled. But so long as economic conditions made Macmillan's remark about 'never having had it so good'[33] approximately true, the purer, or more principled, or more extreme Socialists and Tories were left to fume and fret and write books,[34] but as Britain's economy deteriorated, consensus politics diminished. In December 1970, Richard Crossman, a very pure Socialist, announced with glee that 'There is a cracking sound in the political atmosphere: the sound of the consensus breaking up' (A. Sampson, 1982: p. 75). In 1981, Mrs Thatcher was accused of destroying consensus. She replied as Luther would have replied if he had been accused of Protestantism:

> To me, consensus seems to be the process of abandoning all beliefs, principles, values and policies . . . . It is the process of avoiding the very issues that have got to be solved merely to get people to come to an agreement on the way ahead.

> (ibid.: p. 49)

Butskell was dead and British politics had come to seem like the continuation of war by other means.

Suggested reading

Reilly, 1988(a); Amis, 1957;[35] Paul Foot, 1968; Crosland, 1962, 1974; Crossman, 1960, 1965; Middlemas, 1979; F. Pym, 1984: chs x, xi; A. Sampson, 1962, 1971, 1982.

HAWKEAN CONSENSUS (continued)

10.42 Thus, there was yet another aspect to Mr Hawke's audacity: he took a tired word, associated with stodgy compromise and the fools' paradise of the 1950s and 1960s, polished it up and gave it a visionary gleam. He won the 1983 election and three more. In 1984, opinion pollsters announced that he was the most popular Prime Minister in Australian history. But, eventually, the wheel came full circle, as wheels have a way of doing. In late 1991, it seemed to many that his Liberal opponents were the people with the ideas and the energy, the 'vision'. In November, the Liberal Leader of the Opposition released his much-heralded manifesto for financial and economic reform (*AFR*, 1991; LPA, 1991). One newspaper praised it in these terms:

> It is a victory for 'vision' politics over middle-of-the-road consensus; an indication that here is a leader prepared to state his position and stand by it rather than indulge in the leak-and-deny school of statesmanship practised at both State and Federal level.
>
> (*DTM*, 1991)

Meanwhile, Mr Hawke, still Labor Prime Minister (but only just) waited, like the priest of Nemi, for the decisive stroke from a colleague:

> The priest who slew the slayer,
> And shall himself be slain.
>
> (Macaulay.
> Quoted, Frazer, 1911: p. 1)

Sic transit gloria politica.

THE WILL OF THE PEOPLE

10.43

Military backs land for peace
by Tony Walker
Herald Correspondent

JERUSALEM, Sunday: Israel's retired generals and spy chiefs have overwhelmingly endorsed the principle of territorial compromise with the Arabs in a poll released on the eve of the Israeli elections on Tuesday.

Major General Shlomo Gazit . . . one of the poll's co-ordinators, said it showed that three out of four, or 68 per cent, of those questioned were in favour of yielding territory in exchange for peace provided such a step was accompanied by satisfactory security guarantees.

The bulk of the remainder – 31 per cent – were for annexation under Israeli sovereignty of the West Bank seized in the 1967 war.

(*SMH* 22 June 1992: p. 13)

10.44 The headline is even further astray than General Gazit's arithmetic. If I were an Israeli political leader who favoured 'land for peace' and if the same result were obtained from a survey of generals on the active list, I would not feel reassured, unless I had other reasons for believing that the generals would not take unconstitutional action. And yet, if, in an Australian election, one party received 68 per cent of the vote, that would be an unparalleled landslide and we would have no hesitation in saying that *Australia* had accepted that party and rejected its opponents. We would regard it as a most emphatic expression of *the will of the people*. Why the difference? The beginnings of an answer can be found in the 'unless' clause, four sentences back. An election result is not an expression of the people's will by virtue of its being the will of a majority, even an overwhelming majority. The decisive factor is that virtually everyone either regards it as or is prepared to behave as if it is an expression of the people's will. Despite the extraordinary comminations which opposing parties heap on one another, neither they nor anyone else with any sense believe that an election is a contest between the forces of light and the forces of darkness. Despite some of the things that some of us say on election night, there are very few, if any, Australians for whom an election result is literally an unmitigated disaster. There are none at all for whom the victory of the other side would have been an unmitigated benefit. There will be a scattering of appallingly True Believers[36] (groupuscules and isolated individuals) who reject the whole box-and-dice as illegitimate, but, if one can judge from their behaviour, there are none who believe that overt and violent rejection would be a better bargain than acceptance.

10.45 One might even say that the status of *Will of the People* is not so much conferred by the majority as conceded by the minority, but acceptance is not only an attitude of the minority. The majority must also accept that the minority is as legitimate a part of the polity as the majority and that the majority's claim to speak for all is a hyperbole. This point is made by a very witty sentence from one of Belloc's forgotten novels:

> The populace were wild with joy at their victory, and that portion of them who as bitterly mourned defeat would have been roughly handled had they not numbered quite half the vast assembly of human beings.
>
> (*Mr Clutterbuck's Election* (1908) ch. viii.
> Excerpt, Nicholas, 1956: p. 303)

Near-equality of numbers alone would not be enough. There also needs to be a considerable overlap in interests, attitudes and opinions. A peaceful politics rests on a complicated mixture of principle, habit, prudence and apathy. To call it 'the will of the people' (a claptrap term of political debate) suggests too much and too single-minded determination and striving. To call it 'consensus' (a claptrap term of political theory) suggests too much deliberation, even too much cognition. Whatever it is called, it makes for a more pleasant society than does its absence. (Majority rule in Northern Ireland was not the will of *the* people, but merely of *one of the peoples*. See 8.1–8.27.)

10.46　Thus in countries like Australia, most of the rhetoric of politics is hyperbole and melodrama. But, if the fight and fear are exaggerated, so also are the promises. If fundamental change is needed, it may be impossible to achieve, and, while '*the* minority' may be far from oppressed and doing quite nicely (as it waits to be, once again, 'the majority'), the condition of some minor*ities* may be permanently hopeless (see Rowley, 1970(a), (b), 1971). It is, I agree, unlikely that they would be much helped by the volatility and violence of a more polarised politics (those who have the least are usually those who lose the most in such circumstances). Nevertheless, those of us who talk comfortably of accepting the second-best are seldom those who pay the highest costs of social and moral imperfectibility.[37] There is a further point. W. K. Hancock, rebuking 'publicists and dons who have clung too much to Aristotle', pointed out that, in the West, the general tendency has been to make the 'Have-nots' a diminishing class and that in Australia they have been, except in the most abnormal times, a 'negligible quantity of the population' (1945: p. 165). But if abnormal times seem to have become normal and that general tendency seems to have been actively reversed . . .? Cf. 10.17 above.

For more on *the will of the people*, see 8.18–8.27.

11 Time, change, continuity

11.1 CHANGE, AND THE STATUS QUO

A Change

All change, of whatever kind, or for whatever reason, is generally to be deprecated.

> (Attributed to a nineteenth-century Duke of Cambridge.
> Mason, 1979: p. 23)

All change, of whatever kind, or for whatever reason, is generally to be welcomed.

Those are equal and opposite absurdities and few would find a good word to say about either stated openly. Nevertheless, in the heat of controversy, people often go on as if they accepted one or the other as a fundamental truth. 'This smacks of innovation!' said a senior colonial administrator, faced with a proposal for change, and he really did seem to think that he had produced an argument. On the other hand, proponents of a change sometimes try to evade objections to their proposals by accusing the objectors of being *afraid of change*. The argument seems to go like this:

<u>You object to what I propose.</u>
Therefore, you are afraid of what I propose.

<u>What I propose is a change.</u>
Therefore, you are afraid of change.

The first transition is fallacious if the word 'afraid' is being used pejoratively[1] (and it is). If the second is legitimate, so is:

You do not like porridge.
<u>Porridge is a food.</u>
Therefore, you do not like food.

See Cornford, 1953; Cotta, 1987. See also 11.5 below.

B Status quo

(Pron.: 'STAYtus kwo') Literally: 'condition in which'. As Fowler notes, 'the status quo' can mean 'the position in which things (1) are now or (2) have been till now or (3) were then or (4) had been till then' (1974: pp. 584–585), but the most common contemporary sense is (1). Often 'He supports the status quo' is said as a reproach, but one should always ask '*In what respect* does he support the status quo?' The status quo is not the sort of one-big-something that any sane person could support or oppose in its entirety. See Scruton, 1983: p. 449.

11.2 REFORM; REVOLUTION

A To *reform* something is to *change it for the better*. If someone believes that a proposed change would be a change for the better, s/he is quite entitled to call that proposed change *a reform*, especially if s/he is prepared to argue for it. But merely *calling* it a reform does not *establish* that it *would* be a change for the better. No matter with what emphasis it is recited, no matter how many times it is repeated, the word 'reform' is no substitute for *argument*, even though it is often used as a counterfeit argument. See R. Williams, 1983: pp. 262–264; Nisbet, 1982: pp. 238–243; Sperber & Trittschuh, 1964: pp. 347–352, 365; Turner, 1966. See also *TP* 2.8B.

Trollope's character, Miss Thorne, 'had adopted the Christian religion . . . and always appealed to her doing so as evidence that she had no prejudices against reform, when it could be shown that reform was salutary' (1925: p. 197).

B When the word 'reform' is used as a contraster to '*revolution*', emphasis is being placed on the non-violence, constitutionality and comparatively piecemeal nature of the change, though it need not be true that every revolution has the antithesis of all those characteristics. The word 'revolution' is highly contestable (6.22) and it is still possible to ignite controversy by wondering aloud whether the American Revolution or the Hungarian uprising of 1957 'really was' a revolution. Is 'Tudor revolution' metaphor, hyperbole or literal but atypical? (See, e.g. Elton, 1974: p. 160.) See Scruton, 1983: pp. 397–398, 406–407, 395–396; Calvert, 1970; Kamenka, 1970; Needler, 1991: pp. 3–12; Ritter, 1986: pp. 388–393; J. Davies, 1962; Brinton, 1965; C. E. Welch & Taintor, 1972; Marcuse, 1966; K. Campbell, 1969. For *Tory Reform*, see 7.19.

C For orthodox Communists, '*reformist*' is a very pejorative word, applied to those who believe that significant and beneficial change can be secured without destroying the capitalist system entirely. See Gould, 1960: pp. 43–45; Carew Hunt, 1957: pp. 139–145; Cairns, 1963 and 1975; Summy, 1972. '*Meliorist*' (Latin *melior* = 'better') can also have a derogatory ring. It can suggest a well-meaning, pernicious naivety (cf. 'do-gooder'). It is important, however, not to forget that merely affixing a label is not an argument. (See Flew, 1975: pp. 66–67.) In some circles, 'meliorist' is used as a condemnatory label for anyone who wants to change society. This condemnation is not based on Duke-of-Cambridge grounds (11.1), but on the sheer wickedness of 'imposing your own values on others' (see Docker, 1972: p. 43; Anderson, 1962 and 1980: indexes). Apparently, abstaining from action imposes nothing on anyone. A strange doctrine.

D 'But that's only treating the SYMPTOMS. What about the CAUSES?'

Of medical origin, but frequently used in discussions of social problems. The suggestion is that a proposed treatment is superficial and likely to be less effective than some other which (allegedly) will deal with the cause of the problem. The move is legitimate when:

      (i)   the cause is known,
and (ii)   the cause is accessible,
and (iii) a method of treating the cause is available,
and (iv)   that method has a better chance of success than symptomatic treatment,
and (v)   there is strong reason to believe that the good effects of the method will outweigh any bad effects.

These conditions are not always realised and it is a bad mistake to think that (in medicine or anywhere else) symptomatic treatment should always be avoided or that it is always inferior to treatments of the alleged or even genuine causes. Knife-happy social activists can be even more dangerous than knife-happy surgeons. But it would be a mistake to suggest that the motives behind the illegitimate use of this move are always revolutionary or radical. It can be used for extremely conservative purposes as well: Primus proposes a small change. Secundus dislikes that proposal, but, instead of arguing against it directly, says: 'But that would be merely to treat the symptoms. We must make an in-depth examination of the *whole* problem, not merely of the small part which Primus would have us deal with.' And then it is all shunted off to a committee which, with any luck, will get totally lost and everything will stay precisely as it is. See Cornford, 1953. For 'radical' and 'conservative' in their medical senses, see 11.9A.

11.3 REACTIONARY; REACTIVE; OSTRICHES, LEMMINGS, GADARENE SWINE

A 'Reactionary' is a pejorative word, suggesting either (i) Duke-of-Cambridge-type (11.1) prejudice against change in general, or (ii) defence of established, privileged injustice, or (iii) support for change which would establish privileged injustice (cf. 'obscurantist' (*TP* 2.8B)). It has become a left-wing term of abuse, parallel to such rightist rudenesses as 'trendy' and 'trouble-maker'. See Fowler, 1974: p. 503; K. Hudson, 1977: p. 203; Murray-Smith,

1987: p. 287; Scruton, 1983: pp. 394–395. 'Reactionary' is sometimes mala-propistically misused to mean *someone who reacts against authority*. As if the waters were not muddy enough without that!

For the thesis that Australian politics can be understood as a conflict between the *party of initiative* (the Labor Party) and *parties of resistance*, see Hancock, 1945: chs x, xi; Mayer, 1956, 1966(b), 1969(b); Rawson, 1968, 1969; Goot, 1969. See also 11.8 below.

B Reactive, pro-active

'Reactionary' has so unfavourable a tone and such an unbreakable connection with the 'ultra-right' (11.13A) that it cannot serve as the *mere* adjectival cognate of 'react'. For that job, we have 'reactive': 'Active or operative in return . . . responsive to a stimulus.' Thus, *SOED*, which indicates several other meanings which might (but need not) confuse things. 'Pro-active' is a new word (I have no samples earlier than 1991), coined apparently as a contraster to 'reactive'. The pro-active person does not merely respond to a stimulus: s/he creates stimuli. Instead of being merely active or operative in return, s/he takes the initiative. It is not self-evident that taking the initiative is *always* the best thing to do, though those who use the word always seem to think it is. Though the word is new, it is already being used as a mere posh substitute for 'active'.

C Ostriches, lemmings, Gadarene swine

(a) Ostriches, of course, do not stick their heads in the sand, either because they believe it makes them invisible or for any other reason, but the old yarn that they do makes 'Ostrich!' a suitable rebuke for those who Refuse to Face Facts. See also Brewer, 1970: p. 788.

(b) Lemmings are small rodents, native to some Arctic areas. From time to time, overpopulation results in a serious shortage of food. Large bands of them set out in search of a new habitat. Once they have chosen a direction, they do not deviate from it, eating everything they can find. When they reach the sea, they treat it as a river, but it isn't, so they drown. A resonant, though ambiguous, political symbol.

(c) 'Gadarene' should probably be 'Gerasene',[2] but the former has become semi-proverbial. The Synoptic Gospels report that Christ, on arriving in 'Gadarene' territory, exorcised a multitude of unclean spirits from a man and sent them into a herd of swine 'And the herd with great violence was carried headlong into the sea, . . . and were stifled in the sea'[3] (Mark v. 1–17; Matthew viii. 28–34; Luke viii. 26–39). Thus, to call something *social Gadarenism* is to say that it is headlong, unthinking and self-destructive. Dostoyevsky makes vivid, even lurid use of the metaphor in *The Devils (The Possessed)*, especially pt III, ch. vii.

11.4 PROGRESS, PROGRESSIVE

> If you glance at history's pages
>> In all days and eras known,
> You will find the buried ages
>> Far more wicked than our own.
> As you scan each word and letter
>> You will realise it more
> That the world today is better
>> Than it ever was before.
>>> Ella Wheeler Wilcox(?)
>> (Quoted, Knox, 1958: pp. 98–99)

> When Science has discovered something more
> We shall be happier than we were before.
>> 'Newdigate Poem: A Prize Poem Submitted
>> by Mr Lambkin . . .' (Belloc, 1938: p. 97)

(i) To progress is to move from stage to stage of a process, especially if it has a characteristic or expected end. We can speak of things getting progressively worse, of the progress of a disease, of an occupying power's 'progressive destruction of Xland's identity and culture' (12.17). Thus, the word 'progress' can be evaluatively neutral.

(ii) But the word 'end' in the first sentence above is ambiguous. It can mean simply a *concluding stage*, or it can mean *a goal*. The successive phases leading to a goal are good relative to that goal. We make progress on a journey if our movement brings us closer to the destination. We make progress towards the solution of a problem. If the patient's condition is improving, he is making progress. (Notice, however, that if he is *restored* to health, progress involves going backwards.)

(iii) Because of this association with goals, with wished-for states of affairs, the word 'progress' has acquired a favourable colouring and the instances cited in (i) can have a paradoxical ring (but no one with his wits about him would regard them as self-contradictory). To use the word 'progress' in a favourable fashion does not commit the user to the recognition of a great, beneficent, irresistible social force called 'Progress'. But that notion is always hanging about. So, for some people, to characterise something as 'progress' is not merely to *praise* it, but to *sanctify* it. 'You can't stop progress,' people have told us. (And, all too often, we have forgotten to say in reply: 'How do you know? And what do you mean, anyway? Progress *towards what?*' Cf. 11.6 on *efficiency*.) There may be a trend in some direction or other, but it does not follow *either* that that trend MUST continue *or* that it OUGHT to continue.

People can be intimidated by the label 'progress'. Once it is fastened on something, many believe that it is preposterous to resist that thing or even to ask questions about it. Perhaps the thing is one which it would be wrong or futile to resist. But merely fixing the label to it proves nothing. See 11.5 (modernity), 11.5F (modernisation, development), 11.6 (efficiency).

See R. Williams, 1983: pp. 243–245; Frankel, 1967; Hofstadter, 1959; Plamenatz, 1960: index; Pollard, 1971; Ritter, 1986: pp. 339–344; R. Sampson & Koblernicz, 1973; Spadafora, 1990; C. Welch, 1990; Woollard, 1972.

'A progressive regime', said *The Kabul New Times*, 'is only tolerant to various shades of opinion as long as these do not lead to diversion from its chosen path' (quoted, R. Evans, 1980).

11.5 MODERNITY

> Il faut être absolument moderne.
> Arthur Rimbaud (and Thoroughly Modern Millie)

> . . . the literary world of Germany [in 1909] was surfeited and sickened by the term. 'The Modern', even the adjective 'modern', had become the sign of all that was old-fashioned and bourgeois, a term the connotations of which suggested nothing so much as exhaustion and decay.
> (Malcolm Bradbury & James McFarlane, 1976: p. 39)

> The present is only a period, you know.
> (C. S. Lewis)

A   The strict and primary meaning of the word 'modern' is vague and indeterminate. Its apparent inner core (viz.: 'of our time') looks solid, but can be as slippery as an eel, as intangible as a mirage. Similar bothers afflict the expressions 'contemporary', 'recent', 'now' and 'the present'. From one point of view, my action of beginning this sentence is as utterly past as the assassination of Julius Caesar. From other points of view, the present could begin with the outbreak of the First World War, or the invention of printing, or the emergence of the human species (see *TP* 8.18B (ii)). Point of view is crucial. To predicate modernity of something is to say that it is, *in some significant respect*, of our time. Obviously, then, there need be no one basis on which we predicate modernity. It might be reasonable to expect modern art and modern poetry to have something in common, but that expectation (if reasonable) is founded on the relations between art and poetry, not on a set of intrinsic characteristics which both must share if they are to be modern. To search for the common intrinsic modernity of modern art, modern footware, modern logic, and modern plumbing would be like searching for the intrinsic 'realness' common to real cream, real silk and a real fright (see *TP* 1.16A).
B   Thus, the primary function of the predicate 'modern' is *relational* (*TP* 1.19 (vi)): it merely (and imprecisely) locates a thing in time. The indeterminacy is, much more often than not, sufficiently tamed by context (though it can still trip us up, especially – though not only – when we are theorising). But *because*

of that relational, merely locating function, 'modern' can, *within a given kind of things*, have a more descriptive function as well. A thing which is of our time and of the kind x may be more or less peculiarly, distinctively of our time. It may be more or less different from xs of previous times. When xs of our time have such a peculiar, distinctive character, then the phrase 'modern x' can become more richly descriptive and less a mere locator. 'Modern stuff, eh?' says Ambler's policeman when told of a landscape depicting a blue field under a green sky (1991: p. 56), to which we might reply 'Not very'. The phrases 'modern dance', 'modern poetry', 'modern logic' do not merely locate but also (in at least some contexts and in some circles) describe (or at least awake definite expectations about) intrinsic characteristics. Notice, however, that this operates *within a given kind of things*: modern xs may have certain distinctive intrinsic resemblances, but it would still be a mistake to conclude that there are intrinsic resemblances between modern xs and modern ys.

C   So 'modern' can acquire a more than merely locating descriptive function. This has two paradoxical consequences:

(i)   An x which is of our time (i.e., modern locationally) may not be (in the 'intrinsic' sense) a modern x. (Was Betjeman a modern poet? Are Drysdale's paintings modern art? DO NOT answer 'Yes' or 'No'.)

(ii)   A statement of the type 'Modern x is totally *passé* will not be self-contradictory. (Whether The Modern Novel is dead or alive, whether any of our contemporaries are writing modern literature, are, in some circles, matters for eager debate. See, e.g., Bradbury, 1989: pp. 87–114.)

Thus, one might be able to talk of 'post-modern art' without committing oneself to the proposition that we have entered *a post-modern era*. Contemporary talk of the post-modern tends to be wild and waffly. Margaret A. Rose (in an admirable but depressing book (1991)) finds ambiguities not only in 'modern', but also in 'post'. In some cases, she says (though not in all), whether a writer uses a hyphen or not is significant. Some media-folk use 'post-modern' (or, perhaps, 'postmodern') as a more up-to-date replacement for 'up-to-date'. To call that infantile is unfair to infants.

D   A movement of thought or practice which stresses the differences between the present and the past or tries to make a dramatic break with the past may be called '(a) modernism'. The cautions applying to 'modern' apply here also:

(i)   It is a mistake to think that (e.g.) theological modernism and literary modernism[4] must be two varieties of the same thing, with much in common;

(ii)   A post-modernism is a logical possibility (which does not entail the possibility of a post-modern age).

Whether the world has changed so much that we need to talk about a post-modern age may be an interesting question. If so, it needs to be discussed carefully, clearly, critically and calmly. To react excitedly to a puzzling complex of social phenomena is not always incompatible with trying seriously to understand it (i.e., with *theorising* about it), but the two kinds of activity are not identical and the former should not be confused with the latter. See Arac, 1988; Booker, 1969; Greenberg, 1980; Hoy, 1986; Heller, 1985: ch.vi; McAuley, 1959; M. A. Rose, 1991; S. K. White, 1991; J. F. Wilson, 1987; Wood, 1992.

E   To use 'modern' as a term of evaluation, either favourable or unfavourable, is, at best, a symptom of intellectual fatigue.

F   To *modernise* an x is to bring it into conformity with the way that xs are now. Thus, an editor of *Hamlet* may modernise the spelling (without modernising the text). In talk of socio-economic matters, 'modernisation' has acquired a technical status, though not a precise or complete or agreed definition. Writers tend to begin the same way: modernisation is the complex of developments which characteristically have followed industrialisation and mechanisation. There is, however, room for dispute over just what those changes are (or what the significant ones are). Other disputable issues are the relationship between modernisation and westernisation, whether modernisation is always improvement (see 11.4 on *progress*; 11.6 on *efficiency*), and whether talk of it might be just a bit of ideological flavouring (*TP* 7.2D) to make the world more easily swallowable by the multinationals. The magic word 'development' comes into play in such contexts. It is every bit as tricky as 'progress'. See Needler, 1991: ch. iv; Bendix, 1969; Eisenstadt, 1966; Attir *et al.*, 1981; Gillis *et al.*, 1983: chs ii, iv; Lehmann, 1979; Porter *et al.*, 1991.

11.6   EFFICIENCY

A   *OED* devotes three folio columns to this word and its cognates. The definition most correspondent to contemporary use is:

> The ratio of useful work performed to the total energy expended or heat taken in.[5]

Though this definition is good enough, it might suggest that what is achieved is merely end-*product*, pay-off, or profit – something other than the work by which it is achieved. But how a thing is achieved can be as important an end as any product. (If the whole point of the football competition is to decide who gets the Cup, it would be more efficient to settle the matter by drawing a name out of a hat.) In Australia, over the past few years, we have heard much of 'more efficient teaching in universities'. Such talk, when examined, turns out to have no relation to any goal which a conscientious student or teacher would have in mind. All it means is *fewer lecturers lecturing to more students* with an increased output of graduates popping off the assembly line at the annual Graduation Ceremonies. One must always ask, 'Efficient at producing WHAT?' (cf. 11.4 on *progress*). *How* a goal, X, is achieved can be as much an end or goal as X itself (see *TP* 7.18). Charles Maclean, writing about a vanished civilization, says, 'efficiency as a criterion could easily be misapplied in St Kilda[6] if it failed to take into account the social as well as the economic function of work' (1972: p. 108). Not only in St Kilda! Cf. 2.14F.

It is sometimes said that democracy is less efficient than dictatorship – all that *talk* about what the decision should be, as contrasted with a dictator's instant decision without all that talk – and perhaps without any thought either. An infallible and impeccable dictator would do the job much more efficiently than Parliament and Cabinet, but such dictators are as rare as infallible and impeccable plumbers, and the errors and sins of dictators are much more damaging than a few (or even many) burst pipes and blocked drains. The dictatorial believe (*sincerely*) that anything that hinders them is inefficient. A former Secretary to the [Australian] Cabinet has been reported as having deplored '"destructive and time-wasting mechanisms" such as questions without notice'. He was reported as saying also that

> the efficiency of the public sector was greatly hampered by 'the massive overkill' of accountable processes, such as royal commissions, parliamentary questions, privacy laws and freedom of information legislation.
>
> (Sir Geoffrey Yeend. Reported, Lumby, 1991)

If he is right, elections are equally 'destructive and time-wasting'. But all that expenditure on accountability does mean an enormous saving on bullets, barbed wire and poison gas.

Suggested reading

Midgley, 1979: ch. vi; Bondurant & Fisher, 1966; Hood & Jackson, 1988; Penelhum, 1957; *TP* 10.7 (*relevance*).

B   An infallible and impeccable parliament would be just as good as an infallible and impeccable dictator, but dictators and their admirers are unwilling to admit that fantasy is a game for more than one team of players. Neither do they admit that it is a game. Or that it is fantasy.

11.7   RADICAL

(i)   '*Radix*' is Latin for 'root', so a *radical difference* is a fundamental difference and 'radically wrong' means much more than 'very wrong'. A political radical, Scruton says (1983: p. 391), 'wishes to take his . . . ideas to their roots, and to affirm in a thoroughgoing way the doctrines [thus] . . . delivered.' A radical is likely to be dissatisfied with the status quo (but see 11.1B) and to advocate significant changes which 'make many waves'. People who regard themselves as *revolutionaries* (11.2B) tend to despise radicals as '*mere* radicals'. (See, e.g., Gould, 1960: pp. 42–43.) See also Scruton, 1983: p. 391; Sperber & Trittschuh, 1964: pp. 347–352; MacCoby, 1952; D. Wells, 1978. See also 11.9F (*socialist*). For 'radical' in its medical sense, see 11.9A.

(ii)   Change can be in a variety of directions and there is an all-but-infinite variety of kinds of plants, each with its own roots, so there can be left-wing radicals and right-wing radicals and radicals in between. Scruton

(1983: p. 391) argues that 'radical' is so connected with change that, though 'radical right' (11.11B (iii)) makes sense, 'radical conservative' is oxymoronic (see Fowler, 1974: p. 431). Perhaps, but a complete stand-pattery of the Duke-of-Cambridge variety (11.1A) involves a desire for so much change *in what is happening*, that it may deserve the label. For the radical/conservative distinction, see 11.9.

(iii) A *radical Xist* may also be an *extreme Xist*, even an extremist (11.12A), but he need not be.

(iv) *'The Philosophical Radicals'* is the name given to some of the older nineteenth-century utilitarians (*TP* 7.17). Jeremy Bentham (1748–1832) was their leader. Other notable members were James Mill (1773–1836), David Ricardo (1771–1823) and John Austin (1790–1859: see *TP* 7.12H). They were very active in promoting political, educational and economic change, but abominated socialism and supported *laissez-faire* liberalism (11.10A, D). James Mill's son, John Stuart Mill (1806–1873), was ambivalent about that issue (and many others). See Copleston, 1966: chs i, ii.

11.8 LIBERAL AND CONSERVATIVE

In Gilbert and Sullivan's *Iolanthe*, the sentry outside the Houses of Parliament sings:

I often think it's comical – Fal, lal, la!
How Nature always does contrive – Fal, la, la!
That every boy and every gal
    That's born into the world alive
Is either a little Liberal
    Or else a little Conservative! Fal, la, la!
        (Gilbert, 1926: p. 234)

Gilbert (1836–1911) was satirising the British party system of the late nineteenth century. The satire is not very penetrating or original, though it is amusing enough. According to some, however, Gilbert had stumbled on an important truth without quite realising it, the truth that human beings (or, perhaps, social movements) can be divided into those with a tendency to stress the need for change and those who (or which) tend to stress the value of what is already established and the dangers of departing from it. But it is a very rough-and-ready distinction and any attempt to make it hard and fast would not only group bitter enemies together but also chop most of us into two pieces. (See *TP* 5.21 on *false dichotomies*.) Apart from that, 'radical' (11.9) would be better here than 'liberal'. See also 11.3A (*initiative and resistance*), 11.9A–D (*conservatism*), 11.10 (*liberalism*), 11.11 (*left and right*). For *isms*, see 11.9B.

11.9 CONSERVATIVE AND RADICAL; TORY; SOCIALIST

A The word 'conservative' is at least triply ambiguous:

(i)   Someone can be identified as conservative about a particular issue; i.e., he[7] opposes a change, or supports a lesser change than others might. A stand of that kind may or may not be part of a generally conservative outlook, may or may not commit him to a substantial number of other conservative stands.

(ii) One can speak of conservatism as a tradition or movement of thought and action. Generally, this kind of talk is relative to a culture. What it amounts to in detail depends on the other movements or traditions with which the tradition or movement is contrasted.

(iii) The term 'conservative' can be applied to a constellation of personality traits, preferences, prejudices, etc.

There are links amongst the three, but the links are tenuous and variable.) The third kind of conservatism is connected not quite with *pessimism* but certainly with a vivid awareness of imperfection and imperfectibility. A conservative of that kind is someone whose tendency it is to celebrate the good aspects of the environment in which he finds himself (i.e., his social context), to be conscious of the fragility of things, to count the cost of suggested alterations, and to 'fear disturbance of the quiet seasons'.[8]

By contrast, a radical is someone whose tendency is to be irritated by the faults of his environment, to be conscious of the need for change, and to be optimistic about the chances of improvement. The radical tends to stress the extent to which we can reach an explicit understanding of the working of social institutions. The conservative tends to stress the extent to which an understanding of the workings of social institutions is like knowing how to ride a bicycle or talk a language. (The extent to which one explicitly understands such activities is usually inferior to one's implicit understanding of them. See *TP* 8.13–8.14.) A characteristic fault of the radical is to exaggerate the extent to which intention can govern result. A characteristic fault of the conservative is to understate it. Other characteristic faults of the radical are undue discontent, vainglory and vandalism. Parallel to these are conservative faults of complacency, conformism, contempt for new ideas, and cold feet. At his worst, the radical puts his hand on his heart and says:

> . . . could thou and I with Fate conspire
> To grasp this sorry Scheme of things entire.
> Would not we shatter it to bits – and then
> Re-mould it nearer to the Heart's Desire![9]

(A bloodthirsty and foolish fantasy: cf. 11.6.) At his worst, the conservative puts his hand on his heart and talks like that Duke of Cambridge (11.1A). At their worst, the conservative and the radical are dangerous pains in the neck, but (fortunately for everyone, including themselves) they are not always at their worst. The medical senses of 'conservative' and 'radical' are of interest, but of no uncontroversial political significance:

conservative . . . Designed to restore relatively satisfactory health or function while avoiding radical or surgical measures.

radical . . . Designed to address the root cause of a disorder and by extirpating it effect a cure.

(*IDMB*, 1986)

(For *treating symptoms and causes*, see 11.2D.)

B   Any discussion of complex philosophical, political, moral or religious positions which proceeds by saying 'The Xist says such-and-such, whereas the Yist says something else' can only be partially true. We must never forget the roughness of such predicates as '. . . is a conservative', '. . . is a radical'. 'Is Primus a conservative?' (X) is not like 'Is Primus a graduate?' (Y) or 'Is Primus a regular church-goer?' (Z) A 'Yes' or 'No' answer to Y or Z is informative. Such an answer to X is useless. X is a useful (and well-used) question only when it evokes a fairly detailed account of how Primus goes on (what he says, thinks, does) and of the context(s) in which he does it. Such an account *may* imply a 'Yes' or a 'No' answer, but that answer is not detachable from the account on which it is based (unlike a similar answer to X or Y. Cf. the 'conclusionyness' of '. . . is in the general interest' (6.22)). See Ritter, 1986; Condren, 1989; Höpfl 1981.

It follows that what I have said in A is a tissue of oversimplifications. They are, however, less misleading than such pontifications as the following:

. . . conservatism presupposes poverty of imagination, lack of a spirit of adventure, and a surfeit of prudence. Nations so burdened atrophy.

(Blurb to Métin, 1977 (paperback))

One can make equally rude remarks about radicalism which would be just as good (11.3A). Such sweeping assertions have their place in debating societies and election campaigns. Their place in the study of political concepts corresponds to that of frogs in biology or over-confident company prospectuses in commercial law, i.e., they are objects for dissection, not examples to be imitated. A political system needs both radicals and conservatives, and they need each other.

C   'Conservative' as a label for politicians is used in a bewildering and confusing fashion (and far too few people *feel* bewildered and confused by it). Sir Joh Bjelke-Petersen (of Queensland), President Reagan, and Lady Thatcher have all been called *conservative*. One of Bjelke-Petersen's most noticeable characteristics was a contemptuous disregard for the traditions and forms of parliamentary democracy (see, e.g., Coaldrake, 1989; Lunn, 1984). In economic policy, Reagan was a *laissez-faire* (11.10A) liberal (in a vague fashion), and he talked as if he wished to overturn most of what had been accepted policy in order to 'return' to a mythical past symbolised by John Wayne. Lady Thatcher is another *laissez-fairiste* and, as one of her unhappy backbenchers said, 'She cannot see an institution without hitting it with her handbag.' She made more drastic changes in more ruthless fashion than any previous Prime Minister (see Critchley, 1985; Young & Sloman, 1986).

To take an infinitely more respectable example, people sometimes call Thomas Hobbes a conservative, presumably because of his emphasis on authority, on human imperfectibility, and on the possibility of social breakdown. But Hobbes was no conservative. He was (in a bleakish way) a Utopian[10] with a blueprint for THE good political system, and, every bit as much as Marx, he disparaged 'the tradition of the dead generations [which] weighs like a nightmare on the brain of the living'.

There is little point in calling someone a conservative unless *conserving* is an important element in his or her outlook. 'Conservative' and 'right-wing' (11.11) are *not* synonymous. Membership of a party called 'Conservative' no more entails conservatism than membership of a party called 'Liberal' is an infallible sign of a liberal outlook (11.10).

Suggested reading

Scruton, 1983: pp. 90–92; *OED* 'Conserva' etc.; Muehlenberg, 1990; Buck, 1975; J. Carroll, 1978; Crosland, 1962; Gilmour, 1978; Honderich, 1992; Manne, 1982; O'Sullivan, 1976; Quinton, 1978; Ray, 1974; Sperber & Trittschuh, 1964: pp. 94–97.

D   In Australia, the principal non-Labor parties have had a variety of names, but not since the early twentieth century (and then only in some States: see Jaensch & Teichmann, 1988: pp. 237–240) has any significant party borne the proper name (*TP* 2.9), 'Conservative Party'. Even the descriptive, small 'c' use of the term (i.e., as an adjective or a common noun) was rare in Australian political discourse until the 1970s (though in the universities, Burke-and-Oakeshott fans were proudly styling themselves 'conservatives' in the late 1950s). Now, the term has general acceptance as a generic term, referring primarily to the Liberal and National (*née* Country) Parties. Members of these parties, however, sometimes protest that they are *really* radical reformers. See also 11.11B (ii) (*The New Right*). For discussions and expositions of the general viewpoint of the Liberal Party of Australia, see Brandis *et al.*, 1984; Tiver, 1978; D. M. White, 1978; D. McM. Wells, 1977; Jaensch, 1989; Kemp, 1980; P. O'Brien, 1985; Simms, 1980; Puplick & Southey, 1980. On the National Party, see Aitkin, 1972; Costar & Woodward, 1985. For an overview of party-political onomastics see Murray-Smith, 1987: pp. 257–263.

E Tory

The UK Conservative Party dates from Peel's Tamworth manifesto of 1834, succeeding a faction or group of factions known as *The Tories*. 'Tory', like its (now obsolete) antonym 'Whig', was originally a derogatory nickname, but both sides accepted the other's insult as a name (cf *TP* 1.14D; see Blake, 1972:

pp. 1–9; Scruton, 1983: pp. 466, 493–494). In the UK, the term 'Tory'[11] has never become obsolete and many Conservatives gladly and publicly apply it to themselves. So far as I am aware, no Australian politician has ever publicly called himself a Tory. In public political discourse, it is a derogatory term used by opponents of the non-Labor parties. In private conversation, old-fashioned Australian conservatives sometimes use it of themselves (and of their forebears, going back to Noah). For American uses of 'Whig' and 'Tory' (both bewildering), see Sperber & Trittschuh, 1964: pp. 459–460, 480–482. In *Smithers* v. *Stilt* (6 Georgia 277), the Supreme Court of Georgia (US, not CIS) solemnly pronounced that the word 'Tory' is gravely and eternally defamatory (Sparrow, 1970: pp. 79–83). For *Tory Reform*, see 7.19.

F Socialist

(i)   A form of property or a means of economic production, distribution and exchange is *socialised*[12] to the extent that it is brought under public, rather than private control. A socialist is distinguished from a non-socialist by the extent to which he advocates such socialisation. Thus, it is possible to support some socialisation without being a socialist. It is also possible to be a socialist without being committed to the socialisation of everything, including the corner shop, newspapers and individual tooth-brushes. 'Public' in such contexts usually means 'government', but socialist theories of a more *communitarian* kind are possible (cf. 2.9D and 2.17K on *anarchism* and on *participatory democracy*). Socialists advocate socialisation not merely or even primarily as a more efficient (11.6) organisation of the economy than capitalism, but as a means of preventing exploitation and of promoting social justice and equality (see Boyce *et al.*, 1980: pp.38–39, 247). The rather patchy record of actual programmes of socialisation is the principal reason for the heart-searchings and quarrels alluded to in (iii) below.

(ii) UK and Australian uses of 'socialist' are similar to the uses of 'Tory'. The most common UK use of 'socialist' is as a virtual synonym of 'Labour'. It has the advantage of being, unlike 'Labour', directly applicable both to the party and to each of its members (cf. 'Populist' 8.31). In the UK, people willingly and unexcitedly describe themselves as *socialists* and calmly accept that description from others. In Australia, however, 'He is a socialist' is usually denunciatory;[13] 'I am a socialist' is usually declaratory and defiant (in a 'Here-I-stand' fashion) and is now rarely heard. The outlook of the Australian Labor Party (ALP) has been described as 'Socialism without doctrines' (Métin, 1977). It could also be described as 'Socialism without the name' and very often as 'Socialism without socialism'. In 1921, the Party adopted as an objective 'The socialisation of industry, production, distribution and exchange', but, from the beginning, this was hedged about by qualifications. It has since not merely been watered down but chemically transformed. See, e.g., Jaensch &

Teichmann, 1988: pp. 186–187; O'Meagher, 1983; Cairns, 1963, 1975; Calwell, 1963, 1978; McKinlay, 1979; McManus, 1977: ch. xxv; Nairn, 1989; Hawke, 1984: pp. 163–172; Loveday, 1980; Whitlam, 1978.

(iii) It must be said, however, that that free-and-easy UK use of the label is not universally accepted, even in the UK, and there can be very hot disputes over whether Primus is *really* a socialist. Trying to sort that out would be too much like involving myself in someone else's family squabbles. See Scruton, 1983: pp. 435–437; Bealey, 1970; Samuel & Jones, 1982(b); Terrins & Whitehead, 1984; Crosland, 1962, 1974; Crossman, 1960, 1965, 1969; Feaver, 1987; Heffer, 1991; Lipsey & Leonard, 1981. See also 8.40. For examples of American socialism, see *SRC*, 1992.

(iv) It must also be recognised that, despite the ALP's ambivalence (to put it no stronger) about socialism, all Australian governments, of whatever colour, have, until very recently, been strongly committed to intervention in and support of industry. Only the Chinese Communist Party has been less *laissez-faire* than the very right-wing National (*née* Country) Party of Australia. See Eggleston, 1932; Hancock, 1945; T. Fitzgerald, 1990.

(v) In Communist and Marxist jargon, the word 'socialism' is (or was) used to denote an intermediate stage between the proletarian revolution and the final stage of true communism when the state would have withered away, along with classes, alienation, the distinction between public and private (and, quite possibly, the common cold as well).

11.10 LIBERALISM

A   All 'ism' words are pretty terrible (11.9B; *TP* 7.1) and 'liberalism' is one of the most terrible of all. In America, if you support social services, industrial legislation, legislation to protect the consumer and the environment, you will be called *a liberal*. To advocate such positions is to advocate that government adopt an active, interventionist role. But a look at Bullock and Shock's anthology, *The Liberal Tradition from Fox to Keynes* (1967) shows that some people, called *liberals*, have believed that government should do as little as possible; the idea of *laissez-faire, laissez-aller*: 'Leave enterprise free to go its own way.' See Scruton, 1983: p. 254. Jeremy Bentham (1748–1832) and Herbert Spencer (1820–1903) are nineteenth-century examples. In our own time, F. A. Hayek (1899–1992) has argued a similar case and Hayek regarded himself and is regarded as a liberal. Spencer saw economic planning and social services as 'The Coming Slavery': Hayek, some sixty years later, called them 'The Road to Serfdom'. We cannot dispose of these oddnesses by simply saying that the American meaning of the word 'liberal' differs from the British (like the noun 'flat'). Lord Beveridge (1879–1963), the architect of the welfare state, was an English liberal and is represented in Bullock and Shock's collection as, of course, was John Maynard Keynes (1883–1946), whose view of economics requires the government to be active and interventionist in a way that would have horrified Spencer and Bentham and did horrify Hayek.

In South Africa (at least until recently), if you opposed apartheid, you were *a liberal*, or, as they say there, *a liberalist*. You might combine your opposition to apartheid with support for the restoration of the Holy Roman Empire, but that would not have been enough to lose you the title 'liberalist', or to save you from detention under the ninety-day law if you were not careful. On the other hand, there are some members of the Liberal Party of Australia who think that apartheid is not all *that* bad and believe that that view should be held by all other members of their party. And, if Australian political parties are compared with those of the UK, the Liberal Party of Australia (11.9D) looks more like the Conservative Party than like the UK Liberal Party.

B   So some very diverse, even incompatible political, economic and moral opinions have been given the label 'liberal' or 'liberalism'. Various different reactions to this sort of oddness are possible, e.g.:

(i)   The words really have no or very minimal meaning. People adopt or confer the label. It may identify within a limited context, but it has only the sort of meaning which the colours of a football team or the number of a house has.

(ii)   The words do have a definite meaning, but they have been misapplied. We need to sort out the true liberals from the false. A prerequisite of that is the determination of the *essence* of liberalism: the core of character-istics which all and only liberal people, policies, etc., have.

(iii)   The words do have a definite meaning, but there is no essence to be discovered. 'Liberal' is a relative term – like 'above'. We don't need the word 'aboveness'. We only *just* need the word 'liberalism'. We need to talk about *the liberalism of Fabians* who want peaceful change as compared with *the revolutionariness of Bolsheviks*. We need to talk about *the liberalism of the supporters of the Reform Bill of 1824* as compared with *the conservatism of its opponents*. We need to talk about *the liberalism of the 1824 reformers* as compared with *the liberalism of the supporters of the Parliament Act of 1911*.[14] So there does seem to be a place for the word 'liberalism', but that word does not pick out a body of doctrine (in *that* sense, liberalism is not an ism). There is no one thing, liberalism, which can be an object of study.

None of these positions is adequate. The third has more truth in it (and more awareness of language-as-it-is) than the other two. 'Liberal' does have its relative uses, according to which a position is called 'liberal' because it is more in favour of peaceful change or less in favour of control than some rival position. But that cannot be the whole story. Suppose that the ruling junta of the Republic of Santa Banana believes in gaoling anyone spreading alarm and despondency, and one group in the junta wants to extend this policy to anyone who complains about the weather while another group opposes this. In that case, we might call the second group 'the liberal group in the junta', *but* we might also say, without any self-contradiction, that *no one* in the junta is

liberal. We make this second judgement by reference to criteria (*TP* 2.4) for liberalism, not just by seeing where the junta is placed in relation to other groups of rulers or politicians. Thus, the 'relativistic' meaning of 'liberal' is not the *only* meaning. Further, we must not be too swift in dismissing the existence of 'an ism called "liberalism"'. After all, people write books about liberalism, talk about its history, declare themselves for it or against it or for it up to a point, etc. It may be that all those people are muddled, but, if they are, we can find that out only by taking a good hard look at what they say. And that is the answer to the other two positions as well.
C   Unfortunately, some who write about liberalism prefer to take a quick, easy look and have no doubts about essences. W. H. Walsh (1972), for instance, tells us that a liberal is someone who believes in ineluctable moral laws that are to be put into force regardless of particular circumstances. According to Ronald Dworkin (1978: p. 127), a liberal is someone who believes 'that political decisions must be, so far as is possible, independent of any particular conception of the good life, or of what gives value to life'. Pretty little definitions, nice and neat. But they cannot both be right if they are talking about the same thing. There are other difficulties. Walsh's definition would make liberals of 'Moral Majoritarians' like the Revd Fred Nile and the Revd Jerry Falwell and would exclude many who are usually called liberals: Keynes, D. G. Ritchie, Asquith, indeed almost any reasonably sane politician, almost any administrator who knows his job. Dworkin's definition no doubt includes Dworkin, but that does not make up for its exclusion of Gladstone and John Stuart Mill.[15]

The words 'liberal' and 'liberalism' are *words in use*. They are not algebraic variables hanging about in the hope that some philosopher will give them a job (*TP* 6.2–6.7). They are *alive* and *wild* (1.2). They are used to refer to certain socio-political movements, to various dispositions to thought, action and aspiration. Walsh and Dworkin know that and they profess to be elucidating something that is there to be elucidated. But they do not treat it as something that is there. Instead, they behave like Humpty Dumpty in *Through the Looking Glass*: 'When *I* use a word, it means what I want it to mean, neither more nor less,' and they simultaneously pretend to be telling us something about politics and political theory. Winemakers get threatened with the Trade Practices Act for less. The world, politics, political theory, and the English language have existed for some time. They antedate you, me, Walsh, and Dworkin, and to some extent are independent of us. They are quite likely to survive us. Like it or not (and I rather like it, myself), that's how it is, and the notion of liberalism is part of it. 'The game is played,' as Wittgenstein says. To ignore it and to profess to be talking about liberalism is to indulge in self-deceiving fantasy. As Francis Bacon said:

> . . . the wit and mind of man, if it work upon matter . . . worketh according to the stuff and is limited thereby; but if it work upon itself, as the spider worketh its web, then it is endless, and brings forth indeed cobwebs of

learning, admirable for the fineness of thread and work, but of no substance or profit.

(Bacon, *Advancement* bk I ch. iv, §5, 1951: p. 32)

The word 'liberty' also is part of the historical manifold, the 'matter' which we need to 'work upon'. It would be odd if it and 'liberalism', two words so alike, so closely related in etymology, so often used in close juxtaposition, were quite dissociated in meaning. I do not see that it makes much sense to call someone a liberal unless he puts some special emphasis on freedom and unless he has a certain distrust of power and a strong belief in the need to control power and make it accountable in some way. Am I then saying, after all, that there *is* an essence of liberalism? No. An essence is peculiar to that of which it is the essence and there are many who stress freedom and distrust power who would be more clearly characterised as conservatives or as radicals or as anarchists. An essence, too, is an unchanging thing in that of which it is an essence and it is fairly evident that, in anglophone politics and thought, the stress on freedom and the distrust of power have taken not merely different but mutually antagonistic forms. This stress on freedom combined with a distrust of power is essential to liberalism only in a thin sense of the word 'essential' – i.e., it is a necessary condition for being a liberal (*TP* 4.16). Liberalism must have something to do with the prejudice that, in Lord Devlin's words, 'authority should be a grant and liberty not a privilege' (1965: p. 102), so it is preposterous to call someone like Hobbes a liberal:

. . . that great LEVIATHAN, or rather (to speake more reverently) . . . that *Mortall God*, to which wee owe under the *Immortall God*, our peace and defence.

(Hobbes, *Leviathan* ch. xvii, 1991: p. 120)

A liberal speaking? Not on your life! 'Hobbes was', says Tuck,[16] '. . . a kind of liberal – that is, he believed that public policy should secure a particular level of welfare for all citizens . . . and that once that level is secured there should be no attempt to force policies upon the citizenry' (1989: p. 97). If that makes Hobbes a kind of liberal, then Sukarno, Ataturk and Nasser were liberals of the same kind, a very funny kind. As Bernard Crick once remarked, even if it is true that it is more important to be fed than to be free, that does not imply that being fed is a way of being free. J. E. McTaggart, a quirky philosopher of the early part of this century, said:

compared with the worship of the state, zoolatry is rational and dignified. A bull or a crocodile may not have great intrinsic value, but it has some, for it is a conscious being. The state has none. It would be as reasonable to worship a sewage-pipe, which also possesses considerable value as a means.

(Quoted, Quinton, 1975: p. 13)

Hobbes does not worship the State (or the Commonwealth, or the Sovereign) but he does think it appropriate to use religious language about it. McTaggart goes too far: the State, after all, is the provider and guarantor of sewage-pipes, so is superior to them (though still not deserving worship). But liberalism talking hyperbolically, liberalism (as it were) in its cups sounds much more like McTaggart than like Hobbes.

D The notion of liberalism is embedded in history and is as messy as most things embedded in history. One cannot simply write it off as non-existent because it is messy. One cannot cleanse it of its messiness by waving the magic wand of stipulative (i.e., Humpty Dumptyan) definition (2.1) at it. Liberalism is not so much a *body of doctrine* as a tradition of thought, feeling, aspiration, action. A tradition extends over a substantial period of time, is a moving, developing thing. As D. M. Armstrong says:

> The mechanism of transmission in a tradition is imitation. Now, *the imitation of conduct is not necessarily a transitive relation*. If B imitates A's conduct with tolerable accuracy, and C imitates B's imitation with tolerable accuracy, then C's conduct is not necessarily a tolerably accurate imitation of A's conduct. Imitation, even close imitation, permits a certain 'wander'.
>
> (Armstrong, 1980: p. 99. Emphasis in original)

A tradition, then, would tend to have the sort of unity which Wittgenstein finds in the concept of *game* (see 10.18): not a monolithic unity, but a unity nonetheless. There are those disagreements between alleged liberals such as Spencer, Bentham and Hayek on the one hand and alleged liberals such as Keynes and Beveridge on the other, disagreements so striking and so fundamental as to seem to count against there being any tradition involving all five. But liberalism is not just a matter of the *laissez-fairistes* versus the interventionists. There are also transitional opinions. Bentham, writing towards the end of the eighteenth century, says that the general rule for the government is 'Be quiet' or 'Do Nothing'. He says that any exceptions to that rule are rare and that a heavy onus of proof lies on those who support governmental action (Bullock & Shock, 1967: pp. 28–29). Fifty years later, John Stuart Mill in his uneasy book, *Principles of Political Economy*, seems to be trying to say much the same thing, but it is clear that, in his view, there will be 'some very large and conspicuous exceptions' to the rule that government should leave things alone (bk V, ch. xi, §9, 1970: p. 322). He recognises that 'Freedom of contract, in the case of children, is but another word for freedom of coercion' (ibid.: p. 323). That was an important breach in the wall of *laissez-faire* liberalism (one which Thomas Hill Green was to widen considerably in his *Liberal Legislation and Freedom of Contract* (1881)). Mill also shows a lively awareness that governmental power is only one species of power (2.14) and that there are cases in which governmental power is less susceptible to abuse than non-governmental power.

Round about the time that Mill was working on that book, attempts were being made to legislate for safer working conditions and shorter hours.[17] Some liberals found that very shocking. Speaking against the Factories Bill of 1847, Joseph Hume, MP, declared that any attempt to legislate for better working conditions was an attack on 'the principles of political economy' by which 'the best interests of the community were regulated'. These principles, he said, were 'that masters and men should be allowed to make what arrangements they pleased between themselves, both with regard to the length of hours and the rate of wages; that Government should interfere as little as possible, except in every instance to remove prohibitions and protections' (Bullock & Shock, 1967: pp. 58–60).

To such liberals, that was all obvious common sense, but others took a different view; e.g., Thomas Babington Macaulay who spoke in favour of the Ten Hours Bill of 1846:

> This, they say, is one of those matters about which we ought not to legislate at all; one of those matters which settle themselves far better than any government can settle them. Now it is most important that this point should be fully cleared up . . . . I hardly know which is the greater pest to society . . . a prying, meddlesome government . . . which thinks that it can do everything for everybody better than anybody can do anything for himself; or a careless, lounging government, which suffers grievances, such as it could at once remove, to grow and multiply, and which to all complaint and remonstrance has only one answer: 'We must let things alone: we must let things take their course . . . .' There is no more important problem in politics than to ascertain the just mean between these two most pernicious extremes . . . .
>
> (ibid.: pp. 55–56)

Notice what is happening: a movement from the notion that the duty of government is *laissez-faire* except in rare and urgent cases, to the recognition that those cases may be less rare than had been thought. In Mill, we find also a movement from an exclusive distrust of governmental power to a distrust of other forms of power as well. When we turn to Macaulay's speech, we find that the emphasis has shifted: he says that there is a mean to be struck between governmental activity and governmental busybodyism. Beveridge and Keynes make a further move to the proposition that governmental activity and intervention are *indispensable*. If we look only at the extremes, there seems no such thing as liberalism, merely two incompatible positions, both inexplicably called 'liberalism'. At one extreme, we find Richard Cobden saying

> To make laws for the regulation of trade, is as wise as it would be to legislate about water finding a level, or matter exercising its centripetal force.
>
> (ibid.: p. 54)

At the other extreme, we find Beveridge saying:

> The first condition of full employment is that total outlay should always be high enough to set up a demand for products of industry which cannot be satisfied without using the whole man-power of the country . . . .
> Who is to secure that . . . [this] condition . . . is satisfied? . . . [T]he State.

No one else has the requisite powers; the condition will not get satisfied automatically. It must be a function of the State . . . to protect its citizens against mass-unemployment, as definitely as it is . . . the function of the State to defend the citizens against attack from abroad and against robbery and violence at home . . . .

(ibid.: pp. 263–264)

Two incompatible positions, but if we try to look at the total picture, to take in as much as possible of the arguments, the advocacy, the aspirations of the people usually regarded as contributors to the anglophone liberal tradition, we can map a transition between the two. It is not a transition from concern with liberty to concern with welfare nor is it simply from 'freedom to' to 'freedom from' (want, etc.).[18] Rather, it involves a realisation that there are material and institutional conditions for the effective *general* exercise of freedom and that a concern for freedom which is not also a concern for those conditions is a concern for the freedom, not of human beings generally, but merely for the freedom of the powerful to become more powerful at the expense of the less powerful. (See also Schapiro, 1958: p. 138.)

E   The transition between 'old' and 'new' liberalism is not a purely temporal one. Temporally, there are innumerable overlaps. Macaulay and Mill, whom I have called transitional figures, antedate Spencer, whose main political work, *The Man versus the State* (significant title), appeared in 1884. T. H. Green, who definitely belongs to the Beveridge–Keynes end of the spectrum, died in 1882. 'Old' liberalism (thanks to the newest New Right (11.11B)) is going through a rather noisy revival at the present time. In other words, there is in the liberal tradition an *oscillation* between the view that active government is the foe of freedom and justice, and the view that active government is an indispensable condition for freedom and justice. Indeed, this oscillation is found not merely in the liberal tradition, but also in the thinking of many individual liberals. To those who love tidiness above all things, this will seem logically very unsatisfactory, but it seems to me to be rationally very satisfactory. I am more than merely inclined to think that, in politics, the rational thing to do is to seek an unattainable balance between active government and independent action. The by-products of that self-defeating enterprise may well be as much freedom and justice as we are likely to get. Though the countries in which liberalism is a political force have a very spotty record, they compare rather favourably with those which have rejected or never tried it (see Passmore, 1981).

People have elaborated liberal philosophies of politics and society. It is possible to move from a metaphysical theory (*TP* 7.22) to a socio-political theory of a liberal kind and it is possible to seek a metaphysical justification of a liberal socio-political theory or standpoint. It is possible also to seek a synthesis between such a theory or standpoint and metaphysical positions which one holds on other grounds. But liberalism is not *a philosophy*, except in what can be called *the newspaper sense of the word 'philosophy'*, i.e., a fairly general attitude, a disposition to judge, act, react in a certain roughly specifiable fashion. If we turn to the liberal tradition and ask for 'the' liberal view on the great questions of epistemology and metaphysics, of the nature of man,[19] of the foundations of morality, we find something between a void and a chaos. There has been some association between empiricism (*TP* 7.12B–C) and liberalism, but, of the three great exemplars of British Empiricism, only one (Locke) was a liberal: the other two were Tories (see Hume, 1951, and Berkeley's sermon on Passive Obedience). Sir Karl Popper is certainly a liberal, and one who tries to link his liberalism with his metaphysics, but he is only dubiously an empiricist. (What kind of empiricist says that there is innate knowledge? Popper does. See Popper, 1969: p. 47; Popper, 1972: index.) There has also been some association between liberalism and utilitarianism (*TP* 7.17), but there have been non-liberal utilitarians (e.g., David Hume, Sir James Fitzjames Stephen) and liberal non-utilitarians (e.g., T. H. Green, D. G. Ritchie, Bertrand de Jouvenel); W. E. Gladstone and Samuel Plimsoll were liberal politicians with deep moral convictions, but those convictions have a decidedly deontological smell to them (*TP* 7.18B). What of 'individualism'? There are numerous different theories and attitudes that go by that name (see Lukes, 1973). Hobbes is a proponent of one of them, and also of government unimpeded by constitutional restraints or opposition. The individualism of Mill was strongly criticised by D. G. Ritchie who was certainly a liberal (see Bullock & Shock, 1967: pp. 187–190). Liberalism is not even a comprehensive world-view about whose philosophical expression and justification there is controversy: Mill was an agnostic who moved towards an unworshipful deism; Acton was a Catholic (ibid.: pp. 118–127). This lack of a set of liberal answers to the problems of philosophy is appropriate from a tradition which emphasises the value of liberty. Moral Re-Armers, Marxists and similar sectaries will, of course, see it as a fatal weakness. A disbelief in final solutions, a sort of *hopeful* disbelief in perfectibility is, I think, a necessary or virtually necessary correlate of an emphasis on freedom and a distrust of power. The difference between a liberal and a liberal-minded conservative is that the former tends to have a degree of optimism and a readiness to change which the latter finds it difficult to share. One important difference between a liberal and many socialists is that the latter are *more* ready to restrict liberty in the cause of equality and/or social justice than the former is. (Provided one recognises that the previous two sentences are objectionably glib, they point in the direction of truth.)

Suggested reading

Ritter, 1986: pp. 259–264; R. Williams, 1983: pp. 179–183; Bullock & Shock, 1967; Galston, 1991; Gaus, 1983; T. H. Green, 1964; McCloskey, 1968, 1974; Passmore, 1981; Schapiro, 1958; Hobhouse, 1964; Manning, 1976. For readings on the revived Old Liberalism of the newest New Right, see 11.11B (ii).

11.11 LEFT AND RIGHT

A When the French Estates-General met in joint session in 1789, the nobility sat on the King's right and the representatives of the Tiers Etat (the Third Estate, i.e., the Commoners) sat on his left. That provided a metaphor for attitudes towards the issues involved in the French Revolution, a metaphor which survived the Revolution and still staggers on. At its simplest and crudest: on the Left, the proponents of change; on the Right, the defenders of the existing order, and between the two ends, there is a continuum.

But change can be in all sorts of directions, and the Left/Right distinction has been drawn on other bases as well: egalitarianism and opposition to it, the role of the State in the economy, the ownership of property, etc. Until recently, the Left/Right distinction was usually thought of as a Socialist/Nonsocialist (11.9F) distinction. Even that could be confusing. Primus might say 'Secundus is on the extreme Right wing' on the ground that he was an admirer of Mussolini's exaltation of the State (2.16B) or on the ground that he was an extreme *laissez-fairiste* (11.10A) who wanted the State to do as little as possible. Similarly, an extreme Leftist might be either a devotee of central state planning and the command economy or an anarchist who believed that all authority is slavery. Those are only samples of the complexity and confusion. Given a definite context, the terms could be intelligible and serviceable, even if crude, but even then they *needed* a definite context.

And then came Mr Gorbachev. The more Socialist a Soviet citizen was, the more he opposed the new policies. So it made sense (rather comic sense if you thought about it) to call those opponents 'conservatives', as against the 'radicals' who supported Mr Gorbachev or thought that he should go much further much faster. Then the press began calling 'the conservatives' *Right-wingers*, using the label *'Left-wing'* for the advocates of change. Thus, in a Soviet context, an old-style Stalinist is an extreme Right-winger and admirers of Lady Thatcher and Milton Friedman are on the far Left. Some of the writings most admired by the Right-wingers will be found in a volume called *The Essential Left* (Marx *et al.*, 1960; see also Kagarlitsky, 1992). 'And then there was the man who committed suicide after discovering that Lenin wrote an attack on Left-Wing Communism.'[20] I think that he has come back to haunt us all. For 'Left', 'Right', and 'Centre' as names of factions in the Australian Labor Party, see 5.37. Applying such terms to (e.g.) seventeenth-century figures is at best analogical, at worst (and more likely) tommyrot. See Condren, 1989.

Suggested reading

Labedz, 1988; Labedz & Reilly, 1988(a); Scruton, 1983: pp. 260–262, 408; Arndt, 1980; Crosland, 1974: pp. 97–98; McMurty, 1979; *NS/S*, 1991; A. Sampson, 1971: pp. 36–40.

B New Left and New Right

I have just remarked on rather startling new uses of the terms 'Left' and 'Right'. Please do not think that those have anything to do with the terms 'New Left' and 'New Right'.

(i) The term *'New Left'* came into use in the late 1950s to label various individuals and groups who were Marxist in basic orientation, but had become disillusioned with the 'official' Communist Parties and with most Communist *régimes*. The term was also used for various protest movements which emerged, principally in universities, in the late 1960s. There were similarities and some continuities between the two, but it would be rash to speak of one New Left movement embracing both. Most of the later New Leftists professed opposition to all established authority, devotion to participatory (as opposed to representative) democracy, and enthusiastic admiration for Mao Tse-Tung and the Cultural Revolution (a position not without its logical difficulties). By the mid-1970s, that New Left was old hat.

Suggested reading

Labedz & Reilly, 1988(b); Scruton, 1983: p. 322; Cameron, 1962: ch. iv; Cockburn & Blackburn, 1969; R. Fraser *et al.*, 1988; R. Gordon, 1970; Harrington, 1969; Howe, 1966; Kennan *et al.*, 1968; Lipset & Wolin, 1965; Loebl, 1972; Novak, 1969; Searle, 1972.

(ii) *The New Right*

This expression has been applied to a variety of conflicting positions (i.e., the 'The' is misleading: *TP* 5.30), but seems at present to have come to rest upon those who wish to diminish state intervention in economic matters and to leave as much as possible to the operation of market forces. Some would say that the Hawke and Keating Labor Governments have been, basically, New Right governments. See Jaensch, 1989; North & Weller, 1980.

Suggested reading

Labedz & Reilly, 1988(a); Reilly, 1988(b), (c); Scruton, 1983: pp. 322–323; N. P. Barry, 1979; Butler, 1983; Flew, 1981; Friedman, 1977; Friedman & Friedman, 1962, 1980; Gray, 1984; Hayek, 1944, 1960, 1979, 1988; Ivens, 1975; Keat & Abercrombie, 1991; Machlup, 1976; Minogue, 1989; Nozick, 1974; Nurick, 1989; Pusey, 1991; Sawer, 1982; Skidelsky, 1989; Sterba, 1978.

(iii) *The Radical Right*

Again, the 'The' is misleading. At present, the term is sometimes applied to free-marketeers, extreme small-government libertarians, and 'anarcho-capitalists' (see Swan, 1979; Tier, 1975; Hospers, 1971;[21] Tucker, 1979), but it has been applied also to extreme anti-Communist, racist, authoritarian, nationalist and generally alarmist groups, such as the John Birch Society (American) or the Australian League of Rights. See D. Bell, 1964; Connell & Gould, 1967; Epstein & Forster, 1967; Gott, 1965; Hofstadter, 1967; Ó Maoláin, 1987; Richmond, 1977.

11.12 MIDDLES, CENTRES, EXTREMES, ETC.

A Extremist; Moderate

These are rather vague words, but, usually, to say that someone is an extremist is to say that he demands more than the moderate. At the same time, the moderate is likely to recognise a greater variety of values and ends and to be engaged, much of the time, in arranging 'trade-offs' between them. The extremist, by contrast, is likely to be rather single-minded. He will usually be prepared to accept costs (in terms of disruption and human suffering) which the moderate will regard as unthinkable and to be more ready to use means which the moderate finds regrettable. Solzhenitsyn (1976) portrays Lenin as a pure and extreme extremist. The tone of Kennedy's inaugural address is extremist:

> Let every nation know, whether it wishes us well or ill, that we shall pay any price, bear any burden, meet any hardship, support any friend, oppose any foe to assure the survival and the success of liberty.
> This much we pledge – and more.
>
> (Hofstadter, 1969: p. 453)

Suggested reading

OED 'moder', etc., 'extreme'; Scruton, 1983: pp. 56–57; Berki, 1972; Condren, 1989; Connell & Gould, 1967; Gusfield, 1962; Hoffer, 1980.

B Middle paths

Thomas Hobbes saw himself as trying to tread and map a middle path between two extremes:

> in a way beset with those that contend on one side for too great Liberty, and on the other side for too much Authority, 'tis hard to passe between the points of both unwounded.
>
> (1991: p. 3)

But Hobbes himself is regarded by many as an extremist. The moderate/extremist contrast is often drawn on a basis of greater or less tolerance, though 'extremely tolerant' is not self-contradictory. It begins to seem that 'moderate' and 'extremist' are rather tricky, sticky words. Any use of them should be carefully scrutinised and closely questioned.

If we are offered two alternative courses of action, each with some advantages, it is sensible to see if there is some way of combining as much as possible of the advantages of both with as little as possible of the dis- advantages. In controversy, theoretical or practical (*TP* 5.5E), opposing sides sometimes make exaggerated claims, so that each puts forward a different combination of reason and unreason. The attempt to combine the reasonable- ness of both, with the unreasons trimmed away, is usually a worthwhile enterprise.[22] Although 'He pursues a middle course' is usually (and reasonably) a compliment, it is important not to forget that *any* proposition, theory, or proposal can be represented as standing midway between two others (see Flew, 1975: pp. 42–46; Thouless & Thouless, 1990:[23] p. 63).The words quoted by Honor Tracy from (she says) an Irish sermon should serve as a warning that we must not be too extreme in our pursuit of moderation:

> What we have to do, my dear brethren, is stay on the straight and narrow path between right and wrong.
>
> (Tracy, 1960: p. 7)

See also 11.13A, 10.39. Another point is that assertions of the form 'Yism is *the* middle way between Xism and Zism' assume what is rarely true, i.e., that there is only one conceivable way of trying to combine the good features of Xism and Zism, while avoiding the bad. And, again, even if there were only one, that *does not prove* that Yism deserves our assent or support.

We need to notice also that there is an important ambiguity in 'the (or *a*) way between'. The road between Atown and Btown *connects* Atown with Btown, but the road which runs midway between Rivers C and D may be nowhere near either of them. Unless the Xists and/or Zists give up the struggle, Yism does not reconcile the two parties. It is a new party opposed to both, and the fight may become more rather than less intense. Even if it were true that Anglicanism is the *via media* between Rome and Geneva, it would not be something that joins the two 'cities' together: it would be another *path* running between the Roman and Genevan paths, like the road running between Rivers C and D. It may be neatly parallel to them. And we all know what parallel lines are like (see MacGregor, 1989: p. 643). See also C below.

C The Virtuous Middle; The Sacred (or Majestic) Centre

Though 'middle' and 'centre'/'central' are not synonyms (see Treble & Vallins, 1936: p. 43; *OED*: 'centre', 'middle' and cognates), there are cases in which they are interchangeable. The Chinese Empire called itself *the Middle Kingdom*, because it regarded itself as the centre of the world (*WNWDAL*, 1970). The phrase is still used, sometimes with a semi-ironic flavour, recognising China's importance, smiling at its self-importance (see, e.g.,

Rossabi, 1983; Zhang, 1991). The Chinese phrase could (I expect) be accurately translated as 'the Central Kingdom'. That, perhaps, sounds insufficiently imperial and romantic, too bureaucratic and prosaic, though the notion of the centre of the world (about which Eliade is both learned and lyrical) is anything but bureaucratic (Eliade, 1954; Eliade & Sullivan, 1987). For many of us, 'centre' has been heavily flavoured by such notions as *centralisation* and *democratic centralism* (Fesler, 1968; Scruton, 1983: pp. 57, 117; Kazemzadeh, 1972).

For the Aristotelian doctrine that every virtue consists in keeping a mean (or middle course) between two extremes, see Aristotle, 1973: index heading 'mean, doctrine of'; Copleston, 1947: ch. xxxi; Huby, 1967: ch. iv; Norman, 1983: ch. iii; Ross, 1949: ch. viii. Please note that, even if Aristotle is right, it does *not* follow that every middle course between two extremes is virtuous.

The Buddhist notion of the *Middle Way* has some resemblance to the Aristotelian notion, but only some. It seems to arise in the first place from the Buddha's rejection of both sensual self-indulgence and harsh asceticism but it seems also to have a lot to do with the Plato-like doctrine that the experienceable world is neither real (*strictly* speaking), nor unreal (*strictly* speaking), but *something in between*. It is associated also with the goal of the dissolution of all oppositions and contrasts whatsoever. See Parrinder, 1971: pp. 184, 203–204; Davids, 1909; Vidyabhusana, 1908; Ngawang, 1975.

D The political centre; The middle ground

Synonymous terms from (respectively) the UK and the Australian dialects. To apply one of them to a political position is to say that, of the available options, it is the one least likely to frighten or antagonise most people. It embodies what is (just now) political common sense. The onus of proof (*TP* 8.9A) is on the opponent of any of its constituent propositions or aspirations. To *seize the middle ground* is to be well on the way to winning the next election. The middle ground or centre also embodies (there is no way of *not* mixing metaphors here) 'the mental climate in which Parliament and Government both live and work' (Sidney Webb, quoted, Hawke, 1984: p. 170). Political leaders and party theorisers frequently overrate their capacity to influence that climate. At the same time, it must be recognised that the centre shifts and drifts. In the late 1950s, an Australian political philosopher who was also an active member of the Liberal Party needed to give an example of a totally mad and unthinkable political demand. He chose the 'de-nationalisation' (i.e., 'privatisation') of the postal service. In the mid-1980s, a Labor Prime Minister found it necessary to announce that he did not intend to go quite so far.

The middle ground is normalcy. It is also respectability. *That* word can become very derogatory. The centre can come to seem dull, dreary, lacking in vision, etc.; so much that it becomes the Conventional Wisdom,[24] i.e., the hopelessly unfashionable (cf. 11.14A). Thus, the pursuit of the middle ground can become as perilous as the collection of eagles' eggs. It can also (if practised immoderately) make the pursuer incapable of having opinions, but not of uttering words. See Copi, 1978: pp. 141–142. See also 10.11–10.42 (*consensus*). Scruton's note on *the centre* is superb (1983: p. 57).

E The Dreary Middle; The Dead Centre

'I looked at your work this morning. It was pretty moderate – and in case . . .[you don't] know what that means, it means damn awful.' Thus Evelyn Waugh's Brigadier (1952: pp. 143–144). Euphemism, irony, the attempt to reconcile truth with politeness and self-preservation (and other factors) have played merry hell with these words. The Brigadier's remarks, though odd enough to be arresting, are not so odd as to be baffling.

The middle is associated with wisdom and virtue (see, e.g., Hartshorne, 1987). *The centre* can have sacred and majestic associations. *The middle ground* is usually a very desirable piece of territory. Despite these favourable associations, the *middle/centre*, taken as a whole, is an ambivalent image. 'Mediocre' is a very damning word. Though *moderation* is praised, *fence-sitting* is condemned. To be *at the centre* is to be at the point from which things radiate or round which things revolve.[25] To be *in the middle* is frequently to be in a situation of vulnerability and confusion. '*Compromise*' can suggest statesmanship, broadmindedness and realism. It can also suggest pusillanimity, shiftiness and lack of principles. Even the *middle ground* can turn, almost overnight, into a morass or a trackless desert or a lonely, rocky island (see McCloskey, 1974).

A *very* political family of words.

F Neutrality

When Papua New Guinea joined the United Nations, it was invited to become a member also of the Non-Aligned Group. PNG's reply amounted to 'No thanks. We want to remain neutral.'[26] That indicates some of the complexity of the concept of neutrality. No one can be neutral, *simpliciter*. Neutrality is always between X and Y, and the question 'Neutral against whom?' is by no means as silly as it might look. Neutrality with respect to proposition p may rest on very deep commitment to proposition q. Primus's neutrality with respect to the conflict between Secundus and Tertius might be more advantageous to one of the contenders than his active support. Staff-members of a parliamentary library are required to be politically neutral. They are servants of the Parliament, not of any individual, party or government. But that stance presupposes that parliaments matter and that the parliamentary system is worth working for. Their political neutrality is neutrality *between the parties*, but it is not neutrality between those who support the parliamentary system and those who oppose it. A Communist or a Fascist would say that the activity of those librarians is not neutral, but highly committed, highly partisan, even biased in favour of something he opposes strongly. And, on that matter, he would be right. See 3.42. The neutrality of a civil servant (a different kind of creature from a parliamentary servant) is loyalty to the government of the day, a loyalty which stops (or should stop) short of partisanship. See 2.13A. Neutrality is not always moderation: 'Henry [VIII] signalled his neutrality between the parties by burning three reformers as heretics and executing three conservatives as papalist traitors, all on the same day' (Elton, 1974: p. 194).

A Liberal Premier of Victoria once remarked (while he was in office) that, 'It's about time politically biased people were not in public positions' (Bolte, [1971?]: p. 1).

Suggested reading

(General): Montefiore, 1975; Held *et al.*, 1972: pt III. On neutrality in international relations, see Jaensch & Teichmann, 1988: pp. 140–141; Scruton, 1983: pp. 320–321; Mill, 1963(c).

11.13 ULTRA; ULTRA VIRES

A *'Ultra'* is Latin for 'beyond', not for 'very'. Ultra-violet rays are not *very* violet. They are not violet at all. They are beyond the visible rays at the violet end of the spectrum. Infra-red rays are beyond the visible rays at the other end of the spectrum. They could just as well have been (and once were) called 'ultra-red'. (*'Infra'* is Latin for 'below'.) 'Ultramarine' does not mean 'very sea-blue'. It refers to a blue colour resembling that of lapis lazuli which had to be imported, i.e., it originated *ultra mare*: overseas. Or so *SOED* says.

The political use of 'ultra' seems to have originated in France[27] in words imputing extremism (11.12A): e.g., *'ultrarévolutionnaire'*, *'ultraroyaliste'*. An ultra-Xist went beyond those usually called 'Xist'.[28] In these uses, 'ultra' tended to acquire the meaning 'very', or perhaps 'very, very, very' and thus encouraged such odd expressions as 'ultra-polite' and 'ultra-light aircraft', which, as Eric Partridge says, are 'both ugly and odd'. He also says 'fortunately . . . [this] is obsolescent' (1973: p. 388). Unfortunately, it is not. See *OED* or *SOED* 'ultra'; Fowler, 1974: pp. 657–658; Herbert, 1948: p. 168 n1; Room, 1988: p. 271.

B *Ultra vires* (pron.: 'vyreez'). Literally 'beyond the powers'. An office-holder acts *ultra vires* if he does something beyond his legal entitlements. Unconstitutional legislation is *ultra vires*. See also 2.10 (*sovereignty*), 2.15 (*power and authority*). See Scruton, 1983: pp. 473–474; Sperber & Trittschuh, 1964: pp. 464–466; Yardley, 1988.

11.14 CONFORMISM, CONFORMIST; ELITE; ELITISM; ELITIST

A Conformism, conformist

To assert the proposition that all conformity is wrong, one would have to conform to certain linguistic conventions. It follows that no sane person could assent to that proposition for long. 'Conformism' and 'conformist' are derogatory words. Unless they are also crazy words, not all conformity is conformist. If the concept of conformism makes sense (and it does), only excessive or inappropriate conformity is conformist. Conformism, therefore, is an *essentially contestable concept*. See 6.22 above; *TP* 8.10B. There are social groups in which conformism is so strongly disapproved that anyone with conformist tendencies is condemned and shunned as a pariah – yet more support for the proposition that there are few things so terrible as a flock of mad sheep. Cf. 2.16A (iii). See *TP* 8.10B (*self-stultification*).

B Elite

'Elite' is derived from the Latin '*eligere*', 'to choose', and is therefore an etymological cousin of 'the elect' of theology and of 'election' in its politico-legal sense, though it is not close semantically to either. *SOED* finds it possible to define 'elite' very briefly: 'The choice part or flower (of society, etc.)' but it is a very complicated word. It is fairly safe to say that an elite is

(i)   a minority group within another group (which may be as large as a whole polity, but can be much smaller);

and

(ii) a minority group which is seen as, in some way, superior to the rest of the larger group in which it is included. (See 2.17G.)

There is a multitude of ways in which it is possible to be superior; there is a multitude of ways of seeing a group as superior (ranging from unanimous and profound respect to unanimous and profound detestation): hence, some of the complications of the word. Seeming attempts to give a more precise definition are usually disguised or inadvertent theories of society or political manifestos.

Any activity requiring skill is one at which some will be better than others, so it is hardly possible for a sane person to disapprove consistently of all elites. Some, of course, commit themselves to such a proposition, and it is always impressive to hear someone, in one breath, condemn elites root and branch, and, in the next breath, speak enthusiastically of *revolutionary cadres* and *the vanguard of the proletariat*. See Carew Hunt, 1957: pp. 19–21. See also 8.14, 8.30. How an elite behaves, how exclusive or how open it is, whether it is accountable (and how and to whom) are important questions and 'Are you for or against elites?' may be a very silly one.

Suggested reading

Howard, 1978: pp. 79–81; R. Williams, 1983: pp. 112–115, 60–69; Bottomore, 1966; Docker, 1974; Higley *et al.* 1979; Field & Higley, 1980; Nordlinger, 1967: ch. iv; Rubinstein, 1980; Woodland, 1968; Carew Hunt, 1957: pp. 19–21.

'Elite' came into English as a collective noun, but there is a growing tendency to use it also of each member of an elite: The Xocracy is an elite, so if Tom is an Xocrat, Tom is an elite. That sets my teeth on edge, but I cannot think of a substitute for it. It is certainly better than the insulting French word '*évolué*' (applied to members of Third World elites).

C Elitism, elitist

These are almost invariably terms of reproach, so unless all elites are bad, they can be used reasonably only of elites which should not be elites or which behave or are regarded inappropriately. But they are very often used only because they are the nearest available nasty words, 'missile-words', as Fowler (1974: p. 442) says of 'purism' and 'purist'.

D 'Elitist' and 'conformist' as weapons of argumentative war

Let us suppose that Primus dislikes Secundus and wants to disagree with and discredit anything Secundus says. If Secundus expresses a view in accordance with that of most people, Primus can condemn him as a *conformist*. If Secundus differs from the majority view, Primus can accuse him of the deadly sin of *elitism*. When Primus agrees with the majority, he can invoke The Principle of Democracy. When he disagrees with the majority, he can wrap himself in the mantle of The Individual, fearlessly confronting Society (2.12B). These tactics are often effective. They are also thoroughly dishonest, but who cares about that?

E   In Australia, 'cultural cringe' and 'parochialism' are weapons used in a similar fashion. Primus criticises something Australian and says that they order these things better somewhere else, Secundus can denounce him for exhibiting *the cultural cringe*. When Primus praises something Australian and thinks it better than similar things elsewhere, he can be written off as parochial. The concept of *the cultural cringe* has been blown to bits in L. J. Hume, 1991. Alas, its soul goes marching on and is probably unstoppable.

12 Identity, etc.

BASICS

> What can the England of 1940 have in common with the England of 1840? But then, what have you in common with the child of five whose photograph your mother keeps on the mantelpiece? Nothing, except that you happen to be the same person.
>
> (George Orwell, 1970(b): p. 76)

12.1 Identity-talk is something of a dog's breakfast and has been for a considerable time. Perhaps it might help if we first try to find some basic, literal, uncontroversial,[1] unexciting uses of identity-words:

(i)   A is *identical* with B IFF[2] A is B and B is A. Putting it another way: A is identical with B IFF the expressions 'A' and 'B' refer to the same object. If Tully is identical with Cicero, then there is one person who bears both names. If everyone has one and only one vote, Tully's vote and Cicero's add up to one vote.

(ii) *Identity* is a relation which holds between A and B (or A and B and C, or . . .) IFF A and B (or A and B and C, or . . .) are identical as defined above.

(iii) To *identify* A with B is to find out or assert that A is identical with B as defined above.

Notice that there is something like a *task/achievement* ambiguity in 'identify' so defined (see *TP* 1.27, 8.13). We can say without self-contradiction that Primus identified Secundus as the robber, but that Primus was wrong.

12.2 Those little definitions do not cover all that can be said with the identity-words. They do not even cover all that can be said *sensibly* with them (not the same thing, alas). Further, even what they do say, though it may look simple and obvious enough to be boring, is thin ice on the top of appallingly deep complexity. We do not use the identity-words *only* to assert the identity of A and B at any one tick of the clock. We affirm identity as lasting over time and despite change: not just Cicero and Tully on a particular day, but (e.g.) Cicero (or Tully) at the age of five and Cicero (or Tully) at the age of fifty. We might say 'The first issue of *The Times* appeared in 1788. Its latest issue appeared this morning (Greenwich mean time).' What is that *it*, the one thing that is being said to have existed for all that time? What arguments can support such an assertion? (And does it matter that there was a period in the 1970s when no issues of *The Times* were published?) Once we get on to that tack, many familiar things take on an odd look, e.g., the Hunter (or any other) River. What is so very 'the' about it? ('Everything flows,' said Herakleitos.[3] 'You can't step into the same river twice.' His follower, Kratylos, said, 'You can't even step into it *once*.') Even that vase which (you say) you have had for years: how do you *know* it's the same one? Have you kept it under observation all that time? (See *TP* 1.21, 2.10, 5.30. See also Stroll, 1967; A. E. Taylor, 1914; Poussin, 1914; Viglino, 1967; Wall, 1967.)

12.3   That is just some of the complication underlying those simple little definitions (see P. A. B. Clarke, 1988; Wiggins, 1980), but, even if such awkward questions are not raised, the definitions do not add up to a complete catalogue of our verbal habits; e.g.: To say or show that the perpetrator of crime C is the perpetrator of crime D is an identification according to definitions (i)–(iii), but, despite that, the perpetrator *might remain unidentified*. So here we have a different sense of 'identify':

(iv)   To *identify* the xifier is to complete the sentence 'The xifier is . . .' with a formula which will or purports to enable the location (physical or otherwise) of the person or thing referred to by the subject-term. (*TP* 1.2A (v))

(There is an ambiguity here too (cf. 12.1): 'Jack the Ripper has never been identified'; 'Many identifications of Jack the Ripper have been made'. Those statements can both be true.)

Formulas (i)–(iii) make identity a *relation*, between the bearer of one description and the bearer of another, but formula (iv) yields a different sense of the word:

(v)   Someone's identity in this sense is a body of facts sufficient to distinguish him from all others (i.e. sufficient to *individuate*[4] him).

Names (i.e., proper nouns: *TP* 2.9) play an important part in this, not because someone's name *is* his identity but because it serves as a key to much more information about him.[5]

12.4   In principle, an individuating body of facts might be intrinsically insignificant, might even originate entirely outside the identified person; e.g. a *single identifying number*,[6] like that on a Government-issued *identity card*, or that tattooed on the skin of an inmate of a concentration camp. To say that such a number states *the identity* of its bearer sounds (or, rather, *is*), grossly demeaning. (See *TP* 1.22C on *fungibility*.) Hence we have to say:

Not everything which *identifies* (sense (iii)) adequately states *identity*.

Criteria for adequacy will vary according to context. In ordinary conversation, we do not need the Recording Angel's stock of information to answer the

question 'Who is Sylvia? What is she?' Information of quite that depth and
extent is not available anyway and even approximations to it may be none of
our business. The sort of thing we write in *curricula vitae* or which used to
appear on the backs of Penguin Books might, quite uncontroversially, count as
a minimum set of identifying data: *a* (NOT *the*) statement about (not quite *of*)
X's identity. *The* statement would be much more complicated and far less
easily compilable.

12.5   Primus's identity goes beyond the horizon. There are tricks of the light
and of perspective, so that even what is in plain view may be misinterpreted.
There are patches of 'dead ground' which can come to life most disconcertingly. And that is so even if the observer is Primus himself. The privileged
access which one has to one's own thought and feeling is not as secure or as all-
revealing as one might be inclined sometimes to assert (10.26–10.27). *Image* is
to *identity* as *belief* is to *knowledge*, as *appearance* to *reality* (i.e., not
necessarily in conflict, but not necessarily the same, either).[7] If one is inclined
to be sceptical about the external world on the ground that we are fallible about
it, one must be equally sceptical about oneself. Scepticism (I think) is
unwarranted, but fallibilism is very appropriate (see *TP* 7.3). Hence, some of
the things that are called *'identity crises'* (12.15–12.21).

12.6   I have said that the criteria for adequacy will vary according to context,
but they can also vary in a much more intractable fashion: they can reflect
differences of outlook so basic as to be irresoluble, even perhaps, in some cases
(not all or most) so basic as to diminish mutual intelligibility (see *TP* 5.10). So,
it has been only a short trip from the ordinary, basic and uncontroversial
(12.1) to the highly contestable (see 6.22), but no less basic, even not much less
ordinary.

12.7   In 12.4, I spoke of these as matters concerning *a person's identity*. Can
we also call them matters concerning *personal identity*? If we can manage it, I
think we had better not, because that is not how most anglophone philosophers use the phrase 'personal identity'. They concern themselves with
questions about persistence through change (e.g., Cicero at fifty, Cicero at five:
see 12.2) and with Hume's contention that there is no *self*, only *a bundle of
perceptions* (*Treatise* bk I pt iv ch. vi, 1984: pp. 299–311). The questions
touched on in 12.4 and 12.5, though difficult and even agonising, take for
granted what bothers Hume, Parfit *et al.* Their concerns are not our present
concerns, and it is important that the two kinds of problem be not confused.
(See *TP* 1.24 (ii), (iii) and references therefrom; Penelhum, 1967; C. Taylor,
1989.)

12.8   Identity (as 'defined' in formulas (i)–(iii)) is a relation which a thing has
to itself and to no other thing; hence the phrase 'the identity of X' can also be
used to speak of:

(vi)   the fact that X is a thing distinct from others;
(vii)   the quality or qualities (*TP* 1.20) that make X a thing distinct from
        others;

(viii) the precise nature of X as the singular thing which it is (i.e., its *thisness*, not just its *whatness*. See Wuellner, 1956, or Flew, 1984, on *haecceity*.)

These are not precisely identical (with one another), but clarity does not *always* require us to distinguish them explicitly. Nevertheless, if X is an individual (*TP* 1.22D), the word 'individuality' does the job of (vi) better than 'identity' does. 'Identity' fits (vi) more closely if X is something like a tradition or a culture manifested by different individuals and collective individuals at different times and places (see 11.10D). In the case of such a thing, (vi), (vii) and (viii) tend to merge. That is not so with an individual, hence the relative *im*personality of the personal identity with which Hume *et al.* are concerned. They place much less emphasis on a person's distinctness, much more on his continuity. Where they emphasise distinctness, they are concerned with boundary-drawing, rather than with the precise nature of what is within the boundary (with *thatness*, rather than *thisness* (perhaps)).

12.9 But claims that X possesses the kind of identity sketched in 12.4–12.6 embody (but, when X is a person, usually do not stress) commitments to the proposition that X had a past (and in many cases probably will have a future), so (vi), (vii) and (viii) need also to embody the notion of X as a *continuant* or *persister* and that should be made explicit:

(vi)′ X is and was (and perhaps will be) a thing distinct from others, so that X at time t_1, X at time t_2, and X at time t_3 are/were/will be not only distinct from other things, but identical with one another.

Similar amendments must be made to (vii) and (viii).

NON-LITERAL IDENTITY

12.10 Although formulas (iv)–(viii) depart from the 'simplicity' of formulas (i)–(iii), they are just as literal. There are some uses of identity-words which should not be regarded as literal; e.g., if John James Primus and Thomas Timothy Primus are identical twins, Thomas Timothy is not identical with John James in the way in which John is identical with James and Thomas is identical with Timothy, but the relation between JJ and TT is so close as to be, not just confusing, but *eerie*. Though the word 'identical' does not *literally* apply to them, it is the one we need. The fact that it does not quite fit makes it suitable; hence the phrase, 'uniovular twins' (although it embodies an explanation, and, in that respect, says more than 'identical twins') says far less (indeed, nothing) about the social and psychological aspects of twinhood.

12.11 'Identical' must not be allowed to degenerate into a fancy substitute for 'same' (or 'resembling'). Sameness is a much broader notion than identity.[8] Identity is a special variety of sameness. This care for the identity-words must extend to metaphorical uses of them. Not every case of being-of-the-same-kind should be called *qualitative identity*. That label should be reserved for particularly notable cases of sameness, sameness in so many particulars that confusion is a strong possibility. The tree in Primus's front garden and the tree in Secundus's garden are qualitatively *the same* (i.e., they are of the same sort), since both are melaleucas. They are qualitatively *identical* only if it would be difficult to distinguish them but for their different locations. (See *TP* 1.21.)

12.12   Much the same can be said of talk about *identifying with* someone else (a parent, a character in fiction, someone greatly admired, etc.). Taking terms literally, Tom *cannot* identify with his father, Buck Rogers or Bob Geldof, and (unless Tom is seriously unbalanced) he never believes that he can, but the intensity of his feelings about them and his conscious or unconscious efforts to see things through their eyes or imitate them justifies the use of 'identify with' as a rhetorical trope.[9] If we insist on treating the word as if it were an ice-cold, literal scientific term, we miss the point we began by trying to make, e.g.:

> IDENTIFICATION, a psychological term that denotes the process of becoming or being *like* some other person or persons.
>
> (Higgins, 1967. My italics)

That is probably an accurate report of usage, but it is a usage which guts the term of meaning. If we use 'identification' so widely, what word do we use when we are talking about weird experiences like the one Conrad tries to depict in 'The Secret Sharer'? (And they happen.) *OED* quotes the following from a translation of Freud's *Interpretation of Dreams*:

> An hysterical woman identifies herself most readily . . .with the person with whom she has had sexual relations.

Aristophanes! Thou shouldst be living at this hour. English hath need of thee! (And so hath German.) See 12.45 (*sympathy, empathy*).

12.13   Similar things can be said about *identifying with* a group, class, movement, organisation, cause, etc. The phrase is wasted when used to mean *associating oneself with* or even *taking a strong interest in*. Murray-Smith says that, strictly speaking, a person would be identified with an organisation only if s/he and it were indistinguishable (1987: p. 159). I sympathise with his irritation, but the idiom has its uses *as a vivid hyperbole* (and as nothing else). A vivid hyperbole for what? Gowers says that 'close, constant and well-known association' is a necessary condition for its correct use (Fowler, 1974: p. 260). I do not quite agree. If Primus's association with the Guild of Gladiolus-Growers is close, constant and well-known, then it may be true or almost true that when people think of the Guild, they automatically think of Primus as well and vice versa. They may be said (hyperbolically)[10] to *identify Primus with the Guild*. In the passive voice: 'Primus is identified with the Guild' (cf. Robert Taft's sobriquet 'Mr Republican'). But if even an obscure person works intensely over a long period for a cause or group (etc.), thinks about it for most of his waking hours, and feels its good or bad fortunes as if they were his own, what phrase better suits this than 'He has identified himself with it'? This is an even bolder hyperbole. He and the cause or group are not indistinguishable. Far from it: Most who know of *it* have never heard of him. But 'He takes a pronounced and active interest in it' is too pale and weak. By the same token, using the phrase for any and every affiliation, sympathy or alignment, is *verbicide*,[11] the killing of a word or phrase (in this case, a very useful one). What one *identifies with* in this sense is an important part of one's *identity* as sketched at the end of 12.4.

12.14   In the 1960s, there was a use of the phrase 'relate to' which included some of the things people now do with 'identify with': 'I really relate(d) to Maggie Tulliver/Paul Morel/Elvis Presley/that very unfortunate woman with the dreadful husband,' etc. This had its own unapt aspects because *being disgusted by/bored stiff by/infuriated by* are just as much relations as the one (or those) the speaker is trying to express. Yet, because it is patently vaguer than 'identify with', it may also be less muddling and obfuscating.

DISCOVERIES, CRISES, LOSSES, ETC.

12.15

> The baby new to earth and sky,
> > What time his tender palm is prest
> > Against the circle of the breast,
> Has never thought that 'this is I:'
>
> But as he grows he gathers much,
> > And learns the use of 'I,' and 'me,'
> > And finds 'I am not what I see,
> And other than the things I touch.'
>
> So rounds he to a separate mind
> > From whence clear memory may begin,
> > As thro' the frame that binds him in
> His isolation grows defined.
> *In Memoriam* xlv (Tennyson, 1965: p. 241)[12]

Do we call this 'the child's discovery of his/her *identity*'? That, I think, would be the fashionable thing, but '*individuality*' would be more appropriate (12.8) – not that that is a simple and entirely clear notion (see *TP* 1.22D and references therefrom), but the whole point is that the child is learning his *non*-identity with other things and persons, i.e., his and their *otherness* with respect to one another. When it is not an individual whose otherness is in question, we need another word and (I suppose) 'identity' has to do; e.g.:

> Organisers of this year's inaugural City of Maitland Festival believe it will establish the city's own identity and promote community pride . . . . The festival committee chairman . . . said Maitland had lived for a long time in the shadow of Newcastle [a nearby and larger city]. 'In the past Maitland

had a definite identity but over the years that has disappeared,' . . . [he] said. 'We see the festival as a definite start towards regaining our own identity. We have our own architecture and lifestyle that we should be promoting.'

(Schulha, 1982: p. 11)

12.16   It is typical of such utterances that aspiration and assertion tend to melt into one another. We seem to be urged to make something come to pass because it is already there. This *might* be straightenable-out along potentiality-and-actuality lines (*TP* 1.23), but it is a fairly frequent feature of political talk. The aspiration and assertion concern *the significant otherness* of a collective within or adjacent to another collective. This is a small-scale and harmless instance of something which, on a larger scale, can be explosive. See 7.1–7.15. Significant otherness can also disappear, e.g.:

> Port . . . [was] killed after a brave defence . . . and [his followers,] the Portingas, leaderless, agreed to merge their identity in the common mass of my [i.e., Cerdic's] followers.
>
> (Duggan, 1951: p. 187)

Similarly, the Sorbs had and have a recognised significant otherness within Germany, but Sorbian immigrants to Australia in the late nineteenth century rapidly lost their cultural distinctiveness and were assimilated into the German-Australian community. (The Sorbs are discussed in Stone, 1972, and Futasz & Senff, 1985.)

12.17   The group of the Portingas ceased to exist. It was no longer something significantly other; indeed, it was no longer an other. That was accomplished without the extinction of the individual Portingas. They did not cease to be. They merely ceased to be Portingas by becoming Cerdingas (i.e., followers of Cerdic). Much the same happened to the Sorbs, though much more gradually. This is not the only way in which (an) identity is said to be lost or to fail to exist, though some of the other ways are difficult to characterise:

W

> Ishmaelia . . . cannot conveniently be approached from any part of the world . . . . The European powers independently decided that they did not want that profitless piece of territory; that the one thing less desirable than seeing a neighbour established there, was the trouble of taking it themselves. Accordingly, by general consent, it was ruled off the maps and its immunity guaranteed. As there was no form of government common to the peoples thus segregated, nor tie of language, history, habit or belief, they were called a Republic.
>
> (Evelyn Waugh, *Scoop*, 1948: pp. 79–80)

M

FAIRFIELD: A western area where street after street of ugly flats and the lack of open space demonstrate some of the worst of the suburban sprawl – *opinion of many members of the Royal Australian Institute of Architects.*

'If you drive through Fairfield you realise that there's no identity, no character, a nothingness' – *comment by Fairfield City alderman Sam Morizio.*

(Cribb, 1984)

K

He accused the Indonesia occupying forces in Timor of the 'progressive destruction of East Timor's identity and culture' and of denying the Timorese people the right to cultural, social and political determination.

(Kruger, 1986)

12.18 What is the alleged goal of Indonesian policy, according to the speaker quoted in text **K**? Not, I think, that the Timorese should lose their otherness (as the Portingas lost theirs) by being assimilated into a wider group. My guess is that the speaker is saying that the distinctness of the Timorese which arises out of their own history and out of their adjustment of this-interest-with-that is disappearing and being replaced by a condition of dispossession and dependence. Their group does not cease to exist, but it becomes a different kind of group (or congeries[13] of groups). This condition, it is alleged, is one that is being imposed on them from outside. What is being destroyed is their 'home-grown' or autocthonous identity (see 12.43). They acquire a new one, which is not theirs in that rather special sense.[14] See 12.4.

12.19 The word 'identity' does not appear in **W**, but 'Ishmaelia has no identity' sounds like a summary of it. What is being said is that there was nothing there to associate the various peoples except the decision of the European powers. Hume saw the mind as simply a bundle of perceptions (12.7): Ishmaelia was a bundle of peoples (not just of people: see 8.1–8.3, 8.6). Ishmaelia lacked *unity* (5.12–5.33). Is 'Ishmaelia had no identity' only a rather confusing way of saying this? I think that there is a case for using 'identity' here only if that draws our attention to the fact that, left to himself, no inhabitant of the territory would *identify* himself or anyone else *as* an Ishmaelian or identify anyone not belonging to his people *as* a fellow citizen, nor, of course, would anyone at all *identify with* Ishmaelia (12.12–12.14).

12.20 Text **K** concerns the destruction of an autochthonous culture. Text **W** concerns an attempt to impose a non-autochthonous culture (or a false pretence that a culture exists). **M** does not say either of these things about the Sydney suburb of Fairfield, but what does it say? Not, I think, that Fairfield is indistinguishable from its neighbours, nor that it exists only on a map. It is (it seems) *only too much* part of the furniture of the world and too much unlike the more pleasant urban parts of the world. I once knew a cat called 'Arthur', whose owner lavished affection on him. Arthur refrained from treating her with the violence which he inflicted on everyone else, but otherwise did not reciprocate. 'Poor Arthur,' she would say. 'He just hasn't got a nature.' But, of course, he had: a thoroughly nasty one. Perhaps something similar is being said about Fairfield, perhaps also that no one would want to *identify with* it, any more than with Ishmaelia.

12.21   In *TP* 1.23 (iv), I have given some brief interpretations of what might be meant by 'X is going through an identity crisis.' The Freudian understanding of it, cleansed of its muddle about '*identifying with*', would be better styled an *individuality and independence* crisis. That sort of thing may go along with uncertainty about what kind of person one 'basically' is (i.e., one's identity in the 12.4 sense) and perhaps also a fear or belief that one's own notion of oneself is in conflict with the notions others have of oneself:

> . . . the so-called identity crisis that is observed at various stages of life (e.g., in adolescence) as the person struggles to discern the social role that best fits his self-concept.
>
> (*NEB*, 1987(a): p. 388)

There is also the sudden shock of finding that one is more like some other person (e.g. a parent) than one has habitually believed or that one is not the kind of person that one has habitually believed. These unsettling phenomena have been imaginatively explored in literature, e.g., in Angus Wilson's *Hemlock and After* and in Tom Wolfe's *The Bonfire of the Vanities* (both of which deal with post-adolescent crises). They concern a human being's dual status as subject and object. See T. S. Eliot's *The Cocktail Party* Act I sc. i, 1950: p. 26.

Suggested reading

NEB, 1987(b): p. 720; *EPsy* (Search), 1972: pp. 100–102; Erikson, 1968; Griffiths, 1984; Motet, 1984.

IDENTIFYING . . . AS A . . .

12.22   One of *OED*'s definitions of 'identify' is 'in *Nat. Hist.* to refer a specimen to its proper species',[15] giving these examples:

> The above figure . . . it is hoped is sufficiently accurate to enable the ornithologist to identify this very small bird.
>
> (1847. T. Bewick)

> A sailor identifies a speck on the horizon as a ship of a particular kind.
>
> (1885. A. Bain)

This is 'identifying someone/thing as a [Insert common noun]', not 'identifying someone/thing as [Insert proper noun or uniquely referring description]' as in 12.3. (For common/proper nouns, see *TP* 2.9.) 'Identify' here means much the same as 'recognise' and, generally speaking, 'recognise' is preferable, as being a less muddled and muddling word. There is only one point in favour of this use of 'identify': One can say 'He identified it for me,' whereas one cannot say 'He recognised it for me.'

12.23   It might be said, 'There is another point in favour of this use of "identify": it suggests (as "recognise" does not) a special skill, or, at least, that the identification took a bit of doing.'

Well, yes, but it is just that feature of a word which leads every self-important Tom, Dick and Harriet to misuse it (rather as they substitute 'sight' for 'see').

Is it the case that someone *identifies himself as an X* every time he says that he is an X or acknowledges that he is an X? That might be literally or 'dictionarily' so, but it is a pompous waste of a word except when X is something of deep importance, either in his eyes or in those of others, i.e., a significant part of his thisness (12.8). See Scruton, 1983: p. 213.

CORPORATE IDENTITY

12.24   An Australian bank recently changed the lettering in which it prints its name on forms, signs, etc. and adopted a new trademark (Sorry! *Corporate Symbol*). This, it informed its customers, is 'part of an overall corporate identity change':

> This identity will give the Bank a new physical appearance which is more reflective of our image as a modern and progressive Bank.
>
> (CBA, 1991)

The Bank's identity gives it an appearance which reflects an image, and the identity is taken on by changing trademarks and signs. (*Indeed!*) The announcement concludes with an invitation to ask 'any questions whatsoever about the Bank's new identity'. They really shouldn't tempt us like that. I seem to remember that quite a few people associated with banks have adopted new identities in South America. This is the first instance I know of a bank doing the same thing while staying at home. But it is not really the same thing. The fugitive's new identity, though false, is a more substantial thing than the 'new identity' which the Bank has given itself (12.3 n.). The best one can say is that the Bank has given us a new way of *identifying* its offices and communications. That is hardly 'a new identity'.

12.25   This sort of waffle is not peculiar to banks. In one Australian State, the body which runs the Technical Colleges recently spent more than $50,000 to transform its "dated and conservative" corporate logo into a "friendly, dynamic, assertive and modern visual identity"'. It also said:

> The visual identity of an organisation is part of corporate identity . . . . [A]n organisation may be judged as progressive or old-fashioned, sophisticated or dowdy, on the basis of its visual identity.
>
> (Quoted, Totaro, 1990)

In other words: How you look affects how you are seen. True, true. Apart from the verbosity, look at what has happened to the word 'identity'. Part of its 'charm' or 'mystique' arises from the fact that it can be used to talk about rather mysterious realities: the peculiar *thisness* of a person or collective (see 12.4–12.8 above). And here we have people talking as if an identity is something you can get an advertising agency to cook up for you. Thus, appearance swallows up reality and faces are made entirely out of face-powder and other cosmetics. See Daniel Boorstin's excellent book, *The Image: A Guide to Pseudo-Events in America* and Reeves's biography of John F. Kennedy.

NATIONAL IDENTITY

> Tantantara Tantara Tantara
> Tantara Tantara
> Tzing boom
> > *Iolanthe* Act I

12.26   In 1986, a well-known American magazine began publishing an Australian edition. As might have been expected, the first issue contained a long article on Australia's Search For Its Identity. Various people were asked for their opinions. One was the philosopher, J. A. Passmore, who replied:

> I do not have anything interesting to say about Australian identity except that I wish people would stop talking about it.
>
> > (Attwood, 1986: p. 49)

That was one of the very few intelligent statements in the whole article.

12.27   An Xlander who complains that 'Xlanders lack a sense of national identity' should be asked, NOT to 'define what you mean by "national identity"' but:

(a) Please give two or three examples of polities whose people do have a sense of their national identity;

and

(b) What are your reasons for saying that they have that sense?

These questions are sometimes sufficient to burst the bubble. Some Xlandic complaints about the lack of a sense of Xlandic identity, might boil down to: 'Why can't we have a simple stereotype of ourselves like the ones we have of other peoples?' The answer to that one is: 'Because Xlanders know too much about Xlanders and too little about other peoples.' (See 8.2–8.4.)

12.28   The examples given may reveal that the complaint is based on a misconception of a different kind. They may be polities much smaller than Xland (e.g., San Marino or the Isle of Man), or polities (even Xland itself) involved in total war, or totalitarian polities. In the 1950s and early 1960s, one often heard people say, 'One of the great strengths of the Communists is that they base their policies on a single world-view [*or* "philosophy"]. We should try to do the same.' The people who said that in my hearing were all anti-Communists, few of them McCarthyites, most of them freedom-favouring. They did not realise that one of the things that make polities like ours preferable to Communist polities is this very absence of a single world-view. The identity and unanimity of a totalitarian polity is something manufactured by the Propaganda Ministry and the Secret Police (see 2.16B). I have said enough elsewhere of the inappropriateness of choosing very small polities or wartime polities as paradigms. See 2.4, 5.41–5.45, 10.11–10.17.

12.29 Here is another question which we might ask the complainer:

Does the existence of a sense of Xlandic identity require:

(c) someone with whom all Xlanders can identify (in *some* sense or other)?

12.30 The notion of 'identifying with' is itself somewhat obscure (see 12.12–12.14) and the suggestion that it should be instantiated at polity-level makes it even more nebulous. But (c) does seem to be one of the most busily buzzing bees in the bonnets of Australian identity-hunters. Sooner or later (usually sooner), they pronounce the names of a couple of drawling actors. Evidence is then produced to show that (alas!) many Australians are not like that at all.

12.31 Some who talk about the Search for a Sense of Xlandic National Identity seem to believe that there cannot be such a Sense unless there is a *typical* Xlander, i.e., unless *being an Xlander* can be *typified* by someone whom every (or almost every) Xlander resembles in all (or almost all) significant respects and whom no (or almost no) non-Xlander resembles to that extent. If that is so, i.e., if the existence of such a figure is a *necessary condition* (*TP* 4.16) for the existence of a sense of Xlandic National Identity, then a large polity *cannot* have a Sense of its National Identity and should not want one either. How dull and uniform life would be then! How stagnant and torpid such a society![16]

12.32 But 'identify with' in (c) may have one of its silly senses; e.g. *admire* or *strive to be like* (12.12). The sought-after figure would represent (2.17) Xland in a more prescriptive (*TP* 5.12A) fashion than the one sketched in 12.30–12.31. People do have 'heroes' or at least highly admired figures and a shared habit of regarding the same person(s) in that light can be a very strong bond, but that is no reason why all (or even most) members of the same polity should have the same heroes or representative figures. There are plenty of other social bonds about (even a group of close friends might not admire the same figures). Why cannot Xlanders (or even Australians) be comfortably and untidily polytheistic[17] about their representative figures? And why must there be *just one* bond to bind *all* Xlanders together? I have argued earlier (10.18, 10.29–10.32) that there need not be.

12.33 Does the existence of a sense of Xlandic identity require

(d) that there be something in respect of which all (or almost all) Xlanders are 'identical' (i.e., the same) and in respect of which they differ from non-

Xlanders (e.g., a collection of values or a way of life common and peculiar (*TP* 1.29) to them)?

Here again, I would say that, if the answer is 'Yes', then we cannot have a sense of identity at polity-level and we should not want to have it. Such an 'identity' (i.e. – in this case – uniformity) is found only in clubs which select their members very carefully. It is hardly ever found in families, which usually (as Chesterton points out, 1905: ch. xiv) contain a great deal of incurable variety. He thinks that that is a good thing and so do I, though 'the' family is one of those many things we must not idealise, favourably or unfavourably (cf. 10.14).

12.34   Why do Xlanders want a sense of national identity? One answer seems to be 'Because every other nation has one.' A serious attempt to answer my questions (a) and (b) (12.27) should put paid to *that* idea. Some, however, are convinced that it is of great *practical* importance. In 12.26, I mentioned a magazine article. The contents-page blurb for it said:

> Like the platypus, a distinctive national identity is hard to find, but a sense of cohesion is essential for our survival. We need to find a single voice for a polyglot society; a society in a state of flux.
>
> (*TA*, 1986: p. 1)

The article quoted a very similar pronouncement by the then Minister for Industry and Commerce, Senator Button:

> 'It[18] matters in the sense that we live in a very competitive world – and it matters to the Japanese, to Americans, to Koreans.[19] If we are to survive we have to survive on a cohesive basis . . . we need a sort of *Volksgeist* to survive.'
>
> (Attwood, 1986: p. 49)

Perhaps a dash of *Gleichschaltung* as well? *Ein Volk, Ein Reich* and so forth (2.16C, 5.26–5.28)? *Why* do we need *a single voice*? What's wrong with a society being in a state of flux? All societies are, unless they are ossified.

12.35   Both quotations talk of *cohesion* (5.1–5.33). Is national identity the same as social cohesion or a necessary condition for it? Ask them, not me, but they clearly think that it is one or the other. Where is the evidence for a dangerous lack of cohesion in Australia? There is plenty of evidence for diversity and disagreement, but I do not see that need add up to a lack of cohesion. The language these people use of Australia is pure melodrama. 'The survival of Xland is threatened by a lack of social cohesion.' For 'Xland', read 'Yugoslavia in 1989'. Yes. For 'Xland', read 'India'. Well, 'survival' is a very strong word, but, yes, I see what you are getting at. But *Australia*?! Many politicians cannot talk about their country ('this great country of ours') without saying either that it is about eighteen months off being the New Jerusalem or that it stands on the brink of the bottomless pit. That is all good, fairly clean politics, but neither we nor they should take it literally. Taken literally, it is a

demand for emergency powers and severe restrictions on dissent (cf. 10.33–
10.39).

12.36 No, I don't really think Mr Button is a Nazi, and quite probably the
blurb-writer is a decent enough body when you get to know her, him or it. The
trouble is that the phrase 'Australian national identity' tends to paralyse the
critical faculties and induce sheer babble. According to some of the magazine's
informants, the trouble was that Australia just hadn't had enough disaster in
its history:

> 'Unlike Greece, Australia has never been under foreign occupation or
> endured famine or civil war. The lack of such formative historic events
> means that Australians are indifferent to main issues.'
>
> (ibid.: p. 52)

That suggests a new version of that alleged ancient Chinese curse: 'May you
live in a polity with a strong national identity.'[20] The political scientist, Henry
Mayer, is quoted as saying:

> 'We have never had a unifying crisis in terms of an invasion or civil war.'
>
> (ibid.)

A unifying crisis like a civil war . . . . A vivifying crisis like a bullet through the
head. In the adjoining column, we have the views of the head of a satellite
communications company:

> 'A clear sense of national identity would give people some reason to feel in
> community with each other.'[21]

The two Thoughts belong together. Cf. 5.44.

12.37 Saying 'X has an identity of its own' can amount to saying 'X is
significantly other than T, U, V and W.' It is perfectly sensible to ask 'What
does that otherness consist in?' It is perfectly silly to think that there must be a
simple answer to that question. It is equally silly to expect that there will be
unanimity about the answer. It is sheer Goon-Show gormlessness to believe
that unless there is such a simple, unanimously agreed answer, X is in danger
of disintegration or perhaps was never really there at all. The question, 'What
does it mean to be an Xlander?' is quite unlike 'What is the boiling point of
water?' or 'Who won the Cup in '58?' It is much closer to 'What was it like to
grow up in the seventies?' There is nothing which is *the* answer to that.
Rather, there are quite a lot of different answers which will be neither exactly
the same nor totally at variance. Each will supplement the other and may
correct the other. Some differences of opinion will persist, but that will not
mean that the whole notion of *growing-up-in-the-seventies* is questionable.
One participant's answer to the question may well draw another participant's
attention to features of his own experience which he had overlooked. Not all
divergences are incompatibilities and most incompatibilities of this kind are
tolerable, even valuable. I am assuming, of course, that the participants behave
sensibly. See 10.18, 10.31.

A GREENERY-YALLERY, NATIONAL-ART-GALLERY, MIND-IN-A-FOG YOUNG LAND[22]

12.38

> The establishment of a national art collection is also the establishment of a national identity, the Queen said last night in opening Australia's $63 million National Gallery on the shores of Lake Burley Griffin in Canberra.
>
> The Queen said a national collection helped 'to explain to ourselves what we are and what we value'.
>
> (*NH*, 1982)

Shrewdly chosen words: chiming in with a fashionable Australian preoccupation, giving the journalists a snappy lead paragraph, and stealing some of the clothes of the republicans. There might even be a bit of truth in them, *but can you imagine anyone talking that way about the Louvre or that other National Gallery in Trafalgar Square?* Perhaps we have hit on something not uniquely, but so characteristically Australian as to be part of Australian national identity: an obsessive habit of talking solemnly about the quest for a national identity. It might be a dangerous habit.

As we have seen, identity-talk is highly waffleogenic (12.36). That, in itself, might not be too bad. What worries me more is that the problem of Australian identity might be a *screen problem*, analogous to the psychoanalytic notion of a *screen memory*: a memory which, whether authentic or not, acts both as a censor of and as a censored version of past events which, if consciously remembered, would be intolerable memories, though, perhaps, ones that need attention.[23] A screen problem is like that: it diverts attention from more agonising problems, 'upstages' them. The problem of national identity is well-adapted to that task, because it is both nebulous and labyrinthine. There is no minotaur at its centre, because it has no centre. We can discuss it after dinner on Sunday. Provided that no one loses his temper, it is all very pleasant and we give ourselves the impression of having been engaged in Deep Thought. We can sleep soundly and wake unchanged on Monday. We have got nowhere, we are literally none the wiser, nor even better informed, but it has kept genuine problems away. As we have seen, at least one cabinet minister has attributed the problems of Australian industry to the lack of a *Volksgeist*. This is to shift the responsibility away from government and management and towards the people at large, and – even better – to the absence of a nebulous and elusive abstract entity, i.e., it blames the governed in a way which will not offend them. Cf. the similar use of 'break in morale' (10.8–10.9). This is a 'conservative' version of the symptoms/causes ploy (11.2 D): the cause is buried so deep and is so intangible that anything can be blamed on it. Someone else seems to be blaming social atomisation and interpersonal coldness on the absence of 'a clear sense of national identity' (12.36), i.e., she provides us with a sonorous excuse when 'Only connect'[24] seems a hard saying.

12.39   There is a particularly strong demand in Australia for this intellectual and moral anaesthetic. In 1988, we celebrated the bicentenary of British settlement. Had they got here (say) thirty years earlier, our celebrations might have been more wholehearted. We could have praised our forebears and foregoers without discomfort: the (idealised) convicts, the emancipists, the explorers, the pioneers, the bush-workers, the miners, the Anzacs, etc. That would have involved honouring people who were bitter foes of one another; it may even have involved some self-contradiction. No matter: the sentiment of *national heritage* is almost always 'polytheist' (or, if you prefer it, poly-demitheist (12.32)). On Bastille Day 1989, the façade of Notre Dame de Paris was decorated with *tricolore* rosettes. The Cathedral was joining in a significant French festival. It was not celebrating the two-hundredth anniversary of its own desecration. In London, there are statues of Charles I and of Cromwell, and quite rightly, too. Australians already have no difficulty in honouring both Macquarie and Macarthur,[25] even though they detested each other. Provided the list of venerables is not a closed one, we can cope with it (and there is always the possibility of treating it quietly as a smörgåsbord). Our problem in 1988 was that we knew too much. The skeletons were out of the cupboard and would not go back. In 1951 (the Golden Jubilee of Federation), a collection of well-meaning notables could call on us to (amongst other things) 'remember those whose labours opened this land to the uses of mankind'.[26] They would not have got away with that thirty years later. Indeed, they would not have said it thirty years later. The Aborigines were no longer invisible, nor could we pretend any longer that their decline was (apart from a few deplorable massacres) a sad, but entirely natural phenomenon.[27] In addition, we knew something about ecology (and suspected a great deal more) which made it difficult to be uncritical about those brave and hardworking people who cut down trees and introduced hard-hoofed animals, even though they were indeed brave and hardworking.

12.40 Some feared, some hoped that The Question of Australian Identity would disrupt the celebrations by introducing controversy. (See D. O'Brien, 1991, especially ch. i.) It did not. It enabled us to ignore fears and doubts about our history, economy and ecology. It enabled us to avoid facing up to our own instantiation of what could be called 'Hobbes's law':[28]

> . . . there is scarce a Common-wealth in the world, whose beginnings can in conscience be justified.
>
> (*Leviathan*, 1991: p. 486)

It enabled us to feel cosy while pretending to be critical. 'What is Australian national identity?' was and remains the perfect screen-problem.

SOME RECOMMENDATIONS

12.41 'Identity' is a dangerous word. One can say sensible things with it, but every use of it should be regarded as guilty until proved innocent. Do not use the word 'identity' when one of the following would do instead:

'personality'
'character'
'he'/'she' 'him'/'her'[29]

'self-esteem'

'individuality'
'independence'
'autonomy'

'unity'

'nationality'[30]
'culture'
'background'

Suggested reading

V. Buckley, 1980; Burridge, 1979; R. Campbell, 1971; Dennis, 1955; J. Harris, 1980; Knight, 1990: pp. 109–125; Mackenzie, 1978;[31] A. J. M. Milne, 1968: ch. vi; Rider, 1959; Roe, 1978; A. Smith, 1991.

A VERY TENTATIVE POSTSCRIPT ON THE ABORIGINAL USE OF 'IDENTITY'

12.42   The word 'identity' has a prominent place in the political vocabulary of Australian Aboriginals. So far as I can see, its use has a variety of overlapping facets including the following:

(1) A demand for *recognition* – an obscure and complex notion itself, but something of what is being reacted against can be gathered from the fact that, until 1967, a constitutional provision forbade the counting of Aboriginals in the Census and that the title of Hasluck's *Black Australians* was a deliberate challenge to common opinion. The judgement of the Privy Council in 1788 that Britain had taken possession of land 'practically unoccupied without settled inhabitants or settled laws' (quoted, Detmold, 1985: p. 58) is still deeply entrenched in the minds of most white Australians, even many who consciously repudiate the proposition (cf. 10.22–10.23).

(2) A demand for recognition as something other than an amorphous mass of anomalous individuals; i.e., as a collectivity (or collectivity of collectivities), capable of taking initiatives and having its own internal structures of authority and decision-making.

(3) An insistence on having *rights*, not merely *needs*, especially when the judgement as to what is needed is made by others. An insistence on being subjects, not merely objects (*TP* 8.1B).

(4) The articulation and expression of *Aboriginal* accounts of what it is to be an Aboriginal and an insistence that these are to be taken seriously.

(5) There is still a tendency to believe that the only 'real' Aboriginals are 'full-bloods', living a traditional life-style (in isolated areas, out of sight and out of mind). Aborigines of mixed descent are frequently dismissed as not being 'real Aboriginals' and, therefore, as not having anything to say worth listening to about Aboriginal matters. Since most urban Aboriginals are of mixed descent and since, from among them, rise some of those most skilled in western political discourse, this judgement about their lack of 'reality' is very convenient for those who wish things to stay as they are. At the same time, of course, mixed-race Aboriginals are 'real' enough to be discriminated against as Aboriginals.

Suggested reading

Beckett, 1988; Burger, 1979; Gilbert, 1977; P. Read, 1990; Rowley, 1971.

12.43 Autochthon, autochthony, autochthonous

From Greek *auto* (= 'self') and *chthon, chthonos* (= 'soil'). Literally and etymologically, an autochthon is 'a human being sprung from the soil he inhabits'. Less literally, the autochthons of Xland are its earliest known inhabitants. Bowler dismisses the word as 'a high-falutin synonym for *aboriginal*' (1979: p. 6.).[32] 'Autochthony', however, was given a real job[33] by K. C. Wheare, who spoke of *constitutional autochthony* as a goal of many member-nations of the Commonwealth:

> to be able to say that their constitution has force of law . . . through its own native authority and not because it was enacted . . . by the parliament of the United Kingdom; that it is . . . 'home grown' sprung from their own soil, and not imported.
>
> (1960: p. 89)

Soil is a very powerful symbol, so (if we remember the etymology) 'autochthonous' does this job better than 'home-grown', which suggests nothing more powerful than tomatoes. See Wheare, 1960: ch. iv; K. Robinson, 1961.

12.44 Melting-pot; Multi-culturalism

A   A literal *melting-pot* is, unsurprisingly, a pot in which things are melted, especially metals of different kinds. They melt together, becoming alloys, amalgams. There are two different kinds of metaphorical melting-pot, one of English origin, one American. The English one refers, as *OED* says, to 'thorough remodelling of institutions, etc.'. Bertie Wooster's Uncle Tom, in moments of financial worry or indigestion, declares that civilisation is in the melting-pot. *OED* quotes Morley (1887): 'I think it will be best for the

Constitution of this country not to send it to the melting-pot.' An Australian example is the title of Sax, 1972: *Medical Care in the Melting Pot*. This image of the melting-pot seems to suggest great and troubled uncertainty about the outcome of the process (something not found in well-conducted metallurgical establishments).

The American image of the melting-pot (overlooked by *OED*) is rather different. It is (or was) an optimistic belief that out of the mixture of *many* would arise a homogeneous and very special *one* (cf. 5.26). This, says Moynihan, is an 'idea . . .as old as the Republic'. He quotes a late eighteenth-century New Yorker: 'Here individuals of all nations are melted into a new race of men.' The idea received a dramatic (or, rather, melodramatic) development in Israel Zangwill's play *The Melting Pot* (1908), which contained such lines as these:

> . . . America is God's Crucible, the great Melting Pot where all the races of Europe are melting and re-forming! . . . Germans and Frenchmen, Irishman and Englishman, Jews and Russians – into the Crucible with you all! God is making the American . . . .
>
> The real American has not yet arrived. He is only in the Crucible . . . . [H]e will be the fusion of all the races, perhaps the coming superman.
>
> (1932: pp. 33–34)

That sort of thing went down very well. The play was a huge success. 'Its title', says Moynihan, 'was seized upon as a concise evocation of a profoundly significant American fact' (Glazer & Moynihan, 1963: pp. 288–289). Glazer and Moynihan conclude that 'the melting pot . . . did not happen. At least not in New York and, *mutatis mutandis*, in those parts of America which resemble New York. (ibid.: p. v). More recent observers, academic and journalistic, have echoed this, sometimes much more emphatically (e.g., Tom Wolfe's novel, *The Bonfire of the Vanities*, and many of Alistair Cooke's 'Letter from America' broadcasts in the early 1990s).[34] A non-American non-sociologist who has never set foot in the place must speak with caution of these matters. I shall just raise a couple of questions. Many Americans, most New Yorkers, most Miamians identify themselves not simply as 'Americans', but as 'Xish-Americans'. What is the socio-political significance of this? Clearly, the 'Xish' does not state only a matter of genealogical fact ('I am descended from Xish migrants'), but what beyond that does it state? What does the word 'American' in 'I am an Xish American' state? A mere autobiographical and legal fact ('I am by birth or naturalisation an American citizen')? If more than that, how much more? Those are questions for others to answer. Some rather tricky distinctions must be drawn. There are feelings-of-belongingness. There are loyalties. There are allegiances. The three intersect, but not every instance of each is an instance of each of the others. What does 'I am an Xish American' say in those terms? (e.g., does an Xish American have a divided allegiance?)

Certainly, the melting-pot has not produced a homogeneous American people, but perhaps something else has emerged from it, which has its own 'oneness': a polity which, despite a vast diversity and some very bitter divisions, does nevertheless do something more than merely survive as one thing. It may be appropriate to stop asking 'Is America a melting-pot or is it not?' and try another metaphor such as a *ratatouille* pot which does not produce one homogeneous something, either. Nevertheless, each ingredient modifies every other and the finished product has its own kind of unity.

I shall watch America's future career with interest. And with a little trepidation, some of it due not to misgivings about its capacity to hold together but to its awesome capacity for action as one big thing.

Suggested reading

Defoe, 1975(b); Glazer & Moynihan, 1963.

B *Multiculturalism*: a word to conjure with (and do various other things as well). It is, as Robert Hughes points out (1992: p. 85), dangerously ambiguous. It can be used to advocate 'learning to see through borders'. It can mean something quite contrary to that: 'cultural separatism within the larger whole of America' (or other countries): 'cultural Balkanization'. It can also be used as a vague, soothing expression of unthought-out goodwill, signifying very little. This is a word which should never be taken on trust. For ethnic, see 2.12A n.

Suggested reading

Betts, 1988; Cahill, 1980; Carsaniga, 1986; Chipman, 1980, 1981, 1988; Easson, 1990; Foster & Stockley, 1988, 1989; Hirst, 1990; Jakubowicz, 1980, 1988; Jupp, 1986; O'Reilly, 1989; M. E. Poole *et al.*, 1985; Stockley, 1984; Totaro, 1983; Zubrzycki, 1987.

12.45 Sympathy, empathy

Etymologically, 'sympathy' means 'feeling with'. It has an enormous *range*: from the vaguest, most fleeting, most trivial fellow-feeling to that intense (apparent) awareness of another's consciousness which can be expressed only metaphorically (12.10–12.14). As well, 'sympathy' is often misused as a synonym for 'pity', which need not be a matter of *feeling-with* at all.

So 'sympathy' seemed an inadequate word. Something more precise was needed. In 1904, Vernon Lee coined 'empathy' (etymologically, 'feeling into'), defined thus by *OED*: 'The power of projecting one's personality into (and so fully comprehending) the object of contemplation' (cf. 12.12). The definition is adequate to experience only if we add that the projection can seem to work in the other direction as well. Unfortunately, many people use 'empathy' as if it were only a Learned and Solemn way of saying 'sympathy'. Adrian Room remarks that 'The word has . . . come to mean little more than 'appreciative understanding' (1988: p. 244). Indeed, even less, as the following pomposities indicate:

'. . . there's a lot of . . . party-members who don't like to see the party so factionalised. I have great empathy for that.'

(Quoted, Ramsay, 1987)

. . . Mr Hawke has empathy with the right wing and supports expanded uranium mining.

(*ST*, 1991)

Some have little or no empathy with education . . .

(Pattison, 1988)

See *OED*; Seymour-Smith, 1988; Drever, 1964: p. 83; Rader, 1960: ch. xii; H. Read, 1949: pp. 28–32; Wiseman, 1978.

12.46 *Hic explicit liber.* The book ends here, but, in a certain sense, it is not a book but a wordbook, a different kind of creature. A reader who, despite the advice of the Introduction, has read it from beginning to end may think it needs, not just an end, but a conclusion. That reader should go back and re-read Chapter 1, which is as much conclusion as beginning.

Notes

INTRODUCTION

1 i.e., A. W. Sparkes, *Talking Philosophy*, Routledge, 1991.

1 HUNTING THE WILD CONCEPT

1 For a brief discussion of Socrates's view, see *TP* 1.14. For traditional treatments of definition, see Cohen & Nagel, 1934: ch. xii; Copi, 1978: ch. iv; Creighton & Smart, 1932: ch. v; Latta & MacBeath, 1929: ch. xi; Luce, 1958: pp. 27–30; Maritain, 1937: pp. 76–81; Stebbing, 1950: ch. xxii; etc., etc.
2 Very roughly, because it would be a bad mistake to rule out the possibility of having the concept though lacking the word. See Q. Skinner on *originality* (1989(a): pp. 3–4) and Byron on *longueurs* (*Don Juan* III. xcvii, 1970: p. 697). See Geach, 1957: ch.v.
3 I use the words 'kinwords' and 'contrasters' as less misleading substitutes for 'synonyms' and 'antonyms'. See *TP* 2.6A, 10.1B. The cognates of a word are its 'immediate family', e.g., 'tile', 'tiler', 'tiling'.
4 If the word 'knowledge' seems unnecessarily presumptuous, replace it with 'awareness'.
5 Bk XI ch. xiv, 1944: p. 217.
6 Also known as linguistic philosophers. See *TP* 7.12F.
7 And that might be risky. Wittgenstein liked to play the sage, and sages have a habit of being shocking and paradoxical. The piece quoted is best seen as an exasperated reaction to the disdain for the ordinary shown by Hegelians and logical positivists.

2 HUMPTY DUMPTY AND VARIOUS SOCIAL OBJECTS

1 See Peter Heath's notes to this chapter in L. Carroll, 1974.
2 For discussion of some theories of meaning, see Black, 1972; Cooper, 1973.
3 Cf. Horace *Epistles* bk I epistle 10 line 24 (1979: p. 150).
4 *Second Treatise* §136, 1965: p. 404, and elsewhere (a repetitious writer).
5 See, e.g., Halifax on 'The character of a trimmer' (1969: pp. 45–149).
6 To be pronounced as 'arkies and arks'.
7 For that reason (and others: see Scruton 1983: p. 415), 'monarchism' and 'royalism' are NOT synonymous. When T. S. Eliot declared himself a 'royalist in politics' (1929: pp. vii–viii), he was not saying merely that he was in favour of the House of Windsor! (See Cameron, 1962: pp. 18–33; Chace, 1973; Kojecký, 1971; McDiarmid, 1984; McClelland, 1970: pp. 213–263.)
8 Cf. James Madison (1787): 'A republic, by which I mean a government in which the

scheme of representation takes place. . .' (*Fed*, 1911: p. 45). See also Pangle, 1988; Rahe, 1992. On *representation*, see 2.17.

9 As part of this campaign, the Prime Minister called Dr Hewson a 'feral abacus' (M. Gordon, 1993: p. 211).

10 The up-to-date say 'numbers' (perversely, because, in the Australian political vocabulary, 'the numbers' has for long had the meaning of the *numbers of votes favouring a position or candidate*, not usually in a public election, but in a party branch, conference, or caucus. A *numbers man* is a shrewd calculator, persuader and organiser, an 'operator'. 'You can have all the logic, brother,' said one of them, 'so long as I can have the numbers.' See Cumming, 1991.)

11 Neither of which has much to do with the practice of using 'sovereign' as a synonym for 'monarch'.

12 German '-lich' = English '-ly'.

13 'is set to generate huge losses' and 'in excess of' are Gee-Whiz-Talk for, respectively, 'will lose a lot of money' and 'more than'. Similarly, only a very old-fashioned person would prefer 'X affects Y' to 'X impacts upon Y'.

14 'Ethnic' is a lovely word. 'Primus is an ethnic Chinese' says that Primus is of Chinese descent while not saying that he is of Chinese citizenship. But 'Primus is an ethnic Australian' says that Primus is an Australian citizen of non-Anglophone descent, so Primus can be both an ethnic Chinese and an ethnic Australian. See Howard, 1980: pp. 26–27; Murray-Smith, 1987: p. 115. An Anglo-Australian is not ethnic, but can be *ethnocentric*. Very odd. For *multiculturalism*, see 12.44B.

15 I swear that I saw this one in print. Unfortunately, I did not clip it.

16 Even when 'community' is definitely being used in a *Gemeinschaft* sense, that verbal similarity may cover diverse (and even conflicting) aspirations, desires and values. See Croft & Beresford, 1987.

17 'Between them, anti-psychiatry reformers and cost-cutting politicians have changed the treatment of mental patients. They have many more rights and privileges these days. And, amongst them, schizophrenics are also neglected.' (Julie Rigg, *The Minders*, ABC Radio National, 18 April 1987).

18 Though not perfect: 'Port Stephens Shire Council is battling community apathy in an effort to encourage more measles vaccinations' (Bisset, 1991).

19 '*A society*', however, is an expression of wide and flavourless extension. It may be provisionally defined as *a rule-governed system of interacting individuals*. See Shils, 1975: pp. 17–90.

20 It is related to a civil war and a royal decapitation.

21 'One judge said that . . . some now confused judges with public servants who were subject to Government direction. Judges were, in fact, servants of the Crown and wholly independent' (Hartcher, 1992).

22 '*Front-line troops*', those at '*the coal-face*' or '*the cutting edge*', as distinct from '*base-wallahs*', '*brass-hats*', '*people with shiny trouser-seats*', etc.

23 'The unstated premise in this administrative outlook is that if only faculty and students would go away, the university could be run efficiently' (A character in McInerny, 1981: p. 45).

24 'The computer and the satellite have placed the Book of All Power in the hands of Central Office' (Murray-Smith, 1988: p. 10).

25 With which compare Pfeffer, 1992.

26 Matthew viii. 4; Luke vii. 8

27 He can also manifest contemptuous pity for the ignorance of a passenger who thinks it possible for an Atown–Btown bus to pass through Ctown. Isn't that power, too (though of a different kind)?

28 I say 'For "most", read "a great many significant".'

29 See Jouvenel, 1963: pt III.

30 i.e., the one 'on the receiving end': being a *patient* as distinct from an *agent*. See *SOED* 'Patient' B.3.

31 i.e., 'the defining formula or the thing requiring definition?'

32 As distinct from 'in the power of'. See E above.

33 See Murray-Smith, 1987: pp. 194–195; Gwyn, 1981: pp. 309–311.

34 In one sense, an *ideal* limit (though not in the sense that anyone would strive for it). See *TP* 5.16; Ritter, 1986: pp. 201–206. See also 2.11B.

35 At least, from the layman's point of view. Perhaps there are legal nuances which I have missed.

36 Mozley & Whiteley, 1977: p. 248. The status which Primus has conferred on Secundus is called *power of attorney*! See D above.

37 Probably a cousin of Economic Man. See *TP* 5.16.

38 Like many well-heeled academics.

39 He does not mean physical sustenance only.

40 For MacWhirr, see Conrad's *Typhoon*. Murray was the principal editor of *OED*. His story is told in K. M. E. Murray, 1979, an admirable book.

41 See Hitler's contemptuous dismissal of 'the absurd catchword about safeguarding law and order' (*Mein Kampf* vol. II ch. ii, 1974: pp. 361–362).

42 With a little help from the philosopher, Giovanni Gentile.

43 But not everything. See Scruton, 1983: p. 401.

44 What I have said may seem to make *OED*'s account of those non-political uses seem very complicated. In fact, I have simplified it. Almost all *OED*'s quotations (I have quoted very few of them) illustrate the uses *OED* says they illustrate, but many of them could illustrate other uses as well. That indicates that we are dealing with something *very* complex.

45 I have blended two passages which make the same point.

46 *TP* 2.3.

47 In Australia, the technical legal term. The more colloquial term is 'electorate'. There is also a tendency (baffling to vivid imaginations) to refer to that for which a Member sits as 'his seat'. In the UK, the term is 'constituency'; in the US, 'congressional district'.

48 In Australia, voting is compulsory.

49 Leviticus xvi. We always say 'the scapegoat', but it was the sacrificial goat that really got it in the neck.

50 This would go beyond the democracy of Athens, where women, slaves and residents of non-Athenian origin had no role in the deliberations of the assembly.

3 THE *POLIS* AND THE POLITICAL: OR HAS POLITICS *GOT* A NATURE?

1 For the *harm* paradox, see Plato *The Apology of Socrates* and *Crito*, and Winch, 1972: ch. x. On *love*, see Augustine, 1955: index ('love'); Burnaby, 1938; O'Donovan, 1980.

2 See, e.g., indexes and contents lists of Arendt, 1958, 1988; P. A. B. Clarke, 1988; M. A. Hill, 1979; Kaplan & Kessler, 1989; E. F. Miller, 1980; Parekh, 1981.

3 See, e.g., Bakel *et al.*, 1986; Hogbin & Hiatt, 1966; Ongka, 1979; Standish, 1981.

4 NB the 'that which'. 'Xical activity is Yish activity' does not *identify* (*TP* 1.21) Xical activity with Yish activity. 'Xical activity is that which is Yish activity' does.

5 A slip by the translator. Here, French *politique* should have become English 'political'.

6 Lovely phrase!

7 There is also a rather obfuscating footnote.

8 In New South Wales in 1979, an extremely popular, very able and sublimely self-confident Premier was humiliated by a band of contumacious truck-drivers with virtually no public support and a leader remarkable only for his loquacity. See Painter, 1979: p. 386.
9 Without noticing it, Kate Millett is assuming this as a definition. See 3.12. Oakeshott puts it forward more as an off-the-cuff remark than as a definition, hence I call it simply 'Formula H'. For his concept of politics, see Oakeshott, 1962; Greenleaf, 1966.
10 For 'polis', see 3.1.
11 i.e., a polity or some other 'set of people whom chance or choice have brought together'.
12 It is worth noting that the relationship between 'X is a political activity' and 'X is an activity of political significance' is superimplication, not equivalence (see *TP* 10.3).
13 See, e.g., Pilger, 1991; Meadowcroft, 1991; Thompson, 1990; B. Smith, 1990.

4 POLITICIANS, POLITICKING, LEADERS, LEADING ETC.

1 *Primus inter pares* (i.e., 'first among equals'), as applied to Australian or UK Prime Ministers, has become a bit of a joke, but not the utterly bizarre falsehood it would be if applied to a US President.
2 Cf. the remark of Mr Neville Bonner, Australia's first and, so far, only Aboriginal senator: 'I've been a politician from the age of four. I had to be to survive' (Burger, 1979: p. 1; see also ibid.: pp. 30–31).
3 The officially approved sermons which Tudor and Jacobean clergy were required to read to their flock. See Bibliography under 'Church of England'.
4 See Lear's first speech in Act V scene iii.
5 Hence 'Honesty is the best policy' was once a daring paradox.
6 See, e.g., Trollope's novel, *The Prime Minister*.
7 The words 'statesperson' and 'statespeople' are on the way.
8 He might not be pleased if you call him 'a politician'. 'Parliamentarian' is much safer.
9 *Something* like this is often true in systems which are in form (or even in many respects actually are) autocracies. Cf. Mill on the Czarist bureaucracy (2.14B) and Hume on the emperor's need for his 'praetorian bands' (2.14H). See also Lucas, 1967: pp. 72–78.
10 e.g., Samuel Plimsoll, whose beneficent and eccentric activities are outlined in Turner, 1966: pp. 157–201. The late Senator Alan Missen and the unhappy Mr Barry Jones are Australian examples.
11 To the best of my knowledge, no leader-writer has written the following paragraph, but its day cannot be far off:
> A definite perception exists amongst large sectors of the Australian public of the existence of a profound leadership vacuum in the inmost depths of the very summit of the Australian political and governmental system. Unless this perceived deficiency is rapidly remedied by swift and decisive action, it is unlikely that it will exhibit an adequate degree of improvement in a dramatically short period of time.

5 LOYALTIES AND UNITIES

1 'Relatively' because this 'cashing' involves the concept of action-in-the-general-interest, which, itself, is very complex. See 6.13–6.29.

2 Hyperbole, of course, since neither majority nor minority is entirely homogeneous. I am thinking of the Ulster voices which are audible at a distance.

3 A species of *corruption* (9.31–9.44).

4 For a Japanese counterpart, see Hurst, 1990. For something quite insane, see Heywood, 1964(b).

5 On *open texture*, see Waismann, 1951 and 1953.

6 I would not be happy about this myself, because of the existence of *stateless societies*. See 2.7A.

7 *Total submission* is the *De Cive* version (ch. v sec. 7, Hobbes, 1972: pp. 169–170). In *Leviathan*, Hobbes employs the more complicated notion of *authorisation* (ch. xvi, Hobbes, 1991: pp. 111–115).

8 See, e.g., *Leviathan* chs xi, xvii, 1991: pp. 73–74, 119–120.

9 Cf. C. D. Rowley on the social significance of map-outlines (1965: ch. i) and Benedict Anderson's more complicated notion of the *imagined community* (1983).

10 i.e., Democratic Labor Party, a right-wing breakaway which existed from 1956 to 1978. *APF*, 1990: pp. 50–51; Jaensch & Teichmann, 1988: p. 68; Reynolds, 1974.

11 A newspaper article well worth the bother of chasing up.

12 His *Dictionary* defines 'patriot' as 'One whose ruling passion is the love of his country' but notes that 'It is sometimes used for a factious disturber of the government'

13 'The General Society of the Human Race' (1973: pp. 160–161). Rousseau could on other occasions praise such cosmopolitans (e.g., 1973: p. 90). Rousseau could do lots and lots of very different things. Patrick White's well-known hatred of what he called 'chauvinism' seems to have been a rationalisation of an almost psychotic misanthropy. (See Marr, 1991: index, 'Australia' and *passim*.)

14 See, e.g., Orwell, 1970(a): indexes, 'Communists', 'Fascists', 'Pacifism and pacifists'.

15 See, e.g., M. Gordon, 1993: ch. i; P. Clark, 1990; M. Walsh, 1990.

16 Prime Minister of Australia 1941–1945.

17 Martyn Skinner on Churchill in 1940 (1943: pp. 67–69).

18 See, e.g., Churchill, 1947: pp. 180–210; Addison, 1977; Harrisson, 1978; McCallum & Readman, 1947.

6 INTERESTS

1 From Latin. '*Nasus*' means 'nose'. One sense of '*persona*' is 'mask'.

2 These are all mentioned by Westerway.

3 The context makes it clear that it is the group's subjectivity which is meant, not the 'treater's'.

4 In this section, capital Roman letters ('X', etc.) are used as place-holders for the names of individual persons or groups, Greek letters for objects of need, desire, striving, aversion, etc., and small Roman letters ('a', etc.) for adjectives or for role-ascribing expressions. See *TP* 6.2.

5 To be pronounced Australianly (i.e., as 'Zedland') for rather obvious reasons.

6 A defeasible and qualifiable evaluation (*TP* 9.12). If we assert that X needs money, it does not follow that we are committed to saying that it would be a good thing if X got money, no matter how he got it.

7 Interest-talk is need-regarding, but not all need-talk is interest-talk or interest-regarding. I need a cape and a sword if I am to fight a bull *à la* Hemingway. I need to be a hen if I am to become the mother of chickens. Interest-talk is concerned with actual or possible objects of desire, aspiration and striving. I do not aspire to be a bull-fighter. I do not know how to aspire to henhood, even if I would prefer it, which I do not.

8 As we might – so far as intelligibility goes – *just like* something. 'X likes ice-cream'

is a relatively straightforward assertion; its truth-conditions are obvious; it is easily testable. But need-statements are different: e.g., 'X needs $1000/your advice/ physical exercise/a dose of castor oil.'

9 On which, see Kleinig, 1983.

10 The phrasing is loose, but perhaps it will do. What I am getting at is this: the following expressions all lack referents and so fail to refer:

'Queen Elizabeth II's brother' (i)

'sake' (ii)

'is' (iii)

But (i) is still a referring expression in a way in which (ii) and (iii) are not. See Lacey, 1976: pp. 182–184.

11 And also, according to Strawson, for the falsity of the statement. But there is no need to go into that just now. Strawson's views will be found in his 1971(b). They have been trenchantly criticised by Nerlich, 1965.

12 For a survey of Anderson's social thought, see Baker, 1979: pt I. For some discussion of Truman and Bentley, see Dowling, 1960(a). The rejection of *common good* etc. is a ground-bass to all of Anderson's social thought, but there is no single place where he 'says it all'. See the indexes of Anderson, 1962, 1980, 1982. The relevant entries are *interests*, *social unity*, *solidarism*. For impressions of Andersonianism as a culture, see Horne, 1988: pp. 169–229.

13 Even if one equated general interest with *general welfare* (a mistake) and so considered that justice might be a countervailing consideration, Q would be a most unclear way of raising that possibility.

14 I am not saying that there cannot be authority in morals or expertise in that or other matters of value. But such expertise is a refinement and critique of the ordinary decent and rational person's attempts to cope with himself and the world. Morality is no 'black box' as the inside of a car or of oneself may be. See Anscombe, 1981: pp. 43–50.

15 Did the Sicarii at Masada act in the general interest of their movement? See Josephus VIII, 288–416 (1981: pp. 395–405). It is possible that two rational people might disagree irresolubly over whether such an act was the only thing that morally could be done or whether it was a crazy piece of Gadarenism (or whether it fell somewhere in between). For Gadarenism, see 11.3C.

16 '. . . a small minority, of privileged doctors with *more than* a vested interest in health "chaos".' (*NH*, 1993, my italics). Sinistrissimo!

17 Even when it is not sinister, it means nothing, e.g.: 'As with industrial democracy, the community as a whole has a vested interest in the calibre of trade union officials' (Hawke, 1984: p. 53).

18 The American meaning is different. See Sperber & Trittschuh, 1964: pp. 179–180.

7 NATION

1 The sort of national self-exaltation which leads Xlanders to see Xland as entitled to dominate other polities is sometimes called 'nationalism', but there are clearer ways of saying this: 'imperialism' (2.9F) or 'chauvinism' (5.40, 5.39).

2 The boundary clauses of the Anglo-Irish Treaty of 1921 spoke of 'the wishes of the inhabitants', specifying no areas but the Six Counties and the Twenty-six (Younger, 1968: pp. 515–516).

3 What would be absurd about

a New South Wales (or Sussex) Nationalist movement?

a Hunter Valley (or Thames Valley) Nationalist movement?

a Mayfield (or Notting Hill) Nationalist movement?

What is absurd about them that is or was not absurd about nationalist movements in Ireland, Arabia, Kenya, etc.? (I 'stop not for an answer', but the question is worth thinking about.)

4 'Ethnic cleansing' is a thug's way of making demography coincide with ideology.

5 It is as well to add that he also said, 'A people which finds law an enemy to it will be an enemy to law.'

6 At the time of the Barcelona Olympic Games of 1992, the Catalonian Government described Catalonia as 'a country in Spain', a formula of resonant ambiguity.

7 Respectively, Sir Cecil Spring-Rice (English), Samuel F. Smith (American), and Henry Lawson (Australian). (*What* does Lawson expect his country to do for him?)

8 See Australian daily newspapers, 27 February 1992.

8 THE PEOPLE, DEMOCRACY, POPULISM

1 Is this 'nation' as in 'nationalism' (7.8)? If so, it needs to be stressed that to identify a nation in *OED*'s sense no. 1 or to identify oneself as a member of a nation in that sense is not equivalent to endorsing nationalistic claims made on behalf of that group.

2 And not just in a sense parallel to 'It is possible to be a Catholic and English'. The notion of an English *secular* Jew is not only not self-contradictory: it has many instances. It follows that the totality of those of whom '. . . is a Jew' is usually predicated is far from homogeneous and sharp-edged.

3 Cola di Rienzo was a fourteenth-century (AD) Roman revolutionary. For a summary of his career see 'CdR', 1985, or Monaco, 1967. J. Wright 1975, sketches the background. *LCdR*, 1975, is a translation of a biography by a contemporary. Lytton's novel is still worth reading (and says a lot about *nineteenth*-century political sentiments).

4 Cf. Primo de Rivera's dithyrambic account of what Spain is (1972: p. 58).

5 A Newcastle suburb. Non-Novocastrians should make an appropriate substitution.

6 *The Napoleon of Notting Hill* is G. K. Chesterton's fantastic novel about the development of London boroughs into nation-states marked by fanatical chauvinism.

7 A historical curiosity, since the words are quite distinct in origin. See E. Partridge, 1966: pp. 483–484, 527.

8 Disraeli's Two Nations (7.19) are at one point identified as 'the Rich and the Poor', at another as 'the Privileged and the People' (Disraeli 1927: p. 285).

9 In the terminology of class calculus, *the public* (in this sense) is a *set-complement*. If set S is a set within the universe U, then all the elements of U which are not members of set S constitute the set-complement to set S (i.e., within the universe *birds*, the complement to the set of *emus* is the *set of all birds which are not emus*).

10 A word much misused in contemporary journalese. See Howard, 1978: pp. 50–53.

11 (i) 'People' used this way is usually treated as a plural, but, as we get more excited ideologically, we tend to treat it as a singular.
(ii) The Latin word corresponding to 'people' in this and in the preceding senses is *populus*, whence 'popular'. Normally, this means 'well-liked by many', but there are other uses. When Hobbes says 'popular government', he means 'democracy' (2.9B). When Randolph Bedford says, 'Freetrade is anti-popular, whatever be its country' (1976: p. 80), he meant that it was bad for the less wealthy and the less powerful. Bedford was an old-time Australian Laborite, now dead for half a century. See Pusey, 1991.
Latin *populus* has all the ambiguity of 'people', but *plebs* is pretty much (though not absolutely) restricted to the meaning 'the common people'. See *OxLD*, 1982: pp. 1389, 1403–1405. See also 8.20 n. below.

12 In an attack on the members of the Australian High Court, a journalist jeered at them for having 'to hide from the people behind bullet-proof glass'. It is true that, in the High Court building, there is such a barrier between the bench and the public, but it is not there to protect the judges from *the people*. It is there (like the locks on the journalist's doors) to protect them from *people*, i.e., *some* people.

13 Premier of Queensland, 1968–1987. Eccentric, authoritarian, autocratic. See Patience, 1985; J. Walter, 1990. His belief in popular sovereignty was combined with the maintenance of a remarkable electoral gerrymander.

14 It can also add a splash of colour. In an Australian city, the opening of a pedestrian mall was praised as 'the giving back of the inner-city to its rightful owners, the people' (*NH*, 1980), suggesting that establishing a pleasant, though hardly revolutionary amenity is in the same class as the overthrow of a tyrannical regime or liberation from the rule of an occupying power.

15 'Freedom' here has a Hobbist sense: 'the libertie of the commonwealth', rather than 'the libertie of particular men' (*Leviathan* ch. xxi, 1991: p. 149).

'To call Pearse and his comrades a minority is not quite the truth. They were leaders whose potential followers had not yet realised that they wanted to follow' (Younger, 1968: p. 14). Thus, the word 'minority' is emptied of meaning (and A Terrible Beauty (or something) Is Born).

16 If there had ever been the least chance that the Northern Protestants would regard themselves as members of one Irish people, it was killed stone-dead by the Civil War which De Valera's Republicans launched against the Irish Free State.

17 In New South Wales, not everyone gets Bank Holiday. Not everyone gets into the companionage of the Order of Australia, but that, apparently, is quite all right.

18 Here I am agreeing with just about everyone. For a refreshingly different view, see Vlastos, 1983.

19 Even Ferdinand Marcos put his name to a book called *Today's Revolution: Democracy*, but his former neighbour, Dr Mahathir of Malaysia, has declared that 'democracy is not perfect', not in the tone in which one admits that one's beloved has faults, but as a triumphant *tu quoque* (*TP* 4.27). Dr Mahathir is bolder than most. Cf. 2.9F.

20 The equation, though popular, is false, *demos* and 'people' being not perfectly synonymous (*TP* 6.2A). Greek has three other '"people"-words': *genos*, *laos* and *ethnos*. The relations amongst the four are similar to (though not an exact reflection of) the relations between our various uses of 'people'. In Latin, there are four '"people"-words': *populus*, *quirites*, *plebs* and *gens*, none of them the exact synonym of any of the Greek words or of 'people'. Chasing these up can be quite an illuminating exercise. See the appropriate entries in *OCCL*, 1989; Liddell & Scott, 1940; Woodhouse, 1932; Lampe, 1961; Lewis & Short, 1879; *OxLD*, 1982. The Greek alphabet is transliterated in *TP* 6.1.

21 Schumpeter, 1954: chs xxi–xxiii should be read. I agree with some (but only some) of his criticisms of 'the classical theory of democracy'. His 'Another Theory' seems to me an interesting muddle, no more than that.

22 This phrase was used by Professor Victor Prescott in a radio talk. I do not know whether it is his own. I wish it were mine.

23 As well, the word 'populist' has recently undergone several other meaning-shifts. See 8.36–8.40.

24 Letter to Mary Gladstone 24 April 1881. Excerpt, Bullock & Shock, 1967: pp. 125–127.

25 See, e.g., *On Liberty* and *Representative Government*.

26 Glynn, 1918: p. 6682. See also J. F. H. Wright, 1980.

27 Jeremy Bentham's phrase.

28 From *ploutos* (Greek) = 'wealth'.

29 And others have made their mark, too: 'Julie Christie's sensual charisma first appeared in *Billy Liar*' (*Saturday Evening Post c.* 1965).
30 One of the effects of nomination by primary election is that few except the wealthy or their close dependants have any hope of being elected.
31 i.e., assertions concerned with general principles, world-view, etc. See *TP* 7.2D.
32 It was also applied to Omar Torrijos of Panama, much to the annoyance of his friend, Graham Greene (1984: pp. 93, 95), who quite correctly saw it as a swift 'writing-off', though his appeal to 'My Oxford Dictionary' is naive (1.18–1.20). He also seems to believe that a military ruler doing good turns for suppliants constitutes a 'direct form of democracy'. Ho!
33 This derogatory use of 'populist' is a symptom of unease about simple democratism (8.20). That some who talk this way will also, when it suits them, make simple democratist noises is illogical but unsurprising.

9 MORALITY AND POLITICS

1 As contrasted with 'non-moral', not with 'immoral'. See *TP* 9.3.
2 A and B are borrowed from Philippa Foot. See Foot & Harrison, 1954: p. 104.
3 There are other chapters on the New Testament, Plato and Aristotle. There are good reasons why there should be, but it is funny, just the same.
4 NOT three ways of saying the same thing, though the three things can melt together (12.42 A,D).
5 Some of The Tough-Minded seem not to recognise that these positions are different.
6 In a BBC series on decision-making, an economist called Leonard Joy proposed a short way of dealing with this difficulty: 'the denial . . . that there is a valid distinction between economic and non-economic aspects.' (Audley *et al.*, 1967: p. 73). Quite clearly, there will be no end to the troubles of the world until economists become kings or kings become economists. See also Stockman, 1986.
7 See, e.g., Benn, 1976; Benson, 1983; Downie & Telfer, 1971; Gardner, 1988; R. Young, 1980.
8 Cf.: '"Power politics don't they call it, Jeeves?"
   "Or blackmail, miss."'
               (Wodehouse, 1966: p. 166)
9 See O'Leary, 1962; Hanham, 1959; D. C. Moore, 1976; Cook, 1949. There is quite a large fictional literature on this. See, e.g., Trollope's political novels and the chapters on the election in George Eliot's *Middlemarch*. Nicholas, 1956, is a good anthology.
10 Matthew xxiii. 27.
11 See Jacoby *et al.*, 1977; *TI*, 1989.
12 'If, for example, the chairman of Revlon was hosting a fund-raising dinner for muscular dystrophy or whatever his pet charity was, any magazine that hoped to get Revlon's advertising better take at least one $10,000 table or you simply weren't in the race' (Summers, 1991: p. 20). What do we say about that or things like it?

10 'STATES OF MIND' OF THE PEOPLE AND OF SIMILAR ENTITIES

1 A slightly odd one, since the noun the French use for *discipline and spirit of the troops*, etc. is 'moral' without the 'e'. There are, however, very good reasons why we should spell it as we do. See Fowler, 1974: pp. 370–371.
2 On which, see Webb, 1958; Stoljar, 1973.

3 The connection between this sense of 'moral' and 'moral' as in 'moral principles' is (to me) utterly obscure. See 9.1–9.18.

4 '[The term "morale"]' is usually applied to those aspects of life which are difficult and dangerous, and often has military undertones' (Baynes, 1967: p. 92).

5 'À la guerre, les trois quarts sont des affaires morales, la balance des forces réelles n'est que pour un autre quart' (Baynes, 1967: p. 94).

6 Cf.:

> Just about any hypothesis . . . can be held unrefuted no matter what, by making enough adjustments in other beliefs – though sometimes doing so requires madness.
>
> (Quine & Ullian, 1978: p. 79)

7 'Descriptive' here is short for 'merely descriptive'. A term is diagnostic to the degree that its application implies explanations and predictions, and foreshadows therapeutic or palliative programmes.

8 It would not satisfy rules of definition such as those set out by Stebbing (1950: pp. 425–427). Addison (1977: p. 294 n. 49) says that Taylor 'intelligently defined and analysed' morale, but it is not a definition (and is all the better for not being one). See 1.3–1.9.

9 *Julius Caesar* Act V scene iii [ALMOST].

10 Precisely the same by the rule of transposition (i.e., (If p then q) is equivalent to (If -q then -p)).

11 See Laslett, 1956(b).

12 Cf. Wittgenstein, *Philosophical Investigations* pt I sec. 116.

13 Cf. Murray-Smith, 1988: pp. 8–11, 77, 104, on changes in the administration of Australian Antarctica.

14 Cf. the silly words of Rousseau: 'When, among the happiest people in the world, bands of peasants are seen regulating affairs of State under an oak, and always acting wisely, can we help scorning the ingenious methods of other nations, which make themselves illustrious and wretched with so much art and mystery?' (*The Social Contract* IV. i, 1973: p. 247).

15 Cf. the very sensible words of Owen Harries: 'Many of those who equate the "global village" with amicable relations seem to have little experience of real villages – and the degree of envy, malice, rivalry and vindictiveness that their intimacy can accommodate and even foster' (Harries, 1991: p. 11).

16 See, e.g. Kovesi, 1967: chs i, ii; Midgley, 1981: ch.viii.

17 *Through the Looking Glass* ch. v, L Carroll, 1974: p. 180.

18 Sartre, 1956: pp. 600–615. But, if you want to follow it up, read Mary Warnock first (1960: ch. vii OR 1967: ch. iv).

19 Austin's cat. See Austin, 1979(a): pp. 67–68.

20 See Muschamp, 1986(b); Sparkes, 1984.

21 Apparently one of Rousseau's favourite sayings. Maritain (1928: p. 125) denounces it as 'a formula which is metaphysically hateful'. It is certainly very odd (and especially dangerous in *political* thinking).

22 'I considered that the A.L.P. Executive provided as good a cross-section of public opinion as any available to me . . . . Their views were conveyed to me by the executive officers' (J. T. Lang, Premier of New South Wales 1925–1927, 1930–1932 (1970: p. 107)).

23 J. Cohen *et al.*, 1955; Schwartz, 1955. See also St John-Stevas, 1961: pp. 13–49.

24 From 1927 to 1932 industrial psychologists carried out studies at the Western Electric factory at Hawthorne, Illinois. They discovered that the fact that they took an interest in what the workers were doing affected what the workers did. That seems to have surprised them and to have counted as a discovery (see Barnes, 1979: pp. 40–52). Michael Frayn (1974: sec. 65) points out that the study of nuclear particles would be immeasurably more complicated if they 'had just one human

attribute: the ability to read books on particle theory, and to modify their behaviour as a result'.

25 This is called *qualitative polling* when professionals do it.

26 I borrow this phrase from Musgrave, 1980: p. 14. The words 'toleration' and 'tolerance' (5.6–5.7) often carry with them a suggestion of the gracious or dutiful bearing of an unpleasant burden. The element of mutual respect can considerably mitigate or even, in some cases, completely cancel this element in the *facts* of toleration and tolerance. For a solid, if controversial, study of toleration, see King, 1976, and comments on it by M. James, 1977; King, 1977(b); Kilcullen, 1978. See also 10.20. For a very different view, see Wolff *et al.*, 1969.

27 'Consent' is, perhaps, more a term of political philosophy and jurisprudence than of everyday political discourse. See *TP* 9.11B and references therefrom. See also Beran, 1987; Buchanan & Tullock, 1965; Gough, 1957, Lemos, 1978; Plamenatz, 1968; Simon, 1951. There is also the matter of *informed consent* to medical treatment and to the incurring or imposition of risks. A related matter is the question of when, if ever, it is justifiable to coerce someone for his own good (paternalism). See Gibson, 1982; Faden *et al.*, 1986; Feinberg, 1984, 1986; Gaylin & Macklin, 1982; MacLean, 1981; Scheffler, 1983; Appelbaum *et al.*, 1987; Childress, 1982; Kleinig, 1983; Lidz *et al.*, 1984; Rosoff, 1981; Skegg, 1984; Sperber & Trittschuh, 1964: pp. 93–94; USPCSEPMBBR, 1982. Consent is also central to the law of contract and to the law relating to rape. See entries for the word in *WPLD*, 1986 and 1988; Chamallas, 1988; Faulkner, 1991.

28 The precise relations between these events are rather complex and of no great relevance to my present concerns. They are recounted in Reynolds, 1983: pp. 505–511 and explored in Kelly, 1984, and Summers, 1983.

29 According to a story (which has several versions) one senior Party strategist said 'Consensus and reconciliation are all very well, but there's nothing like a tax-cut. If those greedy bastards out there wanted spirituality, they'd have joined the Hare f***in' Krishnas.'

30 See Reynolds, 1983: pp. 512–513. When the term 'Summit Conference' originated in the mid-1950s, it referred to meetings of heads of government of super- or nuclear powers. In Australia, it has come to mean *an omnium gatherum* of interest groups. So bang goes a metaphor. New South Wales has had a Smog Summit. There have even been regional Smog Summits. And Garbage Summits, too. As Karl Marx said, 'On the level plain, simple mounds look like mountains.' For Mr Hawke's speech to his 'Summit', see his 1984, pp.59–69.

31 Pemberton and Davis (1986: pp. 58–59) maintain that, in at least one of Mr Hawke's speeches, 'The crises of industrial relations and the crisis in the body politic became mutually informing metaphors.' It has also been suggested that his Congregationalist boyhood has contributed to his 'consensusism'.

32 One political scientist called the Summit 'simulated politics'. Another said, 'No, very real *politics*. Anything which screws the Opposition is politics. Simulated consultation.'

33 See Rathbone & Stephenson, 1985: p. 67.

34 As well, the Socialists could make the annual pilgrimage from Aldermaston to Trafalgar Square. Dissident Tories had no such outlet.

35 His salad days, when he was pink in judgement.

36 A phrase introduced by Eric Hoffer in 1951 and much used and misused since. See Hoffer, 1980.

37 Cf. the title of Quinton, 1978.

11 TIME, CHANGE, CONTINUITY

1 'Afraid of X' can mean simply 'regard X as a bad thing'. Obviously something more than that is meant here.
2 O'Flynn, 1951: p. 914; Fenton, 1971: p. 132; Caird, 1963: p. 122.
3 He was then asked to leave.
4 For the former, see Reardon, 1987; Dessouki, 1987. For the latter, see Bradbury & McFarlane, 1976.
5 (i) Oddly, there are no corresponding definitions for 'efficient' or 'efficiently'.
  (ii) Excerpt from a radio discussion:
      'How do you define efficiency?'
      'I define efficiency as producing a product in the most efficient way possible.'
                              (ABC Radio National, 7 July 1992)
6 i.e., the remote Scots island, not Melbourne's principal red-light district.
7 Those who are troubled by the pronouns in this article are implored to read *TP* 1.26.
8 T. S. Eliot, 1968: p. 12.
9 Edward Fitzgerald, 'Rubaiyát of Omar Khayyám of Naishápúr' Stanza 73 (1899: p. 60).
10 See *Leviathan* ch. xxxi, 1991: p. 254.
11 Always with a capital 'T', oddly enough, as if it were an official name.
12 'Nationalised' is sometimes used as a synonym.
13 Helped by the Communist habit of using 'Socialist' to mean 'Communist'. See (v) below.
14 In addition, liberalism/conservatism and liberalism/authoritarianism are NOT the same contrast!
15 Dworkin's phrase 'so far as is possible' might be so stressed as to substitute vacuity for preposterousness.
16 Others with whom I am disagreeing here: C. A. Hooker, 1980; Unger, 1976; Oakeshott, 1975(a): pp. 54–74; Jouvenel, 1957: pp. 231–246.
17 The most energetic supporter of these moves was Anthony Ashley Cooper, seventh Earl of Shaftesbury, a Tory and an Evangelical who also supported sabbatarian legislation. The Evangelicals have been much scorned (by, amongst others, John Stuart Mill). Many of them deserve great credit for their humanitarian work and their refusal to accept the doctrine that starvation and oppression were mere side-effects of progress (11.4) which had to be accepted. Evangelicals like Shaftesbury and Plimsoll made a greater contribution to human happiness than most professed utilitarians. See Best, 1975; Turner, 1966: pp. 37–65, 157–201; Bradley, 1976; Richter, 1964.
18 On freedom (liberty) and its varieties, see Berlin, 1969; G. C. MacCallum, 1972; Ryan, 1979; Pelczynski & Gray, 1984.
19 But see Gaus, 1983.
20 A joke of the late Henry Mayer. For pre-Gorbachev Soviet uses of these terms, see *GSE*, 1983: references under 'Left' and 'Leftist'.
21 In 1971, Professor Hospers was the Libertarian candidate for the American Presidency, gaining one vote in the electoral college. No other professional philosopher has come so close to winning.
22 Cf. Macaulay in 11.10D and the middle ways between socio-economic unpalatabilities alleged by Childs, 1971, and B. J. Cohen, 1989.
23 An overrated and perniciously simplistic book, but its *canvasser* example is magnificent.
24 A phrase originated by J. K. Galbraith (1979: ch. ii and index).
25 See 2.14A, F; A. F. Davies, 1988: pp. 91–115; Shils, 1975: pp. 3–16.
26 PNG later joined the Group.
27 And may have had something to do with those seating arrangements (11.11A).

28 Cf. such phrases as 'more royalist than the King' (Cohen & Cohen, 1960: p. 9), 'more Catholic than the Pope'.

12 IDENTITY, ETC.

1 Except amongst philosophers and logicians.

2 'IFF' means 'if and only if'. See *TP* 4.1, 4.17.

3 Or Heraclitus. See Copleston, 1947: ch. v; Burnet, 1930: ch. iii; Guthrie, 1950: ch. iii; Kirk & Raven, 1957: see index, 'Cratylus', 'Heraclitus'. See also Waugh's account of racing cars as pure 'becoming' with no 'being' (1947: pp. 154–156).

4 Cf. *WPLD*, 1969 'Identity' (about motor vehicles). A *false/new identity* is not merely a *false/new name*, but that plus a life-story with supporting documents allowing Mr X to pass himself off as Mr Y (see, e.g., Rendell, 1978). It is malapropistic pomposity to say 'He has adopted a new identity' when one means only that he has changed his ways and become a different sort of person.

5 Sir Karl Popper (1969: pp. 18–19) suggests that we should 'smile about the policeman who discovers that *the real name* of the man called "Samuel Jones" was "John Smith" . . . no doubt, a last vestige of the magical belief that we gain power over a man or a god or a spirit by gaining knowledge of his *real* name: by pronouncing it we can summon or cite him.' Those are Popper's own ironical italics and perhaps we should risk smiling about *him*. Is there not a quite non-magical and fairly plausible belief that knowing someone's real name *often* does enable us to summon him or make it easier to find him? We can look him up in the telephone book, match this record to that, etc. Still, the relation of name to identity is not entirely so clear and practical as that. For most of us, our names are not *mere identifiers*, but *part of* our identity. Is this a vestige of magical belief? Perhaps, perhaps not. See Harré, 1976: ch. iii.

6 Known in the data-business as 'an S.I.N' (pronounced 'ess-eye-en'). See, e.g., CDC/DJ, 1972: ch. vii.

7 Readers of Old Possum will have realised that a cat's identity (in this sense) is the referent of its Ineffable, Effable, Effanineffable, Deep and Inscrutable Singular Name (T. S. Eliot, 1974(b): p. 10). Others have also got some fun out of such Deep Matters, e.g., Dennis, 1955; Saunders, 1965.

8 i.e., literal identity, formula (i)–(iii) identity.

9 For *rhetoric*, see *TP* 8.4A. For *trope*, see *SOED*. For an important qualification, see 12.21.

10 Cf. the hyperbolical use of 'synonymous with' (*TP* 2.6A).

11 See C. S. Lewis, 1967: pp. 7–8, 130–132, 327–328; G. Hughes, 1988: *passim*.

12 For another example, see Anthony Powell, 1976: pp. 46–47. There is a well-known example in *Kim*, which Ryle misunderstands badly (1949: p. 186). See Kipling, 1949: pp. 167, 264–266, 321–322, 408 (p. 167 shows that what I have called 'fashionable' is not just *newly* fashionable).

13 See *OED*.

14 Cf. *The Destruction of Aboriginal Society* (title of the first volume of Rowley's masterly study, 1970(a)) and Turnbull's picture of the Ik (1974).

15 In '"*identify*" 2.a', which lumps it together with some fundamentally different uses. On identity-talk, *OED* is almost as confused as the rest of us.

16 'I thought a typical Aussie had blonde hair, blue eyes and a tan' (protest of a blonde, blue-eyed, tanned Australian athlete at the choice of a red-haired comrade as the 'typical Australian' for a Commonwealth Games parade: *NH*, 1990).

17 With, of course, a *very* small 'th'. See Knopfelmacher, 1968: pp. 154–156.

18 i.e., Whether there is an Australian identity or Whether Australians have a sense of it – or *Something*.

19 They are, of course, worried sick about the Australian national identity and will buy more of our exports when, but only when, we find out what it is and prove that it exists.

20 Even perhaps a *vibrant* national identity, something which editorial-writers seem to know all about. They like to have their national identity quivering away like a jelly in front of an electric fan (but never in A State of Flux). One thing they do *not* want, however, is (like Jefferson) to 'tremble for my country when I reflect that God is just'. Avoiding *that* kind of vibrancy is the object of the exercise.

21 See 5.38 for Burke's inversion of this view.

22 Not quite *Patience* Act II.

23 See, e.g., Dare, 1984; Stewart, 1979: pp. 117–142; Pincus & Dare, 1978.

24 The epigraph of Forster's *Howard's End*.

25 Lachlan Macquarie, Governor of New South Wales, 1810–1921. John Macarthur (1767–1834), army officer and founder of the wool industry.

26 'A Call to the People of Australia'. Text in major Australian newspapers, 12 November 1951. It is blasted in Wolfsohn, 1969.

27 See Rowley, 1970(a); Blainey, 1991: pp. 46–51, 122–125.

28 His, not as its original, but as its most felicitous, formulator. There is a case for seeing it as implicit in the mythology and sacred books of many peoples. See Jouvenel, 1957: pp. 48–50; Augustine, *De Civ.* XV.5 (1972: pp. 600–601); Machiavelli, *Discorsi* I. ix (1950: pp. 138–141).

29 'Her identity . . . took its biggest and bloodiest sandbagging from Hollywood' (quoted, R. Campbell, 1971). For 'Her identity' read 'She'. For 'its', read 'her'.

30 'Our national identity – are we China or are we Taiwan – will determine our political system' (quoted, Florcruz, 1991: p. 430. For 'national identity', read 'nationality'.

31 One not to be missed.

32 On which, see Murray-Smith, 1987: p. 4. On 'native' and 'indigenous', see Inglis, 1975.

33 Overlooked by *OED*.

34 But see Steinberg, 1974. The best example of the melting-pot is to be found in the Old World. Many typically Irish surnames were once typically Norman or Norse. But you had better not look at the other side of the Irish Sea in this half-century or the next. See Dummett, 1973. See also 8.3 above.

Bibliography

Aberbach, Joel D., R. D. Putnam and B. A. Rockwell 1981 *Bureaucrats and Politicians in Western Democracies* Cambridge, Mass.: Harvard University Press.

Acheson, Dean 1958(a) *Power and Diplomacy* Cambridge, Mass.: Harvard University Press.

—— 1958(b) 'Morality, moralism, and democracy' *The Yale Review* XLVII: pp. 481–493.

Acton, John Emerich Dalberg (Lord Acton) [1934–1902] 1956 *Essays on Freedom and Power* sel. with a new introd. by Gertrude Himmelfarb. London: Meridian/Thames & Hudson.

Adams, Henry 1898 *John Randolph* Boston: Riverside/Houghton Mifflin.

Addison, Paul 1977 *The Road to 1945: British Politics and the Second World War* London: Cape.

Adorno, T. W., Else Frenkel-Brunswik, Daniel J. Levinson, R. Nevitt Sanford in collaboration with Betty Aron, Maria Hertz Levinson and William Morrow 1964 *The Authoritarian Personality* [1950] (2 vols) New York: Science Editions/Wiley.

Aitkin, Don 1972 *The Country Party in New South Wales: A Study of Organisation and Survival* Canberra: Australian National University Press.

Alatas, Syed Hussein 1968 *The Sociology of Corruption: The Nature, Function, Causes and Prevention of Corruption* Singapore: Donald Moore Press.

Albrow, Martin C. 1968 'Bureaucracy' in G. D. Mitchell, 1968.

—— 1970 *Bureaucracy* London: Pall Mall Press.

Allen, R. T. 1989 'When loyalty no harm meant' *Review of Metaphysics* XLIII: pp. 281–294.

Alomes, Stephen 1988 *A Nation At Last?: The Changing Character of Australian Nationalism 1880-1988* North Ryde: Angus & Robertson.

Ambler, Eric 1962 *The Light of Day* London: Heinemann.

—— 1965(a) *Intrigue: Three Famous Novels in One Volume* London: Hodder & Stoughton.

—— 1965(b) *Judgment on Deltchev* pp. 433–634 in Ambler, 1965(a).

—— 1991 *Waiting for Orders: The Complete Short Stories of Eric Ambler* New York: Mysterious Press/Warner.

Amis, Kingsley 1957 *Socialism and the Intellectuals* (Fabian Tract 304) [London]: The Fabian Society.

Anderson, Benedict 1983 *Imagined Communities: Reflections on the Origin and Spread of Nationalism* London: Verso.

Anderson, John 1962 *Studies in Empirical Philosophy* Sydney: Angus & Robertson.

—— 1980 *Education and Inquiry* ed. by D. Z. Phillips. Oxford: Blackwell.

—— 1982 *Art & Reality: John Anderson on Literature and Aesthetics* ed. by Janet Anderson, Graham Cullum and Kimon Lycos. Sydney: Hale & Iremonger.

Andreski, Stanislav L. 1968(a) 'Charisma; routinization of charisma' in G. D. Mitchell, 1968.
—— 1968(b) 'Ideal type' ibid.
Andreski, Stanislav L. and A. L. C. B. Bullock 1988 'Imperialism' in *FDMT*.
Anscombe, G. E. M. 1981 *The Collected Philosophical Papers of G. E. M. Anscombe* vol.
   III: *Ethics, Religion and Politics* Oxford: Blackwell.
Anson, Steve 1992 *Hawke: An Emotional Life* updated edn. Ringwood: McPhee Gribble.
Appelbaum, Paul S., Charles W. Lidz and Alan Meisel 1987 *Informed Consent: Legal
   Theory and Clinical Practice* New York: Oxford University Press.
Apter, David E. and James Joll (eds) 1971 *Anarchism Today* London: Macmillan
Arac, Jonathan (ed.) 1988 *After Foucault: Humanistic Knowledge, Postmodern
   Challenge* New Brunswick, N.J.: Rutgers University Press.
Archer, Jeffrey and Graham Maddox 1976 'The concept of "politics" in Australia'
   Politics XI: pp. 7–12.
Arendt, Hannah 1958 *The Human Condition* Chicago: University of Chicago Press.
—— 1978 *The Life of the Mind* vol. I: *Thinking* New York: Harcourt Brace
   Jovanovich.
Aristotle (384–322 BC) 1941 *The Basic Works of Aristotle* ed. and with an introd. by
   Richard McKeon. New York: Random House.
—— 1973 *Aristotle's Ethics* [sel. with commentary by] J. L. Ackrill. London: Faber.
—— 1976 *The Ethics of Aristotle: The Nicomachean Ethics* trans. by J. A. K.
   Thomson, rev. with notes and appendices by Hugh Tredennick. Introd. and
   bibliography by Jonathan Barnes. Harmondsworth: Penguin.
—— 1981 *The Politics* trans. by T. A. Sinclair, rev. and re-presented by Trevor J.
   Saunders. Harmondsworth: Penguin.
Armstrong, David M. 1980 *'The Nature of Mind' and Other Essays* St Lucia: University
   of Queensland Press.
—— 1983 'An intellectual autobiography' *Quadrant* XXVII no. 1/2 (Jan./Feb.):
   pp. 89–105.
Arndt, Heinz W. 1980 'When a spectrum becomes a circle' *Quadrant* XXIV no. 4
   (Apr.): pp. 46–47.
Attir, Mustafa O., Burkart Holzner and Zdenek Suda (eds) 1981 *Directions of Change:
   Modernization Theory, Research, and Realities* Boulder: Westview Press.
The Attorney's Pocket Dictionary 1981 West Hartford, Conn.: Law and Business
   Publications.
Attwood, Alan 1986 'Our elusive soul. Wanted: a national identity, now lost in a cultural
   casserole' *Time (Australia)* I no. 1 (21 July): pp. 48–55.
Audley, R. J. *et al.* 1967 *Decision Making* London: British Broadcasting Corporation.
Augustine, (Saint) 1944 *The Confessions of St Augustine* trans. by F. J. Sheed. London:
   Sheed & Ward.
—— 1955 *Augustine: Later Works* sel. and trans. with introds by John Burnaby (*The
   Library of Christian Classics* vol.VIII) London: SCM Press.
—— 1972 *Concerning the City of God against the Pagans* a new trans. by Henry
   Bettenson with an introd. by David Knowles. Harmondsworth: Penguin.
Austin, John Langshaw 1979(a) *Philosophical Papers* ed. by J. O. Urmson and G. J.
   Warnock, 3rd edn. Oxford: Oxford University Press.
—— 1979(b) 'A plea for excuses' pp. 175–204 in Austin, 1979(a).
The Australian 1981 'Queenslanders are Australians first' [Editorial] 28 Jan.: p. 8.
The Australian Financial Review 1991 [Reports and articles concerning the Liberal
   Party's *'Fightback!* Package'] 22 Nov.
Australian Political Facts by Ian McAllister, Malcolm Mackerras, Alvaro Ascui and Sue
   Moss 1990 Melbourne: Longman Cheshire.
Bacon, (Sir) Francis (Baron Verulam, Viscount St Albans) (1561–1626) 1951 *'The
   Advancement of Learning' and 'New Atlantis'* with a preface by Thomas Case.
   London: World's Classics/Oxford University Press.

Baier, Kurt 1965 *The Moral Point of View: A Rational Basis of Ethics* abridged edn. New York: Random House.

Bailey, F. G. 1969 *Stratagems and Spoils: A Social Anthropology of Politics* Oxford: Blackwell.

Bakel, Martin A. van, Renée R. Hagesteijn and Pieter van de Velde (eds) 1986 *Private Politics: A Multi-Disciplinary Approach to 'Big-Man' Systems* Leiden: Brill.

Baker, A. J. 1979 *Anderson's Social Philosophy* Sydney: Angus & Robertson.

Balchin, Nigel 1949 *A Sort of Traitors* London: Collins.

Balfour, Campbell (ed.) 1973 *Participation in Industry* London: Croom Helm.

Ball, Terence, James Farr and Russell L. Hanson (eds) 1989 *Political Innovation and Conceptual Change* Cambridge: Cambridge University Press.

Bambrough, Renford 1956 'Plato's political analogies' pp. 98–115 in Laslett, 1956.

Banks, Robert 1979 *Paul's Idea of Community: The Early House Churches in their Historical Setting* Surry Hills, NSW: ANZEA Books.

Barker, (Sir) Ernest 1951 *Essays on Government* 2nd edn. Oxford: Clarendon Press.

Barnes, J. A. 1979 *Who Should Know What? Social Science, Privacy and Ethics* Harmondsworth: Penguin.

Barrass, Tom 1982 'Unconscious youth "denied treatment"' *NH* 7 Sept.: p. 1.

—— 1985 'An extraordinary effort for charity' *NH* 7 Oct.: p. 5.

Barrow, R. H. 1949 *The Romans* Harmondsworth: Penguin.

Barry, Brian 1965 *Political Argument* London: Routledge & Kegan Paul.

—— 1967(a) 'Justice and the common good' pp. 189–193 in Quinton, 1967.

—— 1967(b) 'The public interest' pp. 112–126 in Quinton, 1967.

—— 1975 'Review article: Political accommodation and consociational democracy' *The British Journal of Political Science* V: pp. 477–505.

—— 1979 'Is democracy special?' pp. 155–196 in Laslett & Fishkin, 1979.

Barry, Norman P. 1979 *Hayek's Social and Economic Philosophy* London: Macmillan.

Bartlett, John 1956 *A Complete Concordance or Verbal Index to Words, Phrases and Passages in the Dramatic Works of Shakespeare with a Supplementary Concordance to the Poems* [1894] London: Macmillan.

—— 1980 *Familiar Quotations: A Collection of Passages, Phrases and Proverbs Traced to their Sources in Ancient and Modern Literature* 15th edn. ed. by Emily Morison Beck and the editorial staff of Little, Brown & Co. Boston: Little, Brown.

Bay, Christian 1975 'Gentleness and politics: the case for motherhood reconsidered' *Politics* X: pp. 125–138.

Baynes, J. C. M. 1967 *Morale: A Study of Men and Courage. The Second Scottish Rifles at the Battle of Neuve Chapelle 1915* New York: Praeger.

Bealey, Frank (ed.) 1970 *The Social and Political Thought of the British Labour Party* London: Weidenfeld & Nicolson.

Beckett, Jeremy R. (ed.) 1988 *Past and Present: The Construction of Aboriginality* Canberra: Aboriginal Studies Press.

Bedford, Randolph (1868–1941) 1976 *Naught to Thirty-Three* Melbourne: Melbourne University Press.

Bell, Daniel (ed.) 1964 *The Radical Right: The New American Right* expanded and updated. New York: Anchor/Doubleday.

—— 1988(a) 'Bureaucracy' in *FDMT*.

—— 1988(b) 'Charisma' in *FDMT*.

Bell, Daniel and John Willett 1988 'Proletariat' in *FDMT*.

Bell, David V. J. 1975 *Power, Influence, Authority: An Essay in Political Linguistics* New York: Oxford University Press.

Belloc, Hilaire (1870–1953) 1938 *Sonnets and Verse* new edn. London: Duckworth.

Bendix, Reinhard 1969 *Nation-Building and Citizenship: Studies of our Changing Social Order* New York: Anchor/Doubleday.

Benn, Stanley Isaac 1960 '"Interests" in Politics' *Proceedings of the Aristotelian Society*

NS. LX (1959/60): pp. 123–154.

—— 1967(a) 'Authority' in *EP*.

—— 1967(b) 'Power' in *EP*.

—— 1976 'Freedom, autonomy and the concept of a person' *Proceedings of the Aristotelian Society* NS LXXVI: pp. 109–130.

—— 1983 'Private and public morality: clean living and dirty hands' pp. 155–181 in Benn & Gaus, 1983.

Benn, Stanley Isaac and Gerald F. Gaus (eds) 1983 *Public and Private in Social Life* London: Croom Helm.

Benn, Stanley Isaac and Richard Stanley Peters 1959 *Social Principles and the Democratic State* London: Allen & Unwin.

Benson, John 1983 'Who is the autonomous man?' *Philosophy* LVIII: pp. 5–17.

Bennett, Alan, Peter Cook, Jonathan Miller and Dudley Moore 1987 *The Complete 'Beyond the Fringe'* with an introd. by Michael Frayn, ed. by Roger Wilmut. London: Methuen.

Bentham, Jeremy (1748–1832) 1962 *The Handbook of Political Fallacies* rev. and ed. by Harold A. Larrabee, with an introd. by Crane Brinton. New York: Torchbook/ Harper.

—— 1973 *Bentham's Political Thought* ed. by Bhikhu Parekh. London: Croom Helm.

Bentley, Edmund Clerihew (1875–1956) 1981 *The Complete Clerihews of E. Clerihew Bentley* illus. by Nicolas Bentley, G. K. Chesterton, Victor Reinganum and the author with an introd. by Gavin Ewart. Oxford: Oxford University Press.

Beran, Harry 1987 *The Consent Theory of Political Obligation* London: Croom Helm.

Berkeley, George (1685–1753) 1953(a) *The Works of George Berkeley Bishop of Cloyne* ed. by A. A. Luce and T. E. Jessop: vol. VI ed. by T. E. Jessop. Edinburgh: Nelson.

—— 1953(b)'Passive Obedience or the Christian Doctrine of not resisting the Supreme Power proved and vindicated upon the principles of the Law of Nature. In a Discourse delivered at the College Chapel [Trinity College, Dublin]' pp. 17–46 in Berkeley, 1953(a).

Berki, R. N. 1972 'The distinction between moderation and extremism' pp. 66–80 in Parekh & Berki, 1972.

Berlin, (Sir) Isaiah 1969 *Four Essays on Liberty* Oxford: Oxford University Press.

Best, G. F. A. 1975 *Shaftesbury* London: New English Library.

Betts, Katharine 1988 *Ideology and Immigration: Australia 1976 to 1987* Carlton: Melbourne University Press.

Bierce, Ambrose 1971 *The Enlarged 'Devil's Dictionary'* by Ambrose Bierce (1842–1914?) with 851 newly discovered words and definitions added to the previous thousand-word collection. Research and editing by Ernest Jerome Hopkins. Preface by John Myers Myers. Harmondsworth: Penguin.

Birch, Anthony H. 1964 *Representation and Representative Government: An Essay on The British Constitution* London: Allen & Unwin.

—— 1972 *Representation* London: Macmillan.

Bisset, Kellie 1991 'Port battles apathy on measles vaccinations' *NH* 21 March: p. 6.

Black, Max 1972 *The Labyrinth of Language* Harmondsworth: Penguin

Blainey, Geoffrey 1976 *Triumph of the Nomads: A History of Ancient Australia* Melbourne: Sun Books.

—— 1991 *Eye on Australia: Speeches and Essays* Melbourne: Schwartz & Wilkinson.

Blake, Robert (Lord Blake) 1972 *The Conservative Party from Peel to Churchill* London: Fontana/Collins.

Boas, George 1973 'Vox populi' in *DHI*.

Bogdanor, Vernon 1981 *The People and the Party System: The Referendum and Electoral Reform in British Politics* Cambridge: Cambridge University Press

Bolte, (Sir) Henry [1971?] *Quotations from Chairman Henry Bolte* Hawthorn, Victoria: Gold Star.

Bondurant, Joan V. and Margaret W. Fisher 1966 'Ethics in action: contrasting approaches to social and political problems in modern India' *The Australian Journal of Politics and History* XII: pp. 177–193.

Bone, Ian (ed.) 1991 *Class War: A Decade of Disorder* London: Verso.

Bonjean, Charles M., Terry N. Clark and Robert L. Lineberry (eds) 1971 *Community Politics: A Behavioral Approach* New York: Free Press.

Booker, Christopher 1969 *The Neophiliacs: A Study of the Revolution in English Life in the Fifties and Sixties* London: Collins.

Boorstin, Daniel J. 1973 *The Image: A Guide to Pseudo-Events in America* New York: Atheneum.

Bosanquet, Bernard 1923 *The Philosophical Theory of the State* 4th edn. London: Macmillan.

Bose, Arun 1977 *Political Paradoxes and Puzzles* Oxford: Clarendon Press.

Boswell, James (1740–1795) 1980 *Life of Johnson* ed. by R. W. Chapman, rev. by J. D. Fleeman, with a new introd. by Pat Rogers. Oxford: Oxford University Press.

Bottomore, T. B. 1966 *Elites and Society* Harmondsworth: Penguin.

Bourdieu, P. 1979 'Public opinion does not exist' pp. 124–130 in Mattelart & Siegelaub, 1979.

Bowler, Peter 1979 *The Superior Person's Little Book of Words* Melbourne: Hawthorn Press.

Boyce, P. J. (coordinating ed.), M. N. F. Cribb, R. K. Forward, K. W. Wiltshire and D. E. Drinkwater 1980 *Dictionary of Australian Politics* Melbourne: Longman Cheshire.

Bradbury, Malcolm 1989 *No, Not Bloomsbury* London: Deutsch.

Bradbury, Malcolm and James McFarlane (eds) 1976 *Modernism, 1890–1930* Harmondsworth: Penguin.

Bradley, Ian 1976 *The Call to Seriousness: The Evangelical Impact on the Victorians* London: Cape.

Braham, Colin and Jim Burton 1975 *The Referendum Reconsidered* Fabian Tract 434. London: Fabian Society.

Brandis, George, Tom Harley and Don Maxwell (eds) 1984 *Liberals Face the Future: Essays on Australian Liberalism* Melbourne: Oxford University Press.

Brewer, Ebenezer Cobham 1970 *Brewer's Dictionary of Phrase and Fable* centenary edn rev. by Ivor H. Evans. London: Cassell.

Brinton, Crane 1965 *The Anatomy of Revolution* rev. and expanded edn. New York: Vintage/Random House.

British Political Facts 1900–1985 by David Butler and Gareth Butler 1986 New York: St Martins Press.

Brittan, (Sir) Leon 1990 'The discarded image' *The Spectator* 15 Dec.: pp. 13–14.

Broekmeyer, M. J. (ed.) 1970 *Yugoslav Workers' Self-Management: Proceedings of a Symposium Held in Amsterdam, 7–9 January, 1970* Dordrecht: Reidel.

Brown, Robert 1979 'Bureaucracy: the utility of a concept' pp. 135–155 in Kamenka & Krygier, 1979.

Browne, (Sir) Thomas (1605–1682) 1965 *'Religio Medici' and Other Writings: 'Hydriotaphia: Urn Burial', 'A Letter to a Friend'. 'The Garden of Cyrus', 'Christian Morals'* introd. by M. R. Ridley. London: Everyman/Dent.

Buchanan, James M. and Gordon Tullock 1965 *The Calculus of Consent: Logical Foundations of Constitutional Democracy* Ann Arbor: University of Michigan Press.

Buck, Philip W. (ed.) 1975 *How Conservatives Think* Harmondsworth: Penguin.

Buckley, Amanda 1984 'A call on the radio fuels wrangle on the Franklin dam issue: Mr Hawke insists on an observer' *SMH* 25 Feb.: p. 3.

Buckley, Vincent 1980 'Identity: invention or discovery?' *Quadrant* XXIV no. 8 (Aug.): pp. 12–19.

Bullock, Alan (Lord Bullock) 1988(a) 'Democracy' in *FDMT*.

—— 1988(b) 'Power politics' in *FDMT*.

Bullock, Alan and Maurice Shock (eds) 1967 *The Liberal Tradition from Fox to Keynes* Oxford: Clarendon Press.

Bullock, Alan, *et al.* 1988 'Progressive' in *FDMT*.

Burch, Betty E. 1964 *Dictatorship and Totalitarianism: Selected Readings* New York: Van Nostrand.

Burchfield, R. W. 1976 'A case of mistaken identity: keywords' *Encounter* XLVI no. 6 (June): pp.57–58, 60–64.

Burger, Angela 1979 *Neville Bonner: A Biography* South Melbourne: Macmillan.

Burke, Edmund (1729–1797) 1852 *The Works and Correspondence of the Right Honourable Edmund Burke* a new edition in 8 vols. London: Rivington.

—— 1960 *The Philosophy of Edmund Burke: A Selection from his Speeches and Writings* ed. and with an introd. by Louis I. Bredvold and Ralph G. Ross. Ann Arbor: University of Michigan Press.

—— 1968 *Reflections on the Revolution in France* . . . ed. and with an introd. by Conor Cruise O'Brien. Harmondsworth: Penguin.

—— 1975 *Edmund Burke On Government, Politics and Society* sel. and ed. by B. W. Hill. Glasgow: Fontana/Harvester.

Burnaby, John 1938 *Amor Dei: A Study of the Religion of St Augustine* The Hulsean Lectures for 1938. London: Hodder & Stoughton.

Burnet, John 1930 *Early Greek Philosophy* 4th edn. London: Black.

—— 1964 *Greek Philosophy: Thales to Plato* [1914] London: Macmillan.

Burnheim, John 1985 *Is Democracy Possible?: The Alternative to Electoral Politics* Cambridge: Polity Press in assoc. with Blackwood.

Burns, Robert (1759–1796) [1883] *The Poetical Works of Robert Burns* ed. with introductory biography and notes by Charles Kent. London: George Routledge & Sons.

Burridge, Kenelm 1979 *Someone, No One: An Essay on Individuality* Princeton: Princeton University Press.

Burton, Tom 1991 'Small-minded assault on our culture' *SMH* 20 Feb.: p. 4.

Bury, J. B. 1951 *A History of Greece to the Death of Alexander the Great* 3rd edn. rev. by Russell Meiggs. London: Macmillan.

Buss, Claude A. 1962 *The People's Republic of China* Princeton: Anvil/Van Nostrand.

Butler, Eamonn 1983 *Hayek: His Contribution to the Political and Economic Thought of Our Time* London: Temple Smith.

Byron, Brian 1972 *Loyalty in the Spirituality of St Thomas More* Nieuwkoop: B. de Graaf.

Byron, George Gordon Noel (Lord Byron) (1788–1824) 1970 *Poetical Works* ed. by Frederick Page. A new [3rd] edn, corrected by John Jump. London: Oxford University Press.

Cahill, Desmond 1980 'Australia's multicultural society' *Journal of Intercultural Studies* I: pp. 94–96.

Caird, G. B. 1963 *The Gospel of St Luke* Harmondsworth: Penguin.

Cairns, James Ford (Jim Cairns) (1951) 'A call to the people of Australia' text in major Australian newspapers 12 Nov.

—— 1963 *Socialism and the ALP* . . . [with] comment by Bruce McFarlane (Victorian Fabian Society Pamphlet 8) [Melbourne: The Society].

—— 1975 *The Quiet Revolution* rev. edn. Camberwell, Victoria: Widescope.

Calvert, Peter 1970 *Revolution* London: Macmillan.

Calwell, Arthur Augustus 1963 *Labor's Role in Modern Society* Melbourne: Lansdowne Press.

—— 1978 *Be Just and Fear Not* Adelaide: Rigby in assoc. with Lloyd O'Neill.

Cameron, J. M. 1962 *The Night Battle: Essays* London: Burns & Oates.

—— 1966 *Images of Authority: A Consideration of the Concepts of 'Regnum' and*

'Sacerdotium' London: Burns & Oates.
Campbell, Keith 1969 'Marcuse on the justification of revolution' *Politics* IV: pp. 161–167.
Campbell, Ross 1971 'On being the same, only different' *The Bulletin* 23 Oct.: p. 13.
Canada – Department of Communications/Department of Justice 1972 *Privacy and Computers: A Report of a Task Force Established Jointly by Department of Communications/Department of Justice* Ottawa: Information Canada.
The Canberra Times 1982(a) '60 pc of Britons unwilling to sacrifice any lives' 3 May: p. 5.
—— 1982(b) 'Papers give all the news from the front' 4 May: p. 1.
Carew Hunt, R. N. 1957 *A Guide to Communist Jargon* London: Bles.
Carling, Alan 1991 *Social Division* London: Verso.
Carlyle, Thomas (1795–1881) 1906 *The French Revolution* vol. II. London: Everyman/ Dent.
Carroll, John 1978 'A Conservative credo: principles for a Liberal–Conservative political philosophy' *Quadrant* XXII no. 6 (June): pp. 41–43.
Carroll, Lewis (pseudonym of Charles Lutwidge Dodgson (1832–1898)) 1974 *The Philosopher's Alice: 'Alice's Adventures in Wonderland' & 'Through the Looking-Glass'* with introd. and notes by Peter Heath. London: Academy Editions.
Carsaniga, Giovanni 1986 'Varieties of national identity' Arena no. 74: pp. 39–47.
Cary, Joyce 1955 *Not Honour More* London: Michael Joseph.
Cassen, Robert 1967 'Collective decisions' pp. 61–69 in Audley *et al.*, 1967.
Cassinelli, C. W. 1961 'Political authority: its exercise and possession' *Western Political Quarterly* XIV: pp. 635–646. Reprinted as pp. 74–88 in de Crespigny & Wertheimer, 1971.
The Catholic Worker (Melbourne) 1944 *Design for Democrats: The Autobiography of a Free Journal* by 25 Men, 2nd edn. Melbourne: *The Catholic Worker*.
Chace, William M. 1973 *The Political Identities of Ezra Pound & T. S. Eliot* Stanford: Stanford University Press.
Chamallas, Martha 1988 'Consent, equality, and the legal control of sexual conduct' *Southern California Law Review* LXI: pp. 717–862.
Chamberlain, Neil W. 1967 *The Union Challenge to Management Control* [n.p.] Archon Books.
Chaudhuri, Nirad C. 1975 *Clive of India: A Political and Psychological Essay* London: Barrie & Jenkins.
Chesterton, Gilbert Keith 1905 *Heretics* London: Bodley Head.
—— 1939 Essays . . . sel. with a preface by John Guest, illus. by Newton Whittaker. London: Collins.
—— 1960 *The Napoleon of Notting Hill* [1904] London: World Distribution.
Childress, James 1982 *Who should Decide?: Paternalism in Health Care* New York: Oxford University Press.
Childs, Marquis W. 1971 *Sweden: The Middle Way* [1936] New Haven: Yale University Press.
Chipman, Lauchlan 1980 'The menace of multi-culturalism' *Quadrant* XXIV no. 10 (Oct.): pp. 3–6.
—— 1981 'Of myths and menaces: a rejoinder to Andrew Jacubowicz' *Quadrant* XXV no. 1 (Jan./Feb.): pp. 87–88.
—— 1988 'Bye bye multiculturalism' *Quadrant* XXXII no. 9 (Sept.): pp. 6–8.
Church of England 1987 *'Certain Sermons or Homilies'* (1547) and *'A Homily against Disobedience and Wilful Rebellion'* (1570) a critical edn by Ronald B. Bond. Toronto: University of Toronto Press.
Churchill, (Sir) Winston 1947 *Victory: War Speeches* . . . [vol.VI] 1945 comp. by Charles Eade. Melbourne: Cassell.
Clark, Pilita 1990 'Keating's gone too far: Hand' *SMH* 10 Dec.: p. 1.

Clarke, Paul A. B. 1988 *The Autonomy of Politics* Aldershot: Avebury.

Clarke, (Sir) Richard 1971 *New Trends in Government: Lectures Delivered . . . at the Civil Service College between March 1 and April 5, 1971* London: HMSO.

Clausewitz, Carl von (1780–1831) 1976 *On War* ed. and trans. by Michael Howard and Peter Paret. Princeton: Princeton University Press.

Coaldrake, Peter 1989 *Working the System: Government in Queensland* St Lucia: University of Queensland Press.

Cobban, Alfred 1969 *The Nation State and National Self-Determination* London: Fontana/Collins.

Cockburn, Alexander and Robin Blackburn 1969 *Student Power: Problems, Diagnosis, Action* Harmondsworth: Penguin in assoc. with *New Left Review*.

Cohen, Benjamin J. 1989 *Developing-Country Debt: A Middle Way* Princeton: International Finance Section, Dept of Economics, Princeton University.

Cohen, J. M. and M. J. Cohen 1960 *The Penguin Dictionary of Quotations* Harmondsworth: Penguin.

—— 1971 *The Penguin Dictionary of Modern Quotations* Harmondsworth: Penguin.

Cohen, Julius, Reginald A. H. Robson and Alan Bates 1955 'Ascertaining the moral sense of the community: a preliminary report on an experiment in interdisciplinary research' *Journal of Legal Education* VIII: pp. 137–149.

Cohen, Morris R. and Ernest Nagel 1934 *An Introduction to Logic and Scientific Method* London: Routledge & Kegan Paul.

'Cola di Rienzo' in *NEB Micropedia*.

Coleman, James 1972 'Collective decisions and collective action' pp. 208–219 in Laslett, *et al.*, 1972.

Commonwealth Bank of Australia 1991 'Helpful information: your mastercard account statement' [Leaflet] [n.p.].

The Concise Oxford Dictionary of Current English 1976, 6th edn., ed. by J. B. Sykes. Oxford: Clarendon Press.

Condren, Conal 1989 'Radicals, conservatives and moderates in early modern thought: a case of Sandwich Islands syndrome' *History of Political Thought* X: pp. 525–542.

Connell, R. W. and Florence Gould 1967 *Politics of the Extreme Right: Warringah 1966* (Sydney Studies in Politics 7) Sydney: Sydney University Press.

Connolly, William E. 1983 *The Terms of Political Discourse* 2nd edn. Oxford: Martin Robertson.

Conrad, Joseph (1857–1924) 1986 *'Typhoon' and Other Tales* ed. with an introd. by Cedric Watts. Oxford: World's Classics/Oxford University Press.

Cook, Hartley Kemball 1949 *The Free and Independent: The Trials, Temptations and Triumphs of the Parliamentary Elector* London: Allen & Unwin.

Coombs, Herbert C. 1970 *The Fragile Pattern: Institutions and Man* (The Boyer Lectures 1970) Sydney: Australian Broadcasting Commission.

Cooper, David E. 1973 *Philosophy and the Nature of Language* London: Longman.

Copi, Irving M. 1978 *Introduction to Logic* 5th edn. New York: Macmillan.

Copleston, Frederick 1947 *A History of Philosophy* vol. I: *Greece and Rome* rev. edn. London: Burns, Oates & Washbourne.

—— 1966 *ibid.* vol. VIII: *Bentham to Russell* London: Burns & Oates.

Cornford, Francis MacDonald 1953 *Microcosmographia Academica, Being a Guide for the Young Academic Politician* [1908] 5th edn. Cambridge: Bowes & Bowes.

Costar, Brian and Dennis Woodward 1985 *Country to National: Australian Rural Politics and Beyond* Sydney: Allen & Unwin.

Cotta, Sergio 1987 'Innovation and the public good: on understanding the logic of liberty' pp. 173–184 in Feaver & Rosen, 1987.

Cowden-Clarke, (Mrs) 1881 *The Complete Concordance to Shakespeare: Being a Verbal Index to All The Passages in the Dramatic Works Of the Poet* new and rev. edn. London: Bickers & Son.

Cowen, (Sir) Zelman 1977 *The Fragile Consensus* (The George Judah Cohen Memorial Lecture 1976) Sydney: University of Sydney.

Cranston, Maurice 1968 *Political Dialogues* London: British Broadcasting Corporation.

—— 1977 'Politics and ethics' pp. 279–299 in King, 1977.

Creighton, James Edward and Harold R. Smart 1932 *An Introductory Logic* 5th edn. New York: Macmillan.

Creighton, Mandell 1956 Letter to Lord Acton, 9 April 1887, pp. 341–345 in Acton, 1956.

Cribb, Timothy 1984 'A suburb with "no identity, no character, a nothingness"' *SMH* 11 Oct.: p. 3.

Crick, Bernard 1973 *Basic Forms of Government: A Sketch and a Model* London: Macmillan.

—— 1977 'Freedom as politics' pp. 301–322 in King, 1977.

—— 1982 *In Defence of Politics* 2nd Pelican edn. Harmondsworth: Penguin.

Crisp, Leslie Finlay 1972 'Politics and the Commonwealth Public Service' *Public Administration* (Royal Institute of Public Administration, Australian Regional Groups) XXXI: pp. 287–309.

Critchley, Julian 1985 *Westminster Blues: Minor Chords* London: Futura

Croft, Suzy and Peter Beresford 1987 'The politics of nostalgia' *New Society* 17 July: pp. 18–20.

Crombie, I. M. 1964 *Plato: The Midwife's Apprentice* London: Routledge & Kegan Paul.

Crosland, C. A. R. (Anthony Crosland) 1962 *The Conservative Enemy: A Programme of Radical Reform for the 1960s* London: Cape.

—— 1974 *'Socialism Now' and Other Essays* . . . ed. by Dick Leonard. London: Cape.

Crossman, R. H. S. (Richard Crossman) 1958 *'The Charm of Politics' and Other Essays in Political Criticism* London: Hamish Hamilton.

—— 1960 *Labour in the Affluent Society* (Fabian Tract no. 325) London: Fabian Society.

—— 1965 *Planning for Freedom* London: Hamish Hamilton.

—— 1969 *Government and the Governed: A History of Political Ideas and Political Practice* 5th edn. London: Chatto & Windus.

Cumming, Fia 1991 *Mates: Five Champions of the Labor Right* Sydney: Allen & Unwin.

Currie, H. MacL. (ed.) 1973 *The Individual and the State* London: Dent.

Dahl, Robert A. 1968 'Power' in IESS.

—— 1970 *Modern Political Analysis* 2nd edn. Englewood Cliffs: Prentice-Hall.

—— 1979 'Procedural democracy' pp. 97–133 in Laslett & Fishkin, 1979.

—— 1989 *Democracy and its Critics* New Haven: Yale University Press.

The Daily Telegraph (Sydney) 1982 'Aussie general enters the fray' 21 Dec.: p. 9.

The Daily Telegraph Mirror (Sydney) 1991 'A grand vision for the future' (Editorial) 22 Nov.: p. 12.

Dare, Christopher 1984 'Memory and forgetting: psychoanalytic theories' in *DPCP*.

Davids, C. A. F. Rhys 1909 'Asceticism (Buddhist)' in *ERE*.

Davidson, Kenneth 1991 'Reception fades for pay TV' *NH* 14 Oct.: p. 10 (*The Age*).

Davie, Donald 1969 'On hobbits and intellectuals' *Encounter* XXIII no. 4 (Oct.): pp. 87–92.

Davies, Alan F. 1988 *The Human Element: Three Essays in Political Psychology* Fitzroy: McPhee Gribble/Penguin.

Davies, James C. 1962 'Towards a theory of revolution' *American Sociological Review* XXVII: pp. 5–18.

Debusman, Bernd 1990 'Chamorro inherits economic ruin, Ortega's army' *NH* 28 Feb.: pp. 1, 3 (Reuter).

de Crespigny, Anthony 1968 'Power and its forms' *Political Studies* XVI: pp. 192–205.

Reprinted in de Crespigny & Wertheimer, 1971.

de Crespigny, Anthony and Alan Wertheimer (eds) 1971 *Contemporary Political Theory* London: Nelson.

Defoe, Daniel (1660-1731) 1975(a) *Selected Writings* . . . ed. by James T. Boulton Cambridge: Cambridge University Press.

—— 1975(b) 'The true born Englishman: a satyr' pp. 52-81 in Defoe, 1975(a).

De George, Richard T. (ed.) 1966 *Ethics and Society: Original Essays on Contemporary Moral Problems* New York: Anchor/Doubleday.

—— 1976 'Authority: a bibliography' pp. 141-170 in R. B. Harris, 1976.

de Grazia, Alfred 1968 'Representation: theory' in *IESS*.

Dejevsky, Mary 1992 'Community faces cruelty of Darwin's theory' *The Weekend Australian* 4/5 Jan.: p. 11 (*The Times*).

Dennis, Nigel 1955 *Cards of Identity* London: Weidenfeld & Nicolson

d'Entrèves, Alexander Passerin 1973 'The State' in *DHI*.

Derber, Milton 1970 *The American Idea of Industrial Democracy, 1865-1965* Urbana: University of Illinois Press.

Derrick, P. and J.-F. Phipps (eds) 1969 *Co-ownership Co-operation and Control: An Industrial Objective* London: Longmans Green.

Dessouki, Ali E. Hillal 1987 'Modernism: Islamic modernism' in *ER*.

Detmold, Michael J. 1985 *The Australian Commonwealth: A Fundamental Analysis of its Constitution* Sydney: Law Book Company.

Devambez, Pierre, *et al.* 1970 *A Dictionary of Ancient Greek Civilisation* London: Methuen.

Devlin, (Sir) Patrick (Lord Devlin) 1965 *The Enforcement of Morals* London: Oxford University Press.

Dictionary of the History of Ideas: Studies of Selected Pivotal Ideas: editor-in-chief: Philip P. Wiener 1973 New York: Scribner.

The Dictionary of Physiological and Clinical Psychology ed. by Rom Harré and Roger Lamb 1984 Oxford: Blackwell.

Disraeli, Benjamin (1804-1881) 1911 *Coningsby or, The New Generation* London: Everyman/Dent.

—— 1927 *Sybil or The Two Nations* London: Peter Davies.

Docker, John 1972 'Sydney intellectual history and Sydney libertarianism' *Politics* VII: pp. 40-47.

—— 1974 *Australian Cultural Elites: Intellectual Traditions in Sydney and Melbourne* Cremorne: Angus & Robertson.

Dominian, Jack 1976 *Authority: A Christian Interpretation of the Psychological Eolution of Authority* London: Burns & Oates.

Dostoyevsky, Fyodor 1953 *The Devils (The Possessed)* trans. with an introd. by David Magarshack. London: Penguin.

Douhet, Giulio 1943 *The Command of the Air* trans. by Dino Ferrari. London: Faber.

Dowling, Richard Eric 1960(a) 'Pressure group theory: its methodological range.' *American Political Science Review* LIV: pp. 944-954.

—— 1960(b) Review of A. P. Rowe's *If the Gown Fits in Semper Floreat* (11 July): pp. 6-7.

Downie, R. S. 1972 'The distinction between moderation and extremism' pp. 66-80 in Parekh & Berki, 1972.

Downie, R. S. and Elizabeth Telfer 1971 'Autonomy' *Philosophy* XLVI: pp. 293-301.

Doyle, (Sir) Arthur Conan (1859-1930) 1950 *The Memoirs of Sherlock Holmes* Harmondsworth: Penguin.

Drever, James 1964 *A Dictionary of Psychology* rev. by Harvey Wallerstein [further rev. by B. R. Singer] Harmondsworth: Penguin.

Dreyfus, Herbert and Bryan Magee 1987 'Husserl, Heidegger and modern existentialism' Dialogue 12 in Magee [*et al.*], 1987.

Duffy, Ann 1986 'Reformulating power for women' *Canadian Review of Sociology and Anthropology* XXXIII: pp. 22–46.

Duggan, Alfred 1951 *Conscience and the King* London: Faber.

Dummett, Ann 1973 *A Portrait of English Racism* Harmondsworth: Penguin.

Duncan-Jones, Austin 1958 'Authority' *Proceedings of the Aristotelian Society: Supplementary Volume* XXXII: pp. 241–260.

Dunn, Frank 1989 'All cultures are good except our own' *Quadrant* XXXIV no. 6 (June): pp. 40–43.

Dworkin, Ronald 1978 'Liberalism' pp. 113–143 in Hampshire, 1978.

Dwyer, Peter 1989 *Public and Private Lives* Melbourne: Longman Cheshire.

Earl, Donald 1967 *The Moral and Political Tradition of Rome* London: Thames & Hudson.

Easson, Michael (ed.) 1990 *Australia and Immigration: Able to Grow?* Leichardt: Pluto Press/Lloyd Ross Forum.

Edwards, Allen L. 1946 'Morale' in *EPsy* (Citadel).

Edwards, David L. 1988 'Antinomianism' in *FDMT*.

Eggleston, F. W. (Sir Frederick Eggleston) 1932 *State Socialism in Victoria* London: P. S. King.

Ehrlich, Howard J., Carol Ehrlich, David De Leon and Glenda Morris (eds) 1979 *Reinventing Anarchy: What are Anarchists Thinking These Days?* Routledge & Kegan Paul.

Eisenstadt, S. N. 1966 *Modernization: Protest and Change* Englewood Cliffs: Prentice Hall.

Eliade, Mircea 1954 'Psychology and comparative religion: a study of the symbolism of the centre' pp. 17–43 in Hastings & Nicholl, 1954.

Eliade, Mircea and Lawrence E. Sullivan 1987 'Center of the world' in *ER*.

Eliot, George (pseudonym of Mary Ann Evans) (1819–1880) 1965 *Middlemarch* ed. by W. J. Harvey. Harmondsworth: Penguin.

Eliot, Thomas Stearns 1929 *For Lancelot Andrewes: Essays on Style and Order* New York: Doubleday, Doran.

—— 1939 *The Idea of a Christian Society* London: Faber.

—— 1950 *The Cocktail Party: A Comedy* 4th impression (rev.) London: Faber.

—— 1968 *Murder in the Cathedral* [1935] London: Faber.

—— 1974(a) *Collected Poems 1909–1962* London: Faber.

—— 1974(b) *The Illustrated Old Possum: Old Possum's Book of Practical Cats* [1940] Nicolas Bentley drew the pictures. London: Faber.

Elliott, John 1978 *Conflict or Cooperation: The Growth of Industrial Democracy* London: Kogan Page.

Elliott, Robert and Arran Gare (eds) 1983 *Environmental Philosophy* St Lucia: University of Queensland Press.

Elster, Jon and John E. Riemer (eds) 1991 *Interpersonal Comparisons of Well-Being* Cambridge: Cambridge University Press

Elton, G. R. 1974 *England under the Tudors* 2nd edn. London: Methuen.

Emery, F. E. and Einer Thorsrud 1969 *Form and Content in Industrial Democracy: Some Experiences from Norway and Other European Countries* London: Tavistock.

Emmet, Dorothy 1966 *Rules, Roles and Relations* London: Macmillan.

—— 1972 *Function, Purpose and Powers: Some Concepts in the Study of Individuals and Societies* . . . with a foreword by Victor Turner, 2nd edn. London: Macmillan.

Emmet, E. R. 1968 *Learning to Philosophize* rev. edn. Harmondsworth: Penguin.

Emy, H. V. 1972 'The roots of Australian politics: a critique of a culture' *Politics* VIII: pp. 12–30.

—— 1974 *The Politics of Australian Democracy* Melbourne: Macmillan.

Encyclopedia of Philosophy editor-in-chief: Paul Edwards 1967 New York: Macmillan & Free Press.

Encyclopedia of Psychology ed. by Philip Lawrence Harriman, 1946 New York: Citadel Press.

Encyclopedia of Psychology ed. by H. J. Eysenck, W. Arnold and R. Meili 1972 London: Search Press.

Encyclopedia of Psychology ed. by Raymond J. Corsini and Bonnie D. Ozaki 1984 New York: Wiley-Interscience.

The Encyclopedia of Religion editor-in-chief: Mircea Eliade 1987 New York: Macmillan.

Encyclopedia of Religion and Ethics ed. by James Hastings, John A. Selbie *et al.* 1908 vol. I: A-Art. Edinburgh: T. & T. Clark.

—— 1909 vol. II: Arthur–Bunyan.

—— 1914 vol. VIII: Hymns–Liberty.

Epstein, Benjamin and Arnold Forster 1967 *The Radical Right: Report on the John Birch Society and its Allies* New York: Vintage/Random House.

Erikson, Erik 1968 'Identity, psychosocial' in *IESS*.

The Essential Left: see Marx *et al.*, 1960.

Euclid (323–283 BC) 1933 *The Elements of Euclid* with an introd. by Sir Thomas L. Heath. London: Everyman/Heath.

Evans, David 1991'Ground attack dents detente' *DTM* 26 Feb.: p. 10.

Evans, Raymond 1987 *Loyalty and Disloyalty: Social Conflict on the Queensland Homefront 1914-18* Sydney: Allen & Unwin.

Evans, Robert 1980 'Outbreak may curtail "moderate" rule' *NH* 6 May: p. 2 (AAP-Reuter).

Ewin, R. E. 1990 'Loyalty: the police' *Criminal Justice Ethics* IX: pp. 3–15.

Faden, Ruth R. and Tom Beauchamp in collaboration with Nancy M. P. King 1986 *A History and Theory of Informed Consent* New York: Oxford University Press.

Fairlie, Henry 1968 *The Life of Politics* London: Methuen.

Farrar, L. L. (Jr) 1989 'Porous vessels: a critique of the nation, nationalism and national character as analytical concepts' *History of European Ideas* X: pp. 705–720.

Faulkner, James 1991 '*Mens rea* in rape: *Morgan* and the inadequacy of subjectivism, or why no ahould not mean yes in the eyes of the law' *Melbourne University Law Review* XVIII: pp. 60–82.

Feaver, George 1987 'Two minds or one?: the Mills, the Webbs, and liberty in British social democracy' pp. 139–172 in Feaver & Rosen, 1987.

Feaver, George and Frederick Rosen (eds) 1987 *Lives, Liberties and the Public Good: New Essays in Political Theory* Basingstoke: Macmillan in assoc. with the London School of Economics and Political Science.

The Federalist or, The New Constitution [1787-1788] by Alexander Hamilton, James Madison & John Jay 1911 London: Everyman/Dent.

Feinberg, Joel 1977 'Harm and self-interest' pp. 285–308 in Hacker & Raz, 1977.

—— 1984 *The Moral Limits of the Criminal Law* vol. I: *Harm to Others* New York: Oxford University Press.

—— 1986 *ibid.* vol. III: *Harm to Self.*

Feith, Herbert 1962 *The Decline of Constitutional Democracy in Indonesia* Ithaca: Cornell University Press.

Felknor, Bruce 1975 *Dirty Politics* [1966] Westport, Conn.: Greenwood Press.

Fenton, J. C. 1971 *The Gospel of St Matthew* Harmondsworth: Penguin.

Fesler, James W. 1968 'Centralization and decentralization' in *IESS*.

Field, G. Lowell and John Higley 1980 *Elitism* London: Routledge & Kegan Paul.

Finley, M. I. 1971 *The Ancient Greeks* rev. reprint. Harmondsworth: Penguin in assoc. with Chatto & Windus.

Fishkin, James 1979 'Tyranny and democratic theory' pp. 197–226 in Laslet & Fishkin, 1979.

Fitzgerald, Ross (ed.) 1977 *Human Needs and Politics* Rushcutters Bay: Pergamon.

Fitzgerald, Tom 1990 *Between Life and Economics* (Boyer Lectures 1990) Crows Nest, NSW: ABC Enterprises.

Fitzgibbon, Constantine 1974 *The Blitz* London: Corgi/Transworld.

Flathman, Richard E. 1980 *The Practice of Authority: Authority and the Authoritative* Chicago: University of Chicago Press.

Fletcher, George P. 1993 *Loyalty: An Essay in the Morality of Relationships* New York: Oxford University Press.

Flew, Antony (ed.) 1956 *Essays in Conceptual Analysis* London: Macmillan.

—— 1975 *Thinking about Thinking* London: Fontana/Collins.

—— 1981 *The Politics of Procrustes: Contradictions of Enforced Equality* Buffalo: Prometheus Books.

—— (ed.) 1984 *A Dictionary of Philosophy* 2nd edn. London: Pan/Macmillan.

Florcruz, Jaime A. 1991 'Playing with Fire' *Time (Australia)* 21 Oct.: pp. 42–43.

The Fontana Dictionary of Modern Thought ed. by Alan Bullock and Oliver Stallybrass; new and rev. edn. by Alan Bullock and Stephen Trombley assisted by Bruce Eadie 1988 London: Fontana.

Foot, Paul 1968 *The Politics of Harold Wilson* Harmondsworth: Penguin.

Foot, Philippa R. and Jonathan Harrison 1954 'When is a principle a moral principle?' [Symposium] *Proceedings of the Aristotelian Society: Supplementary Volume* XXVIII: pp. 95–134.

Forster, Edward Morgan 1941 *Howards End* [1910] Harmondsworth: Penguin.

Foster, Lois and David Stockley 1988 'The rise and decline of Australian multi-culturalism: 1973–1988' *Politics* XXIII: pp. 1–10.

—— 1989 'The politics of ethnicity: multiculturalism in Australia' *Journal of Intercultural Studies* X no. 2: pp. 16–33.

Fowler, Henry W. 1974 *A Dictionary of Modern English Usage* 2nd edn. rev. by Sir Ernest Gowers. Corrected reprint. Oxford: Clarendon Press.

Fox, James J., Ross Garnaut, Peter McCawley and J. A. C. Mackie (eds) 1980 *Indonesia: Australian Perspectives* Canberra: Research School of Pacific Studies, Australian National University.

Fox, William T. R. and Annette Baker Fox 1968 'International politics' in *IESS*.

Frankel, Charles 1967 'Progress, the idea of' in *EP*.

Frankena, W. K. 1973 *Ethics* 2nd edn. Englewood Cliffs: Prentice-Hall. Chapters i–ii, iv–vi.

Frankena, William K. and John T. Granrose (eds) 1974 *Introductory Redings in Ethics* Englewood Cliffs: Prentice-Hall.

Fraser, John Malcolm 1981 Ministerial Statement: Review of Commonwealth Functions. House of Representatives Debates, 30 Apr.

Fraser, Ronald *et al.*, 1988 *1968: A Student Generation in Revolt* London: Chatto & Windus.

Frayn, Michael 1974 *Constructions* London: Wildwood.

Frazer, (Sir) James George 1911 *The Magic Art and the Evolution of Kings* vol. I rev. edn. London: Macmillan.

Freeling, Nicholas 1988 *Lady Macbeth* Harmondsworth: Penguin.

Freeman, Derek 1983 *Margaret Mead and Samoa: The Making and Unmaking of an Anthropological Myth* Canberra: Australian National University Press.

French, Derek and Heather Saward 1983 *Dictionary of Management* 2nd edn. Aldershot: Gower.

Friedman, Milton 1977 *From Galbraith to Economic Freedom* [London]: The Institute of Economic Affairs.

Friedman, Milton and Rose D. Friedman 1962 *Capitalism and Freedom* Chicago: University of Chicago Press.

—— 1980 *Free to Choose: A Personal Statement* Melbourne: Macmillan.

Friedrich, Carl J. 1958 'Authority, reason and discretion' pp. 28–48 in *Nomos*, 1958.

284   *Bibliography*

—— (ed.) 1964 *Totalitarianism* New York: Universal Library/Grosset & Dunlap.
—— 1966 'Political pathology' *The Political Quarterly* XXXVII. pp. 70–85.
—— 1967 *An Introduction to Political Theory: Twelve Lectures at Harvard* New York: Harper & Row.
Futasz, Mira and Hans-Dieter Senff 1985 *History of Sorb Education* Swansea, NSW: Sumptibus Publications for the Newcastle Branch of the Australian–German Democratic Republic Friendship Society.
Galbraith, John Kenneth 1979 *The Affluent Society* 3rd edn. Harmondsworth: Penguin.
Gallie, W. B. 1964 *Philosophy and the Historical Understanding* London: Chatto & Windus.
Galston, William A. 1991 *Liberal Purposes: Goods, Virtues and Diversity in the Liberal State* Cambridge: Cambridge University Press
Gardner, Peter 1988 'Religious upbringing and the liberal ideal of religious autonomy' *Journal of Philosophy of Education* XXII: pp. 89–105.
Gaus, Gerald F. 1983 *The Modern Liberal Theory of Man* London: Croom Helm.
Gaylin, Willard and Ruth Macklin 1982 *Who Speaks for the Child: The Problems of Proxy Consent* New York: Plenum Press.
Geach, Peter Thomas 1957 *Mental Acts: Their Content and their Objects* London: Routledge & Kegan Paul.
—— 1972 *Logic Matters* Oxford: Blackwell.
—— 1976 *Reason and Argument* Oxford: Blackwell.
Gefter, M. I 1976 'Imperialism' pp. 162–168 in *GSE* vol. X.
Gellner, Ernest 1987 *Culture, Identity, and Politics* Cambridge: Cambridge University Press.
Gibson, Mary 1982 *To Breathe Freely: Risk, Consent, and Air* (Working Paper) College Park: Center for Philosophy and Public Policy, University of Maryland.
Gierke, Otto von (1844–1921) 1957 *Natural Law and the Theory of Society 1500 to 1800* trans. with an introd. by Ernest Barker. Boston: Beacon Press.
Gilbert, Kevin 1977 *Living Black: Blacks Talk to Kevin Gilbert* Ringwood: Allen Lane.
Gilbert, W. S. (Sir William Gilbert) (1836–1911) 1926 *The Savoy Operas, Being the Complete Text of the Gilbert and Sullivan Operas as Originally Produced in the Years 1875–1896* London: Macmillan.
Gill, Alan 1984 'Sir Alan Walker cannot be silenced' *SMH* 15 Nov.: p. 18.
Gillis, Malcolm, Dwight H. Perkins, Michael Roemer and Donald R. Snodgrass 1983 *Economics of Development* New York: Norton.
Gilmore, (Dame) Mary 1954 *Fourteen Men: Verses* Sydney: Angus & Robertson.
Gilmour, Ian 1978 *Inside Right: A Study of Conservatism* London: Quartet Books.
Glazer, Nathan and Daniel Patrick Moynihan 1963 *Beyond the Melting Pot: The Negroes, Puerto Ricans, Jews, Italians and Irish of New York City* Cambridge, Mass.: Massachusetts Institute of Technology Press and Harvard University Press.
Glynn, Patrick McMahon 1918 Electoral Bill, 1918: Second Reading Speech *Commonwealth of Australia Parliamentary Debates* LXXXVI: pp. 6669–6682.
Gogarty, Oliver St John 1937 *As I Was Going Down Sackville Street* London: Rich & Cowan.
Goldsmith, Oliver (c. 1728–1774) 1906 *The Poetical Works of Oliver Goldsmith* ed. with an introd. and notes by Austin Dobson. London: Oxford University Press.
Goot, Murray 1969 'Parties of initiative and resistance: a reply' *Politics* IV no. 1 (May): pp. 84–99.
Gordon, Michael 1993 *A Question of Leadership: Paul Keating Political Fighter* St Lucia: University of Queensland Press.
Gordon, Richard (ed.) 1970 *The Australian New Left: Critical Essays and Strategy* Melbourne: Heinemann.
Gott, K. D. 1965 *Voices of Hate: A Study of the Australian League of Rights and its Director Eric D. Butler* Melbourne: Dissent Publishing Association.

Gough, J. W. 1957 *The Social Contract: A Critical Study of its Development* 2nd edn. Oxford: Clarendon Press.

Gould, L. Harry 1960 *Marxist Glossary* 3rd rev. edn. Sydney: Current Book Distributors.

Gowers, (Sir) Ernest: *see* Fowler, H. W.

Grabovsky, Peter Nils 1989 *Wayward Governance: Illegality and its Control in the Public Sector* [Canberra]: Australian Institute of Criminology.

Grant, Bruce 1972 *The Crisis of Loyalty: A Study of Australian Foreign Policy* Sydney: Angus & Robertson in assoc. with the Australian Institute of International Affairs.

Graubard, Stephen R. (ed.) 1980 *The State* New York: Norton. Reprint of *Daedalus* CVIII no. 4 (Fall 1979).

Gray, John 1984 *Hayek on Liberty* Oxford: Blackwell.

Great Soviet Encyclopedia a translation of the 3rd edn, vol. X 1976 New York: Macmillan.

—— 1983 *Index to Vols I-XXXI.*

Green, Antony 1991 'Greiner clears the deck for early election' *SMH* 25 March: p. 4.

Green, Thomas Hill 1964 *The Political Theory of Thomas Hill Green: Selected Writings* ed. by John R. Rodman. New York: Appleton-Century-Crofts.

Greenberg, Clement 1980 'Modern and post-modern' *Quadrant* XXIV no. 3 (March): pp. 30–33.

Greene, Graham 1950 *The Ministry of Fear: An Entertainment* [1943] London: Heinemann.

—— 1984 *Getting to Know the General: The Story of an Involvement* London: The Bodley Head.

Greenleaf, W. H. 1966 *Oakeshott's Philosophical Politics* London: Longmans.

Grene, Marjorie 1966 *The Knower and the Known* London: Faber.

Griffiths, A. Phillips 1984 'Child adoption and identity' *Royal Institute of Philosophy Lecture Series* XVIII: Supplement to *Philosophy* 1984 (*Philosophy and Practice*: pp. 275–285.

Griffiths, A. Phillips and Richard Wollheim 1960 'How can one person represent another?' [Symposium] *Proceedings of the Aristotelian Society: Supplementary Volume* XXIV: pp. 187–224.

Grosman, Brian A. 1989 'Corporate loyalty, does it have a future?' *The Journal of Business Ethics* VIII: pp. 565–568.

Groth, Alexander J. 1964 'The "isms" in totalitarianism' *The American Political Science Review* LVIII: pp. 888–901.

Grunberger, Richard 1974 *A Social History of the Third Reich* Harmondsworth: Penguin.

Guérin, Daniel 1970 *Anarchism From Theory to Practice* introd. by Noam Chomsky, trans. by Mary Klopper. New York: Monthly Review Press.

Gunn, J. A. W. (ed.) 1972 *Factions No More: Attitudes to Party in Government and Opposition in Eighteenth-Century England: Extracts from Contemporary Sources* London: Cass.

Gusfield, Joseph R. 1962 'Mass society and extremist politics' *American Sociological Review* XXVII: pp. 19–30.

—— 1975 *Community: A Critical Response* Oxford: Blackwell.

Guthrie, W. K. C. 1950 *The Greek Philosophers from Thales to Plato* London: Methuen.

—— 1971 *Socrates* Cambridge: Cambridge University Press.

Gwyn, Richard 1981 *The Northern Magus: Pierre Trudeau and Canadians . . .* ed. by Sandra Gwyn. Toronto: PaperJacks.

Gyford, John and Stephen Haseler 1971 *Social Democracy: Beyond Revisionism* (Fabian Research Series 292) London: Fabian Society.

Hacker, P. M. S. and Joseph Raz (eds) 1977 *Law, Morality, and Society: Essays in Honour of H. L. A. Hart* Oxford: Clarendon Press.

Hackney, Alan 1958 *Private Life* London: Gollancz.
Halifax (George Savile, first Marquess of Halifax) (1633–1695) 1969 *Complete Works* ed. with an introd. by J. P. Kenyon. Harmondsworth: Penguin.
Hall, Greg 1990 'Aboriginal ministry appeals for clemency in Savage case' *The Catholic Weekly* [Sydney] 31 Jan.: p. 3.
Hampshire, (Sir) Stuart (ed.) 1978 *Public and Private Morality* Cambridge: Cambridge University Press.
Hancock, W. K. (Sir Keith Hancock) 1945 *Australia* [1930] London: Australian Pocket Library/Benn.
Hanham, H. J. 1959 *Elections and Party Management: Politics in the Time of Disraeli and Gladstone* London: Longman.
Hanson, Russell L. 1989 'Democracy' pp. 68–89 in Ball *et al.*, 1989.
Hardy, Thomas (1840–1928) 1975 *Tess of the d'Urbervilles: A Pure Woman Faithfully Presented* by Thomas Hardy, introd. by P. N. Furbank. London: Macmillan.
Hare, Richard Mervyn 1952 *The Language of Morals* Oxford: Clarendon Press.
—— 1963 *Freedom and Reason* Oxford: Clarendon Press.
Harman, Gilbert 1977 *The Nature of Morality: An Introduction to Ethics* New York: Oxford University Press.
Harré, Rom (ed.) 1976 *Personality* Oxford: Blackwell.
Harries, Owen 1991 'The new world order? Take your pick' (edited version of the 1991 Latham Memorial Lecture) *SMH* 19 Sep.: p. 11.
Harrington, Michael 1969 *Toward a Democratic Left: A Radical Program for a New Majority* Baltimore: Penguin.
Harris, J. 1980 *Identity: A Study of the Concept in Education for a Multicultural Australia* (Education and Development Committee Report no. 22) Canberra: AGPS.
Harris, Nigel 1992 *National Liberation* London: Penguin.
Harris, R. Baine (ed.) 1976 *Authority: A Philosophical Analysis* University, Tuscaloosa, AL.: University of Alabama Press.
Harris, Stewart 1972 *Political Football: The Springbok Tour of Australia, 1971* Melbourne: Gold Star Publications.
Harrisson, Tom 1978 *Living Through the Blitz* Harmondsworth: Penguin.
Hart, Herbert Lionel Adolphus 1961 *The Concept of Law* Oxford: Clarendon Press.
Hartcher, Peter 1992 'Judges lash politicians over status' *SMH* 29 Jan.: p. 3.
Hartshorne, Charles 1987 *Wisdom as Moderation: A Philosophy of the Middle Way* Albany, N.Y.: State University of New York Press.
Hasluck, (Sir) Paul 1970 *Black Australians: A Survey of Native Policy in Western Australia* 2nd edn. Melbourne: Melbourne University Press.
Hastings, Cecily and Donald Nicholls (eds) 1954 *Selection II* London: Sheed & Ward.
Hawke, Robert James Lee 1979 *The Resolution of Conflict* (Boyer Lectures, 1979) Sydney: Australian Broadcasting Commission.
—— 1984 *National Reconciliation: The Speeches of Bob Hawke Prime Minister of Australia* sel. by John Cook. Sydney: Fontana/Collins.
Hawker, Geoffrey 1981 *Who's Master, Who's Servant?* Sydney: Allen & Unwin.
Hayek, Friedrich August von 1944 *The Road to Serfdom* Sydney: Dymock.
—— 1960 *The Constitution of Liberty* London: Routledge & Kegan Paul.
—— 1979 *Social Justice, Socialism and Democracy: Three Australian Lectures* [Turramurra]: The Centre for Independent Studies.
—— 1988 *The Fatal Conceit: The Errors of Socialism (The Collected Works of F. A. Hayek* vol. I ed. by W. W. Bartley III) Chicago: University of Chicago Press.
Head, Brian W. 1984 'Recent theories of the state' *Politics* XIX no. 1 (May): pp. 36–45.
Head, Brian W. and Allan Patience (eds) 1989 *From Fraser to Hawke* Melbourne: Longmans Cheshire.
Heffer, Eric 1991 *Never a Yes Man: The Life and Politics of an Adopted Liverpudlian* London: Verso.

Heidenheimer, Arnold J., Michael Johnston and Victor T. LeVine (eds) 1989 *Political Corruption: A Handbook* New Brunswick, N.J.: Transaction Publishers.

Held, Virgina, Sidney Morgenbesser and Thomas Nagel (eds) 1974 *Philosophy, Morality, and International Affairs* Essays ed. for the New York Group of the Society for Philosophy and Public Affairs. New York: Oxford University Press.

Held, Virginia, Kae Nielsen and Charles Parsons (eds) 1972 *Philosophy and Political Action* Essays ed. for the New York Group of the Society for Philosophy and Public Affairs. New York: Oxford University Press.

Heller, Agnes 1985 *The Power of Shame: A Rational Perspective* London: Routledge & Kegan Paul.

Herbert, A. P. (Sir Alan Herbert) 1948 *What a Word! Being an Account of 'The Word War' conducted in 'Punch' to the great Improvement and Delight of the People and the lasting Benefit of the King's English with many Ingenious Exercises and Horrible Examples* 9th edn. London: Methuen.

Hermens, F. A. 1938 'The Trojan horse of democracy' *Social Research* V: pp. 379–423.

Heywood, Thomas (*c*.1574–1641) 1964(a) *The Dramatic Works of Thomas Heywood, Now First collected With Illustrative Notes and a Memoir of the Author in Six Volumes* [1874] Volume the Sixth. New York: Russell & Russell.

—— 1964(b) *The Royall King and The Loyall Subject* [1637] pp. 1–83 in Heywood, 1964(a).

Hickey, T. J. O. 1971 'The ambiguity of "sovereignty"' *The Times* 29 Jan.: p. 14.

Hickie, David 1985 *The Prince and the Premier: The Story of Perce Galea, Bob Askin and the Others who gave Organised Crime its Start in Australia* North Ryde: Angus & Robertson.

Hicks, John D. 1968 'The populist contribution' [1931] pp. 14–23 in Saloutos, 1968(a).

Higgins, J. W. 1967 'Identification' in *NCE*.

Higley, John, Desley Deacon and Don Smart, with the collaboration of Robert G. Cushing, Gwen Moore and Jan Pakulski 1979 *Elites in Australia* London: Routledge & Kegan Paul.

Higley, John and Robert G. Cushing 1977 'Consensus and conflict among Australia's leaders' *Politics* no. 1 (May): pp. 38–58.

Hill, Christopher 1958 *Puritanism and Revolution: Studies in Interpretation of the English Revolution of the 17th Century* London: Secker & Warburg.

—— 1970 *God's Englishman: Oliver Cromwell and the English Revolution* London: Weidenfeld & Nicolson.

—— 1975 *The World Turned Upside Down: Radical Ideas During the English Revolution* Harmondsworth: Penguin.

Hill, Melvyn A. (ed.) 1979 *Hannah Arendt: The Recovery of the Public World* New York: St Martins Press.

Hindess, Barry 1971 *The Decline of Working-Class Politics* London: Paladin.

Hinsley, F. H. 1966 *Sovereignty* London: New Thinker's Library/Watts.

Hirst, John 1990 'Australia's absurd history: a critique of multiculturalism' *Overland* no. 118 (Feb.): pp. 5–10.

Hitler, Adolf 1974 *Mein Kampf* [1925–1932] with an introd. by D. C. Watt, trans. by Ralph Mannheim. London: Hutchinson.

Hobbes, Thomas (1588–1679) 1972 *Man and Citizen*: Thomas Hobbes's *De Homine* trans. by Charles T. Wood, T. S. K. Scott-Craig and Bernard Gert, and *De Cive*, trans. by Thomas Hobbes, also known as *Philosophical Rudiments Concerning Government and Society*, ed. with an introd. by Bernard Gert. New York: Anchor/Doubleday.

—— 1991 *Leviathan* ed. by Richard Tuck Cambridge: Cambridge University Press.

Hobhouse, Leonard Trelawny 1964 *Liberalism* introd. by Alan P. Grimes New York: Oxford University Press.

Hobsbawm, E. J. 1990 *Nations and Nationalism since 1780: Programme, Myth, Reality* Cambridge: Cambridge University Press.

Hockenos, Paul 1991 'Free to hate' *New Statesman/Society* 12 Apr.: pp. 18–19.

Hoffer, Eric 1980 *The True Believer: Thoughts on the Nature of Mass Movements* [1951] with an introd. by Sidney Hook. Alexandria, Virginia: Time-Life Books.

Hofstadter, Richard 1959 *Social Darwinism in American Thought* rev. edn. New York: Braziller.

—— 1967 *'The Paranoid Style in American Politics' and Other Essays* New York: Vintage/Random House.

—— 1968 'The folklore of populism' [1955] pp. 58–68 in Saloutos, 1968(a).

—— (ed.) 1969 *Great Issues in American History: From Reconstruction to the Present Day, 1864–1969* New York: Vintage/Random House.

Hogbin, Ian and L. R. Hiatt (eds) 1966 *Readings in Australian and Pacific Anthropology* Melbourne: Melbourne University Press.

Honderich, Ted 1992 *Conservatism* London: Penguin.

Hood, Christopher and Michael Jackson 1988 'Fifth column. The rhetoric of relevance: decoding Dawkinspeak' *'The Age' Monthly Review* (March): pp. 12–13.

Hooker, Clifford A. 1980 'Science as a human activity, human activity as . . .' *Contact* XII: pp. 1–29.

—— 1983 'On deep versus shallow theories of environmental pollution' pp. 58–84 in Elliott & Gare, 1983.

Höpfl, H. 1981 'Isms' *The British Journal of Political Science* XIII: pp. 1–17.

Horace 1979 Horace: *Satires and Epistles*, Persius: *Satires*, a verse trans. with an introd. and notes by Niall Rudd. Harmondsworth: Penguin.

Horne, D. R. (Donald Horne) 1988 *The Education of Young Donald* rev. edn. Ringwood: Penguin.

Hospers, John 1971 *Libertarianism: A Political Philosophy for Tomorrow* Los Angeles: Nash.

Housman, Alfred Edward 1939 *The Collected Poems of A. E. Housman* London: Cape.

Howard, Philip 1978 *Weasel Words* London: Hamish Hamilton.

—— 1980 *New Words for Old* [1977] London: Unwin Paperbacks.

Howe, Irving (ed.) 1966 *The Radical Papers* New York: Anchor/Doubleday.

Howson, Peter 1984 *The Life of Politics (The Howson Diaries)* ed. by Don Aitkin. Ringwood: Viking.

Hoy, David Couzens (ed.) 1986 *Foucault: A Critical Reader* Oxford: Blackwell.

Huby, Pamela M. 1967 *Greek Ethics* London: Macmillan.

Hudson, Kenneth 1977 *The Dictionary of Diseased English* London: Macmillan.

—— 1978 *The Language of Modern Politics* London: Macmillan.

Hudson, W. J. 1989 *Blind Loyalty: Australia and the Suez Crisis, 1956* Carlton: Melbourne University Press.

Hughes, Geoffrey 1988 *Words in Time: A Social History of the English Vocabulary* Oxford: Blackwell.

Hughes, Robert 1992 'The fraying of America' *Time (Australia)* VII no. 5 (3 Feb.): pp. 82–85.

Hume, David (1711–1776) 1951 *Theory of Politics: Containing 'A Treatise of Human Nature', Book III Parts I and II and Thirteen of the 'Essays Moral, Political and Literary'* ed. by Frederick Watkins. Edinburgh: Nelson.

—— 1984 *A Treatise of Human Nature* ed. with an introd. by Ernest C. Mossner. London: Penguin.

Hume, L. J. 1991 'Another look at the cultural cringe' *Political Theory Newsletter* III no. 1 (Apr.): pp. 1–36.

Hurst, G. Cameron III 1990 'Death, honor, and loyalty: the Bushidō Ideal' *Philosophy East and West* XL: pp. 511–527.

Hynd, Douglas 1983 *The Local Church as Community: Reading Guide* Ainslie, A.C.T.: Zadok Centre.

The Independent Monthly (Surry Hills, NSW) 1991 'The illusion of leadership' Oct.: pp. 25–31.

Inglis, Kenneth S. 1975 'Papua New Guinea: naming a nation' *New Guinea and Australia, The Pacific and South-East Asia* IX no. 4 (Jan.): pp. 2–20.

International Dictionary of Medicine and Biology editor-in-chief: Sidney I. Landau 1986 New York: Wiley.

International Encyclopedia of the Social Sciences ed. by David L. Sills 1968 New York: Macmillan & Free Press.

Ionescu, Ghita and Ernest Gellner (eds) 1969 *Populism: Its Meanings and National Characteristics* London: Weidenfeld & Nicolson.

Ivens, Michael (ed.) 1975 *Prophets of Freedom and Enterprise* London: Kogan Page for Aims of Industry.

Jackson, Michael 1993 'Democratic theory and practice' ch.iii in R. Smith, 1993(a).

Jacoby, Neil H., Peter Nehemkis and Richard Eels 1977 *Bribery and Extortion in World Business: A Study of Corporate Payments Abroad* New York: Studies of the Modern Corporation, Graduate School of Business, Columbia University/Macmillan.

Jaensch, Dean 1983 *Power Politics: Australia's Party System* Sydney: Allen & Unwin.

—— 1989 *The Hawke-Keating hijack: The ALP in Transition* Sydney: Allen & Unwin.

Jaensch, Dean and Max Teichmann 1988 *The Macmillan Dictionary of Australian Politics* 3rd edn. South Melbourne: Macmillan.

Jakubowicz, Andrew 1980 'The myth of the menace of multiculturalism: a reply to Lauchlan Chipman' *Quadrant* XXV no. 1 (Jan./Feb.): pp. 85–87.

—— 1988 'The celebration of (moderate) diversity in a racist society: multiculturalism and education in Australia' *Discourse* VIII no. 2 (Apr.): pp. 37–75.

James I (1566–1625) 1965 *The Political Works of James I* reprinted from the edn. of 1616, with an introd. by Charles Howard McIlwain. New York: Russell & Russell.

James, Fredric 1992 *Postmodernism, Or the Cultured Logic of Late Capitalism* London: Verso.

James, Michael 1977 'On "Toleration"' [Review of P. King, 1976] *Politics* XII: pp. 174–178.

—— 1981 'Public interest and majority rule in Bentham's democratic theory' *Political Theory* IX: pp. 49–64.

James, William (1842–1910) 1975 *Pragmatism* Cambridge, Mass.: Harvard University Press.

Janda, Kenneth 1968 'Representation: representational behavior' in *IESS*.

Janowitz, Morris (ed.) 1961 *Community Political Systems* Glencoe: Free Press.

Jenkins, David 1973 *Job Power: Blue and White Collar Democracy* New York: Doubleday.

Jennings, W. I. (Sir Ivor Jennings) 1961 'How to transfer authority' *The Listener* 23 Jan.: pp. 337–338.

John XXIII, (Pope) 1962 *Right Order in Human Society* trans. from the Latin text of the encyclical letter *Mater et Magistra* with an explanation by John Farrar. Sydney: Catholic Press Newspaper Co.

Johnson, Samuel (1709–1784) 1843 *The Dictionary of the English Language . . .* London: Bohn.

Joll, James 1979 'Politicians and the freedom to choose: the case of July 1914' pp. 99–114 in Ryan, 1979.

Josephus (Flavius Josephus) (AD 37 – c.100) 1981 *The Jewish War* trans. by G. A. Williamson, rev. with a new introd., notes and appendixes by E. Mary Smallwood. Harmondsworth: Penguin.

Jouvenel, Bertrand de 1952 *Power: The Natural History of its Growth* rev. edn. London: Batchworth.

—— 1957 *Sovereignty: An Inquiry into the Political Good* Cambridge: Cambridge University Press.

—— 1961 'Seminar exercise: the chairman's problem' *American Political Science Review* LV: pp. 368–372.

—— 1963 *The Pure Theory of Politics* Cambridge: Cambridge University Press.

Jupp, James 1981 'The British Social Democrats and the crisis in British Labour politics' *Politics* XVI: pp. 253–260.

—— 1982 *Party Politics: Australia 1966–1981* Sydney: Allen & Unwin.

—— 1986 'The politics of multiculturalism' *The Australian Quarterly* LVIII no. 1 (Autumn): pp. 93–101.

Kagarlitsky, Boris 1992 *The Disintegrating Monolith* London: Verso.

Kamenka, Eugene (ed.) 1970 *A World in Revolution?: The University Lectures 1970* Canberra: Australian National University.

—— (ed.) 1973 *Nationalism: The Nature and Evolution of an Idea* Canberra: Australian National University Press.

—— (ed.) 1982 *Community as a Social Ideal* London: Arnold.

—— 1989 *Bureaucracy* Oxford: Blackwell.

Kamenka, Eugene and Martin Krygier (eds) 1979 *Bureaucracy: The Career of a Concept* Port Melbourne: Arnold.

Kamenka, Eugene and Alice Erh-Soon Tay (eds) 1980 *Law and Social Control* London: Arnold.

Kaplan, Gisela T. and Clive S. Kessler (eds) 1989 *Thinking, Judging, Freedom* Sydney: Allen & Unwin.

Kaufman, Herbert 1968 'Administration I: the administrative function' in *IESS*.

Kazemzadeh, Firuz 1972 'Democratic Centralism' in *MCWS*.

Keat, Russell and Nicholas Abercrombie (eds) 1991 *Enterprise Culture* London: Routledge.

Kedourie, Elie 1961 *Nationalism* rev. edn. New York: Praeger.

Kelly, Paul 1984 *The Hawke Ascendancy: A Definitive Account of its Origins and Climax 1975–1983* Sydney: Angus & Robertson.

Kemp, David 1980 'The Liberal Party' pp. 313–320 in Mayer & Nelson, 1980.

Kemp Smith, Norman 1923 *A Commentary to Kant's 'Critique of Pure Reason'* 2nd edn. London: Macmillan.

Kennan, George *et al.* 1968 *Democracy and the Student Left* London: Hutchinson.

Kennedy, John Fitzgerald (alleged author) 1957 *Profiles in Courage* New York: Cardinal/Pocket Books.

Kennedy, Kett 1990 'William McCormack: forgotten Labor leader' ch. xii in Murphy *et al.*, 1980.

Kernohan, Andrew 1989 'Social power and human agency' *The Journal of Philosophy* LXXXVI: pp. 712–726.

Kilcullen, John 1978 'Toleration' Quadrant XXII no. 2 (Feb.): pp. 77–79.

King, Preston 1976 *Toleration* London: Allen & Unwin.

—— (ed.) 1977(a) *The Study of Politics: A Collection of Inaugural Lectures* London: Cass.

—— 1977(b) 'A reply to Michael James' *Politics* XII: pp. 179–180.

King, Roger 1986 *The State in Modern Society: New Directions in Political Sociology* . . . with chapter 8 by Graham Gibbs. London: Macmillan.

Kipling, Rudyard 1949 *Kim* [1901] London: Macmillan.

Kirk, G. S. and Raven, J. E. 1957 *The Presocratic Philosophers: A Critical History with a Selection of Texts* Cambridge: Cambridge University Press.

Kitto, Humphrey Davy Findley 1951 *The Greeks* Harmondsworth: Penguin.

Kleinig, John 1983 *Paternalism* Manchester: Manchester University Press.

Klueg, F. E. 1967 'Sin, occasion of' in *NCE*.

Knight, Stephen 1990 *The Selling of the Australian Mind: From First Fleet to Mercedes* Port Melbourne: Heinemann.

Knopfelmacher, Frank 1968 *'Intellectuals and Politics'* and *Other Essays* Melbourne: Nelson.

Knox, Ronald A. 1958 *Literary Distractions* London: Sheed & Ward.

Koch, Tony 1990 'Goss boosts building to retain jobs' *The Courier-Mail* 18 Dec.: p. 3.

Koestler, Arthur 1967 *The Ghost in the Machine* London: Hutchinson.

Kohn, Hans 1968 'Nationalism' in *IESS*.

—— 1973 'Nationalism' in *DHI*.

Kojecký, Roger 1971 *T. S. Eliot's Social Criticism* London: Faber.

König, René 1968 *The Community* London: Routledge & Kegan Paul.

Kovesi, Julius 1967 *Moral Notions* London: Routledge & Kegan Paul.

Krader, Lawrence 1968 *Formation of the State* Englewood Cliffs: Prentice-Hall.

Kreyche, G. F. 1967 'Occasion' in *NCE*.

Kruger, Andrew 1986 'UN hears fresh charges of murder in E. Timor. Fretilin still fighting guerrilla war: report' *NH* 18 Aug.: p. 5.

Labedz, Leopold 1988 'Left, the'; 'Left Book Club' in *FDMT*.

Labedz, Leopold and Steve Reilly 1988(a) 'Right, The' in *FDMT*.

—— 1988(b) 'New Left' in *FDMT*.

Labedz, Leopold and Alan Ryan 1988 'Anarchism' in *FDMT*.

Lacey, A. R. 1976 *A Dictionary of Philosophy* London: Routledge & Kegan Paul.

Lampe, G. W. H. 1961 *A Patristic Greek Lexicon* Oxford: Clarendon Press.

Lane, Max 1991 *'Openness', Political Discontent and Succession in Indonesia: Political Developments in Indonesia, 1989-1991* [Nathan]: Centre for the Study of Australia-Asian Relations, Griffith University.

Lang, John Thomas 1970 *The Turbulent Years* Sydney: Alpha Books.

Laslett, Peter (ed.) 1956(a) *Philosophy, Politics and Society* Oxford: Blackwell.

—— 1956(b) 'The face to face society' pp. 157-184 in Laslett, 1956(a).

Laslett, Peter and James Fishkin (eds) 1979 *Philosphy, Politics and Society: A Collection* 5th series. Oxford: Blackwell.

Laslett, Peter and W. G. Runciman (eds) 1962 *Philosophy, Politics and Society: A Collection* 2nd series. Oxford: Blackwell.

Laslett, Peter, W. G. Runciman and Quentin Skinner (eds) 1972 *Philosophy, Politics and Society: A Collection* 4th series. Oxford: Blackwell.

Latta, Robert and Alexander Macbeath 1929 *The Elements of Logic* London: Macmillan.

Laurance, Jeremy 1987 'In search of asylum' *New Society* 17 Apr.: pp. 18-19.

Laver, Michael 1979 *Playing Politics* Harmondsworth, Penguin.

—— 1983 *Invitation to Politics* Oxford: Blackwell.

Leeder, Stephen 1984 'Entertaining but without political purpose' *NH* 26 May: p. 6.

Lefever, Ernest W. (ed.) 1972(a) *Ethics and World Politics: Four Perspectives* Baltimore: Johns Hopkins University Press.

—— 1972(b) 'Morality versus moralism in foreign policy' pp. 1-20 in Lefever, 1972(a).

Legge, J. D. (convenor) 1973 *Traditional Attitudes and Modern Styles in Political Leadership* Papers presented to the 28 International Congress of Orientalists. Sydney: Angus & Robertson.

Lehmann, David (ed.) 1979 *Development Theory: Four Critical Studies* London: Case.

Leigh, Edward E. (comp.) 1979 *Right Thinking: A Personal Collection of Quotations Dating from 3000 BC to the Present Day which might be Said to Cast some Light on the Workings of the Tory Mind* London: Hutchinson Benham.

Lemos, Ramon M. 1978 *Hobbes and Locke: Power and Consent* Athens: University of Georgia Press.

Lewis, Charlton T. and Charles Short 1879 *A Latin Dictionary Founded on Andrews' Edition of Freund's Latin Dictionary* rev., enl., and in great part rewritten. Oxford: Clarendon Press.

Lewis, Clive Staples (1898–1963) 1963 *The Four Loves* London: Fontana/Collins.
—— 1967 *Studies in Words* 2nd edn. Cambridge: Cambridge University Press.
Lewis, (Sir) George Cornewall 1898 *Remarks on the Use and Abuse of some Political Terms* . . . a new edn with notes and introd. by Thomas Raleigh. Oxford: Clarendon Press.
Liberal Party of Australia 1991 *Fightback!: Taxation and Expenditure Reform for Jobs and Growth* Canberra: Liberal Party of Australia.
Lichtheim, George 1974 *Imperialism* Harmondsworth: Penguin.
Liddell, Henry George and Robert Scott 1940 *A Greek-English Lexicon* 9th edn. Oxford: Clarendon Press.
Lidz, Charles W., Alan Meisel, Eviatur Zerubavel, Mary Carter, Regina M. Sestak and Loren H. Roth 1984 *Informed Consent: A Study of Decisionmaking in Psychiatry* with a foreword by Alan A. Stone. New York: Guilford Press.
The Life of Cola di Rienzo trans. with an introd. by John Wright 1975 Toronto: Pontifical Institute of Mediaeval Studies.
Lijphart, Arend 1977 *Democracy in Plural Societies: A Comparative Exploration* New Haven: Yale University Press.
Lindsay, A. D. (First Lord Lindsay of Birker) (1879–1952) 1962 *The Modern Democratic State* New York: Galaxy/Oxford University Press.
Lipset, Seymour Martin and Sheldon S. Wolin (eds) 1965 *The Berkeley Student Revolt: Facts and Interpretations* New York: Anchor/Doubleday.
Lipsey, David and Dick Leonard (eds) 1981 *The Socialist Agenda: Crosland's Legacy* London: Cape.
Lipsitz, Lewis 1968 'Consensus II: the study of consensus' in *IESS*.
Little, Graham 1989 'Leadership styles: Fraser and Hawke' ch. ii in Head & Patience, 1989.
Lively, Jack 1975 *Democracy* Oxford: Blackwell.
Lockard, Duane 1973 'The "great tradition" of American corruption' *New Society* (May): pp. 486–488.
Locke, John 1965 *Two Treatises of Government* a critical edn with an introd. and apparatus criticus by Peter Laslett, rev. edn. New York: Mentor/New American Library.
Loebl, Eugen 1972 *Conversations with the Bewildered* London: Allen & Unwin.
Longford (Earl of) [i.e., Pakenham, Frank] and Thomas P. O'Neill 1974 *Eamon de Valera* [rev. edn.] London: Arrow.
Loomis, C. P. and J. A. Beagle 1957 *Rural Sociology* rev. edn. Englewood Cliffs: Prentice-Hall.
Loudon, Bruce and M. G. G. Pillai 1990 'PM's demise raises spectre of return to military regime' *The Australian* 8 Aug.: p. 7.
Loveday, Peter 1971 'Representation – or interests? Two themes in Australian political thought, 1850 to the present' Australasian Political Studies Association. Thirteenth Annual Conference.
—— 1980 'Labor and democratic socialism' pp. 73–87 in North & Weller, 1980.
Lucas, John Randolph 1967 *The Principles of Politics* corrected reprint. Oxford: Clarendon Press.
—— 1976 *Democracy and Participation* Harmondsworth: Penguin.
Luce, A. A. 1958 *Logic* London: Teach Yourself Books/English Universities Press.
Lucy, Richard 1979 'Wran's our man: the 1978 NSW state elections' *Politics* XIV no. 1 (May): pp. 89–96.
Lukes, Steven 1973 *Individualism* Oxford: Blackwell.
—— 1974 *Power: A Radical View* London: Macmillan.
—— 1977 *Essays in Social Theory* London: Macmillan.
Lumby, Catherine 1991 'Archbishop raps Govt tax reform' *SMH* 3 May: p. 4.

Lunn, Hugh 1984 *Joh: The Life and Political Adventures of Sir Johannes Bjelke-Petersen* 2nd edn. St Lucia: University of Queensland Press.

Lyttleton, Adrian (ed.) 1975 *Italian Fascisms from Pareto to Gentile* trans. from the Italian by Douglas Parmée [*et al.*] New York: Torchbooks/Harper & Row.

Lytton, (Lord) (Edward Lytton Bulwer-Lytton) 1911 *Rienzi* [1835, 1848] London: Everyman/Dent.

Mabbott, J. D. 1947 *The State and the Citizen: An Introduction to Political Philosophy* London: Hutchinson's University Library.

McAuley, James 1959 *The End of Modernity: Essays on Literature, Art and Culture* Sydney: Angus & Robertson.

—— 1971 *Collected Poems 1936-1970* Sydney: Angus & Robertson.

McCabe, Herbert 1979 *Law, Love and Language* 2nd edn. London: Sheed & Ward.

MacCallum, Gerald C. (Jr) 1972 'Negative and positive freedom' pp. 174–193 in Laslett *et al.*, 1972.

MacCallum, Ronald Buchanan and Alison Readman 1947 *The British General Election of 1945* London: Oxford University Press.

McClelland, J. S. (ed.) 1970 *The French Right (from de Maistre to Maurras)* London: Cape.

McCloskey, H. J. 1968 'Some arguments for a liberal society' *Philosophy* XLII: pp. 324–344.

—— 1974 'Liberalism' *Philosophy* XLIX: pp. 13–32.

MacCoby, S. (ed.) 1952 *The English Radical Tradition 1763-1914* London: Kaye.

McCoy, A. W. 1980 *Drug Traffic: Narcotics and Organized Crime in Australia* Sydney: Harper & Row.

McCoy, Charles A. and John Playford (eds) 1967 *Apolitical Politics: A Critique of Behavioralism* New York: Crowell.

McDiarmid, Lucy 1984 *Saving Civilization: Yeats, Eliot and Auden between the Wars* Cambridge: Cambridge University Press.

Mace, C. A. (ed.) 1957 *British Philosophy in the Mid-Century: A Cambridge Symposium* London: Allen & Unwin.

MacGregor, Geddes 1989 *Dictionary of Religion and Philosophy* New York: Paragon House.

Machiavelli, Niccolò (1469–1527) 1950 *'The Prince' and 'The Discourses'* with an introd. by Max Lerner. New York: Modern Library/Random House.

Machlup, Fritz (ed.) 1976 *Essays on Hayek* New York: New York University Press.

McInerny, Ralph 1981 *The Search Committee* New York: Atheneum.

McKenzie, Robert and Allen Silver 1968 *Angels in Marble: Working Class Conservatives in Urban England* London: Heinemann.

Mackenzie, W. J. M. 1975 *Power, Violence, Decision* Harmondsworth: Penguin.

—— 1978 *Political Identity* Harmondsworth: Penguin.

McKinlay, Brian (ed.) 1979 *A Documentary History of the Australian Labor Movement 1950-1975* Richmond, Victoria: Drummond.

Maclean, Charles 1972 *Island on the Edge of the World: Utopian St Kilda and its Passing* London: Stacey.

MacLean, Douglas 1981 *Risk and Consent: A Survey of the Issues for Centralized Decision Making* (Working Paper) College Park: Center for Philosophy and Public Policy, University of Maryland.

McManus, Frank 1977 *The Tumult and the Shouting* Adelaide: Rigby.

McMorrow, G. J. 1967 'Authority' in *NCE*.

McMurty, John 1979 'How to tell the Left from the Right' *Canadian Journal of Philosophy* IX: pp. 387–412.

Macpherson, Crawford Brough 1966 *The Real World of Democracy* Oxford: Clarendon Press.

—— 1973 *Democratic Theory: Essays in Retrieval* Oxford: Clarendon Press.

—— 1977 *The Life and Times of Liberal Democracy* Oxford: Oxford University Press.

The Macquarie Encyclopedic Thesaurus: The Book of Words general ed.: J. R. L. Bernard 1990 Chatswood, NSW: Macquarie Library.

McRae, Kenneth (ed.) 1974 *Consociational Democracy: Political Accommodation in Segmented Societies* Toronto: Carleton Library/McClelland & Stewart.

McShea, Robert J. 1978 'How power corrupts' *Journal of Value Inquiry* XII: pp. 37–48.

Maddox, Graham 1974 'Democratic theory and the face to face society' *Politics* IX: pp. 56–62.

—— 1986 'Contours of a democratic polity' *Politics* XXI no. 2 (Nov.): pp. 1–11.

Madge, John 1962 *The Origins of Scientific Sociology* New York: Free Press.

Magee, Bryan [*et al.*] 1987 *The Great Philosophers: An Introduction to Western Philosophy* London: BBC Books.

Mair, Lucy 1962 *Primitive Government* Harmondsworth: Penguin.

—— 1965 *An Introduction to Social Anthropology* Oxford: Clarendon Press.

Manley, Gordon D. 1968 'Gemeinschaft' pp. 84–85 in Mitchell, 1968.

Manne, Robert (ed.) 1982 *The New Conservatism in Australia* Melbourne: Oxford University Press.

Manning, D. J. 1976 *Liberalism* London: Dent.

Mannison, D. S., *et al.* (eds) 1980 *Environmental Philosophy* Canberra: Department of Philosophy, Research School of Social Sciences, Australian National University.

Manschrek, Clyde L. (ed.) 1971 *Erosion of Authority* Nashville: Abingdon Press.

Marcos, Ferdinand E. 1971 *Today's Revolution: Democracy* [n.p.].

Marcuse, Herbert 1966 'Ethics and revolution' pp. 133–147 in De George, 1966.

Maritain, Jacques 1928 *Three Reformers: Luther-Descartes-Rousseau* London: Sheed & Ward.

—— 1937 *An Introduction to Logic* London: Sheed & Ward.

Marr, David 1991 *Patrick White: A Life* Milson's Point: Random House.

Marsh, Arthur 1979 *Concise Encyclopedia of Industrial Relations* Westmead, Hants: Gower Press.

Marshall, S. L. A. 1978 *Men against Fire: The Problem of Battle Command in Future War* Gloucester, Mass.: Peter Smith.

Marx, Karl, Friedrich Engels and V. I. Lenin 1960 *The Essential Left: Four Classic Texts on the Principle of Socialism* London: Unwin.

Marxism, Communism and Western Society: A Comparative Encyclopaedia ed. by C. D. Kernig 1973, New York: Herder.

Mason, Peter 1979 *Cauchu the Weeping Wood: A History of Rubber* Sydney: Australian Broadcasting Commission.

Mattelart, Armand and Seth Siegelaub (eds) 1979 *Communication and Class Struggle: Capitalism, Imperialism* vol. I New York: International General.

Mayer, Henry 1956 'Some conceptions of the Australian party system, 1910–1950' *Historical Studies, Australia and New Zealand* VII no. 27 (May): pp. 253–270.

—— (ed.) 1966(a) *Australian Politics: A Reader* Melbourne: Cheshire.

—— 1966(b) 'Parties: initiative and resistance' pp. 223–230 in Mayer, 1966.

—— 1969(a) *Australian Politics: A Second Reader* Melbourne: Cheshire.

—— 1969(b) 'Initiative and resistance: a comment' *Politics* IV: pp. 212–215.

Mayer, Henry and Helen Nelson (eds) 1980 *Australian Politics: A Fifth Reader* Melbourne: Longman Cheshire.

Meadowcroft, Michael 1991 'Means to an end' [Letter] *New Statesman/Society* 31 May: p. 23.

Meggitt, M. J. 1966 'Indigenous forms of government among the Australian Aborigines' pp. 57–74 in Hogbin & Hiatt, 1966.

Merson, John *et al.* 1982 *Science & Ethics 3: Genetic Engineering - Who Decides?* [Audiotape] Sydney: Australian Broadcasting Commission.

Métin, Albert (1871–1918) 1977 *Socialism without Doctrine* [1901] trans. by Russel Ward. Chippendale, NSW: Alternative Publishing Co-operative.

Middlemas, Keith 1979 *Politics in Industrial Society: The Experience of the British System since 1911* London: Deutsch.

Midgley, Mary 1979 *Beast and Man: The Roots of Human Nature* Hassocks: Harvester.

—— 1981 *Heart and Mind: The Varieties of Moral Experience* London: Methuen.

Mill, John Stuart (1806–1973) 1963(a) *Essays on Politics and Culture* ed. by Gertrude Himmelfarb. New York: Anchor/Doubleday.

—— 1963(b) 'Thoughts on parliamentary reform' pp. 304–333 in Mill, 1963(a).

—— 1963(c) 'A few words on non-intervention' pp. 368–384 in Mill, 1963(a).

—— 1970 *Principles of Political Economy with some of their Applications to Social Philosophy Books IV and V* [1848] ed. with an introd. by Donald Winch. Harmondsworth: Penguin.

—— 1972 *'Utilitarianism', 'Liberty', 'Representative Government', Selections from 'Auguste Comte and Positivism'* ed. by H. B. Acton. London: Everyman/Dent.

Miller, Eugene F. 1980 'What does "Political" Mean?' *The Review of Politics* XLII: pp. 56–72.

Miller, John Donald Bruce 1960 *Politicians: An Inaugural Lecture Delivered at the University, Leicester 25 February, 1958* Leicester: Leicester University Press.

—— 1965 *The Nature of Politics* Harmondsworth: Penguin.

Millett, Kate 1972 *Sexual Politics* London: Abacus/Sphere.

Milne, A. J. M. 1968 *Freedom and Rights* London: Allen & Unwin.

—— 1972 'Reason, morality and politics' pp. 31–51 in Parekh & Berki, 1972.

Milne, Glenn 1991 'Liberal loyalists portray the human face of Hewson' *The Australian* 29 Oct.: pp. 1, 5.

Milton, John (1609–1674) 1951 *'Areopagitica' and 'Of Education' with Autobiographical Passages from Other Prose Works* ed. by George H. Sabine. New York: Crofts Classics/Appleton-Century-Crofts.

Minogue, K. R. 1972 'Theatricality and politics: Machiavelli's concept of fantasia' pp. 148–162 in Parekh & Berki, 1972.

—— 1987 'Loyalty, liberalism and the State' pp. 203–227 in Feaver & Rosen, 1957.

—— 1989 'The emergence of the New Right' ch. vii in Skidelsky, 1989.

Mitchell, Basil 1970 *Law, Morality, and Religion in a Secular Society* London: Oxford University Press.

Mitchell, G. Duncan (ed.) 1968 *A Dictionary of Sociology* London: Routledge & Kegan Paul. Articles are arranged alphabetically by title.

Monaco, M. 1967 'Cola di Rienzo' in *NCE*.

Montefiore, Alan (ed.) 1975 *Neutrality and Impartiality: The University and Political Commitment* Cambridge: Cambridge University Press.

Moore, David Cresap 1976 *The Politics of Deference: A Study of the Mid-Nineteenth Century English Political System* Hassocks: Harvester.

Moore, George Edward 1903 *Principia Ethica* Cambridge: Cambridge University Press.

Morgan, H. Wayne 1971 *Unity and Culture: The United States, 1877–1900* Harmondsworth: Penguin.

Morgan, Hugh M. 1989 'Mining and political power' *Quadrant* XXIV no. 7 (July): pp. 15–19.

Morgan, Patrick 1980 'The paradox of Australian nationalism' *Quadrant* XXIV no. 3 (March): pp. 7–10.

Morris-Jones, W. H. 1949 *Socialism and Bureaucracy* (Fabian Tract no. 277) London: Fabian Publications and Gollancz.

Mosse, George L. 1966 *Nazi Culture: Intellectual Cultural and Social Life in the Third Reich* trans. by Salvator Attanasio and others. London: W. H. Allen.

Motet, D. 1984 'Identity Crisis' in *EPsy* (Wiley).

Mozley and Whiteley's Law Dictionary 9th edn by John B. Saunders 1977 London: Butterworth.

Muehlenberg, Bill 1990 *Modern Conservative Thought: An Annotated Bibliography* Melbourne: Institute of Public Affairs.

Munro-Clark, Margaret (ed.) 1992 *Citizen Participation in Government* Sydney: Hale & Iremonger.

Murphy, Denis, Roger Joyce and Margaret Cribb (eds) 1990 *The Premiers of Queensland* rev. edn. St Lucia: University of Queensland Press. First edn (ed. by Murphy & Joyce) was published in 1978 as *Queensland Political Portraits 1859-1952*.

Murray, K. M. Elisabeth 1979 *Caught in the Web of Words: James A. H. Murray and the 'Oxford English Dictionary'* Oxford: Oxford University Press.

Murray, Robert 1970 *The Split: Australian Labor in the Fifties* Melbourne: Cheshire.

Murray-Smith, Stephen 1987 *Right Words: A Guide to English Usage in Australia* Ringwood: Viking.

—— 1988 *Sitting on Penguins: People and Politics in Australian Antarctica* Surry Hills, NSW: Hutchinson.

Muschamp, David (ed.) 1986(a) *Political Thinkers* London: Macmillan.

—— 1986(b) 'Rousseau and the general will.' pp. 123-137 in Muschamp, 1986(a).

Musgrave, Peter William 1980 'The core curriculum: a case study in cultural planning in a pluralist society' Adelaide: 50th ANZAAS Congress.

Mussolini, Benito [and Giovanni Gentile] 1939 'The doctrine of Fascism' [1932] pp. 164-179 in Oakeshott, 1939.

Nairn, Bede 1989 *Civilising Capitalism: The Beginnings of the Australian Labor Party* Carlton: Melbourne University Press.

Namier, (Sir) Lewis 1957 *The Structure of Politics at the Accession of George III* 2nd edn. London: Macmillan.

Nathanson, Stephen 1989 'In defense of "moderate patriotism"' *Ethics* XCIX: pp. 535-552.

—— 1990 'On deciding whether a nation deserves our loyalty' *Public Affairs Quarterly* IV: pp. 287-298.

Needler, Martin C. 1991 *The Concepts of Comparative Politics* New York: Praeger.

Nerlich, Graham 1965 'Presupposition and entailment' *American Philosophical Quarterly* II: pp. 33-42.

Neumann, Franz 1950 'Approaches to the study of political power' *Political Studies Quarterly* LXV: pp. 161-180. Reprinted as ch.i of Neumann, 1957.

—— 1957 *The Democratic and the Authoritarian State: Essays in Political and Legal Theory* . . . ed. and with a preface by Herbert Marcuse. Glencoe: Free Press.

The New Catholic Encyclopedia 1967 New York: McGraw-Hill.

The New Encyclopaedia Britannica 15th edn 1987 Chicago: Encyclopaedia Britannica Inc.

—— 1987(a) 'Related fields: social psychology' vol. XXVII: p. 388.

—— 1987(b) 'The development of human behavior' vol. XIV: pp. 708-723.

The New Encyclopaedia Britannica: Micropedia 15th edn 1991 Chicago: Encyclopaedia Britannica Inc.

New Statesman/Society 1991 'What's left of the Left?' 3 May: pp. 4-21.

The Newcastle Herald (New South Wales) 1980 'Opening the new mall' [Editorial] 17 Nov.: p. 2.

—— 1982 '$63m art gallery "provides national identity"' 13 Oct.: p. 1.

—— 1985 'Stewart asks for details' 3 Oct.: p. 5.

—— 1988 'Liberals' winter of discontent' [Editorial] 29 Aug.: p. 4.

—— 1990 'Games curtain to open as backstage bickering rages' 24 Jan.: p. 1.

—— 1991(a) 'Life term for murder of wife' 4 Oct.: p. 2.

—— 1991(b) 'Man who followed thief praised by judge' 4 Oct.: p. 3.

—— 1992 'Medicare target of fear campaign: Howe' 1 Feb.: p.4.

Ngawang Lobsang Yishey Fensing Gyatso (14th Dalai Lama) 1975 '*The Buddhism of*

Tibet' and *'The Key to the Middle Way'* trans. in the main by Jeffrey Hopkins and Lati Rimpoche. London: Allen & Unwin.

Nicholas, H. G. (ed.) 1956 *To the Hustings: Election Scenes from English Fiction* London: Cassell.

Nisbet, Robert A. 1973 'The nemesis of authority' *Quadrant* XVII no. 4 (July/Aug.): pp. 11–22.

—— 1976 *The Quest for Community* New York: Oxford University Press.

—— 1982 *Prejudices: A Philosophical Dictionary* Cambridge, Mass.: Harvard University Press.

Niskanen, William A. 1973 *Bureaucracy and Representative Government* New York: Aldine-Atherton.

Nolan, Richard 1986 'Don't ignore economy's victims' [Letter] *SMH* 21 Aug.: p. 12.

Nolte, Ernst 1969 *Three Faces of Fascism: Action Française. Italian Fascism. National Socialism* trans. from the German by Leila Vennewitz. New York: Mentor/New American Library.

Nomos: Yearbook of the American Society for the Philosophy of Law 1958 vol. I: *Authority* ed. by Carl Friedrich.

—— 1987 vol. XXIX: *Authority Revisited* ed. by J. Roland Pennock and John W. Chapman.

Nordlinger, Eric A. 1967 *The Working-Class Tories: Authority, Deference and Stable Democracy* London: Macgibbon & Kee.

Norington, Brad 1991 'Labor Council blasts ACTU's call for big cuts in migrants' *SMH* 12 Apr.: p. 4.

Norman, Richard 1983 *The Moral Philosophers: An Introduction to Ethics* Oxford: Clarendon Press.

North, Jane and Patrick Weller (eds) 1980 *Labor: Directions for the Eighties* Sydney: Novak.

Novak, Michael 1969 *A Theology for Radical Politics* New York: Herder.

Nozick, Robert 1974 *Anarchy, State and Utopia* Oxford: Blackwell.

Nurick, John 1989 *Wet, Dry and Privatise* [Perth, W.A.]: Australian Institute for Public Policy.

Oakeshott, Michael (ed.) 1939 *The Social and Political Doctrines of Contemporary Europe* Cambridge: Cambridge University Press.

—— 1962 *'Rationalism in Politics' and Other Essays* London: Methuen.

—— 1975(a) *Hobbes on Civil Association* Oxford: Blackwell.

—— 1975(b) *On Human Conduct* Oxford: Clarendon Press.

O'Brien, Denis 1991 *The Bicentennial Affair: The Inside Story of Australia's 'Birthday Bash'* Crow's Nest, NSW: Australian Broadcasting Commission.

O'Brien, Patrick 1980 'Political conflict and the sense of permanent crisis in the Australian polity' ch. vii in Weller & Jaensch, 1980.

—— 1985 *The Liberals: Factions, Feuds and Fancies* Ringwood: Viking.

O'Connor, Ulick 1967 *Oliver St John Gogarty: A Poet and his Times* London: New English Library.

O'Donovan, Oliver 1980 *The Problem of Self-Love in St Augustine* New Haven: Yale University Press.

O'Flynn, J. A. 1951 *'The Gospel . . . according to St Mark'* pp. 905–934 in Orchard, *et al.*, 1951.

O'Leary, Cornelius 1962 *The Elimination of Corrupt Practices in British Elections 1868-1911* Oxford: Clarendon Press.

Ó Maoláin, Ciarán (comp.) 1987 *The Radical Right: A World Directory* (A Keesing's Reference Publication) Harlow, Essex: ABC-CLIO/Longman.

Omar Khayyám 1899 *Rubáiyát of Omar Khayyám the Astronomer-Poet of Persia* rendered into English verse [by Edward Fitzgerald] London: Golden Treasury/Macmillan.

O'Meagher, Brian (ed.) 1983 *The Socialist Objective* Sydney: Hale & Iremonger.

Ongka 1979 *Ongka: A Self-Account by a New Guinea Big-Man* trans. by Andrew Strathern. London: Duckworth.

Orchard, Bernard *et al.* (eds) 1951 *A Catholic Commentary on Holy Scripture* Edinburgh: Nelson.

O'Reilly, T. D. 1989 'Alienation: embracing the destroyer' *Quadrant* XXXIV no. 6 (June): pp. 44–45.

Orwell, George 1954 *Nineteen Eighty-Four: A Novel* (1949) Harmondsworth: Penguin.

—— 1970(a) *The Collected Essays, Journalism and Letters of George Orwell* vol. I: '*An Age Like This*' *1920–1940* ed. by Sonia Orwell and Ian Angus. Harmondsworth: Penguin in assoc. with Secker & Warburg.

—— 1970(b) *ibid.* vol. II: '*My Country Right or Left*' *1940–1943*.

—— 1970(c) *ibid.* vol. III: '*As I Please*' *1943–1945*.

—— 1970(d) *ibid.* vol. IV: '*In Front of Your Nose*' *1945–1950*.

—— 1970(e) 'Politics and the English language' (1946) pp. 156–170 in Orwell, 1970(d).

Osborn's Concise Law Dictionary 6th edn by John Burke 1976 London: Sweet & Maxwell.

O'Sullivan, Noël 1976 *Conservatism* London: Dent.

The Oxford Companion to Classical Literature 2nd edn, ed. by M. C. Howatson 1989 Oxford: Clarendon Press.

The Oxford Companion to the Mind ed. by Richard L. Gregory with the assistance of O. L. Zangwill 1987 Oxford: Oxford University Press.

The Oxford Dictionary of the Christian Church ed. by F. L. Cross and E. A. Livingstone 1974 London: Oxford University Press.

The Oxford Dictionary of Quotations 2nd edn with revisions. London: Oxford University Press.

The Oxford English Dictionary 2nd edn, prepared by J. A. Simpson and E. S. C. Weiner 1989 Oxford: Clarendon Press.

Oxford Latin Dictionary ed. by P. W. Glare. Oxford: Clarendon Press.

Page, Barbara and Martin Painter 1993 'The public service' ch. viii in R. Smith, 1993(b).

Painter, Martin 1979 'Australian political chronicle: New South Wales' *Australian Journal of Politics and History* XXV: pp. 383–387.

Pangle, Thomas L. 1988 *The Spirit of Modern Republicanism: The Moral Vision of the American Founders and the Philosophy of Locke* Chicago: University of Chicago Press.

Parekh, Bhikhu 1981 *Hannah Arendt and the Search for a New Political Philosophy* London: Macmillan.

Parekh, Bhikhu and R. N. Berki (eds) 1972 *The Morality of Politics* London: Allen & Unwin.

Parfit, Derek 1971 'Personal identity' *Philosophical Review* LXXX: pp. 3–27.

Parker, R. S. 1976 'The meaning of responsible government' *Politics* XI: pp. 178–184.

Parkin, Andrew and John Warhurst (eds) 1983 *Machine Politics in the Australian Labor Party* Sydney: Allen & Unwin.

Parkin, Frank 1967 'Working class Conservatives: a theory of political deviance' *The British Journal of Sociology* XVIII: pp. 278–290.

Parrinder, Geoffrey 1971 *Dictionary of Non-Christian Religions* Amersham: Hulton.

Partridge, Eric 1966 *Origins: A Short Etymological Dictionary of Modern English* 4th edn. London: Routledge & Kegan Paul.

—— 1973 *Usage and Abusage: A Guide to Good English* rev. edn. Harmondsworth: Penguin in assoc. with Hamish Hamilton.

Partridge, P. H. 1963 'Some notes on the concept of power' *Political Studies* XI: pp. 107–125. Reprinted as pp. 18–35 in de Crespigny & Wertheimer (eds) *Contemporary Political Theory*.

—— 1971 *Consent and Consensus* London: Pall Mall.

—— 1980 'Law and internal peace' pp. 86–92 in Kamenka & Tay, 1980.

Pasquinelli, Carla 1986 'Power without the State' *Telos* XLVIII: pp. 79–92.
Passmore, John A. 1981 *The Limits of Government* (Boyer Lectures 1981) Sydney: Australian Broadcasting Commission.
Pateman, Carole 1970 *Participation and Democratic Theory* Cambridge: Cambridge University Press.
Patience, Allan (ed.) 1985 *The Bjelke-Petersen Premiership 1968–1983: Issues in Public Policy* Melbourne: Longman Cheshire.
Pattison, Allan 1988 'TAFE: empathy with education is vital' [Letter] *SMH* 8 Dec.: p. 20.
Peabody, Robert L. 1968 'Authority' in *IESS*.
Pelczynski, Zbigniew and John Gray (eds) 1984 *Conceptions of Liberty in Political Philosophy* London: Athlone Press.
Pemberton, Joanne and Glyn Davis 1986 'The rhetoric of consensus' *Politics* XXI no. 1 (May): pp. 55–62.
Penelhum, Terence 1957 'The logic of pleasure' *Philosophy and Phenomenological Research* XVII: pp. 488–503.
—— 1967 'Personal identity' in *EP*.
Percy, Eustace (Lord Percy of Newcastle) 1954 *The Heresy of Democracy: A Study in the History of Government* London: Eyre & Spottiswoode.
Peters, John C. and Susan Welch 1978 'Political corruption in America: a search for a definition and a theory' *The American Political Science Review* LXXIV: pp. 697–708.
Peters, R. S. (Richard Peters), P. G. Winch and A. E. Duncan-Jones 1958 'Authority' [Symposium] *Proceedings of the Aristotelian Society: Supplementary Volume* XXXII: pp. 207–260. Peters's paper is reprinted as pp. 60–73 in de Crespigny & Wertheimer, 1971.
Pettit, Philip 1988 'The paradox of loyalty' *American Philosophical Quarterly* XXV: pp. 163–171.
Pettman, Ralph (ed.) 1979 *Moral Claims in World Affairs* Canberra: Australian National University Press.
Pfeffer, Jeffrey 1981 *Power in Organizations* Boston: Pitman.
—— 1992 *Managing with Power, Politics and Influence in Organisation* Cambridge, Mass.: Harvard Business School Press.
Pilger, John 1991 'In defence of Oxfam: the Charity Commission has been used by the right' *New Statesman/Society* 17 May: p. 8.
Pilgrim, John 1965 'Anarchism and stateless societies' *Anarchy* V: pp. 353–368.
Pincus, Lily and Christopher Dare 1978 *Secrets in the Family* London: Faber.
Pitkin, Hanna Fenichel 1967 *The Concept of Representation* Berkeley and Los Angeles: University of California Press.
—— 1989 Representation' pp. 132–154 in Ball *et al.*, 1989.
Plamenatz, John 1960 *On Alien Rule and Self-Government* London: Longman.
—— 1968 *Consent, Freedom and Political Obligation* . . . 2nd edn. London: Oxford University Press.
Plant, Raymond 1974 *Community and Ideology: An Essay in Applied Social Philosophy* London: Routledge and Kegan Paul.
Plato (428–348 BC) 1961 *The Collected Dialogues of Plato including the Letters* ed. by Edith Hamilton and Huntington Cairns. New York: Bollingen/Pantheon.
—— 1974 *The Republic* trans. with an introd. by Desmond Lee, 2nd edn. Harmondsworth: Penguin.
Polanyi, Michael 1958 *Personal Knowledge: Towards a Post-Critical Philosophy* London: Routledge & Kegan Paul.
Political Parties of the World 3rd edn, ed. by Alan J. Day 1988 Harlow: Keesing/ Longman.
Political Scandals and Causes Célèbres since 1945: An International Reference Compendium 1989. Chicago: St James Press.

Pollard, Sidney 1971 *The Idea of Progress* Harmondsworth: Penguin.

Poole, Michael 1978 *Workers' Participation in Industry* London: Routledge & Kegan Paul.

Poole, Millicent E., P. P. R. de Lacey and B. S. Randhawa (eds) 1985 *Australia in Transition: Culture and Life Possibilities* Sydney: Harcourt Brace Jovanovich.

Pope, Alexander 1966 *Poetical Works* ed. by Herbert Davis. London: Oxford University Press.

Popper, K. R. (Sir Karl Popper) 1966 *The Open Society and its Enemies* 5th edn. London: Routledge & Kegan Paul.

—— 1969 *Conjectures and Refutations: The Growth of Scientific Knowledge* 3rd edn. London: Routledge & Kegan Paul.

—— 1972 *Objective Knowledge: An Evolutionary Approach* Oxford: Clarendon Press.

Porter, Doug, A. Bryant and G. Thompson 1991 *Development in Practice: Paved with Good Intentions* London: Routledge.

Post, Gaines 1973 'Medieval and Renaissance ideas of nation' in *DHI*.

Poussin, L. de la Vallée 1914 'Identity (Buddhist)' in *ERE*.

Powell, Anthony 1976 *To Keep the Ball Rolling* (The Memoirs of Anthony Powell) vol. I: *Infants of the Spring* London: Heinemann.

Prasser, Scott *et al.* (eds) 1990 *Corruption and Reform: The Fitzgerald Vision* St Lucia: University of Queensland Press.

Priestland, David 1988 'All people's state' in *FDMT*.

Primo de Rivera, Jose Antonio 1972 *Selected Writings* ed. by Hugh Thomas. London: Cape.

Punch, Maurice 1985 *Conduct Unbecoming: The Social Construction of Police Deviance and Control* London: Tavistock.

Puplick, Christopher I. and R. J. Southey 1980 *Liberal Thinking* South Melbourne: Macmillan.

Pusey, Michael 1991 *Economic Rationalism in Canberra: A Nation-Building State Changes its Mind* Melbourne: Cambridge University Press.

Pym, Barbara 1984 *A Very Private Eye: The Diaries, Letters and Notebooks of Barbara Pym* ed. by Hazel Holt and Hilary Pym. London: Macmillan.

Pym, Francis 1984 *The Politics of Consent* London: Hamish Hamilton.

Queensland Parliamentary Debates (Hansard) 1957 11–12 June.

Quiddington, Peter 1990 'Tunnel cost blowout: taxpayers face $1 bn bill' *SMH* 30 March: pp. 1, 6.

Quine, Willard van Orman and J. S. Ullian 1978 *The Web of Belief* 2nd edn. New York: Random House.

Quinton, Anthony (Lord Quinton) 1975 'Social objects' *Proceedings of the Aristotelian Society* NS LXXVI (1975/76): pp. 1–27.

—— 1978 *The Politics of Imperfection: The Religious and Secular Traditions of Conservative Thought in England from Hooker to Oakeshott* (The T. S. Eliot lectures delivered at the University of Kent at Canterbury in October 1976) London: Faber.

Rader, Melvin (ed.) 1960 *A Modern Book of Esthetics: An Anthology* 3rd edn. New York: Holt Rinehart & Winston.

Radice, Giles (ed.) 1974 *Working Power: Policies for Industrial Democracy* (Fabian Tract 431) London: Fabian Society.

Rahe, Paul A. 1992 *Republics Ancient and Modern: Classical Republicanism and the American Revolution* Chapel Hill: University of North Carolina Press.

Ramsay, Alan 1987 'The faction be with you – or else' *SMH* 18 July: p. 29.

Raphael, David Daiches 1976 *Problems of Political Philosophy* rev. edn. London: Macmillan.

Rathbone, Catherine and Michael Stephenson 1985 *Pocket Companion Guide to Political Quotations* Harlow: Longman.

Rawson, D. W. 1968 'Another look at "initiative and resistance"' *Politics* III: pp. 41–54.
—— 1969'"Initiative and resistance": a brief rejoinder' *Politics* IV: pp. 215–216.
Ray, John J. (ed.) 1974 *Conservatism as Heresy: An Australian Reader* Sydney: Australian and New Zealand Book Company.
Raz, Joseph (ed.) 1990 *Authority* Oxford: Blackwell.
Read, (Sir) Herbert 1949 *The Meaning of Art* [rev. edn] Harmondsworth: Penguin in assoc. with Faber.
Read, Peter 1990 *Charles Perkins: A Biography* Ringwood: Viking.
Reading, Geoffrey 1989 *High Climbers: Askin and Others* Sydney: John Ferguson.
Reardon, Bernard M. G. 1987 'Modernism: Christian modernism' in *ER*.
Reeves, Thomas C. 1991 *A Question of Character: A Life of John F. Kennedy* London: Bloomsbury.
Reid, Alan 1972 *The Power Struggle* 2nd edn. St Ives, NSW: Tartan Press.
Reilly, Steve A. 1988(a) 'Consensus politics' in *FDMT*.
—— 1988(b) 'Reaganism' in *FDMT*.
—— 1988(c) 'Thatcherism' in *FDMT*.
Rendell, Ruth 1978 *A Sleeping Life* London: Hutchinson.
Reynolds, Paul L. 1974 *The Democratic Labor Party* Milton: Jacaranda Press.
—— 1983 'Australian political chronicles: the Commonwealth' *The Australian Journal of Politics and History* XXIX: pp. 505–516.
Rhodes, Clifford (ed.) 1969 *Authority in a Changing Society* London: Constable.
Richardson, F. M. 1978 *Fighting Spirit: A Study of the Psychological Factors in War* London: Leo Cooper.
Richler, Mordecai 1991 'A reporter at large: inside/outside' *The New Yorker* 23 Sept.: pp. 40–92.
Richmond, Keith 1977 'The Australian League of Rights and the process of political conversion' *Politics* XII no. 1 (May): pp. 70–71.
Richter, Melvin 1964 *The Politics of Conscience: T. H. Green and his Age* London: Weidenfeld & Nicolson.
Ricklefs, Merle Calvin 1981 *A History of Modern Indonesia: c. 1300 to the Present* London: Macmillan.
Rider, Priscilla L. 1959 'Legal protection of the manifestations of individual personality – the identity indicia' *Southern California Law Review* XXXIII: pp. 34–40.
Riker, William H. 1964 'Some ambiguities in the notion of power' *American Political Science Review* LVIII: pp. 342–349.
Ritter, Harry 1986 *Dictionary of Concepts in History* New York: Greenwood Press.
Roberts, Simon 1979 *Order and Dispute: An Introduction to Legal Anthropology* Harmondsworth: Penguin.
Robinson, Kenneth 1961 'Constitutional autochthony in Ghana' *Journal of Commonwealth Studies* I: pp. 41–55.
Robinson, Richard 1962 *Plato's Earlier Dialectic* 2nd edn, corrected reprint. Oxford: Clarendon Press.
——1964 *An Atheist's Values* Oxford: Blackwell.
Roe, Michael 1978 'Challenges to Australian identity' *Quadrant* XXII no. 4 (Apr.): pp. 34–40.
Roget, Peter Mark 1984 *The Penguin Roget's Thesaurus of English Words and Phrases* new edn completely rev., updated and abridged by Susan M. Lloyd. Harmondsworth: Penguin.
Rokeach, Milton [*et al.*] 1960 *The Open and Closed Mind: Investigations into the Nature of Belief Systems and Personality Systems* New York: Basic Books.
Rollin, H. R. 1987 'Asylums: are they really necessary?' pp. 54–56 in *OCM*.
Rolph, C. H. (pseudonym of C. R. Hewitt) 1987 *Further Particulars* Oxford: Oxford University Press.

Room, Adrian 1988 *Dictionary of Confusing Words and Meanings* illus. reprint. New York: Dorset Press.

Rose, Margaret A. 1991 *The Post-Modern and the Post-Industrial* Cambridge: Cambridge University Press.

Rose, Richard (ed.) 1974(a) *Electoral Behavior: A Comparative Handbook* New York: Free Press.

—— 1974(b) 'Britain: simple abstractions and complex realities' ch. x in Rose, 1974(a).

Rosoff, Arnold J. 1981 *Informed Consent: A Guide for Health Care Providers* Rockville, M.D.: Aspen.

Ross, W. D. (Sir David Ross) 1949 *Aristotle* 5th edn. London: Methuen.

Rossabi, Morris (ed.) 1983 *China among Equals: The Middle Kingdom and its Neighbours 10th-14th Centuries* Berkeley and Los Angeles: University of California Press.

Rousseau, Jean-Jacques 1972 *Du contrat social* ed. with an introd. and notes by Ronald Grimsley. Oxford: Clarendon Press.

—— 1973 *'The Social Contract' and 'Discourses'* trans. and introd. by G. D. H. Cole, rev. and augmented by J. H. Brumfitt and John C. Hall. London: Everyman/Dent.

Routley, Val and Richard Routley 1980 'Social theories, self management, and environmental problems' pp. 217-332 in Mannison *et al.*, 1980.

Rowley, Charles Dunford 1965 *The New Guinea Villager: A Retrospect from 1964* Melbourne: Cheshire.

—— 1970(a) *The Destruction of Aboriginal Society: Aboriginal Policy and Practice* vol. I Canberra: Australian National University Press.

—— 1970(b) *Outcasts in White Australia ibid.* vol. II.

—— 1971 *The Remote Aborigines ibid.* vol. III.

—— 1973 'The stateless politics of Melanesia' *Quadrant* (March/April): pp. 52-58.

—— 1980 'Aboriginals and the Australian political system' ch. xxiii in Weller & Jaensch.

Rowse, Tim 1988 'Middle Australia and the noble savage: a political romance' pp. 161-177 in Beckett, 1988.

Rubinstein, W. D. 1980 'The upper crust' *Quadrant* XXIV no. 8 (Aug.): pp. 77-78.

Russell, Bertrand 1928 *Power: A New Social Analysis* London: Allen & Unwin.

Rustow, Dankwart A. 1968 'Nation' in *IESS*.

Ryan, Alan (ed.) 1979 *The Idea of Freedom: Essays in Honour of Isaiah Berlin* Oxford: Oxford University Press.

—— 1988(a) 'Anarcho-syndicalism' in *FDMT*.

—— 1988(b) 'Populism' in *FDMT*.

Ryle, Gilbert 1949 *The Concept of Mind* London: Hutchinson.

—— 1957 'Theory of meaning' pp. 239-264 in Mace, 1957. Reprinted as pp. 350-372 in Ryle, 1971.

—— 1971 *Collected Papers* vol. II: *Collected Essays 1929-1968* London: Hutchinson.

Sabini, J. and M. Silver 1989 'Loyalty as good and duty: a critique of Stocker' *International Journal of Moral and Social Studies* IV: pp. 131-138.

St John-Stevas, Norman (Lord St John of Fawsley) 1961 *Life, Death and the Law: A Study in the Relationship between Law and Christian Morals in the English and American Legal Systems* London: Eyre & Spottiswoode.

Saloutos, Theodore (ed.) 1968(a) *Populism: Reaction or Reform?* New York: Holt, Rinehart & Winston.

—— 1968(b) 'The professors and the populists' pp. 104-118 in Saloutos, 1968(a).

Sampson, Anthony 1962 *The Anatomy of Britain* London: Hodder & Stoughton.

—— 1971 *The New Anatomy of Britain* London: Hodder & Stoughton.

—— 1982 *The Changing Anatomy of Britain* London: Hodder & Stoughton.

Sampson, Ronald and Casimir N. Koblernicz 1973 'Progress' in *MCWS*.

Samuel, Raphael and Gareth Stedman Jones (eds) 1982(a) *Culture, Ideology and Politics: Essays for Eric Hobsbawm* London: Routledge & Kegan Paul.
—— 1982(b) 'The Labour Party and social democracy' pp. 320–329 in Samuel & Jones, 1982(a).
Sartori, Giovanni 1968(a) 'Democracy' in *IESS*.
—— 1968(b) 'Representation: representational systems' in *IESS*.
Sartre, Jean-Paul 1956 *Being and Nothingness: An Essay in Phenomenological Ontology* New York: Philosophical Library.
Saunders, James 1965 *Next Time I'll Sing to You* London: Heinemann Educational.
Sawer, Marian (ed.) 1982 *Australia and the New Right* London: Allen & Unwin.
Sax, Sidney 1972 *Medical Care in the Melting Pot: An Australian Review* Sydney: Angus & Robertson.
Schapiro, J. Selwyn 1958 *Liberalism: Its Meaning and History* New York: Anvil/Van Nostrand Reinhold.
Scheffler, Samuel 1983 *The Role of Consent in the Legitimation of Risky Activity* (Working Paper) College Park: Center for Philosophy and Public Policy, University of Maryland.
Schlesinger, Arthur (Jr) 1972 'National interests and moral absolutes.' pp. 21–42 in Lefever, 1972(a).
Schmidt, Helmut Dan and Wolfgang J. Mommsen 1972 'Imperialism' in *MCWS*.
Schmidt-Mummendey, A. 1972 'Authoritarianism', 'Authoritarian personality' in *EPsy* (Search).
Schulha, Alek 1982 'Festival aims to help regain city's identity' *NH* 18 Oct.: p. 11.
Schumpeter, Joseph Alois 1954 *Capitalism, Socialism and Democracy* 4th edn. London: Unwin University Books.
Schwartz, Louis Brown 1955 'Ascertaining the moral sense of the community' *Journal of Legal Education* VIII: pp. 319–320.
Scriven, Michael 1976 *Reasoning* New York: McGraw-Hill.
Scruton, Roger 1980 *The Meaning of Conservatism* Harmondsworth: Penguin.
—— 1983 *A Dictionary of Political Thought* London: Pan in assoc. with Macmillan.
Searle, John R. 1972 *The Campus War* Harmondsworth: Penguin.
Seddon, George 1973 'Jet-set and parish pump' *Quadrant* XVII no. 3 (May/June): pp. 46–52.
Sellars, Wilfrid and John Hospers (eds) 1952 *Readings in Ethical Theory* New York: Appleton-Century-Crofts.
Serving the People with Dialectics: Essays on the Study of Philosophy by Workers and Peasants 1972 Peking: Foreign Languages Press.
Seymour-Smith, Martin 1988 'Empathy' in *FDMT*.
Shafer, Boyd C. 1955 *Nationalism: Myth and Reality* London: Gollancz.
Shernock, Stan K. 1990 'The effects of patrol officers' defensiveness toward the outside world on their ethical orientations' *Criminal Justice Ethics* IX: pp. 24–42.
Sherrard, D. G. 1985 'Private problems' [Letter] *The Australian* 11 Dec.: p. 12.
Shils, Edward 1968 'Consensus I: the concept of consensus' in *IESS*.
—— 1975 *Center and Periphery: Essays in Macrosociology* Chicago: University of Chicago Press.
The Shorter Oxford English Dictionary on Historical Principles 1947 prepared by William Little, H. W. Fowler and J. Coulson, rev. and ed. by C. T. Onions, 3rd edn reprinted with corrections. Oxford: Clarendon Press.
Shumer, S. M. 1979 'Machiavelli: republican politics and its corruption' *Political Theory* VII: pp. 5–34.
Simms, Marian 1980 '"Private enterprise and progress": the genesis of Liberal Party ideology' pp. 306–312 in Mayer & Nelson, 1980.
Simon, Yves R. 1951 *Philosophy of Democratic Government* Chicago: University of Chicago Press.

Simons, Jack 1985 [Telephoned comment] *NH* 14 Aug.: p. 2.

Sinclair, T. A. 1951 *A History of Greek Political Thought* London: Routledge & Kegan Paul.

Singer, Peter 1973(a) Democracy and Disobedience Oxford: Clarendon Press.

—— 1973(b) 'The triviality of the debate over "ought" and the definition of "Moral"' *American Philosophical Quarterly* X: pp. 51–56.

Sitwell, (Sir) Osbert 1949 *Demos the Emperor: A Secular Cantata* London: Macmillan.

Skegg, P. D. G. 1984 *Law, Ethics and Medicine: Studies in Medical Law* Oxford: Clarendon Press.

Skidelsky, Robert (ed.) 1989 *Thatcherism* Oxford: Blackwell.

Skinner, Martyn 1943 *Letters to Malaya III & IV: Written from England to Alexander Nowell M.C.S. of Ipoh* London: Putnam.

Skinner, Quentin 1989(a) 'Language and political change' pp. 6–23 in Ball *et al.*, 1989.

—— 1989(b) 'The state' pp. 90–131, in Ball *et al.*, 1989.

Smith, Anthony 1991 *National Identity* London: Penguin.

Smith, B. C. 1988 *Bureaucracy and Political Power* Brighton: Wheatsheaf Books.

Smith, Bernard 1990 'Christian cant' [Letter] *The Spectator* 18 Aug.

Smith, Rodney (ed.) 1993(a) *Politics in Australia* 2nd edn. St Leonard's, NSW: Allen & Unwin.

—— 1993(b) 'The party system' ch. ix in R. Smith, 1993(a).

Snyder, Louis L. 1990 *Encyclopedia of Nationalism* New York: Paragon House.

The *Socialist Review* Collective 1992 *Unfinished Business: Twenty Years of 'Socialist Review'* London: Verso.

Solzhenitsyn, Alexander 1976 *Lenin in Zürich: Chapters* trans. by H. T. Willette. London: Book Club Associates.

Sommerfeldt, J. R. 1967 'Identity, principle of' in *NCE*.

Spadafora, David 1990 *The Idea of Progress in Eighteenth-Century Britain* New Haven: Yale University Press.

Sparkes, A. W. 1973 'Surveys: a preliminary survey' *Politics* VIII: pp. 369–370.

—— 1984 'Rousseau on the general will' *Cogito* [Quezon City] II no. 4 (Dec.): pp. 79–101.

—— 1991 *Talking Philosophy: A Wordbook* London: Routledge.

Sparrow, Gerald 1970 *The Great Defamers* London: John Long.

The Spectator 1966 'And now, an election broadcast' 25 March: pp. 349–350.

—— 1990 'Britain's sovereignty' [Editorial] 15 Dec.: p. 5.

Sperber, Hans and Travis Trittschuh 1964 *Dictionary of American Political Terms* New York: McGraw-Hill.

Spiro, Herbert J. 1968 'Totalitarianism' in *IESS*.

Srzednicki, Jan 1987 *The Democratic Perspective: Political and Social Philosophy* Dordrecht: Reidel.

Standish, W. A. (Bill Standish) 1981 'Power to the people?: implementing constitutional change in Papua New Guinea' *Australasian Political Studies Association: 23rd Annual Conference.*

Stankiewicz, W. J. (ed.) 1969 *In Defense of Sovereignty* New York: Oxford University Press.

Stassinopoulos, Arianna 1974 *The Female Woman* London: Fontana/Collins.

Stebbing, Lizzie Susan 1950 *A Modern Introduction to Logic* 7th edn. London: Methuen.

Stein, Maurice R. 1960 *The Eclipse of Community* New York: Harper & Row.

Steinberg, Stephen 1974 *The Academic Melting Pot: Catholics and Jews in American Higher Education* New York: McGraw-Hill.

Steintrager, James 1977 *Bentham* London: Allen & Unwin.

Steketee, Mike 1981 'Feuds that fuel the ALP' *SMH* 1 Aug.: p. 12.

Sterba, James F. 1978 'Neo-libertarianism' *American Philosophical Quarterly* XV: pp. 115–121.

Stevenson, Burton n.d. *Stevenson's Book of Quotations* London: Cassell.

Stevenson, Robert Louis (1850–1894) 1923 *Kidnapped, being Memoirs of the Adventures of David Balfour in the Year MDCCLI* . . . London: Heinemann *et al.*

Stewart, J. I. M. 1979 '*Our England Is A Garden*' and Other Stories London: Gollancz.

Stockley, David 1984 'The politics of multiculturalism: Australian and Canadian comparisons' *Australian-Canadian Studies* III: pp. 21–35.

Stockman, David A. 1986 *The Triumph of Politics* London: The Bodley Head.

Stoljar, S. J. 1973 *Groups and Entities: An Inquiry into Corporate Theory* Canberra: Australian National University Press.

Stone, Gerald 1972 *The Smallest Slavonic Nation: The Sorbs of Lusatia* London: The Athlone Press of the University of London.

Strangwayes-Booth, Joanna 1976 *A Cricket in the Thorn Tree: Helen Suzman and the Progressive Party of South Africa* London: Hutchinson.

Strawson, P. F. (Sir Peter Strawson) 1952 'Ethical intuitionism' pp. 250–259 in Sellars & Hospers, 1952.

—— 1971(a) *Logico-Linguistic Papers* London: Methuen.

—— 1971(b) 'On referring' pp. 1–27 in Strawson, 1971(a). Reprinted from *Mind* NS LIX (1950) and from Flew, 1956.

Stretton, Hugh 1969 *The Political Sciences: General Principles of Selection in the Social Sciences and History* London: Routledge & Kegan Paul.

Stroll, Avrum 1967 'Identity' in *EP*.

Summers, Anne 1983 *Gamble for Power: How Bob Hawke beat Malcolm Fraser. The 1983 Election* Melbourne: Nelson.

—— 1991 *The Curse of the Lucky Country* (The Inaugural Donald Horne Lecture) Clayton: Ideas for Australia 1991–92 Program in assoc. with National Centre for Australian Studies, Monash University.

Summy, Gay 1972 'The revolutionary democracy of J. F. Cairns' *Politics* VII no. 1 (May): pp. 55–66.

The Sunday Telegraph (Sydney) 1991 'Hawke looks left and right again' [Editorial] 23 June: p. 46.

Swan, Peter L. 1979 'The libertarian challenge to Big Government' *Quadrant* XXIII no. 9 (Sept.): pp. 5–11.

The Sydney Morning Herald 1951 'Call to the nation: "Australia in Danger"' 12 Nov.: p. 1.

—— 1991(a) 'A growing chaos that is India' [Editorial] 20 May: p. 16.

—— 1991(b) 'PM blasts foreign protesters' 10 July: p. 9 (Australian Associated Press, Reuters).

Tabb, J. Yanai and Amira Goldfarb 1970 *Workers' Participation in Management: Expectations and Experience* Oxford: Pergamon Press.

Talmon, Jacob Leib 1970 *The Origins of Totalitarian Democracy* London: Sphere.

Tate, John 1982 'Newcastle's air quality "alarming"' *NH* 20 Sep.: p. 8.

Taylor, A. E. 1914 'Identity' in *ERE*.

Taylor, Charles 1989 *Sources of the Self: The Making of the Modern Identity* Cambridge: Cambridge University Press.

Tennyson, Alfred (Lord Tennyson) (1809–1892) 1965 *Poems and Plays* London: Oxford University Press.

Terrins, Deirdre and Phillip Whitehead (eds) 1984 *100 Years of Fabian Socialism 1884–1984* London: The Fabian Society.

Theological Dictionary of the New Testament vol. I, ed. by Gerhard Kittel, trans. and ed. by Geoffrey W. Bromiley 1964(a) Grand Rapids: Eerdmans.

—— 1964(b) *ibid.* vol. II.

Thompson, Damian 1990 'Politics begins at home' *The Spectator* 28 July: pp. 16–17.

Thouless, R. H. and C. R. Thouless 1990 *Straight and Crooked Thinking* 4th edn. London: Headway/Hodder & Stoughton.

Thynne, Ian and Goldring, John 1981 'Government "responsibility" and responsible government' *Politics* XVI: pp. 197–207.

Tier, Mark 1975 'Libertarians: radicals on the right' *Politics* X no. 2 (Nov.): pp. 164–168.

Time (Australia) 1986 Contents page. 21 July: p. 1.

'*The Times' Index* 1989 References under 'India: corruption Bofors arms deal 1986' (Jan.–Dec.): p. 461.

Tiver, Peter G. 1978 *The Liberal Party: Principles and Performance* Milton: Jacaranda Press.

Tönnies, Ferdinand 1955 *Community and Association (Gemeinschaft und Gesellschaft)* trans. and supplemented by Charles P. Loomis. London: Routledge & Kegan Paul.

Totaro, Paola 1990 'Teachers oppose $50,000 update for TAFE's image' *SMH* 26 June p. 5.

Totaro, Paolo 1983 'Multiculturalism for some Australians: a personal view' *Meanjin* XLII: pp. 63–69.

Townsend, Derek 1983 *Jigsaw: The Biography of Johannes Bjelke-Petersen, Statesman - Not Politician* Brisbane: Sneyd & Morley.

Tracy, Honor 1960 *The Straight and Narrow Path* Harmondsworth: Penguin in assoc. with Methuen.

Treble, H. A. and G. H. Vallins 1936, *An ABC of English Usage* Oxford: Clarendon Press.

Trollope, Anthony (1815–1882) 1925 *Barchester Towers* London: World's Classics/ Oxford University Press.

—— 1973 *The Prime Minister* London: Panther.

Tuck, Richard 1972 'Why is authority such a problem?' pp. 194–207 in Laslett *et al.*, 1972.

—— 1989 *Hobbes* Oxford: Oxford University Press.

Tucker, David 1979 *Radical Individualism* Oxford: Blackwell.

Turnbull, Colin M. 1974 *The Mountain People* London: Picador/Pan.

Turner, Ernest Sackville 1961 *The Phoney War on the Home Front* London: Michael Joseph.

—— 1966 *Roads to Ruin: The Shocking History of Social Reform* Harmondsworth: Penguin.

Uhr, John 1981 'Democratic theory and consensus: roots of the civic culture' *Politics* XVI no. 1 (May): pp. 103–118.

—— 1984 'Political sociology and political reality: the concept of democratic consensus' *Politics* XIX no. 2 (Nov.): pp. 93–101.

Unger, Roberto Mangabeira 1976 *Knowledge and Politics* New York: Free Press.

United States - President's Commission for the Study of Ethical Problems in Medicine and Biomedical and Behavioral Research (USPCSEPMBBR) 1982 *Making Health Care Decisions: A Report on the Ethical and Legal Implications of the Informed Consent in the Patient-Practitioner Relationship* vol. I: Washington: [The Commission].

Urmson, J. O. 1968 *The Emotive Theory of Ethics* London: Hutchinson.

Vanier, Jean 1979 *Community and Growth* Sydney: St Paul Publications.

Vasser, M. M. 1976 '"Imperialism, the highest stage of"' pp. 168–169 in *GSE*, 1976.

Victoria - Parliamentary Debates (Hansard) 1955 19 Apr.: pp. 2840–2932.

Vidyabhusana, Satis Chandra 1908 'Absolute (Vedantic and Buddhistic)' in *ERE*.

Viglino, U. 1967 'Identity, principle of' in *NCE*.

Vinson, T. and R. Homel 1976 *Indicators of Community Well-being* Canberra: Department of Social Security/Australian Government Publishing Service.

Vlastos, Gregory 1983 'The historical Socrates and Athenian democracy' *Political Theory* XI: pp. 495–516.

Vogler, Carolyn M. 1985 *The Nation State: The Neglected Dimension of Class* Aldershot: Gower.

Waismann, Friedrich 1951 'Verifiability' pp. 116–144 in Flew, 1951.

—— 1953 'Language strata.' pp. 11–31 in Flew, 1953.

Walker, Tony 1992 'Military backs land for peace' *SMH* 22 June: p. 13.

Wall, K. A. 1967 'Identity' in *NCE*.

Wallace, G. and Walker, A. D. M. (eds) 1970 *The Definition of Morality* London: Methuen.

Walsh, Geraldine 1991 'Postscript' *SMH* 20 May: p. 16.

Walsh, Max 1990 'Treasurer provokes a showdown with Hawke' *SMH* 10 Dec.: pp. 1, 6.

Walsh, W. H. 1972 'Open and closed morality' pp. 17–30 in Parekh & Berki, 1972.

Walter, E. V. 1964 'Power and violence' *American Political Science Review* LVIII: pp. 350–360.

Walter, James 1979 *The Acculturation to Political Work: New Members of the Federal Backbench* [Canberra]: Australasian Political Studies Assoc. and the Parliament of Australia.

—— 1990 'Johannes Bjelke-Petersen: the populist autocrat' pp. 494–526 in Murphy, *et al.*, 1990.

Walter, James and Kay Dickie 1985 'Johannes Bjelke-Petersen: a political profile' ch. iii in Patience, 1985.

Ward, Russel 1970 'Two kinds of Australian patriotism' *Victorian Historical Magazine* XLI: pp. 225–243.

Warhurst, John 1986 'In defence of single-issue interest groups' *The Australian Quarterly* LVIII (Autumn): pp. 102–109.

Warner, Rex 1944 *The Professor: A Novel* [1938] London: The Bodley Head.

Warnock, (Sir) Geoffrey J. 1967 *Contemporary Moral Philosophy*. London: Macmillan. Ch. v.

—— 1971 *The Object of Morality* London: Methuen.

Warnock, Mary (Baroness Warnock) 1960 *Ethics since 1900* London: Oxford University Press.

—— 1967 *Existentialist Ethics* London: Macmillan.

Wartenberg, Thomas E. 1988 'The concept of power in feminist theory' *Praxis International* VIII: pp. 301–316.

Watkins, Alan 1966 'The politics of consensus' *Spectator* 25 March: p. 348.

Watt, Donald Cameron 1988 'Realpolitik' in *FDMT*.

Watt, E. D. 1982 *Authority* London: Croom Helm.

Waugh, Evelyn 1947 *Vile Bodies* [1930] uniform edn. London: Chapman and Hall.

—— 1948 *Scoop: A Novel about Journalists* [1938] uniform edn. London: Chapman and Hall.

—— 1952 *Men at Arms: A Novel* London: Chapman and Hall.

Webb, Leicester Chisholm (ed.) 1958 *Legal Personality and Political Pluralism* Melbourne University Press on behalf of Australian National University.

—— 1960 *Politics and Polity: An Inaugural Lecture Delivered at Canberra on 13th August 1959* [Canberra]: Australian National University.

Weber, Eugen (ed.) 1964 *Varieties of Fascism: Doctrines of Revolution in the Twentieth Century* Princeton: Anvil/Van Nostrand.

Weber, Max (1864–1920) 1948(a) *From Max Weber: Essays in Sociology* trans., ed. and with an introd. by H. H. Gerth and C. Wright Mills. London: Routledge & Kegan Paul.

—— 1948(b) 'Politics as a vocation' pp. 77–128 in M. Weber, 1948(a).

Webster's New World Dictionary of the American Language editor-in-chief: David B. Guralnik, 2nd college edn 1970 New York: The World Publishing Co.

Wedgwood, C. V. (Dame Veronica Wedgwood) 1964 *The Trial of Charles I* London: Collins.

Welch, Claud E. and Mavis Bunker Taintor (eds) 1972 *Revolution and Social Change* North Scituate: Duxbury Press.

Welch, Colin 1990 'The march of mind' *The Spectator* 18 Aug.: pp. 27–28.

Weller, Patrick 1989 'Politicisation and the Australian public service' *Australian Journal of Public Administration* XLVIII: pp. 369–381.

Weller, Patrick and Michelle Grattan 1981 *Can Ministers Cope?: Australian Federal Ministers at Work* Melbourne: Hutchinson.

Weller, Patrick and Dean Jaensch (eds) 1980 *Responsible Government in Australia* Richmond, Victoria: Drummond on behalf of the Australasian Political Studies Association.

Wells, David 1978 'Radicalism, conservatism and environmentalism' *Politics* XIII: pp. 299–306.

Wells, Deane McM. 1977 *Power with Theory: A Critical Analysis of the Liberal Party Philosophers* Collingwood: Outback Press.

—— 1980 'The Fuhrer principle' *Opus* [University of Newcastle (NSW) Students' Association] no. 7.

Werth, Alexander 1965 *De Gaulle: A Political Biography* Harmondsworth: Penguin.

Wesker, Arnold 1976 *Words as Definitions of Experience* . . . with an afterword by Richard Appignanesi. London: Writers and Readers Publishing Cooperative.

Westerway, Peter B. 1963 'Pressure groups' pp. 120–166 in Wilkes, 1963.

Wheare, K. C. 1960 *The Constitutional Structure of the Commonwealth* Oxford: Clarendon Press.

—— 1966 *Modern Constitutions* 2nd edn. London: Opus/Oxford University Press.

Wheelwright, Philip 1954 *The Burning Fountain: A Study in the Language of Symbolism* Bloomington: Indiana University Press.

White, D. M. 1978 *The Philosophy of the Australian Liberal Party* Richmond, Victoria: Hutchinson.

White, Stephen K. 1991 *Political Theory and Postmodernism* Cambridge: Cambridge University Press.

White, Terence Hanbury 1962 *The Once and Future King* London: Fontana/Collins.

Whitlam, Edward Gough 1978 *Reform during Recession: The Way Ahead* (The inaugural T. J. Ryan Memorial Lecture) Toowong: University of Queensland ALP Club.

Wiggins, David 1980 *Sameness and Substance* Oxford: Blackwell.

Wight, Martin 1978 *Power Politics* ed. by Hedley Bull and Carsten Holbraad. Leicester: Leicester University Press and Royal Institute of International Affairs.

Wiles, Peter 1969 'A syndrome, not a doctrine: some elementary theses on populism' ch. vii in Ionescu & Gellner, 1969.

Wilkes, John (ed.) 1963 *Forces in Australian Politics* Sydney: Australian Institute of Political Science/Angus & Robertson.

Willey, (Sir) Basil 1964 *The English Moralists* London: Chatto & Windus.

Williams, Bernard 1976 *Morality: An Introduction to Ethics* Cambridge: Cambridge University Press.

Williams, R. D. 1977 *An Introduction to Virgil's 'Aeneid'* Sydney: Australian Broadcasting Commission.

Williams, Raymond 1983 *Keywords: A Vocabulary of Culture and Society* 2nd edn. London: Flamingo/Fontana.

Wilson, Angus 1952 *Hemlock and After* London: Secker & Warburg.

Wilson, Bryan R. 1975 *The Noble Savage: The Primitive Origins of Charisma and Its Contemporary Survival* Berkeley: Quantum/University of California Press.

Wilson, John F. 1987 'Modernity' in *ER*.

Wilson, Paul Richard 1971 *The Sexual Dilemma: Abortion, Homosexuality, Prostitution and the Criminal Threshold* St Lucia: University of Queensland Press.

Winch, Peter 1972 *Ethics and Action* London: Routledge & Kegan Paul.

Wisdom, John 1953 *Philosophy and Psycho-Analysis* Oxford: Blackwell.

Wiseman, Mary Bittner 1978 'Empathetic identification' *American Philosophical Quarterly* XV: pp. 107–113.

Wittgenstein, Ludwig 1958(a) *Philosophical Investigations* 2nd edn. Oxford: Blackwell.

—— 1958(b) *Preliminary Studies for the 'Philosophical Investigations' Generally Known as 'The Blue and Brown Books'* Oxford: Blackwell.

Wodehouse, P. G. 1966 *Stiff Upper Lip, Jeeves* (1963) Harmondsworth: Penguin.

Wolfe, Tom 1987 *The Bonfire of the Vanities* New York: Farrar Straus Giroux.

Wolff, Robert Paul, Barrington Moore Jr and Herbert Marcuse 1969 *A Critique of Pure Tolerance* London: Cape.

Wolfsohn, Hugo 1969 'The ideology makers' [1964] pp. 42–51 in Mayer, 1969(a).

Wolin, Sheldon Seymour 1961 *Politics and Vision: Continuity and Innovation in Western Political Thought* London: Allen & Unwin.

Wollheim, Richard 1962 'A paradox in the theory of democracy' pp. 71–87 in Laslett *et al.*, 1962.

Wood, Ellen Meiksins 1972 *Mind and Politics: An Approach to the Meaning of Liberal and Socialist Individualism* Berkeley and Los Angeles: University of California Press.

—— 1992 *The Pristine Culture of Capitalism: A Historical Essay on Old Regimes and Modern States* London: Verso.

Woodhouse, S. C. 1932 *English-Greek Dictionary: A Vocabulary of the Attic Language* 2nd impression (with a supplement) London: Routledge & Kegan Paul.

Woodland, D. J. A. W. 1968 'Elite' in G. D. Mitchell, 1968.

Woodward, C. Vann 1968 'The populist heritage and the intellectual' [1959/60] pp. 78–88 in Saloutos, 1968(a).

Woollard, A. G. B. 1972 *Progress: A Christian Doctrine?* London: SPCK.

Words and Phrases Legally Defined under the general editorship of John B. Saunders, 2nd edn 1969 London: Butterworth.

—— 1986 Supplement.

—— 1988 3rd edn.

Worsley, Peter 1969 'The concept of populism' ch. x in Ionescu & Gellner, 1969.

Wright, J. F. H. 1980 *Mirror of the Nation's Mind: Australia's Electoral Experiments* Sydney: Hale & Iremonger.

Wright, John 1975 Introduction pp. 13–28 in *LCdR*, 1975.

Wuellner, Bernard 1956 *A Dictionary of Scholastic Philosophy* Milwaukee: Bruce.

Xenophon (*c.*435–354 BC) 1964 *The March up Country: A Translation of Xenophon's Anabasis* W[trans. by] W. H. D. Rouse. Ann Arbor: University of Michigan Press.

Yardley, D. C. M. 1988 '*Ultra vires*' in *FDMT*.

Young, Hugo 1991 'Europe: ostensibly the inescapable conclusion' *The Guardian Weekly* 23 June: p. 4.

Young, Hugo and Anne Sloman 1986 *The Thatcher Phenomenon* London: British Broadcasting Corporation.

Young, Robert 1980 'Autonomy and the "inner self"' *American Philosophical Quarterly* XVII: pp. 35–41.

Younger, Calton 1968 *Ireland's Civil War* London: Muller.

Zangwill, Israel 1932 *The Melting Pot: Drama in Four Acts* [1908] new and rev. edn. New York: Macmillan.

Zhang Yongjin 1991 *China in the International System, 1918–20: The Middle Kingdom at the Periphery* Basingstoke: Macmillan in assoc. with St Antony's College Oxford.

Zubrzycki, Jerzy 1987 'Public policy in multicultural Australia' *Quadrant* XXXI no. 7 (July): pp. 48–52.

Index